Advanced French

Edited by

Shaina Malkin and Cindy Hazelton

LIVING LANGUAGE®

Published in the United States by Living Language, an imprint of Random House, Inc.

www.livinglanguage.com

Editor: Shaina Malkin
Production Editor: Carolyn Roth
Production Manager: Tom Marshall
Interior Design: Sophie Chin
Illustrations: Sophie Chin

First Edition

ISBN: 978-0-307-97155-5

This book is available at special discounts for bulk purchases for sales promotions or premiums. Special editions, including personalized covers, excerpts of existing books, and corporate imprints, can be created in large quantities for special needs. For more information, write to Special Markets/ Premium Sales, 1745 Broadway, MD 3-1, New York, New York 10019 or e-mail specialmarkets@ randomhouse.com.

PRINTED IN THE UNITED STATES OF AMERICA

15 14 13 12 11 10

Acknowledgments

Thanks to the Living Language team: Amanda D'Acierno, Christopher Warnasch, Suzanne McQuade, Shaina Malkin, Erin Quirk, Laura Riggio, Amanda Munoz, Fabrizio La Rocca, Siobhan O'Hare, Sophie Chin, Sue Daulton, Alison Skrabek, Carolyn Roth, Ciara Robinson, and Tom Marshall.

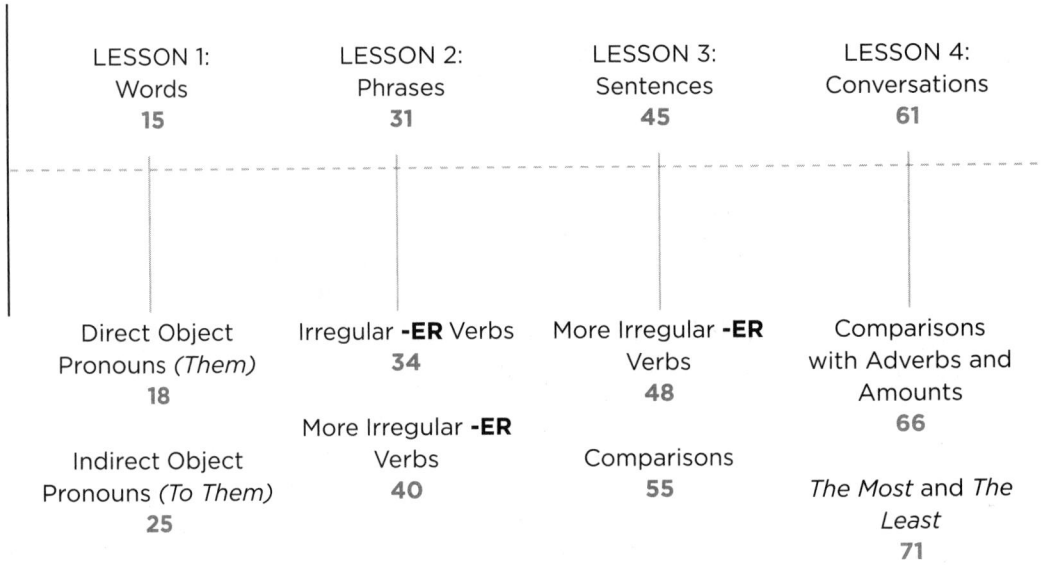
C O U R S E

OUTLINE

COURSE

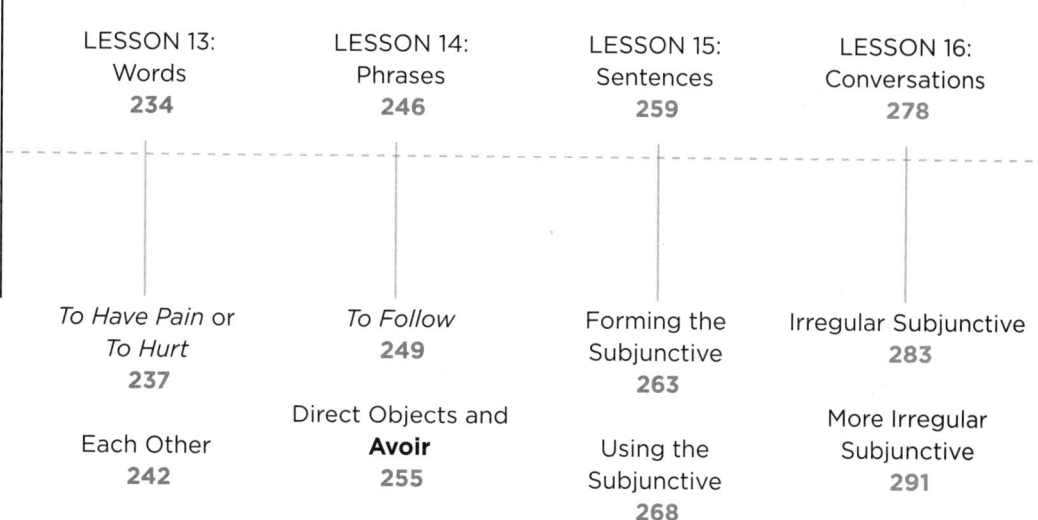

OUTLINE

How to Use This Course

Bienvenue à *Living Language Advanced French*!

Before we begin, let's take a quick look at what you'll see in this course.

CONTENT

Advanced French is a continuation of *Intermediate French*.

Now that you've mastered the basics with *Essential* and *Intermediate French*, you'll take your French even further with a comprehensive look at irregular verbs, advanced verb tenses, and complex sentences.

UNITS

There are four units in this course. Each unit has four lessons arranged in a "building block" structure: the first lesson will present essential *words*, the second will introduce longer *phrases*, the third will teach *sentences*, and the fourth will show how everything works together in everyday *conversations*.

At the beginning of each unit is an introduction highlighting what you will learn in that unit. At the end of each unit you'll find the Unit Essentials, which review the key information from that unit, and a self-graded Unit Quiz, which tests what you've learned.

LESSONS

There are four lessons per unit for a total of 16 lessons in the course. Each lesson has the following components:

- **Introduction** outlining what you will cover in the lesson.

- **Word Builder 1** (first lesson of the unit) presenting key words and phrases.

- **Phrase Builder 1** (second lesson of the unit) introducing longer phrases and expressions.

- **Sentence Builder 1** (third lesson of the unit) teaching sentences.

- **Conversation 1** (fourth lesson of the unit) for a natural dialogue that brings together important vocabulary and grammar from the unit.

- **Take It Further** providing extra information about the new vocabulary you just saw, expanding on certain grammar points, or introducing additional words and phrases.

- **Word / Phrase / Sentence / Conversation Practice 1** practicing what you learned in Word Builder 1, Phrase Builder 1, Sentence Builder 1, or Conversation 1.

- **Word Recall** reviewing important vocabulary and grammar from any of the previous lessons in *Essential, Intermediate,* or *Advanced French.*

- **Grammar Builder 1** guiding you through important French grammar that you need to know.

- **Work Out 1** for a comprehensive practice of what you saw in Grammar Builder 1.

- **Word Builder 2 / Phrase Builder 2 / Sentence Builder 2 / Conversation 2** for more key words, phrases, or sentences, or a second dialogue.

- **Take It Further** for expansion on what you've seen so far and additional vocabulary.

- **Word / Phrase / Sentence / Conversation Practice 2** practicing what you learned in Word Builder 2, Phrase Builder 2, Sentence Builder 2, or Conversation 2.

- **Word Recall** reviewing important vocabulary and grammar from any of the previous lessons in *Essential, Intermediate,* or *Advanced French.*

- **Grammar Builder 2** for more information on French grammar.

- **Work Out 2** for a comprehensive practice of what you saw in Grammar Builder 2.

- **Drive It Home** ingraining an important point of French grammar for the long term.

- **Tip or Culture Note** for a helpful language tip or useful cultural information related to the lesson or unit.

- **How Did You Do?** outlining what you learned in the lesson.

UNIT ESSENTIALS

You will see the **Unit Essentials** at the end of every unit. This section summarizes and reviews key grammar from the unit, and tests your knowledge of vocabulary by allowing you to fill in your very own "cheat sheet," with hints directing you back to the vocabulary in the lessons. Once you complete the blanks with the missing vocabulary, the Unit Essentials will serve as your very own reference for the most essential vocabulary and grammar from each unit.

UNIT QUIZ

After each Unit Essentials, you'll see a **Unit Quiz** testing your progress. Your quiz results will allow you to see which sections, if any, you need to review before moving on to the next unit.

PROGRESS BAR

You will see a **Progress Bar** on each page that has course material. It indicates your current position within each unit and lets you know how much progress you're making. Each line in the bar represents a Grammar Builder section.

AUDIO

Look for this symbol ⊙ to help guide you through the audio as you're reading the book. It will tell you which track to listen to for each section that has audio. When you see the symbol, select the indicated track and start listening! If you don't see the symbol, then there isn't any audio for that section. You'll also see ⅠⅠ, which will tell you where that track ends.

The audio can be used on its own—in other words, without the book—when you're on the go. Whether in your car or at the gym, you can listen to the audio on its own to brush up on your pronunciation or review what you've learned in the book.

PHONETICS

Phonetics will occasionally be used in this course (in other words, [eh-truh] in addition to être), usually in order to highlight a point about French pronunciation. Remember that phonetics are not exact—they're just a general approximation of sounds—and so you should rely most on the audio, *not* the phonetics, to further your pronunciation skills.

For a guide to our phonetics system, see the **Pronunciation Guide** at the end of the course.

PRONUNCIATION GUIDE, GRAMMAR SUMMARY, GLOSSARY

At the back of this book you will find a **Pronunciation Guide**, **Grammar Summary**, and **Glossary**. The Pronunciation Guide provides information on French pronunciation and the phonetics system used in this course. The Grammar Summary contains a brief overview of key French grammar from *Essential, Intermediate,* and *Advanced French.* The Glossary (French-English and English-French) includes all of the important words from *Essential, Intermediate,* and *Advanced French,* as well as additional vocabulary.

FREE ONLINE TOOLS

Go to *www.livinglanguage.com/languagelab* to access your free online tools. The tools are organized around the units in this course, with audiovisual flashcards, and interactive games and quizzes. These tools will help you to review and practice the vocabulary and grammar that you've seen in the units, as well as provide some bonus words and phrases related to the unit's topic.

Unit 1:
Shopping

Welcome to *Advanced French*! In this course, you'll learn how to form complex sentences and use more advanced verb tenses. By the end of the course, you'll have all the skills and knowledge necessary to speak and understand conversational French.

There are four units in *Advanced French*, and four lessons in each unit. As in *Intermediate French*, each unit will gradually build from words to conversations.

Ready to get started?

By the end of this unit, you should be able to:

☐ Name different types of clothing

☐ Say *I understand them*

☐ Name different types of accessories

☐ Say *I speak to them*

☐ Talk about hundreds, thousands, or millions of something

☐ Discuss what to *throw out* and what to *buy*

☐ Name items you might find at a French market

☐ Discuss what you *prefer*

☐ Talk about price and size when you go shopping

☐ Discuss what you *use* and who is *paying*

☐ Make comparisons

☐ Say whether something was done *more slowly* or *less quickly*

☐ Talk about *the most* and *the least*

Lesson 1: Words

By the end of this lesson, you will be able to:

☐ Name different types of clothing

☐ Say *I understand them*

☐ Name different types of accessories

☐ Say *I speak to them*

Word Builder 1

Let's get started with different types of vêtements *(m.)* *(clothes, clothing)*.

▶ 1A Lesson 1 Word Builder 1 (CD 7, Track 1)

(man's) suit	le complet
pants	le pantalon
jacket	le veston
coat	le manteau
(fashion) scarf	le foulard
hat	le chapeau
sweater	le pull(-over), le tricot
raincoat	l'imperméable *(m.)*
glove	le gant
shirt (usually button)	la chemise

skirt	la jupe
blouse	la blouse*, le chemisier
sock	la chaussette
shoes	les chaussures (*f.*)

* Note that blouse can also mean *coat*. For example, a doctor might wear une blouse blanche (*a white coat*).

Take It Further

In these sections, we'll expand on what you've seen so far or introduce additional grammar and vocabulary.

For instance, let's talk more about scarves. Scarves are very popular in France, so it's important to know the difference between the two words for *scarf*:

fashion scarf	le foulard
winter scarf	l'écharpe (*f.*)

Un foulard is often made out of silk. It is worn as a fashion accessory, not as a way to keep warm. However, une écharpe could be made of other fabric such as wool when it's cold outside, or worn as a belt or around the shoulders.

Also, you learned that le complet means *suit*. However, there are actually multiple words for *suit* in French. Here are the others:

man's suit	le costume
woman's suit	le tailleur

Le complet is more of a formal word for a man's suit and is often used when referring to a three-piece suit or complet-veston.

✎ Word Practice 1

Identify the following items by filling in the blanks with the correct French word. Make sure to include le, la, l', or les before each word.

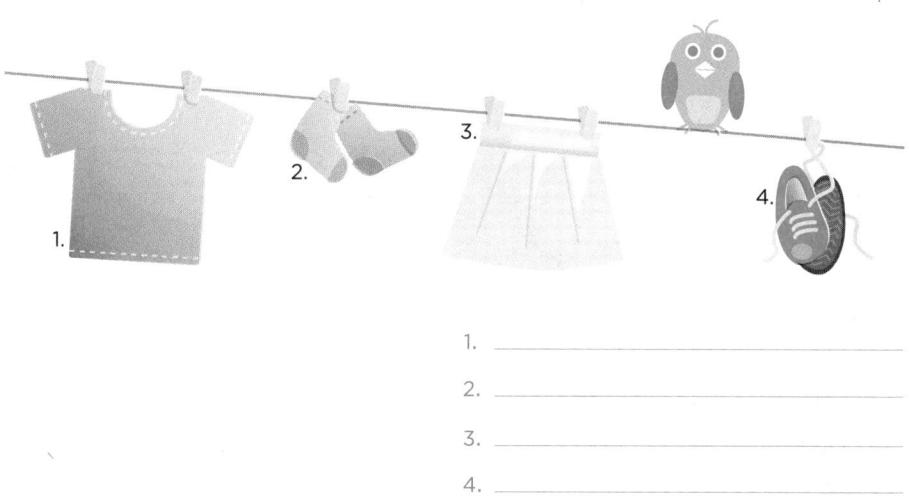

1. _____

2. _____

3. _____

4. _____

ANSWER KEY:

1. la chemise; 2. la chaussette; 3. la jupe; 4. les chaussures

✎ Word Recall

Remember that these exercises will review important vocabulary and grammar from any of the previous lessons in the program, from the first lesson of *Essential French* through *Intermediate French* up to your current point in *Advanced French*. The exercises will reinforce what you've learned so far and help you retain the information for the long term.

Match the French question words on the left to the correct English translations on the right.

1. quand	a. *how much, how many*
2. combien	b. *when*
3. quel/quelle/quels/quelles	c. *where*
4. où	d. *what, which*

ANSWER KEY:
1. b; 2. a; 3. d; 4. c

Grammar Builder 1
DIRECT OBJECT PRONOUNS (*THEM*)

▶ 1B Lesson 1 Grammar Builder 1 (CD 7, Track 2)

In *Advanced French*, you're going to learn how to form more complex sentences in French. To start, let's talk about "direct object pronouns."

Take a look at the following sentence:

Je prends le livre.
I take the book.

In technical terms, je (*I*) is the subject of that sentence, prends (*take*) is the verb, and le livre (*the book*) is what's known as the "direct object." A direct object is a noun that receives the action of a verb. In this case, it is the "thing that is taken."

However, in English, you know that it is also possible to say *I take **it** instead of I take **the book**. In other words, you replace the noun *the book* with the pronoun *it*. In this example, *it* is therefore the "direct object pronoun" that replaces the "direct object" noun *the book.* Simply put, direct object pronouns take the place of direct object nouns in sentences.

Here are the direct object pronouns in French:

me (m')	me	nous	us
te (t')	you	vous	you
le (l')	him, it (m.)	les	them (m.)*
la (l')	her, it (f.)	les	them (f.)*

* Note that les can also mean *it* when replacing certain French plural nouns, like les fruits (*fruit*) and les vacances (*vacation*), that are singular in English. You'll see an example of this below.

As you can see, in French, direct object pronouns must agree in number and gender with the nouns they replace. So if you want to replace la porte (*the door*), you must use la (*it, f.*) and not le (*it, m.*). If you want to replace les portes (*the doors*), you must use les (*them*). Notice that *them* has the same form in both the masculine and feminine.

While the direct object pronoun comes after the verb in English (*I take it*), it always comes **before** the verb in French. Here are a few examples, the first one using the verb fermer (*to close*):

Elle ferme la porte. Elle la ferme.
She closes the door. She closes it.

Il aime le film. Il l'aime.
He likes the movie. He likes it.

Aimez-vous les fruits ? Non, je ne les aime pas.
Do you like fruit? No, I don't like it.

Direct object pronouns can also replace the proper names of people, places, etc. So instead of saying *I understand* **Sophie**, you can say *I understand* **her**.

Here are some examples:

Je vous comprends.
I understand you.

Je la comprends.
I understand her./I understand it.

Je le comprends.
I understand him./I understand it.

Je les comprends.
I understand them. (I understand it [pl.].)

Il ne me comprend pas.
He doesn't understand me.

Me comprends-tu ?
Do you understand me?

In some sentences, a verb may be followed by a verb in the infinitive. For example: vous pouvez aider (*you can help*). If you want to use a direct object pronoun in this type of sentence, place the pronoun ***directly before the verb it is referring to***, which is usually the verb in the infinitive.

Vous pouvez nous aider ?
Can you help us?

In this case, you put the direct object pronoun nous (us) directly before aider (lit., to help) and not pouvez (can). This is because you're saying help us, and not can us, which of course wouldn't make sense.

Finally, note that, in the positive imperative, the direct object pronouns me and te become moi and toi. Also, the pronoun normally comes after the verb in the positive imperative. For example: Vous me quittez. Quittez-moi ! (You're leaving me. Leave me!). This only applies to the positive imperative, not the negative imperative: Ne me quittez pas. (Don't leave me.)

(II)

✎ Work Out 1

Rewrite the following sentences in French by replacing the direct object nouns with direct object pronouns.

1. Nous chantons une chanson. (We sing a song.)

_____

2. Elle prépare le déjeuner. (She prepares lunch.)

_____

3. Il vend les fruits. (He sells fruit.)

_____

4. Est-ce que vous aimez les foulards ? (Do you like scarves?)

_____

5. Ils prennent la voiture. (They take the car.)

_____

6. **Je n'aime pas le poulet.** (*I don't like chicken.*)

ANSWER KEY:

1. **Nous la chantons.** (*We sing it.*) 2. **Elle le prépare.** (*She prepares it.*) 3. **Il les vend.** (*He sells it.*) 4. **Est-ce que vous les aimez ?** (*Do you like them?*) 5. **Ils la prennent.** (*They take it.*) 6. **Je ne l'aime pas.** (*I don't like it.*)

Word Builder 2

Now let's look at **les accessoires** (*m.*) (*accessories*).

▶ 1C Lesson 1 Word Builder 2 (CD 7, Track 3)

handkerchief (tissue)	**le mouchoir**
purse, bag	**le sac**
stocking (hose)	**le bas**
bathing suit	**le maillot (de bain)**
pajamas	**le pyjama**
jewelry	**les bijoux** (*m.*)
watch	**la montre**
earring	**la boucle d'oreille**
ring	**la bague**
bracelet	**le bracelet**
umbrella	**le parapluie**
tie	**la cravate**
cap	**la casquette**
glasses	**les lunettes** (*f.*)
sunglasses	**les lunettes** (*f.*) **de soleil**
briefcase	**la serviette***

⏸ *La serviette can mean *briefcase*, *towel*, or *napkin* depending on the context.

Take It Further

Note that la bague can only refer to a *ring* that you wear on your finger and that usually has a gem or other design element on it. The word anneau (m.), on the other hand, means almost any kind of *ring*, not just jewelry. When referring to jewelry, anneau usually means a basic band without a setting.

Here are some more French words and phrases related to rings:

wedding ring	l'alliance (*f.*)
engagement ring	la bague de fiançailles
diamond ring	la bague en diamant
diamond	le diamant
gold	l'or (*m.*)
silver	l'argent (*m.*)*

* Remember that argent can also mean *money* or *cash*.

Finally, here are some other words and phrases related to shopping that will be helpful to know:

salesman/saleswoman	le vendeur/la vendeuse
merchant, vendor, dealer	le marchand/la marchande
to wear	porter
outfit	l'ensemble (*m.*), la tenue
clothing size	la taille
shoe size	la pointure
tennis shoes, sneakers	les baskets (*f.*), les chaussures (*f.*) de basket/tennis
t-shirt	le T-shirt*

* Pronounced [tee-shehrt].

jeans	le jean**
dress	la robe
belt	la ceinture
necklace	le collier
well-dressed	bien habillé/bien habillée
casual	décontracté/décontractée
formal, in formal dress/attire	en tenue de soirée
dress code	le code vestimentaire

** Pronounced just as in English: [dzheen].

Est-ce qu'il y a un code vestimentaire ?

Is there a dress code?

✎ Word Practice 2

Fill in the blanks with the appropriate French word.

1. Il fait du soleil ce matin. J'ai besoin de mes _____ (sunglasses).

   (*It's sunny this morning. I need my sunglasses.*)

2. Elle a beaucoup de _____ (jewelry). (*She has a lot of jewelry.*)

3. Martine a vendu son _____ (bag) et sa _____ (watch).

   (*Martine sold her bag and her watch.*)

4. Il pleut. Est-ce que vous avez votre _____ (umbrella) ?

   (*It's raining. Do you have your umbrella?*)

5. Gérard n'a pas de _____ (ties). (*Gérard doesn't have any ties.*)

   ANSWER KEY
   1. lunettes de soleil; 2. bijoux; 3. sac, montre; 4. parapluie; 5. cravates

✎ Word Recall

Write out the following numbers in French.

1. *eleven* _____

2. *four* _____

3. *seventy-three* _____

4. *forty* _____

5. *fifty-seven* _____

ANSWER KEY
1. onze; 2. quatre; 3. soixante-treize; 4. quarante; 5. cinquante-sept

Grammar Builder 2
INDIRECT OBJECT PRONOUNS (*TO THEM*)

▶ 1D Lesson1 Grammar Builder 2 (CD 7, Track 4)

In Grammar Builder 1, you learned that direct objects receive the action of a verb, and direct object pronouns replace direct objects in sentences.

As opposed to direct objects, **indirect** objects receive the action of a verb indirectly and are usually separated from the verb by a preposition like *to, at, for,* etc.

For example, compare the following two sentences:

I understand Mark.
I speak to Mark.

In the first sentence, *Mark* is a **direct** object. However, in the second sentence, *Mark* is an **indirect** object because it is separated from the verb *speak* by the preposition *to*. As a result, if you said *I speak to him* instead of *I speak to Mark*, the word *him* would be an indirect object pronoun, not a direct object pronoun.

The same is true in French. Indirect objects in French are usually preceded by a preposition like à (*to*). Note, however, that indirect object pronouns in French replace both the indirect object **and** the preposition in the sentence. So they don't just mean *me, you, him, her*, etc.; they mean *to me, to you, to him, to her*, and so on, depending on the preposition.

Here are the French indirect object pronouns, using the preposition *to* as an example:

me (m')	to me	nous	to us
te (t')	to you	vous	to you
lui	to him/her/it	leur	to them*

* Leur can also mean *to it* when replacing certain French plural nouns that are singular in English.

Keep in mind that if, for instance, the pronoun is replacing the preposition **pour** (*for*) and not à (*to*), then the pronouns would translate as *for me, for you*, etc. The same is true for any other preposition.

Also note that there is only one pronoun for *to him, to her*, and *to it*: **lui**. Similarly, there is only one pronoun for *to them (m.)* and *to them (f.)*: **leur**.

Like direct object pronouns, indirect object pronouns are placed immediately before the verb.

Je parle à Luc. Je lui parle.
I speak to Luc. I speak to him.

Advanced French

Je parle à ma fille. Je lui parle.
I speak to my daughter. I speak to her.

Il me parle.
He speaks to me.

Il te parle.
He speaks to you.

Il lui parle.
He speaks to him./He speaks to her. (He speaks to it.)

Il nous parle.
He speaks to us.

Il vous parle.
He speaks to you.

Il leur parle.
He speaks to them. (He speaks to it [pl.].)

Note that in a sentence where a verb is followed by a verb in the infinitive, indirect object pronouns behave in the same way as direct object pronouns: **je vais te parler** (*I'm going to talk to you*).

Finally, as with direct object pronouns, the indirect object pronouns **me** and **te** become **moi** and **toi** in the positive imperative. Also, the pronoun normally comes after the verb in the positive imperative. For example: **Vous me parlez. Parlez-moi !** (*You speak to me. Speak to me!*). Again, this doesn't apply to the negative imperative: **Ne me parlez pas.** (*Don't speak to me.*)

✎ Work Out 2

Rewrite the following French sentences by replacing the underlined indirect objects with indirect object pronouns.

1. Suzanne parle à ses amis. (*Suzanne speaks to her friends.*)

   _____

2. Nous parlons à toi et à Claude. (*We speak to you and to Claude.*)

   _____

3. Ils donnent les livres à leurs enfants. (*They give the books to their children.*)

   _____

4. Vous parlez à votre ami. (*You speak to your friend.*)

   _____

ANSWER KEY:
1. Suzanne leur parle. (*Suzanne speaks to them.*) 2. Nous vous parlons. (*We speak to you.*) 3. Ils leur donnent les livres. (*They give them the books.*) 4. Vous lui parlez. (*You speak to him.*)

✎ Drive It Home

Remember that this exercise is designed to instill key information about French grammar. Although it may seem repetitive, it is **very** important that you read through each question carefully, write out each response, and then read the whole question out loud. It will help you to retain the information beyond just this lesson and course.

A. Fill in the blanks with the correct direct object pronoun.

1. Je _____ aide. (*I help her.*)

2. Tu _____ aides. (*You help me.*)

3. Elle _____ aide. (*She helps him.*)

4. Nous _____ aidons. (We help you, infml.)

5. Vous _____ aidez. (You help them, m.)

6. Elles _____ aident. (They help us.)

7. Ils _____ aident. (They help you, pl./fml.)

8. Il _____ aide. (He helps them, f.)

B. Now fill in the blanks with the correct indirect object pronoun.

1. Je _____ donne la bague. (I give the ring to her.)

2. Tu _____ donnes la bague. (You give the ring to me.)

3. Elle _____ donne la bague. (She gives the ring to him.)

4. Nous _____ donnons la bague. (We give the ring to you, infml.)

5. Vous _____ donnez la bague. (You give the ring to them, m.)

6. Elles _____ donnent la bague. (They give the ring to us.)

7. Ils _____ donnent la bague. (They give the ring to you, pl./fml.)

8. Il _____ donne la bague. (He gives the ring to them, f.)

ANSWER KEY:

A. 1. l'; 2. m'; 3. l'; 4. t'; 5. les; 6. nous; 7. vous; 8. les

B. 1. lui; 2. me; 3. lui; 4. te; 5. leur; 6. nous; 7. vous; 8. leur

Tip

It's important to note that there are some verbs that are followed by **indirect** objects in English, but by **direct** objects in French. Here are two of the most common ones:

attendre*	to wait for
regarder*	to look at

* Attendre can also simply mean *to wait* and regarder can also mean *to watch*, depending on the context.

In other words, **attendre** and **regarder** should be followed by direct objects and direct object pronouns in French, even though they would be followed by indirect objects and indirect object pronouns in English. This is because the English verbs contain a preposition (*to wait **for**, to look **at***), while their French equivalents are not followed by a preposition.

J'attends ma femme. Je l'attends.
I'm waiting for my wife. I'm waiting for her.

Je regarde la porte. Je la regarde.
I'm looking at the door. I'm looking at it.

The opposite is also true. There are some verbs that take direct objects in English, but require indirect objects in French. Here are three common ones:

obéir à	*to obey*
répondre à	*to answer*
téléphoner à	*to call*

So, for example, you would follow *to obey* with a direct object in English: *I obey the teacher. I obey him.* However, you would use an indirect object in French because **obéir** is usually followed by the preposition **à**. You literally say *I obey to the teacher. I obey to him.* in French.

Il obéit à son père. Il lui obéit.
He obeys his father. He obeys him. (lit., He obeys to his father. He obeys to him.)

Je réponds à mon ami. Je lui réponds.
I answer my friend. I answer him.

Je téléphone à mon amie. Je lui téléphone.
I call my friend. I call her.

Advanced French

How Did You Do?

Let's see how you did! By now, you should be able to:

☐ Name different types of clothing
  (Still unsure? Jump back to page 15)

☐ Say *I understand them*
  (Still unsure? Jump back to page 18)

☐ Name different types of accessories
  (Still unsure? Jump back to page 22)

☐ Say *I speak to them*
  (Still unsure? Jump back to page 25)

Lesson 2: Phrases

By the end of this lesson, you will be able to:

☐ Talk about hundreds, thousands, or millions of something

☐ Discuss what to *throw out* and what to *buy*

☐ Name items you might find at a French market

☐ Discuss what you *prefer*

Phrase Builder 1

Let's review numbers higher than 100.

▶ 2A Lesson 2 Phrase Builder 1 (CD 7, Track 5)

one hundred one	cent un
two hundred	deux cents

two hundred six	deux cent six
one thousand	mille
one thousand one	mille un
one million	un million

Take It Further

Multiples of cent (*one hundred*) are written with a final s:

trois cents
three hundred

However, that final s is dropped when it is followed by a number:

trois cent quatorze
three hundred fourteen

Multiples of mille (*one thousand*), on the other hand, do not add a final s:

deux mille
two thousand

Note that, unlike un million (*one million*), mille (*one thousand*) and cent (*one hundred*) are never preceded by un or une in order to say *one thousand* or *one hundred*.

If million is followed by a noun, then you need to place de in between million and the noun:

un million de dollars
a million dollars

However, if million is followed by other numbers and then the noun, you don't add de:

trois millions cinq cents personnes
three million five hundred people

Finally, un milliard is *one billion* and un trillion is *a trillion*. If you're *a billionaire,* you're un/une milliardaire. If you're *a millionaire,* you're un/une millionnaire.

✎ Phrase Practice 1

Translate the following numbers into English.

1. cent un _____

2. mille six cents _____

3. deux mille dix _____

4. trois cent cinquante _____

5. deux millions huit cent soixante-six _____

ANSWER KEY:
1. one hundred one; 2. one thousand six hundred; 3. two thousand (and) ten; 4. three hundred (and) fifty; 5. two million eight hundred (and) sixty-six

✎ Word Recall

Fill in the blanks with the correct family member in French.

1. La sœur de mon père est ma _____.

2. Le père de ma mère est mon _____.

3. Les filles de ma tante sont mes _____ .

4. Le frère de mon père est mon _____ .

5. Le fils de ma sœur est mon _____ .

ANSWER KEY:

1.tante (*The sister of my father is my aunt.*) 2.grand-père (*The father of my mother is my grandfather.*) 3.cousines (*The daughters of my aunt are my female cousins.*) 4.oncle (*The brother of my father is my uncle.*) 5.neveu (*The son of my sister is my nephew.*)

Grammar Builder 1
IRREGULAR -ER VERBS

▶ 2B Lesson 2 Grammar Builder 1 (CD 7, Track 6)

You know that most-er verbs follow the same pattern:je parle ,tu marches , il/elle dîne ,nous jouons ,vous lavez ,ils/elles demandent .

However, you also know that some-er verbs are slightly irregular, such asmanger (*to eat*) andappeler (*to call*).Manger adds ane in thenous form andappeler doubles thel in every form except for thenous andvous forms.

Let's review the full conjugation ofappeler in the present tense:

APPELER (TO CALL) - PRESENT			
j'appelle	*I call*	nous appelons	*we call*
tu appelles	*you call*	vous appelez	*you call*
il appelle	*he calls*	ils appellent	*they call*
elle appelle	*she calls*	elles appellent	*they call*

Notice the difference in pronunciation betweenappelle andappelons/appelez in the audio. The firste inappelle is pronounced [eh], while the firste inappelons/ appelez (and in the infinitive formappeler) is pronounced [uh].

The verb jeter (*to throw, to throw out/away*) is conjugated and pronounced in a very similar way.

JETER (TO THROW, TO THROW OUT/AWAY) - **PRESENT**			
je jette	*I throw*	nous jetons	*we throw*
tu jettes	*you throw*	vous jetez	*you throw*
il jette	*he throws*	ils jettent	*they throw*
elle jette	*she throws*	elles jettent	*they throw*

As you can see, the t is doubled in every form except for the nous and vous forms. Also, the first e in jette is pronounced [eh], while the first e in jetons/jetez (and in the infinitive form jeter) is pronounced [uh].

However, it is important to note that, in the future and conditional tenses, both appeler and jeter double their respective letters for **all** forms, including nous and vous .

Tu appelleras ton ami demain.
You will call your friend tomorrow.

Nous jetterons les papiers dans la poubelle.
We will throw the papers in the garbage.

Notice the new words le papier (*paper*) and la poubelle (*garbage, trash can*) in the sentence above.

Other verbs like appeler and jeter include:

rappeler	*to call back*
projeter	*to plan*
rejeter	*to reject*

Another -er verb that is slightly irregular is acheter (*to buy*).

ACHETER *(TO BUY)* - **PRESENT**			
j'achète	*I buy*	nous achetons	*we buy*
tu achètes	*you buy*	vous achetez	*you buy*
il achète	*he buys*	ils achètent	*they buy*
elle achète	*she buys*	elles achètent	*they buy*

In this case, instead of doubling a letter, the first e is changed to an è in every form except for nous and vous. But, conveniently enough, the pronunciation is just like appeler and jeter. The è in achète is pronounced [eh], while the first e in achetons/achetez (and acheter) is pronounced [uh].

Again similar to appeler and jeter, the è is used for *all* forms of acheter in the future and conditional tenses.

ACHETER *(TO BUY)* - **FUTURE**			
j'achèterai	*I will buy*	nous achèterons	*we will buy*
tu achèteras	*you will buy*	vous achèterez	*you will buy*
il achètera	*he will buy*	ils achèteront	*they will buy*
elle achètera	*she will buy*	elles achèteront	*they will buy*

Other verbs conjugated like acheter include:

lever	*to lift, to raise, to pick up*
enlever	*to remove, to take off*
mener	*to lead*
emmener	*to take (someone)*
promener	*to walk (to take someone or something for a walk)*
peser	*to weigh*

Marie achète des bijoux au grand magasin.
Marie buys some jewelry at the department store.

Jean emmène ses amis au restaurant.
Jean takes his friends to the restaurant.

Ils enlèvent leurs manteaux.
They take off their coats.

✎ Work Out 1

Fill in the blanks with the correct present tense form of the verb in parentheses.

1. Elle _____ (acheter) des chaussures. (*She is buying shoes.*)

2. _____ -ils (jeter) les chaussettes ? (*Are they throwing out the socks?*)

3. Tu _____ (jeter) tes vêtements sur le lit. (*You throw your clothes on the bed.*)

4. Vous _____ (acheter) des blouses. (*You buy some blouses.*)

5. Ils _____ (acheter) des bijoux. (*They buy jewelry.*)

6. Nous _____ (appeler) nos amis. (*We call our friends.*)

7. Est-ce qu'il _____ (acheter) un costume ? (*Is he buying a suit?*)

8. Comment t'_____-tu (appeler) ? (*What's your name?*)

ANSWER KEY:
1. achète; 2. Jettent; 3. jettes; 4. achetez; 5. achètent; 6. appelons; 7. achète; 8. appelles

Phrase Builder 2

Here is some vocabulary for specialty foods that you might find at un marché (*a market*).

▶ 2C Lesson 2 Phrase Builder 2 (CD 7, Track 7)

Dijon mustard	la moutarde de Dijon
a piece of cheese	un morceau de fromage
chestnut paste	la crème de marrons
a box of sugar-coated chestnuts	une boîte de marrons glacés
black currant syrup	le sirop de cassis
a basket of strawberries	un panier de fraises
a bunch of asparagus	une botte d'asperges*
waffles	les gaufres (*f.*)

⏸ *Botte can also mean *bundle*, as in, *a bundle of leeks or straw*.

Take It Further

Les marrons (*m.*) (*chestnuts*) are popular in France. La crème de marrons (*chestnut paste*) is often used to create spreads, desserts, or fillings for pastries. Les marrons glacés (*sugar-coated chestnuts*) are sweet, candy-coated chestnuts that are served as candy or with dessert. You'll frequently see them in chocolate and candy stores.

Another popular nut is la noisette (*hazelnut*). You will also find hazelnut paste in many spreads, desserts, and pastry fillings. Furthermore, hazelnut is frequently added to chocolate in France. If a piece of chocolate is labeled as praliné, for example, that usually means it's filled with a noisette or amande (*f.*) (*almond*) ganache.

Phrase Practice 2

Match the English words on the left to the correct French translations on the right.

1. *bunch*	a. panier
2. *box*	b. morceau
3. *mustard*	c. botte
4. *basket*	d. boîte
5. *piece*	e. moutarde

ANSWER KEY:
1. c; 2. d; 3. e; 4. a; 5. b

Word Recall

Fill in the blanks with the correct French word.

1. Je fais du _____. *(I play sports.)*

2. Je fais la _____. *(I'm waiting in line.)*

3. Je fais des _____. *(I'm shopping.)*

4. Je fais des _____. *(I'm running errands.)*

5. Je fais le _____. *(I'm cleaning the house.)*

ANSWER KEY:
1. sport ; 2. queue ; 3. courses ; 4. achats ; 5. ménage

Grammar Builder 2
MORE IRREGULAR **-ER** VERBS

▶ 2D Lesson 2 Grammar Builder 2 (CD 7, Track 8)

Another irregular -er verb is préférer (*to prefer*). Here is its full conjugation:

PRÉFÉRER (*TO PREFER*) - **PRESENT**			
je préfère	*I prefer*	nous préférons	*we prefer*
tu préfères	*you prefer*	vous préférez	*you prefer*
il préfère	*he prefers*	ils préfèrent	*they prefer*
elle préfère	*she prefers*	elles préfèrent	*they prefer*

Notice that the last é changes to an è in all forms except for nous and vous.

Qu'est-ce que vous préférez, le café ou le thé ?
Which (What) do you prefer, coffee or tea?

Je préfère l'eau.
I prefer water.

In the future and conditional, the last é doesn't change for any form.

Vous préférerez le chocolat.
You will prefer chocolate.

Vous préféreriez le chocolat.
You would prefer chocolate.

Other verbs that conjugate like **préférer** include:

célébrer	to celebrate
compléter	to complete
espérer	to hope
posséder	to own
protéger	to protect
répéter	to repeat

Il espère aller en France.
He hopes to go to France.

Nous célébrons les fêtes avec notre famille.
We celebrate the holidays with our family.

The verb **suggérer** (*to suggest*) is also formed like **préférer**: je suggère d'aller (*I suggest going*).

✎ Work Out 2

Fill in the blanks with the correct present tense form of the verb **préférer**.

1. Elle _____ la blouse blanche. (*She prefers the white blouse.*)

2. Je _____ les croissants. (*I prefer croissants.*)

3. Elles _____ les robes. (*They prefer dresses.*)

4. Il _____ la cravate rouge. (*He prefers the red tie.*)

5. Nous _____ les gants noirs. (*We prefer black gloves.*)

ANSWER KEY:
1. préfère; 2. préfère; 3. préfèrent; 4. préfère; 5. préférons

✎ Drive It Home

A. Fill in the blanks with the correct present tense form of the verb jeter.

1. Nous _____ nos vêtements sur la chaise.

   (*We throw our clothes on the chair.*)

2. Tu _____ tes vêtements sur la chaise.

   (*You throw your clothes on the chair.*)

3. Elle _____ ses vêtements sur la chaise.

   (*She throws her clothes on the chair.*)

4. Ils _____ leurs vêtements sur la chaise.

   (*They throw their clothes on the chair.*)

5. Je _____ mes vêtements sur la chaise.

   (*I throw my clothes on the chair.*)

6. Vous _____ vos vêtements sur la chaise.

   (*You throw your clothes on the chair.*)

7. Elles _____ leurs vêtements sur la chaise.

   (*They throw their clothes on the chair.*)

8. Il _____ ses vêtements sur la chaise.

   (*He throws his clothes on the chair.*)

B. Now fill in the blanks with the correct present tense form of the verb acheter.

1. Vous _____ des chaussures au grand magasin.

   (*You buy some shoes at the department store.*)

2. Il _____ des chaussures au grand magasin.

   (He buys some shoes at the department store.)

3. J' _____ des chaussures au grand magasin.

   (I buy some shoes at the department store.)

4. Elles _____ des chaussures au grand magasin.

   (They buy some shoes at the department store.)

5. Tu _____ des chaussures au grand magasin.

   (You buy some shoes at the department store.)

6. Elle _____ des chaussures au grand magasin.

   (She buys some shoes at the department store.)

7. Nous _____ des chaussures au grand magasin.

   (We buy some shoes at the department store.)

8. Ils _____ des chaussures au grand magasin.

   (They buy some shoes at the department store.)

C. Finally, fill in the blanks with the correct present tense form of the verb préférer.

1. Je _____ le thé. (I prefer tea.)

2. Tu _____ le thé. (You prefer tea.)

3. Nous _____ le thé. (We prefer tea.)

4. Elle _____ le thé. (She prefers tea.)

5. Elles _____ le thé. (They prefer tea.)

6. Vous _____ le thé. (You prefer tea.)

7. Ils _____ le thé. (*They prefer tea.*)

8. Il _____ le thé. (*He prefers tea.*)

ANSWER KEY:
A. 1. jetons; 2. jettes; 3. jette; 4. jettent; 5. jette; 6. jetez; 7. jettent; 8. jette
B. 1. achetez; 2. achète; 3. achète; 4. achètent; 5. achètes; 6. achète; 7. achetons; 8. achètent
C. 1. préfère; 2. préfères; 3. préférons; 4. préfère; 5. préfèrent; 6. préférez; 7. préfèrent; 8. préfère

 ## Tip

Let's go back to numbers for a second. Now that you know how to talk about *thousands* of something, you actually also know how to talk about the year in French.

To say a year in French, spell out the entire number using mille (*thousand*):

deux mille dix	2010 (*lit., two thousand ten*)
mille neuf cents	1900 (*lit., one thousand nine hundred*)
mille neuf cent quatre-vingt-dix	1990 (*lit., one thousand nine hundred ninety*)
mille sept cent soixante-seize	1776 (*lit., one thousand seven hundred seventy-six*)

How Did You Do?

Let's see how you did! By now, you should be able to:

☐ Talk about hundreds, thousands, or millions of something
(Still unsure? Jump back to page 31)

☐ Discuss what to *throw out* and what to *buy*
(Still unsure? Jump back to page 34)

☐ Name items you might find at a French market
(Still unsure? Jump back to page 38)

☐ Discuss what you *prefer*
(Still unsure? Jump back to page 40)

Lesson 3: Sentences

By the end of this lesson, you will be able to:

☐ Talk about price and size when you go shopping

☐ Discuss what you *use* and who is *paying*

☐ Make comparisons

Sentence Builder 1

▶ 3A Lesson 3 Sentence Builder 1 (CD 7, Track 9)

I would like to buy some clothes.	**Je voudrais acheter des vêtements.**
What do you have?	**Qu'est-ce que vous avez ?**
It's how much? (How much is it?)	**C'est combien ?**
It's too expensive.	**C'est trop cher.**
That's inexpensive./It's a good buy. (lit., It's good market.)	**C'est bon marché.**
Is there a discount?	**Y a-t-il une remise ? (Il y a une remise ?)**
May I try it on? (Can I try it on?)	**Est-ce que je peux l'essayer ?**
Where are the dressing rooms?	**Où sont les cabines d'essayage ?**
What size? (clothing)	**Quelle taille ?**
It's a good choice.	**C'est un bon choix.**
It's on sale.	**Il/Elle est en solde.**
I'll take it. (I'm going to take it.)	**Je vais le/la prendre.**

Take It Further

Let's review *this* and *that*, also known as the "demonstratives." They're very useful words to know when shopping.

DEMONSTRATIVES		
Masculine Singular	ce	*this, that*
Masculine Singular (before a vowel or silent h)	cet	*this, that*
Feminine Singular	cette	*this, that*
Masculine Plural	ces	*these, those*
Feminine Plural	ces	*these, those*

Notice that the plural form is the same for both the masculine and feminine.

Ce pull est jaune.
This sweater is yellow./That sweater is yellow.

Cet imperméable est joli.
This raincoat is pretty./That raincoat is pretty.

Ces chaussures sont marron.
These shoes are brown./Those shoes are brown.

If you want to specify that you mean *this* or *that*, remember that you can add **-ci** (*here*) and **-là** (*there*) after the noun. For example:

Vous voudriez ce manteau-ci ou ce manteau-là ?
Do you want this coat or that coat? (lit., Do you want this coat here or that coat there?)

J'achète cette robe-ci. Je n'aime pas cette robe-là.
I'm buying this dress. I don't like that dress.

You can do the same thing with *these* and *those*:

Ces chaussettes-ci ou ces chaussettes-là ?
These socks or those socks?

Finally, if you want to say *this one* or *that one* in French, use the following words:

celui-ci/celle-ci	*this one, this one here (m./f.)*
celui-là/celle-là	*that one, that one there (m./f.)*
ceux-ci/celles-ci	*these ones, these ones here (m./f.)*
ceux-là/celles-là	*those ones, those ones there (m./f.)*

Notice the different forms depending on gender.

Vous voulez quel chapeau ? Celui-ci.
Which hat do you want? This one.

Je préfère celui-là.
I prefer that one.

Je n'aime pas ces chaussures-ci. J'aime celles-là.
I don't like these shoes. I like those (ones).

✎ Sentence Practice 1

Translate the following words and phrases into French.

1. *the (clothing) size* _____

2. *the dressing rooms* _____

3. *a discount* _____

4. *on sale* _____

5. *inexpensive* _____

ANSWER KEY:
1. la taille; 2. les cabines d'essayage; 3. une remise; 4. en solde; 5. bon marché

✎ Word Recall

Let's review some more question words. Match the French words on the left to the correct English translations on the right.

1. qu'est-ce que	a. *why*
2. comment	b. *who*
3. pourquoi	c. *what*
4. qui	d. *how*

ANSWER KEY:
1. c; 2. d; 3. a; 4. b

Grammar Builder 1
MORE IRREGULAR -**ER** VERBS

▶ 3B Lesson 3 Grammar Builder 1 (CD 7, Track 10)

Let's look at the full conjugation of the verb employer (to use, to employ).

EMPLOYER (TO USE, TO EMPLOY) - PRESENT			
j'emploie	I use	nous employons	we use
tu emploies	you use	vous employez	you use
il emploie	he uses	ils emploient	they use
elle emploie	she uses	elles emploient	they use

As you can see, the y in the verb changes to an i for every form except nous and vous.

In the future and conditional, the y in employer changes to an i for **all** forms, including nous and vous. For example: nous emploierons (we will employ), vous emploieriez (you would employ).

Here are two other verbs like employer:

ennuyer	to bore, to annoy
nettoyer	to clean

Estelle emploie le téléphone pour son travail.
Estelle uses the phone for her work.

Le jeudi, je nettoie la maison.
On Thursdays, I clean the house.

Verbs in -yer are conjugated in the future and conditional using the third person singular form of the present tense rather than the infinitive as the stem.

The verb envoyer (to send, to throw) is also conjugated like employer in the present tense: j'envoie, nous envoyons, etc. However, it is irregular in the future and conditional. Those tenses are formed with enverr- + ending for all forms: j'enverrai (I will send), nous enverrions (we would send), and so on.

Now let's look at another verb that ends in -yer: payer(*to pay, to pay for*).

Interestingly, payer can actually be conjugated with or without the i change. In other words, you can change the y to i for the forms that change, or just keep the y as is. Either one is fine, and you will see both ways used.

PAYER(*TO PAY, TO PAY FOR*) - **PRESENT**			
je paye/je paie	*I pay*	nous payons	*we pay*
tu payes/tu paies	*you pay*	vous payez	*you pay*
il paye/il paie	*he pays*	ils payent/ils paient	*they pay*
elle paye/elle paie	*she pays*	elles payent/elles paient	*they pay*

Notice that nous and vous only have one possible form.

Also note that payer is one of those verbs that takes a direct object in French even when it would take an indirect object in English.

Je paye/paie les billets.
I pay for the tickets.

Or: Je les paye/paie.(*I pay for them.*)

In the future and conditional, either all forms of verbs like payer keep the y or all forms change the y to i Both ways are correct.

The verb essayer(*to try, to try on/out*) is formed like payer.

J'essaie/essaye de parler français.
I'm trying to speak French.

Ⅱ

✎ Work Out 1

Complete the sentences by filling in the correct present tense forms of the verbs in parentheses.

1. Il _____ (employer) l'ordinateur. *(He's using the computer.)*

2. Nous _____ (nettoyer) la maison. *(We're cleaning the house.)*

3. Est-ce que tu _____ (payer) l'addition ? *(Are you paying the bill?)*

4. Vous _____ (essayer) le pantalon. *(You're trying on the pants.)*

ANSWER KEY:
1. emploie, 2. nettoyons, 3. payes/paies, 4. essayez

Sentence Builder 2

▶ 3C Lesson 3 Sentence Builder 2 (CD 7, Track 11)

I would like to buy some souvenirs.	Je voudrais acheter des souvenirs.
I'd like to buy some perfume for my girlfriend.	Je voudrais acheter du parfum pour ma petite amie.
I'd like to buy some cologne for my boyfriend.	Je voudrais acheter de l'eau de cologne pour mon petit ami.
I would like to buy a (fashion) scarf.	Je voudrais acheter un foulard.
You don't have anything else?	Vous n'avez rien d'autre ?
Do you have something less expensive?	Avez-vous quelque chose de moins cher ?
Do you have something of the same kind ? (lit., Do you have something in the same kind/type?)	Avez-vous quelque chose dans le même genre ?
That costs a lot. (That costs dearly.)	Ça coûte cher.

That's three euros per pair. (lit., It/That costs three euros the pair.)	Ça coûte trois euros la paire.
Excuse me, but where is the register?	Excusez-moi, mais où est la caisse ?
You must pay at the register.	Il faut payer à la caisse.

Take It Further

Quelque chose (*something*) is what's known as an "indefinite pronoun." Indefinite pronouns are used to talk generally, referring to nothing or no one specific. You actually already know a few of them. Here's a list of the most common indefinite pronouns:

something	quelque chose
someone, somebody	quelqu'un
each (one)	chacun
another, another one	un/une autre
several	plusieurs
nothing, anything	ne... rien
no one, anyone, nobody, anybody	ne... personne
whatever/whoever/wherever, anything/anyone/anywhere/anytime	n'importe quoi/qui/où/quand

On can also be used as an indefinite pronoun when it means *one, people in general,* or a non-specific *you/they.*

Comment va-t-on au musée ?
How does one get to the museum?

Quelqu'un t'a téléphoné.
Somebody called you.

Il n'y a personne ici.
There's no one here./There's nobody here.

Il fait n'importe quoi pour gagner de l'argent.
He does anything to make money.

You can use **d'autre** or **autre** with some of the indefinite pronouns to mean *else*: **quelqu'un d'autre** (*someone else*), **ne... rien d'autre** (*nothing else, anything else*), etc. If you want to say *something else*, use **autre chose**. **Autre chose** can also mean *anything else*.

And here are some of the other words you saw in Sentence Builder 2. You already knew **le parfum**, which can mean *perfume*, *fragrance*, or *flavor*.

(cash) register	**la caisse**
souvenir, memory	**le souvenir**
cologne	**l'eau** (*f.*) **de cologne**
pair	**la paire**
same, even	**même**
kind, type, genre	**le genre**

Finally, you saw that you can use a definite article (**le, la**) when you want to say *per* something: **trois euros la paire** (*three euros per pair*). Another, more general way is to use **par** (*per*):

trois euros par jour
thirty euros per day

par personne
per person

✎ Sentence Practice 2

Translate the following conversation into English.

\- Je voudrais acheter quelque chose pour ma petite amie.

_____

\- Qu'est-ce que tu veux acheter ?

_____

\- Un foulard ?

_____

\- Voici un foulard.

_____

\- C'est combien ?

_____

\- Ça coûte 60 euros.

_____

\- C'est bon marché. Où est la caisse ?

_____

ANSWER KEY:
- *I would like to buy something for my girlfriend.*
- *What do you want to buy?*
- *A scarf?*
- *Here's a scarf.*
- *How much is it?/It's how much?*
- *It's sixty euros./It costs sixty euros. or That's sixty euros./That costs sixty euros.*
- *That's inexpensive./It's a good buy. Where is the (cash) register?*

✎ Word Recall

Match these expressions.

1. **C'est vrai !**	a. *Okay!*
2. **Pas de chance !**	b. *It's true!*
3. **Formidable !**	c. *Of course!*
4. **D'accord !**	d. *No luck!*
5. **Bien sûr !**	e. *Fantastic!*

ANSWER KEY:
1. b; 2. d; 3. e; 4. a; 5. c

Grammar Builder 2
COMPARISONS

▶ 3D Lesson 3 Grammar Builder 2 (CD 7, Track 12)

You've learned how to form and use adjectives in basic sentences. Now let's look at how to use them in comparisons.

For example, you may want to say that someone or something has *more* or *less* of a characteristic *than* someone or something else. Or you may want to say that they have the same degree of it.

It's very easy to do this in French. Just use the following constructions:

plus + adjective + **que**	*more … than*
moins + adjective + **que**	*less … than (not as … as)*
aussi + adjective + **que**	*as … as*

Il est plus actif que moi.
He is more active than I am. (He is more active than me.)

Il est moins actif que moi.
He is less active than I am. (He is less active than me./He is not as active as me.)

Il est aussi actif que moi.
He is as active as I am. (He is as active as me.)

Note that "**plus** + adjective + **que**" can also be translated as:

-er form of the adjective ... *than*

In other words: *shorter than, taller than,* etc.

Robert est plus grand que Michel.
Robert is taller than Michel.

Don't forget that the adjective must agree with the noun it is describing in gender and number.

Jeanne est plus grande que Robert.
Jeanne is taller than Robert.

Les robes sont plus jolies que les jupes.
The dresses are prettier than the skirts.

Les adultes sont moins actifs que les enfants.
Adults are less active than children. (Adults are not as active as children.)

Les garçons sont aussi grands que les filles.
The boys are as tall as the girls.

In French, you can also use "**plus/moins/aussi** + adjective" without the **que**.
This is like saying *the dress is longer* instead of *the dress is longer than the skirt* in English.

La robe est plus longue.
The dress is longer.

Les parents sont plus gentils.
The parents are kinder.

L'appartement est aussi cher.
The apartment is just as expensive.

Notice that, in this case, "aussi + adjective" translates as *just as ...* .

The adjectives bon/bonne (*good*) and mauvais/mauvaise (*bad*) are irregular when used to make comparisons, just as they are in English.

For example, you wouldn't say plus bon/bonne (*lit., more good*) in French or in English. That's incorrect. Instead, you would use the word meilleur/meilleure (*better*):

Le vin est bon, mais le champagne est meilleur.
The wine good, but the champagne is better.

To say that something is *worse*, change the adjective mauvais/mauvaise (*bad*) to plus mauvais/mauvaise (*worse*) or use the irregular form pire (*worse*). The two forms are interchangeable.

Ce restaurant est pire/plus mauvais que l'autre.
This restaurant is worse than the other.

If you want to say something is *as good* or *as bad*, just use aussi always: Le vin est bon, mais le champagne est aussi bon. (*The wine is good, but the champagne is just as good*). Ce restaurant est aussi mauvais que l'autre. (*This restaurant is as bad as the other.*)

Moins can also be used normally with those two adjectives: moins bon/bonne (*not as good*), moins mauvais/mauvaise (*not as bad*).

Finally, if you're using beaucoup de (*many, much, a lot of*) as an adjective, you don't use aussi beaucoup de if you want to make an equal comparison. Instead, you use autant de:

Il a beaucoup de problèmes.
He has many problems.

Il a autant de problèmes que nous.
He has as many problems as we do. (lit., He has as many problems as us.)

✎ Work Out 2

Complete the sentences by filling in the blanks with the correct French words.

1. Le livre est _____ intéressant _____ le film. (*as ... as*)

2. André est _____ intelligent _____ Gérard. (*less ... than*)

3. Les gants sont _____ beaux _____ les sacs. (*more ... than*)

4. Le manteau est _____ long _____ l'imperméable. (*as ... as*)

ANSWER KEY:
1. aussi... que (*The book is as interesting as the movie.*) 2. moins... que (*André is less intelligent than Gérard./André is not as intelligent as Gérard.*) 3. plus... que (*The gloves are more beautiful than the bags.*) 4. aussi... que (*The coat is as long as the raincoat.*)

✎ Drive It Home

A. Fill in the blanks with the correct present tense form of the verb employer.

1. J' _____ l'ordinateur. (*I'm using the computer.*)

2. Vous _____ l'ordinateur. (*You're using the computer.*)

3. Elle _____ l'ordinateur. (*She's using the computer.*)

4. Tu _____ l'ordinateur. (*You're using the computer.*)

5. Ils _____ l'ordinateur. (*They're using the computer.*)

6. Il _____ l'ordinateur. (*He's using the computer.*)

7. Nous _____ l'ordinateur. (*We're using the computer.*)

8. Elles _____ l'ordinateur. (*They're using the computer.*)

B. Now complete the sentences by filling in the blanks with plus... que . Make sure to read each sentence out loud once you're done.

1. Elle est _____ petite _____ moi.

   (*She is shorter than me.*)

2. Il est _____ petit _____ moi.

   (*He is shorter than me.*)

3. Vous êtes _____ petit(e)(s) _____ moi.

   (*You are shorter than me.*)

4. Tu es _____ petit(e) _____ moi.

   (*You are shorter than me.*)

5. Ils sont _____ petits _____ moi.

   (*They are shorter than me.*)

ANSWER KEY:

A. 1. emploie ; 2. employez ; 3. emploie ; 4. emploies ; 5. emploient ; 6. emploie ; 7. employons ; 8. emploient

B. all plus... que

⊕ Culture Note

Paris has a reputation for being one of the centers of the fashion world. And, in fact, fashion is one of the most important industries in France. French haute couture (*high fashion*) includes many famous names of couturiers (*designers*) from the past and present, including Coco Chanel, Yves Saint Laurent, Christian Dior, and so on.

If you're interested in high fashion, the rive droite (*right bank*), between Opéra and Place Charles de Gaulle, or the neighborhood near Saint-Germain-des-Prés on the rive gauche (*left bank*), is where you need to go in Paris. There are also many small boutiques scattered throughout Paris, as well as famous department stores like Galeries Lafayette, Printemps, and Le Bon Marché. There are various shopping malls scattered throughout the city as well.

How Did You Do?

Let's see how you did! By now, you should be able to:

☐ Talk about price and size when you go shopping
(Still unsure? Jump back to page 45)

☐ Discuss what you *use* and who is *paying*
(Still unsure? Jump back to page 48)

☐ Make comparisons
(Still unsure? Jump back to page 55)

Lesson 4: Conversations

By the end of this lesson, you will be able to:

☐ Say whether something was done *more slowly* or *less quickly*

☐ Talk about *the most* and *the least*

Conversation 1

Mme Martin is at the marché (*market*) shopping for the items she needs to make a soup containing poireaux (*m.*) (*leeks*) and pommes (*f.*) de terre (*potatoes*).

▶ 4A Lesson 4 Conversation 1 (CD 7, Track 13)

Mme Martin :	Bonjour monsieur. Est-ce que vous avez des poireaux aujourd'hui ?
Le marchand :	Bien sûr, madame, combien en voulez-vous ?
Mme Martin :	Combien coûtent les poireaux ?
Le marchand :	Deux euros la livre.
Mme Martin :	Donnez-moi une livre, s'il vous plaît.
Le marchand :	Voilà. Il vous faut autre chose, madame ?
Mme Martin :	Ah, oui. Je fais une bonne soupe ce soir—aux poireaux et aux pommes de terre—donc il me faut des pommes de terre.
Le marchand :	Combien en voulez-vous, madame ?
Mme Martin :	Je voudrais trois livres, s'il vous plaît.
Le marchand :	Et voilà, de belles pommes de terre. Et avec ça ?
Mme Martin :	Ça suffit, pour le moment. Je vous dois combien, monsieur ?
Le marchand :	Ça fait cinq euros, madame.

Ms. Martin:	*Hello sir. Do you have leeks today?*
Merchant:	*Of course, ma'am, how many of them do you want?*
Ms. Martin:	*How much do the leeks cost?*

Merchant:	*Two euros per pound.*
Ms. Martin:	*Give me one pound, please.*
Merchant:	*Here it is. Do you need anything else, ma'am?*
Ms. Martin:	*Oh, yes. I'm making a good soup tonight—leek (and) potatoes—so I need some potatoes.*
Merchant:	*How many of them do you want, ma'am?*
Ms. Martin:	*I would like three pounds, please.*
Merchant:	*And here they are, beautiful potatoes. And with that?*
Ms. Martin:	*That's enough, for the moment. How much do I owe you, sir?*
(II) Merchant:	*That's five euros, ma'am.*

Take It Further

You know that the word en can be used to mean *in, on,* or *to.*

Je vais en vacances.
I'm going on vacation.

Il est allé en France.
He went to France.

Je suis en France.
I'm in France.

However, en can also be used as a pronoun. Like the pronoun y (*there*), it is used to replace a phrase.

En is used to replace "de/du/de la/de l'/des + noun." As a result, it can mean *some, of it, of them, from it,* etc. For example, instead of saying:

Combien voulez-vous de poireaux ?
How many leeks do you want?

You could say:

Combien en voulez-vous ?
How many of them do you want?

Notice that, likey ,en comes before the verb.

Here are some more examples:

Nous buvons du thé.
We drink tea.

Nous en buvons.
We drink some (of it)./We drink it.

J'ai besoin de deux pommes de terre.
I need two potatoes.

J'en ai besoin.
I need some (of them)./I need them.

Whenen is used with a quantity expression likebeaucoup de (*a lot of*) orune livre de (*a pound of*), thede is removed but the quantity (beaucoup, une livre) remains. Notice that English works the same way.

Je voudrais une livre et demie de champignons.
I would like a pound and (a) half of mushrooms.

J'en voudrais une livre et demie.
I would like a pound and (a) half of them.

Je mange beaucoup de fromage.
I eat a lot of cheese.

J'en mange beaucoup.
I eat a lot of it.

In Conversation 1, you also saw that you can use a form of il faut to mean *I need, she needs*, etc. instead of the general *you need to* or *it's necessary to*. Just insert the appropriate **indirect** object pronoun between il and faut:

il faut	it's necessary to, you have to, you need to, you must
il me faut	I need
il vous faut	you need
il lui faut	he needs, she needs

Finally, you saw the very helpful phrase Ça suffit, which means *That's it* or *That's enough*. A related phrase is C'est tout, which means *That's all*. So if the clerk in a store asks you if C'est tout ? (*Is that all?*), you can respond Oui, c'est tout. (*Yes, that's all.*)

✎ Conversation Practice 1

Re-read Conversation 1. Then say whether each sentence below is vrai (*true*) or faux (*false*). Next to each sentence, write down V for vrai or F for faux.

1. Mme Martin voudrait faire une soupe. _____

2. Mme Martin voudrait trois livres de poireaux. _____

3. Mme Martin voudrait une livre de pommes de terre. _____

4. Les poireaux coûtent cinq euros la livre. _____

5. Mme Martin doit cinq euros. _____

ANSWER KEY:

1. V (*Yes, she does want to make a soup.*) 2. F (*No, Mme Martin would like one pound of leeks.*) 3. F (*No, Mme Martin would like three pounds of potatoes.*) 4. F (*No, the leeks cost two euros per pound.*) 5. V (*Yes, she does owe five euros.*)

✎ Word Recall

Translate the following avoir expressions into English.

1. avoir froid _____

2. avoir soif _____

3. avoir besoin de _____

4. avoir tort _____

5. avoir faim _____

6. avoir envie de _____

7. avoir raison _____

ANSWER KEY:

1. *to be cold;* 2. *to be thirsty;* 3. *to need;* 4. *to be wrong;* 5. *to be hungry;* 6. *to feel like;* 7. *to be right*

Grammar Builder 1
COMPARISONS WITH ADVERBS AND AMOUNTS

▷ 4B Lesson 4 Grammar Builder 1 (CD 7, Track 14)

You can also make comparisons with adverbs.

For example, here are the three ways you can make a comparison using
poliment (*politely*):

plus poliment que	more politely than
moins poliment que	less politely than (not as politely as)
aussi poliment que	as politely as

Here are some more examples of comparisons with adverbs:

Marc parle plus lentement que Joseph.
Marc speaks more slowly than Joseph.

Le train va moins vite que l'avion.
*The train goes less quickly than the plane. (The train does not go as quickly as the
plane.)*

L'autobus va aussi vite que la voiture.
The bus goes as quickly as the car.

Like the adjective bon (*good*), the adverb bien (*well*) has an irregular comparative
form when talking about more. Instead of plus bien (*lit., more well*), which is
incorrect, you say mieux (*better*).

Marie parle bien, mais Jean parle mieux.
Marie speaks well, but Jean speaks better.

And like the adjective mauvais (bad), the adverb mal (bad, badly) has two possible comparative forms when talking about more: plus mal (worse) or pire (worse). However, pire is mainly used in informal conversation and is generally not considered correct in writing or formal speech.

When used as adverbs, beaucoup (many, a lot, much) and peu (little) also have some irregular comparative forms. Instead of plus beaucoup, you simply say plus (more). And instead of plus peu, you say moins (less). In equal comparisons, beaucoup becomes autant.

Je travaille beaucoup.
I work a lot.

Je travaille autant que toi.
I work as much as you do. (I work as much as you.)

You can also compare amounts of things. Just use "plus de + noun + que" (more ... than) or "moins de + noun + que" (less ... than).

Il y a plus de baguettes dans la boulangerie que dans la pâtisserie.
There are more baguettes in the bakery than in the pastry shop.

✎ Work Out 1

Complete the following sentences with the correct missing words.

1. Paul parle _____ Christine. (Paul speaks better than Christine.)

2. Il conduit _____ moi. (He drives worse than me.)

3. Elle travaille _____ lui. (She works as much as him.)

4. Nos parents conduisent _____ vous.

(*Our parents drive as slowly as you.*)

5. Tu parles _____ moi. (*You speak more quickly than me.*)

ANSWER KEY:

1. mieux que; 2. plus mal que/pire que; 3. autant que; 4. aussi lentement que; 5. plus vite que

Conversation 2

Cheyann and Jeanne are shopping for a special event next Saturday evening.

▶ 4C Lesson 4 Conversation 2 (CD 7, Track 15)

Cheyann :	Je voudrais acheter une nouvelle paire de chaussures pour la soirée de samedi prochain.
Jeanne :	Et moi, je vais regarder les robes.
Cheyann :	Regarde ces belles chaussures rouges ! Je les aime ! Qu'est-ce que tu penses ?
Jeanne :	Elles sont très belles, mais je pense que les chaussures noires sont plus belles et plus chic. Essaye-les.
Cheyann :	Voici ma pointure... Je les aime beaucoup ! Tu as raison. Les chaussures noires sont les plus belles.
Jeanne :	Et maintenant, qu'est-ce que tu penses, la robe bleue ou la robe noire ?
Cheyann :	La robe bleue est la plus jolie. J'adore la couleur. Essaye-la.
Jeanne :	Regarde cette belle robe que je porte !
Cheyann :	Oh là là ! Elle te va à ravir.
Jeanne :	À mon avis, nous serons les plus jolies femmes à la soirée.
Cheyann :	De toute façon, nous serons bien habillées !

Cheyann:	*I'd like to buy a new pair of shoes for the party next Saturday (lit., of next Saturday).*
Jeanne:	*And me, I'm going to look at dresses.*
Cheyann:	*Look at these beautiful red shoes! I like them! What do you think?*
Jeanne:	*They're very beautiful, but I think that the black shoes are more beautiful and more stylish. Try them on.*
Cheyann:	*Here's my (shoe) size ... I like them a lot! You're right. The black shoes are the most beautiful.*
Jeanne:	*And now, what do you think, the blue dress or the black dress?*
Cheyann:	*The blue dress is the prettiest. I love the color. Try it on.*
Jeanne:	*Look at this beautiful dress that I'm wearing!*
Cheyann:	*Wow! It looks great on you.*
Jeanne:	*In my opinion, we'll be the most beautiful women at the party.*
Cheyann:	*At any rate, we'll be well-dressed!*

Take It Further

You just saw some good expressions to use in conversation. Let's review:

in my opinion	à mon avis
at any rate, in any case, anyhow	de toute façon
to look great on someone, to suit someone well	aller à ravir à quelqu'un

La jupe va à ravir à Sophie. Elle lui va à ravir.
The skirt looks great on Sophie. It looks great on her.

Also notice the use of que to mean *that* in je pense que... (*I think that ...*) and cette belle robe que je porte (*this beautiful dress that I'm wearing*). You'll learn more about how to use que in Unit 3.

Finally, here are some new words you'll see in Grammar Builder 2:

student, pupil	un/une élève
class, grade, classroom	la classe
famous	célèbre

✎ Conversation Practice 2

Translate the following sentences into English.

1. Je les aime ! _____

2. Essaye-les. _____

3. Essaye-la. _____

4. Elle te va à ravir. _____

ANSWER KEY:
1. *I like them!* 2. *Try them on.* 3. *Try it on.* 4. *It looks great on you.*

✎ Word Recall

Fill in the blanks with the correct French word.

1. Il me faut une _____ . (*I need a fork.*)

2. Il me faut un _____ . (*I need a knife.*)

3. Il me faut une _____ . (*I need a napkin.*)

4. Il me faut une _____ . (*I need a spoon.*)

5. Il me faut du _____ . (*I need salt.*)

6. Il me faut du _____ . (*I need pepper.*)

ANSWER KEY:
1. fourchette; 2. couteau; 3. serviette; 4. cuiller/cuillère; 5. sel; 6. poivre

Grammar Builder 2
THE MOST AND THE LEAST

▶ 4D Lesson 4 Grammar Builder 2 (CD 7, Track 16)

If you want to talk about *the most* or *the least* of something, then you need to use the "superlative" form of the adjective.

In French, the superlative is formed by using:

le/la/les + plus + adjective	the most ...
le/la/les + moins + adjective	the least ...

Don't forget that the adjective has to agree in gender and number with the noun. Here are some examples with *the most*:

le plus beau
the most handsome

la plus belle
the most beautiful

les plus beaux
the most handsome

les plus belles
the most beautiful

Note that the plus superlative can also be translated as the -*est* form of an adjective: *the tallest, the smallest,* etc. For example: le plus joli (*the prettiest*).

Now here are some examples with *the least*:

le moins joli
the least pretty

la moins jolie
the least pretty

les moins jolis
the least pretty

les moins jolies
the least pretty

Now let's look at how to use the superlative in sentences. Remember that most adjectives in French follow the noun. As a result, their superlatives also follow the noun. Note that the definite article (le, la, l', les) appears twice as a result.

Où est le restaurant le plus cher ?
Where is the most expensive restaurant? (lit., Where is the restaurant the most expensive?)

Les restaurants les plus célèbres sont à New York.
The most famous restaurants are in New York. (lit., The restaurants the most famous are in New York.)

In French, the word *in* is translated by the partitive (du, de la, etc.) when it follows the superlative:

C'est la ville la plus riche du monde.
It's the richest city in the world. (lit., It's the city the richest of the world.)

Keep in mind, however, that some adjectives come before the noun in French. For those adjectives, you usually put their superlatives before the noun as well. In this case, the definite article only appears once.

Henri est le meilleur élève de la classe.
Henri is the best pupil in the class.

As you can see, the plus superlative of bon/bonne (*good*) is irregular. So, if you want to say *the best*, use le/la/les + meilleur(s)/meilleure(s). Not surprisingly, the plus superlative of mauvais/mauvaise (*bad*) is irregular as well. If you want to say *the worst*, use le/la/les + pire(s) or le/la/les + plus mauvais/mauvaise(s).

✎ Work Out 2

Translate the following sentences into English.

1. C'est la plus jolie maison. _____

2. C'est la jupe la moins chère. _____

   _____

3. Elle est la plus belle femme. _____

   _____

4. Elle est la meilleure amie de Sophie. _____

5. Il est l'homme le plus heureux du monde. _____

   _____

ANSWER KEY:
1. *This is/That is/It is the prettiest house/home.* 2. *This is/That is/It is the least expensive skirt.* 3. *She is the most beautiful woman.* 4. *She is Sophie's best friend./She is the best friend of Sophie.* 5. *He is the happiest man in the world.*

✎ Drive It Home

A. Complete the sentences by filling in the blanks with moins... que.

1. Elle marche _____ vite _____ lui.

   (She does not walk as quickly as him.)

2. Tu marches _____ vite _____ lui.

   (You do not walk as quickly as him.)

3. Je marche _____ vite _____ lui.

   (I do not walk as quickly as him.)

4. Nous marchons _____ vite _____ lui.

   (We do not walk as quickly as him.)

5. Ils marchent _____ vite _____ lui.

   (They do not walk as quickly as him.)

B. Now complete the following sentences by filling in the blanks with le plus.

1. C'est _____ grand restaurant. *(It's the biggest restaurant.)*

2. C'est le livre _____ cher. *(It's the most expensive book.)*

3. C'est _____ long film. *(It's the longest movie.)*

4. C'est le grand magasin _____ célèbre.

   (It's the most famous department store.)

5. C'est _____ joli magasin. *(It's the prettiest store.)*

ANSWER KEY:
A. all moins... que
B. all le plus

 Tip

You know a lot about French pronouns by now. You've learned about subject pronouns, direct object pronouns, indirect object pronouns, y, en, etc.

You've also learned that they all come before the verb in French.

Elle la ferme.
She closes it.

Il me parle.
He speaks to me.

J'y vais.
I'm going there.

Nous en buvons.
We drink some.

However, what do you do when you need to use more than one of those pronouns in a sentence? Well, there's a specific order for that as well. In sentences, place the pronouns in the following order:

ORDER OF PRONOUNS IN SENTENCES						
subject pronouns	me (m')	le	lui	y	en	verb
	te (t')	la	leur			
	se (s')	l'				
	nous	les				
	vous					

Il me le donne.

He gives it to me.

Il le lui donne.

He gives it to him/her/it.

Il y en a trois.

There are three of them.

Je leur en parlerai.

I'll speak to them about it. (lit., I'll speak to them of it.)

How Did You Do?

Let's see how you did! By now, you should be able to:

☐ Say whether something was done *more slowly* or *less quickly*
(Still unsure? Jump back to page 66)

☐ Talk about *the most* and *the least*
(Still unsure? Jump back to page 71)

Unit 1 Essentials

Test your knowledge of the materials in Unit 1 by filling in the blanks in the following charts and sentences. Once you've completed these pages, you'll have your very own reference for the most essential vocabulary and grammar from this unit.

Don't forget to go to ***www.livinglanguage.com/languagelab*** to access your free online tools for this lesson: audiovisual flashcards, and interactive games and quizzes.

Vocabulary Essentials

CLOTHING

clothing		raincoat	
(man's) suit		glove	
pants		shirt	
jacket		skirt	
coat		blouse	
(fashion) scarf		sock	
hat		shoes	
sweater			

[Pg. 15] (If you're stuck, visit this page to review!)

ACCESSORIES

accessories		ring	
purse, bag		umbrella	
bathing suit		tie	

pajamas		glasses	
jewelry		sunglasses	
watch		briefcase	

[Pg. 22]

NUMBERS ABOVE 100

one hundred one		one thousand	
two hundred		one thousand one	
two hundred six		one million	

[Pg. 31]

SPECIALTY FOODS

Dijon mustard	
a piece of cheese	
a box of sugar-coated chestnuts	
a basket of strawberries	

[Pg. 38]

SHOPPING EXPRESSIONS

It's how much?/How much is it?	
It's too expensive.	
That's inexpensive./It's a good buy.	
Is there a discount?	
May I try it on?/Can I try it on?	
Where are the dressing rooms?	
What size? (clothing)	

It's on sale.	
I'll take it./I'm going to take it.	

[Pg. 45]

MORE SHOPPING EXPRESSIONS

Do you have something less expensive?	
Excuse me, but where is the register?	
You must pay at the register.	

[Pg. 51]

IRREGULAR -ER VERBS

to eat		*to buy*	
to call		*to lift, to raise, to pick up*	
to call back		*to take (someone)*	
to throw, to throw out, to throw away		*to walk, to take someone or something for a walk*	

[Pgs. 34–36]

MORE IRREGULAR -ER VERBS

to prefer		*to repeat*	
to celebrate		*to suggest*	
to hope			

[Pgs. 40 & 41]

MORE IRREGULAR -ER VERBS

to use, to employ		to send	
to bore, to annoy		to pay, to pay for	
to clean		to try, to try on, to try out	

[Pgs. 49 & 50]

Grammar Essentials ·

DIRECT OBJECT PRONOUNS

1. Direct object pronouns in French always come before the verb in a sentence.

2. If a verb is followed by another verb in the infinitive, place the direct object pronoun directly before the verb it is referring to, which is usually the verb in the infinitive.

3. The direct object pronouns me and te become moi and toi in the positive imperative. Also, the pronoun normally comes after the verb in the positive imperative.

DIRECT OBJECT PRONOUNS			
me	me (m')	us	nous
you	te (t')	you	vous
him, it (m.)	le (l')	them (m.), it (m. pl.)	les
her, it (f.)	la (l')	them (f.), it (f. pl.)	les

INDIRECT OBJECT PRONOUNS

1. Indirect objects in French are usually preceded by a preposition like à (to).

2. Indirect object pronouns in French replace both the indirect object **and** the preposition in the sentence.

3. Indirect object pronouns are placed immediately before the verb.

Advanced French

4. The indirect object pronouns me and te become moi and toi in the positive imperative. Also, the pronoun normally comes after the verb in the positive imperative.

INDIRECT OBJECT PRONOUNS			
to me	me (m')	to us	nous
to you	te (t')	to you	vous
to him/her/it	lui	to them, to it	leur

COMPARISONS WITH ADJECTIVES

more ... than, -er ... than	plus + adjective + que
less ... than, not as ... as	moins + adjective + que
as ... as	aussi + adjective + que

IRREGULAR COMPARISONS WITH ADJECTIVES

better	meilleur/meilleure
worse	plus mauvais/mauvaise, pire
as many, as much	autant de

COMPARISONS WITH ADVERBS

more ... than	plus + adverb + que
less ... than, not as ... as	moins + adverb + que
as ... as	aussi + adverb + que

IRREGULAR COMPARISONS WITH ADVERBS

better	mieux
worse	plus mal, pire
more	plus
less	moins
as much	autant

COMPARISONS WITH AMOUNTS

more ... than	plus de + noun + que
less ... than	moins de + noun + que

THE SUPERLATIVE

1. If an adjective normally follows the noun, then its superlative follows the noun.
2. If the adjective normally comes before the noun, then its superlative comes before the noun.

The superlative is formed by using:

the most ... , the -est	le/la/les + plus + adjective
the least ...	le/la/les + moins + adjective

IRREGULAR SUPERLATIVES

the best	le/la/les + meilleur(s)/meilleure(s)
the worst	le/la/les + pire(s), le/la/les + plus mauvais/mauvaise(s)

VERBS

ACHETER *(TO BUY)* - **PRESENT**

I buy	j'achète	we buy	nous achetons
you buy (infml.)	tu achètes	you buy (pl./fml.)	vous achetez
he buys	il achète	they buy (m.)	ils achètent
she buys	elle achète	they buy (f.)	elles achètent

ACHETER *(TO BUY)* - **FUTURE**

I will buy	j'achèterai	we will buy	nous achèterons
you will buy (infml.)	tu achèteras	you will buy (pl./fml.)	vous achèterez
he will buy	il achètera	they will buy (m.)	ils achèteront
she will buy	elle achètera	they will buy (f.)	elles achèteront

APPELER *(TO CALL)* - **PRESENT**

I call	j'appelle	we call	nous appelons
you call (infml.)	tu appelles	you call (pl./fml.)	vous appelez
he calls	il appelle	they call (m.)	ils appellent
she calls	elle appelle	they call (f.)	elles appellent

EMPLOYER *(TO USE, TO EMPLOY)* - **PRESENT**

I use	j'emploie	we use	nous employons
you use (infml.)	tu emploies	you use (pl./fml.)	vous employez
he uses	il emploie	they use (m.)	ils emploient
she uses	elle emploie	they use (f.)	elles emploient

JETER *(TO THROW, TO THROW OUT/AWAY)* - **PRESENT**			
I throw	je jette	*we throw*	nous jetons
you throw (infml.)	tu jettes	*you throw (pl./fml.)*	vous jetez
he throws	il jette	*they throw (m.)*	ils jettent
she throws	elle jette	*they throw (f.)*	elles jettent

JETER *(TO THROW, TO THROW OUT, TO THROW AWAY)* - **FUTURE**			
I will throw	je jetterai	*we will throw*	nous jetterons
you will throw (infml.)	tu jetteras	*you will throw (pl./fml.)*	vous jetterez
he will throw	il jettera	*they will throw (m.)*	ils jetteront
she will throw	elle jettera	*they will throw (f.)*	elles jetteront

PAYER *(TO PAY, TO PAY FOR)* - **PRESENT**			
I pay	je paye/je paie	*we pay*	nous payons
you pay (infml.)	tu payes/tu paies	*you pay (pl./fml.)*	vous payez
he pays	il paye/il paie	*they pay (m.)*	ils payent/ils paient
she pays	elle paye/elle paie	*they pay (f.)*	elles payent/elles paient

PRÉFÉRER *(TO PREFER)* **- PRESENT**

I prefer	je préfère	we prefer	nous préférons
you prefer (infml.)	tu préfères	you prefer (pl./fml.)	vous préférez
he prefers	il préfère	they prefer (m.)	ils préfèrent
she prefers	elle préfère	they prefer (f.)	elles préfèrent

PRÉFÉRER *(TO PREFER)* **- FUTURE**

I will prefer	je préférerai	we will prefer	nous préférerons
you will prefer (infml.)	tu préféreras	you will prefer (pl./fml.)	vous préférerez
he will prefer	il préférera	they will prefer (m.)	ils préféreront
she will prefer	elle préférera	they will prefer (f.)	elles préféreront

Unit 1 Quiz

Now let's see how you've done so far!

In this section you'll find a short quiz testing what you learned in Unit 1. After you've answered all of the questions, score your quiz and see how you did! If you find that you need to go back and review, please do so before continuing on to Unit 2.

As in *Intermediate French*, there will be a quiz at the end of every unit.

A. Match the clothing and accessories on the left to the correct French translations on the right.

1. *watch*	a. **le manteau**
2. *sweater*	b. **le parapluie**
3. *coat*	c. **la montre**
4. *bag*	d. **le pull**
5. *umbrella*	e. **le sac**

B. Translate the following phrases into French.

1. *How much is it?* _____

2. *Can I try it on?* _____

3. *What size?* _____

4. *It's on sale.* _____

5. *Where is the register?* _____

C. Give the correct present tense form of the verb in parentheses.

1. tu _____ (employer)

2. elles _____ (appeler)

3. nous _____ (jeter)

4. il _____ (acheter)

5. je _____ (payer)

D. Rewrite the following sentences in French by replacing the underlined phrases with direct or indirect object pronouns.

1. **Tu parles <u>à moi</u>.** (*You speak to me.*)

   _____

2. **Je donne le bracelet <u>à toi</u>.** (*I give the bracelet to you.*)

   _____

3. **Elle prend <u>le train</u>.** (*She takes the train.*)

   _____

4. **Il parle <u>à Nathalie et Paul</u>.** (*He speaks to Nathalie and Paul.*)

   _____

5. **Vous allez aider <u>Sophie</u>.** (*You're going to help Sophie.*)

   _____

ANSWER KEY:
A. 1. c; 2. d; 3. a; 4. e; 5. b
B. 1. C'est combien ? 2. Est-ce que je peux l'essayer ? 3. Quelle taille ? 4. Il/Elle est en solde. 5. Où est la caisse ?
C. 1. emploies; 2. appellent; 3. jetons; 4. achète; 5. paie/paye
D. 1. Tu me parles. 2. Je te donne le bracelet. 3. Elle le prend. 4. Il leur parle. 5. Vous allez l'aider.

How Did You Do?

Give yourself a point for every correct answer, then use the following key to determine whether or not you're ready to move on:

0-7 points: It's probably best to go back and study the lessons again to make sure you understood everything completely. Take your time; it's not a race! Make sure you spend time reviewing the vocabulary and reading through each grammar note carefully.

8-16 points: If the questions you missed were in Section A or B, you may want to review the vocabulary again; if you missed answers mostly in Section C or D, check the Unit 1 Essentials to make sure you have your conjugations and other grammar basics down.

17-20 points: Feel free to move on to the next unit! You're doing a great job.

Points

The Imperfect Tense (*I Was Speaking*)   The Imperfect Tense vs. The Past Tense

Irregular Imperfect Tense

I Read, I Write, I Say

Unit 2:
Work and School

In this unit, you'll learn the vocabulary you need to talk about school and jobs. You'll also learn another very important past tense: l'imparfait *(m.) (the imperfect)*. Knowing the difference between l'imparfait and le passé composé *(the past tense)* is an essential part of learning to speak naturally in French.

By the end of this unit, you should be able to:

☐ Name different professions

☐ Talk about what you *used to have*

☐ Identify the different departments in a company

☐ Say what you *used to eat* and who you *used to be*

☐ Talk about applying for a job

☐ Describe what was going on when something happened

☐ Talk about school

☐ Say *I read, I write,* and *I say*

☐ Describe your work environment

☐ Talk about duration

☐ Talk about classes, tests, and activities at school

☐ Say *I leave* and *I sleep*

☐ Tell someone what you *see*

☐ Say what you *know* and whom you *know*

Lesson 5: Words

By the end of this lesson, you will be able to:

☐ Name different professions

☐ Talk about what you *used to have*

☐ Identify the different departments in a company

☐ Say what you *used to eat* and who you *used to be*

Word Builder 1

Let's get started with les professions (*f.*) (*professions*). You should already be familiar with some of them.

▶ 5A Lesson 5 Word Builder 1 (CD 7, Track 17)

accountant	le comptable/la comptable
bank clerk	l'employé de banque/l'employée de banque
civil servant	le fonctionnaire/la fonctionnaire
pharmacist	le pharmacien/la pharmacienne
homemaker	l'homme au foyer/la femme au foyer
construction worker	l'ouvrier en bâtiment/l'ouvrière en bâtiment
author	l'auteur/l'auteure
writer	l'écrivain/l'écrivaine*
computer programmer	l'informaticien/l'informaticienne

* As you learned in Essential French, écrivain can be and often is used for both men and women; écrivaine exists, but is less common.

The Imperfect Tense (*I Was Speaking*)   The Imperfect Tense vs. The Past Tense

Irregular Imperfect Tense   *I Read, I Write, I Say*

dentist	le dentiste/la dentiste
nurse	l'infirmier/l'infirmière
actor/actress	l'acteur/l'actrice
plumber	le plombier
farmer	le fermier/la fermière
carpenter	le charpentier
policeman/policewoman	le policier/la femme policier, l'agent de police/l'agente de police
businessman/businesswoman	l'homme d'affaires/la femme d'affaires
beautician	l'esthéticien/l'esthéticienne

Take It Further

Remember that some professions have both masculine and feminine forms, while certain professions only have a masculine form that's used for both men and women. For example, *plumber* and *carpenter* usually only have a masculine form, but you can use it to talk about a man or a woman.

Also remember that French does not use an indefinite article between être and professions:

Je suis écrivain.
I am a writer.

✎ Word Practice 1

Match the following professions to the correct French translations on the right.

1. *nurse*	a. le fonctionnaire/la fonctionnaire
2. *plumber*	b. l'écrivain/l'écrivaine
3. *accountant*	c. le comptable/la comptable
4. *carpenter*	d. l'infirmier/l'infirmière
5. *civil servant*	e. le plombier
6. *writer*	f. le charpentier

ANSWER KEY:

1. d; 2. e; 3. c; 4. f; 5. a; 6. b

✎ Word Recall

Now let's review some of the professions you saw in *Essential French*. Translate each sentence into French.

1. *My father is a doctor.* _____

2. *She is a singer.* _____

3. *My son is a lawyer.* _____

4. *He is a cook.* _____

5. *Sandrine is a manager.* _____

ANSWER KEY:

1. Mon père est médecin. 2. Elle est chanteuse. 3. Mon fils est avocat. 4. Il est cuisinier. 5. Sandrine est gérante. (Sandrine est directrice.)

The Imperfect Tense (*I Was Speaking*)   The Imperfect Tense vs. The Past Tense

Irregular Imperfect Tense   *I Read, I Write, I Say*

Grammar Builder 1
THE IMPERFECT TENSE (*I WAS SPEAKING*)

▶ 5B Lesson 5 Grammar Builder 1 (CD 7, Track 18)

You've already learned one way to talk about the past in French: le passé composé (*the past tense*). For example: j'ai mangé (*I ate*), je suis allé(e) (*I went*), etc.

However, you can also talk about the past using l'imparfait (*m.*) (*the imperfect tense*). L'imparfait usually corresponds to the following forms in English: *used to + verb* (*used to talk*) and *was/were + -ing* (*was talking, were talking*). In Lesson 6, we'll look more in-depth at when to use l'imparfait, and the difference between le passé composé and l'imparfait. For now, just focus on learning how to form the tense.

Fortunately, it's very easy to form the imperfect tense. All three groups of verbs form the imperfect in the same way:

1. Take the nous form of the verb in the present tense and drop the -ons ending.

2. Next, add one of the following endings:

PRONOUN	ENDING	PRONOUN	ENDING
je	-ais	nous	-ions
tu	-ais	vous	-iez
il	-ait	ils	-aient
elle	-ait	elles	-aient

And that's it!

Let's look at an example of an -er verb in the imperfect: parler *(to speak)*. In the present tense, the nous form of parler is parlons. So just drop the -ons from parlons (leaving you with parl-) and add the endings to form the imperfect.

PARLER *(TO SPEAK)* - **IMPERFECT**			
je parlais	*I was speaking, I used to speak*	nous parlions	*we were speaking, we used to speak*
tu parlais	*you were speaking, you used to speak*	vous parliez	*you were speaking, you used to speak*
il parlait	*he was speaking, he used to speak*	ils parlaient	*they were speaking, they used to speak*
elle parlait	*she was speaking, she used to speak*	elles parlaient	*they were speaking, they used to speak*

Notice that the endings for the imperfect tense are the same as the endings for the conditional tense. Of course, the tenses are not identical; the first part is formed differently. For instance, *I would speak* is je parlerais, while *I was speaking* is je parlais.

Also note that a verb like étudier *(to study)* will have two ?s in a row in the nous and vous imperfect forms. It may look a little strange, but it is correct.

nous étudiions	*we were studying (we used to study)*
vous étudiiez	*you were studying (you used to study)*

The Imperfect Tense (*I Was Speaking*)   The Imperfect Tense vs. The Past Tense

Irregular Imperfect Tense   *I Read, I Write, I Say*

Now let's look at an -ir verb in the imperfect: finir (*to finish*). In the present tense, the nous form of finir is finissons. By dropping the -ons from finissons, you get finiss-, and then you just add the endings.

FINIR (TO FINISH) - **IMPERFECT**			
je finissais	*I was finishing, I used to finish*	nous finissions	*we were finishing, we used to finish*
tu finissais	*you were finishing, you used to finish*	vous finissiez	*you were finishing, you used to finish*
il finissait	*he was finishing, he used to finish*	ils finissaient	*they were finishing, they used to finish*
elle finissait	*she was finishing, she used to finish*	elles finissaient	*they were finishing, they used to finish*

Next, let's look at an -re verb: vendre (*to sell*). In the present tense, the nous form of vendre is vendons. So drop the -ons from vendons and then add the endings.

VENDRE (TO SELL) - **IMPERFECT**			
je vendais	*I was selling, I used to sell*	nous vendions	*we were selling, we used to sell*
tu vendais	*you were selling, you used to sell*	vous vendiez	*you were selling, you used to sell*
il vendait	*he was selling, he used to sell*	ils vendaient	*they were selling, they used to sell*
elle vendait	*she was selling, she used to sell*	elles vendaient	*they were selling, they used to sell*

Finally, let's look at the imperfect of avoir (*to have*). Avoir forms the imperfect normally. In the present tense, the nous form of avoir is avons, so just drop the -ons from avons and then add the endings.

AVOIR *(TO HAVE)* - **IMPERFECT**			
j'avais	*I had, I was having, I used to have*	nous avions	*we had, we were having, we used to have*
tu avais	*you had, you were having, you used to have*	vous aviez	*you had, you were having, you used to have*
il avait	*he had, he was having, he used to have*	ils avaient	*they had, they were having, they used to have*
elle avait	*she had, she was having, she used to have*	elles avaient	*they had, they were having, they used to have*

Notice that the imperfect of avoir is usually translated as *had, was/were having*, or *used to have*.

As an additional note, remember the expression il y a (*there is, there are*)? Its imperfect form is il y avait (*there was, there were*).

Il y a un concert samedi soir.
There is a concert on Saturday evening.

Il y avait un concert samedi soir.
There was a concert on Saturday evening.

The Imperfect Tense (*I Was Speaking*)   The Imperfect Tense vs. The Past Tense

Irregular Imperfect Tense   *I Read, I Write, I Say*

Also keep in mind that if a verb has an irregular nous form in the present tense, then that irregular form will carry over into the imperfect. For example, the nous form of boire (*to drink*) is buvons, so the imperfect of boire would be je buvais, tu buvais, etc. Same goes for faire, conduire, prendre, etc.

✎ Work Out 1

Fill in the blanks with the correct imperfect tense form of the verbs in parentheses. Note that vouloir (*to want*) and aller (*to go*) form the imperfect normally.

1. il ne _____ (finir) pas

2. elle _____ (vendre)

3. tu _____ (danser)

4. nous ne _____ (marcher) pas

5. il _____ (boire)

6. vous _____ (aller)

7. nous _____ (étudier)

8. je n' _____ (avoir) pas

9. elles _____ (vouloir)

ANSWER KEY:
1. finissait; 2. vendait; 3. dansais; 4. marchions; 5. buvait; 6. alliez; 7. étudiions; 8. avais; 9. voulaient

Word Builder 2

Here is some more useful vocabulary related to work.

▶ 5C Lesson 5 Word Builder 2 (CD 7, Track 19)

job, work	le boulot, le travail
factory	l'usine *(f.)*
company	la société
accounting	la comptabilité
computer science (IT)	l'informatique *(f.)*
computer	l'ordinateur *(m.)*
software	le logiciel
meeting	la réunion
staff	le personnel
colleague	le collègue/la collègue
boss	le patron/la patronne
salary	le salaire

Take It Further

Instead of just la comptabilité or l'informatique, you might also hear le service de comptabilité (*accounting department*) or le service d'informatique (*IT department*). As you can probably tell, le service means *department*.

Here are some other services within a company:

finance department	le service financier
sales department	le service des ventes
legal department	le service juridique

The Imperfect Tense (*I Was Speaking*)   The Imperfect Tense vs. The Past Tense

Irregular Imperfect Tense   *I Read, I Write, I Say*

marketing department	le service de marketing
public relations (PR) department	le service des relations publiques
shipping department, mail room	le service du courrier
customer service department	le service clientèle, le service client

And of course:

| management | la direction |

✎ Word Practice 2

Translate the following phrases into French:

1. *my salary* _____

2. *their computer* _____

3. *her (female) boss* _____

4. *our company* _____

5. *your (plural/polite) job* _____

ANSWER KEY

1. mon salaire; 2. leur ordinateur; 3. sa patronne; 4. notre société; 5. votre boulot/travail

✎ Word Recall

Rewrite the following verbs in the **passé composé** (*past tense*).

1. je finis _____

2. vous travaillez _____

3. elles vendent _____

4. j'ai _____

5. nous buvons _____

6. elle arrive _____

ANSWER KEY:
1. j'ai fini; 2. vous avez travaillé; 3. elles ont vendu; 4. j'ai eu; 5. nous avons bu; 6. elle est arrivée

Grammar Builder 2
IRREGULAR IMPERFECT TENSE

▶ 5D Lesson 5 Grammar Builder 2 (CD 7, Track 20)

Unfortunately, there are some verbs with irregular forms in the imperfect.

As you know, verbs like manger (*to eat*) and commencer (*to begin, to start*) have a spelling change in the present tense nous form: nous mangeons, nous commençons. You also know that since the imperfect is based on the nous form, this spelling change should carry over into the imperfect.

Well, it does, but, somewhat ironically, that spelling change **does not** carry over for the nous and vous forms. In other words, in the imperfect, verbs like manger and commencer carry over the spelling change for all forms except nous and vous.

Here are the full conjugations of manger and commencer in the imperfect:

MANGER *(TO EAT)* - **IMPERFECT**			
je mangeais	*I was eating, I used to eat*	nous mangions	*we were eating, we used to eat*
tu mangeais	*you were eating, you used to eat*	vous mangiez	*you were eating, you used to eat*

The Imperfect Tense (*I Was Speaking*)   The Imperfect Tense vs. The Past Tense

Irregular Imperfect Tense   *I Read, I Write, I Say*

MANGER *(TO EAT)* - **IMPERFECT**			
il mangeait	*he was eating, he used to eat*	ils mangeaient	*they were eating, they used to eat*
elle mangeait	*she was eating, she used to eat*	elles mangeaient	*they were eating, they used to eat*

COMMENCER *(TO BEGIN, TO START)* - **IMPERFECT**			
je commençais	*I was beginning, I used to begin*	nous commencions	*we were beginning, we used to begin*
tu commençais	*you were beginning, you used to begin*	vous commenciez	*you were beginning, you used to begin*
il commençait	*he was beginning, he used to begin*	ils commençaient	*they were beginning, they used to begin*
elle commençait	*she was beginning, she used to begin*	elles commençaient	*they were beginning, they used to begin*

Finally, it is probably not surprising that the verb être (*to be*) is entirely irregular in the imperfect. Here are its forms:

ÊTRE *(TO BE)* - **IMPERFECT**			
j'étais	*I was, I used to be*	nous étions	*we were, we used to be*
tu étais	*you were, you used to be*	vous étiez	*you were, you used to be*
il était	*he was, he used to be*	ils étaient	*they were, they used to be*
elle était	*she was, she used to be*	elles étaient	*they were, they used to be*

(II) Notice that the imperfect of être is usually translated as *was/were* or *used to be*.

✎ Work Out 2

Put the verbs in parentheses in the imperfect tense.

1. je _____ (manger)

2. vous _____ (commencer)

3. j' _____ (être)

4. nous _____ (manger)

5. elle _____ (commencer)

6. vous _____ (être)

ANSWER KEY:

1. mangeais; 2. commenciez; 3. étais; 4. mangions; 5. commençait; 6. étiez

✎ Drive It Home

Fill in the blanks with the imperfect form of each verb.

1. J' _____ (avancer).

2. J' _____ (avoir).

3. Je _____ (danser).

4. J' _____ (être).

5. Je _____ (voyager).

6. J' _____ (étudier).

7. Je _____ (choisir).

The Imperfect Tense (*I Was Speaking*)   The Imperfect Tense vs. The Past Tense

Irregular Imperfect Tense   *I Read, I Write, I Say*

8. Je _____ (répondre).

9. J' _____ (aller).

10. Je _____ (boire).

ANSWER KEY:
1. avançais; 2. avais; 3. dansais; 4. étais; 5. voyageais; 6. étudiais; 7. choisissais; 8. répondais;
9. allais; 10. buvais

How Did You Do?

Let's see how you did! By now, you should be able to:

☐ Name different professions
(Still unsure? Jump back to page 91)

☐ Talk about what you *used to have*
(Still unsure? Jump back to page 94)

☐ Identify the different departments in a company
(Still unsure? Jump back to page 99)

☐ Say what you *used to eat* and who you *used to be*
(Still unsure? Jump back to page 101)

Lesson 6: Phrases

By the end of this lesson, you will be able to:

☐ Talk about applying for a job

☐ Describe what was going on when something happened

☐ Talk about school

☐ Say *I read*, *I write*, and *I say*

Phrase Builder 1

Ever thought about working abroad? Here is some vocabulary that will come in handy if you're looking for a job or just talking about salary, hours, and other similar issues in French.

▶ 6A Lesson 6 Phrase Builder 1 (CD 7, Track 21)

at work	**au travail**
at the office	**au bureau**
to earn money	**gagner de l'argent**
personnel manager (human resources manager)	**le directeur du personnel**
to apply for a job	**faire une demande d'emploi**
to have an interview	**avoir une entrevue**
full-time	**à plein temps**
part-time	**à temps partiel**
retired	**à la retraite**
unemployment	**le chômage**
to be unemployed	**être sans emploi (être sans travail)**

The Imperfect Tense (*I Was Speaking*)   The Imperfect Tense vs. The Past Tense

Irregular Imperfect Tense

I Read, I Write, I Say

summer job	l'emploi (*m.*) saisonnier
to work hard	travailler dur
to be busy	être occupé/occupée
to be growing (as in, the company is growing)	être en pleine expansion

Take It Further

We're going to take a look at the difference between l'imparfait and le passé composé in Grammar Builder 1. But first, let's look at l'imparfait on its own.

Here's a short paragraph in l'imparfait to help give you a better sense of the tense.

Quand j'étais jeune, j'avais un petit chien. Il était brun. Il aimait aller se promener avec mes amis et moi. Nous jouions toujours ensemble.

When I was young, I used to have a little dog. He was brown. He liked to go take a walk with my friends and me. We always used to play together.

✎ Phrase Practice 1

Translate the following dialogue into English:

A: Bonjour mademoiselle. _____

B: Bonjour monsieur. Je voudrais faire une demande d'emploi. _____

_____

C: À temps plein ou à temps partiel ? _____

_____

D: À temps partiel. Je cherche un emploi saisonnier. _____

_____

ANSWER KEY:
A: Hello, miss.
B: Hello, sir. I would like to apply for a job.
C: Full-time or part-time?
D: Part-time. I'm looking for a summer job.

✎ Word Recall

Fill in the blanks with the most appropriate verb from the word bank below.

chante	écrit
joue	pratique

1. Le médecin _____ la médecine.

2. La chanteuse _____ des chansons.

3. L'actrice _____ des rôles.

4. L'écrivain _____ des livres.

ANSWER KEY:
1. pratique (*The doctor practices medicine.*) 2. chante (*The singer sings songs.*) 3. joue (*The actress plays roles.*) 4. écrit (*The writer writes books.*)

Grammar Builder 1
THE IMPERFECT TENSE VS. THE PAST TENSE

▶ 6B Lesson 6 Grammar Builder 1 (CD 7, Track 22)

You saw a paragraph with l'imparfait in Take It Further. Here are a few more examples of l'imparfait in use:

The Imperfect Tense (*I Was Speaking*)   The Imperfect Tense vs. The Past Tense

Irregular Imperfect Tense   *I Read, I Write, I Say*

Je lui parlais tous les jours.
I used to talk to him (her) every day.

Quand j'étais jeune, je dansais bien.
When I was young, I used to dance well.

Quand j'étais jeune, ma mère me chantait une chanson tous les soirs.
When I was young, my mother used to sing a song to me every night.

Hier, j'avais un problème avec ma voiture...
Yesterday, I was having a problem with my car ...

Now let's review some of the sentences you've seen with le passé composé:

J'ai fait des achats.
I ran some errands. (lit., I did some purchases.)

Tu n'as pas mangé à neuf heures.
You didn't eat at 9:00.

Vous avez parlé ?
Did you speak?/Have you spoken?/You spoke?

Quand êtes-vous arrivée, Marie ?
When did you arrive, Marie?

Le petit garçon est tombé.
The little boy fell.

And now let's take a look at a sentence that contains both l'imparfait and le passé composé:

Il faisait froid quand j'ai quitté la maison ce matin.
It was cold when I left the house this morning.

So why do you use the imperfect in the first part of the sentence and the past tense in the second part? Although both tenses describe the past, they're used in different ways.

Here is how they're used:

TENSE	HOW IT'S USED	EXAMPLES
Imperfect	actions that are continuous, habitual, or repetitive; descriptions	set the scene; describe the weather, the time of day, an emotion, a wish, what someone used to do, or what someone was doing when something else happened; express a condition or state without a specified duration
Past	actions that have been completed	express something that happened all of a sudden or a specified number of times; express a completed action

So, when the two tenses are used together, the imperfect often sets the scene for an action expressed in the past tense. An even bigger clue to use the passé composé is if the action happens soudain (*suddenly*) or tout à coup/tout d'un coup (*all of a sudden*).

In the example sentence you saw, il faisait froid (*it was cold*) is in the imperfect because it describes the weather, setting the scene for the completed action: j'ai quitté la maison (*I left the house*).

The Imperfect Tense (*I Was Speaking*)   The Imperfect Tense vs. The Past Tense

Irregular Imperfect Tense

I Read, I Write, I Say

Let's look at some more examples:

Elles commençaient à parler quand il est entré dans la salle.
They were beginning to speak when he entered the room.

Il était minuit quand je suis revenu(e).
It was midnight when I returned.

Je prenais un bain quand le téléphone a sonné.
I was taking a bath when the phone rang.

J'ai entendu la chanson que tu chantais.
I heard the song that you were singing.

Tu chantais, for example, is in the imperfect because it expresses what someone was doing (*singing*) when something else happened (*heard the song*).

If you're confused, don't worry. It'll get much easier to identify which tense to use with—what else?—practice, practice, practice.

⏸

✎ Work Out 1

Fill in the blanks with either l'imparfait or le passé composé of the verb in parentheses. Pay attention to the English translations. Don't forget that the past participle agrees with the subject if the verb uses être in the passé composé.

1. Je n' _____ (être) pas à la maison quand tu

   _____ (téléphoner). (*I was not at home when you called.*)

2. Tout le monde _____ (parler) quand l'auteur

   _____ (entrer). (*Everyone was talking when the author entered.*)

3. Il _____ (faire) beau quand ils

_____ (aller) au parc dimanche. (*It was beautiful outside*

when they went to the park on Sunday.)

4. Elle nous _____ (regarder). (*She was watching us.*)

5. Nous _____ (chanter) beaucoup. (*We used to sing a lot.*)

6. Nous _____ (décider) d'aller au restaurant.

(*We decided to go to the restaurant.*)

7. Je _____ (arriver) au restaurant à neuf heures du soir.

(*I arrived at the restaurant at 9:00 in the evening.*)

8. Il y _____ (avoir) quatre voitures. (*There were four cars.*)

ANSWER KEY:
1. étais, as téléphoné; 2. parlait, est entré; 3. faisait, sont allés; 4. regardait; 5. chantions; 6. avons décidé; 7. suis arrivé(e); 8. avait

Phrase Builder 2

Now let's move on to vocabulary related to l'école (*f.*) (*school*).

▶ 6C Lesson 6 Phrase Builder 2 (CD 7, Track 23)

at school	à l'école
in middle school	au collège
in high school	au lycée
in college	à l'université
classroom	la salle de classe
to teach	enseigner

The Imperfect Tense (*I Was Speaking*)   The Imperfect Tense vs. The Past Tense

Irregular Imperfect Tense   *I Read, I Write, I Say*

diploma	le diplôme
bachelor's degree	la licence
master's degree	la maîtrise (le master)
academic year	l'année (*f.*) scolaire
back-to-school	la rentrée
difficult subjects	les matières (*f.*) difficiles
literature	la littérature
foreign language	la langue étrangère
gym (physical education)*	la gym(nastique)
report card	le bulletin scolaire

* If you want to say *gym* in the sense of the location (a school gymnasium, or a health club) and not *gym* class, then you need to say le gymnase.

Take It Further

In the first Take It Further of this lesson, you saw a short paragraph using just l'imparfait. Now let's look at a paragraph using both l'imparfait and le passé composé. Study it carefully. The more exposure you get to the two tenses, the more comfortable you'll be knowing when to use each one.

Ce week-end, j'étais très occupée. Mon mari et moi, nous avons décidé d'aller au parc parce qu'il faisait beau. Nous sommes arrivés au parc à midi. C'était très joli ! Au parc, il y avait beaucoup de monde. À deux heures, nous avons quitté le parc et nous sommes allés au musée. Je voulais voir les vieux tableaux. Nous regardions les tableaux quand nous avons entendu nos amis Joelle et Robert. Quelle coïncidence ! Après la visite au musée, nous avons mangé dans un bon restaurant en ville avec Joelle et Robert.

This weekend, I was very busy. My husband and I (lit., me), we decided to go to the park because it was beautiful (outside). We arrived at the park at noon. It was very pretty! In the park, there were a lot of people. At 2:00, we left the park and we went to the museum. I wanted to see the old paintings. We were looking at the paintings when we heard our friends Joelle and Robert. What a coincidence! After the visit to the museum, we ate in a good restaurant in town with Joelle and Robert.

✎ Phrase Practice 2

Circle the word that best completes each sentence.

1. Ma sœur a dix-sept ans. Elle est étudiante (au lycée, au collège, à l'université).
2. Mon frère a vingt et un ans. Il est étudiant (au lycée, au collège, à l'université).
3. Pour moi, la littérature n'est pas (une matière difficile, une rentrée, un bulletin scolaire).
4. Le prof et tous les étudiants étaient dans (la salle de classe, la licence, la maîtrise).
5. C'est le premier jour de l'école. C'est (le bulletin scolaire, la rentrée, la maîtrise).

ANSWER KEY:
1. au lycée (*My sister is 17 years old. She's a student in high school.*) 2. à l'université (*My brother is 21 years old. He's a student in college.*) 3. une matière difficile (*For me, literature isn't a difficult subject.*) 4. la salle de classe (*The professor/teacher and all of the students were in the classroom.*) 5. la rentrée (*It's the first day of school. It's back-to-school.*)

The Imperfect Tense (*I Was Speaking*)   The Imperfect Tense vs. The Past Tense

Irregular Imperfect Tense   *I Read, I Write, I Say*

✎ Word Recall

Match the places on the left to the correct English translations on the right.

1. la bibliothèque	a. *store*
2. la librairie	b. *office*
3. le bureau	c. *library*
4. l'usine	d. *factory*
5. le magasin	e. *bookstore*

ANSWER KEY:
1. c; 2. e; 3. b; 4. d; 5. a

Grammar Builder 2
I READ, I WRITE, I SAY

▶ 6D Lesson 6 Grammar Builder 2 (CD 7, Track 24)

If you want to talk about schools and education, then you need to learn how to use the irregular verbs **lire** (*to read*), **écrire** (*to write*), and **dire** (*to say*).

You've seen all of these verbs in some form already, whether in *Essential French* or *Intermediate French*. In fact, you saw the full conjugation of **lire** in *Essential French*. However, let's review. Here is **lire** in the present tense:

LIRE *(TO READ)* - **PRESENT**			
je lis	*I read*	**nous lisons**	*we read*
tu lis	*you read*	**vous lisez**	*you read*
il lit	*he reads*	**ils lisent**	*they read*
elle lit	*she reads*	**elles lisent**	*they read*

Les enfants lisent une bonne histoire.
The children are reading a good story.

The past participle of lire is lu.

Pendant le voyage, nous avons lu beaucoup de livres.
During the trip, we read a lot of books.

Now let's look at écrire.

ÉCRIRE *(TO WRITE)* - **PRESENT**			
j'écris	*I write*	nous écrivons	*we write*
tu écris	*you write*	vous écrivez	*you write*
il écrit	*he writes*	ils écrivent	*they write*
elle écrit	*she writes*	elles écrivent	*they write*

J'écris une lettre à mes amis à l'université.
I'm writing a letter to my friends in college.

The past participle of écrire is écrit.

Le petit garçon a écrit une lettre au Père Noël.
The little boy wrote a letter to Santa Claus (lit., Father Christmas).

Finally, here is the verb dire (*to say, to tell*):

DIRE *(TO SAY, TO TELL)* - **PRESENT**			
je dis	*I say*	nous disons	*we say*
tu dis	*you say*	vous dites	*you say*
il dit	*he says*	ils disent	*they say*
elle dit	*she says*	elles disent	*they say*

Qu'est-ce que vous dites ?
What are you saying?

The Imperfect Tense (*I Was Speaking*)   The Imperfect Tense vs. The Past Tense

Irregular Imperfect Tense   *I Read, I Write, I Say*

The past participle of dire is dit.

J'ai dit qu'elle avait une jolie robe.
I said (that) she had a pretty dress.

The future and conditional of écrire, lire, and dire are formed normally, in the same way as other -re verbs: drop the final e from the infinitive and add the appropriate ending. The imperfect is also formed normally: just drop the -ons from the present tense nous form and add the ending.

Going forward in *Advanced French*, if you don't see a note about a specific tense when discussing an irregular verb, that means the tense is formed normally.

✎ Work Out 2

Fill in the blanks with the correct present tense forms.

1. Qu'est-ce que tu _____ (lire) ? (*What are you reading?*)

2. Nous _____ (écrire) en français. (*We're writing in French.*)

3. Ils _____ (lire) très bien. (*They read very well.*)

4. Elle _____ (dire) bonjour à Sophie. (*She's saying hello to Sophie.*)

5. Vous n'_____ (écrire) pas à votre mère ? (*You're not writing to your mother?*)

ANSWER KEY:
1. lis; 2. écrivons; 3. lisent; 4. dit; 5. écrivez

✎ Drive It Home

A. Conjugate each verb in the imparfait.

1. Il _____ (téléphoner).

2. Il _____ (vendre).

3. Il _____ (être).

4. Il _____ (tomber).

5. Il _____ (finir).

6. Il _____ (regarder).

7. Il _____ (faire).

B. Now conjugate each verb in the passé composé.

1. Il _____ (téléphoner).

2. Il _____ (vendre).

3. Il _____ (être).

4. Il _____ (tomber).

5. Il _____ (finir).

6. Il _____ (regarder).

7. Il _____ (faire).

The Imperfect Tense (*I Was Speaking*)   The Imperfect Tense vs. The Past Tense

Irregular Imperfect Tense   *I Read, I Write, I Say*

C. Finally, decide if you need **le passé composé** or **l'imparfait** to complete each of these sentences.

1. Il _____ (être) au bureau quand elle

_____ (vendre) la maison.

2. Il _____ (regarder) la télé ; tout à coup, elle

_____ (téléphoner).

3. **La nuit dernière, il** _____ (faire) froid.

ANSWER KEY:
A. 1. téléphonait; 2. vendait; 3. était; 4. tombait; 5. finissait; 6. regardait; 7. faisait
B. 1. a téléphoné; 2. a vendu; 3. a été; 4. est tombé; 5. a fini; 6. a regardé; 7. a fait
C. 1. était, a vendu (*He was at the office when she sold the house.*) 2. regardait, a téléphoné (*He was watching television; all of a sudden, she called.*) 3. faisait/a fait (*Last night, it was cold.*)

☀ Tip

Earlier in the lesson, you saw some vocabulary for school **matières** (*subjects*). Here is a more comprehensive list:

math	les maths (*f.*), les mathématiques (*f.*)
calculus	le calcul
geometry	la géométrie
history	l'histoire (*f.*)*
spelling	l'orthographe (*f.*)
English literature	la littérature anglaise
English	l'anglais (*m.*)
French	le français
foreign language	la langue étrangère
science	la science
chemistry	la chimie

* Remember that **histoire** can mean *history, story,* or *tale.*

biology	la biologie
physics	la physique
gym, physical education	la gym, la gymnastique, l'éducation physique
art	l'art (m.)
drawing	le dessin
music	la musique
computer science	l'informatique (f.)
extracurricular activities	les activités (f.) extra-scolaires/ parascolaires

If you want to say that you're taking a class in a certain subject, just use cours (*class*) + de (d'). For example, you could say mon cours de français (*my French class*), un cours de maths (*a math class*), etc.

How Did You Do?

Let's see how you did! By now, you should be able to:

☐ Talk about applying for a job
(Still unsure? Jump back to page 105)

☐ Describe what what was going on when something happened
(Still unsure? Jump back to page 107)

☐ Talk about school
(Still unsure? Jump back to page 111)

☐ Say *I read, I write*, and *I say*
(Still unsure? Jump back to page 114)

The Imperfect Tense (*I Was Speaking*)   The Imperfect Tense vs. The Past Tense

Irregular Imperfect Tense   *I Read, I Write, I Say*

Lesson 7: Sentences

By the end of this lesson, you will be able to:

☐ Describe your work environment

☐ Talk about duration

☐ Talk about classes, tests, and activities at school

☐ Say *I leave* and *I sleep*

Sentence Builder 1

▶ 7A Lesson 7 Sentence Builder 1 (CD 8, Track 1)

I get along well with my boss.	Je m'entends bien avec mon patron/ ma patronne.
The people where I work are great.	Les gens où je travaille sont super.
Here is my office.	Voici mon bureau.*
Here is my cubicle.	Voici mon cubicule.**
I'm a salesman/saleswoman.	Je suis vendeur/vendeuse.
I'm on vacation.	Je suis en vacances.
(I) can't wait for the end of the day!	Vivement la fin de la journée !
I work very hard.	Je travaille très dur.
I work forty hours a week (per week).	Je travaille quarante heures par semaine.

* Notice that bureau can mean *office* in the sense of the building where you work, but also the room that you are assigned to work in. It can also mean *desk*.
**Colloquially, box is the French word for *cubicle*.

| I've been working for this company for two months. (lit., I work for this company for two months.) | Je travaille pour cette société depuis deux mois. |
| I worked for that company for two years. | J'ai travaillé pour cette société pendant deux ans. |

Take It Further

You know that indefinite articles are not used between être and professions in French. However, you should use an indefinite article if the profession is preceded by an adjective.

Je suis vendeur.
I am a salesman.

Je suis un bon vendeur.
I am a good salesman.

In Sentence Builder 1, you saw some good expressions to use in conversation:

| to get along with | s'entendre avec |
| to get along well with | s'entendre bien avec |

And you saw the word vivement, which literally means *strongly* (as in, *I strongly feel that ...*), but is often used to mean *can't wait for*:

Vivement vendredi !
Can't wait for Friday!

Vivement les vacances !
Can't wait for vacation!

The Imperfect Tense (*I Was Speaking*)   The Imperfect Tense vs. The Past Tense

Irregular Imperfect Tense   *I Read, I Write, I Say*

Vivement la suite !
Can't wait for what happens next!/Can't wait for the rest!

Note that la suite can mean *the rest, the next part,* or *what happens next.*

✎ Sentence Practice 1

Translate the following sentences into English.

1. Voici mon bureau. _____

2. Voici mon box. _____

3. Voici mon patron. _____

4. Voici mon comptable. _____

ANSWER KEY:
1. *Here is my office.* 2. *Here is my cubicle.* 3. *Here is my boss.* 4. *Here is my accountant.*

✎ Word Recall

Fill in the blanks using the following word bank:

une carafe	un verre
une bouteille	une tasse

1. Elle voulait _____ d'eau. (*She wanted a pitcher of water.*)

2. Paul m'a donné _____ de vin. (*Paul gave me a bottle of wine.*)

3. J'ai bu _____ d'eau parce que j'avais soif.

   (*I drank a glass of water because I was thirsty.*)

4. **Il faisait froid, donc j'ai bu** _____ **de chocolat chaud.**

(It was cold, so I drank a cup of hot chocolate.)

ANSWER KEY:
1. une carafe; 2. une bouteille; 3. un verre; 4. une tasse

Grammar Builder 1
DURATION

▶ 7B Lesson 7 Grammar Builder 1 (CD 8, Track 2)

Depuis *(since, for)*, **pour** *(for)*, and **pendant** *(during, for)* are helpful words to know when talking about lengths of time. You've already seen these words in various sentences, but let's look at them in detail and see when and how they're used.

Pour *(for)* is used to express how long an action will take in the future or near future.

Je vais travailler pour cette société pour un an.
I'm going to work for this company for one year.

If a situation or action began in the past and is still going on, use the present tense + **depuis** *(since, for)* to talk about the time that has elapsed. For example, if someone asks if you are working at a company and you still work there, you might say:

Je travaille pour cette société depuis un an.
I've been working for this company for a year. (lit., I work for this company for a year.)

Use the past tense or the imperfect + **pendant** *(during, for)* to talk about an action that was completed in the past, and is not connected to the present at all. For example, if you no longer work at the company, you could say:

The Imperfect Tense (*I Was Speaking*)   The Imperfect Tense vs. The Past Tense

Irregular Imperfect Tense   *I Read, I Write, I Say*

J'ai travaillé pour cette société pendant un an.
I worked for that company for one year.

Pendant can also be used instead of **pour** to talk about the future. In this case, you would use the near future/future tense + pendant: **Je vais travailler pour cette société pendant un an.** (*I'm going to work for this/that company for a year.*)

So, to summarize:

1. To talk about the duration of a completed action in the past, use the past tense or the imperfect + **pendant**.

2. To talk about the duration of an action that started in the past and continues in the present, use the present tense + **depuis**.

3. To talk about the duration of an action that will take place in the future or near future, use the near future or future tense + **pour** or **pendant**.

Depuis can be used in certain expressions as well. For instance, you can use **depuis combien de temps ?** with the present tense to ask (*for*) *how long?*

Depuis combien de temps attend-il ?
How long has he been waiting?

Il attend depuis dix minutes.
He's been waiting for ten minutes.

The expression **depuis quand ?** means *since when?* It is also used with the present tense.

Depuis quand travaillez-vous ici ?
Since when have you been working here?

Je travaille ici depuis janvier.
I've been working here since January.

Work Out 1

Use depuis, pour, or pendant.

1. **Nous sommes ici _____ trois heures.** *(We've been here since 3:00.)*

2. **Mes amis vont aller au Canada _____ trois semaines.**

   (My friends are going to go to Canada for three weeks.)

3. **J'étais en France _____ un mois.** *(I was in France for a month.)*

4. **_____ combien de temps est-ce que tu habites à New York ?**

   (How long have you been living in New York?)

5. **Il travaille en ville _____ deux ans.**

   (He's been working in the city for two years.)

6. **_____ l'hiver, nous sommes allés en Floride.**

   (During the winter, we went to Florida.)

   ANSWER KEY:
   1. depuis; 2. pour/pendant; 3. pendant; 4. Depuis; 5. depuis; 6. Pendant

Sentence Builder 2

7C Lesson 7 Sentence Builder 2 (CD 8, Track 3)

I did my homework.	**J'ai fait mes devoirs.**
I made a spelling mistake.	**J'ai fait une faute d'orthographe.**

The Imperfect Tense (*I Was Speaking*)   The Imperfect Tense vs. The Past Tense

Irregular Imperfect Tense   *I Read, I Write, I Say*

I'm taking a class. (I'm attending a class.)	J'assiste à un cours.
I'm going to the (school) cafeteria.	Je vais à la cantine.
The children play in the schoolyard (playground).	Les enfants jouent dans la cour de récréation.
She's a member of the French club.	Elle fait partie du cercle français.
It's necessary to learn the poem by heart.	Il faut apprendre le poème par cœur.
I'm taking my calculus test.	Je passe mon examen de calcul.
I did well on my test.	J'ai réussi à mon examen.
I failed my test.	J'ai échoué à mon examen.
I failed.	J'ai raté.

Take It Further

You learned a lot of helpful words, phrases, and verbs for talking about school in the sentences above. Let's review, and look at some related terms:

school cafeteria	la cantine
cafeteria (general term)	la cafétéria
schoolyard, playground	la cour de récréation
recess, break	la récré, la récréation
club	le cercle, le club
member	le membre
to be a member of	faire partie de, être membre de
by heart	par cœur
to learn by heart	apprendre par cœur
poem	le poème
test, exam	l'examen (*m.*)

Irregular -IR Verbs   To Know

lesson	la leçon
class, course	le cours
to attend (a class), to take (a class)	assister à (un cours)
to take (a test)	passer (un examen)
to do well, to succeed	réussir
to pass a test/class, to do well on a test/in a class	réussir à un examen/cours
to fail (a test/class)	échouer à (un examen/cours), rater (un examen/cours)
mistake	la faute, l'erreur (f.)
to make a mistake	faire une faute/erreur

Note that **passer** is a "false" similar word when talking about school. For example, **passer un examen** does not mean *to pass a test*, it means *to take a test*.

✎ Sentence Practice 2

Match the following English phrases to the correct French translations.

1. *to take a test*	a. **assister à un cours**
2. *to fail a test*	b. **faire une faute**
3. *to do well on a test*	c. **réussir à un examen**
4. *to attend a class*	d. **passer un examen**
5. *to be a member of*	e. **échouer à un examen**
6. *to make a mistake*	f. **faire partie de**

ANSWER KEY:
1. d; 2. e; 3. c; 4. a; 5. f; 6. b

The Imperfect Tense (*I Was Speaking*)   The Imperfect Tense vs. The Past Tense

Irregular Imperfect Tense   *I Read, I Write, I Say*

Word Recall

Now match the following verbs to the correct French translations.

1. *to pay*	a. **employer**
2. *to throw*	b. **payer**
3. *to prefer*	c. **acheter**
4. *to use*	d. **préférer**
5. *to buy*	e. **jeter**

ANSWER KEY:
1. b; 2. e; 3. d; 4. a; 5. c

Grammar Builder 2
IRREGULAR -IR VERBS

▶ 7D Lesson 7 Grammar Builder 2 (CD 8, Track 4)

As you know, there are groups of irregular -er verbs that follow specific patterns.

For example, you've already learned about verbs that are similar to **manger**, **commencer**, **appeler**, **acheter**, **préférer**, **employer**, and **payer**.

Now let's look at a group of irregular -ir verbs known as the "SST" verbs. They're called SST verbs because their je, tu, and il/elle forms end in -s, -s, and -t.

To create the je, tu, and il/elle forms of SST verbs in the present tense, drop the last ***three*** letters of the infinitive form and add the endings shown below. To create the nous, vous, and ils/elles forms, drop the last ***two*** letters of the infinitive form and add the endings.

Irregular **-IR** Verbs   *To Know*

	DROP THE LAST *THREE* LETTERS OF THE INFINITIVE AND ADD …		DROP THE LAST *TWO* LETTERS OF THE INFINITIVE AND ADD …
je	-s	nous	-ons
tu	-s	vous	-ez
il	-t	ils	-ent
elle	-t	elles	-ent

Dormir (*to sleep*), for example, is an SST verb. So to create its je, tu, and il/elle forms, drop the last three letters of the infinitive (leaving you with dor-) and add the endings. To create its nous, vous, and ils/elles forms, drop the last two letters of the infinitive (leaving you with dorm-) and add the endings.

DORMIR *(TO SLEEP)* - **PRESENT**			
je dors	*I sleep*	nous dormons	*we sleep*
tu dors	*you sleep*	vous dormez	*you sleep*
il dort	*he sleeps*	ils dorment	*they sleep*
elle dort	*she sleeps*	elles dorment	*they sleep*

Partir (*to leave*) is also an SST verb:

PARTIR *(TO LEAVE)* - **PRESENT**			
je pars	*I leave*	nous partons	*we leave*
tu pars	*you leave*	vous partez	*you leave*
il part	*he leaves*	ils partent	*they leave*
elle part	*she leaves*	elles partent	*they leave*

Other common SST verbs include:

sentir	*to feel*
servir	*to serve*
sortir	*to go out, to leave*

You actually saw the full conjugation of sortir already, in *Essential French*.

The Imperfect Tense (*I Was Speaking*)   The Imperfect Tense vs. The Past Tense

Irregular Imperfect Tense

I Read, I Write, I Say

Here are some examples of SST verbs in sentences:

Le samedi soir, je sors avec mes amis.
On Saturday night, I go out with my friends.

Quand partez-vous en vacances ?
When are you leaving on vacation?

Mon mari dort toujours devant la télévision.
My husband always sleeps in front of the television.

The past participles of SST verbs are formed normally: cut off the -ir from the infinitive form and add -i. For example, the past participle of partir is parti and the past participle of dormir is dormi.

Vous avez bien dormi hier soir ?
Did you sleep well last night?

J'ai servi le dessert avec le café.
I served the dessert with coffee.

Remember that the verbs partir and sortir form the passé composé with the verb être, so their past participles need to agree in gender and number with the subject of the sentence.

Marie est sortie avec Jean.
Marie went out with Jean.

⏸

Irregular **-IR** Verbs | To Know

✎ Work Out 2

Conjugate the following verbs in the present tense.

1. Les filles _____ (dormir). *(The girls are sleeping.)*

2. À quelle heure est-ce que nous _____ (partir) ?

   (At what time are we leaving?)

3. _____ -elle (sortir) avec Jean ? *(Is she going out with Jean?)*

4. Vous _____ (servir) le dîner. *(You serve dinner.)*

   ANSWER KEY:
   1. dorment; 2. partons; 3. Sort; 4. servez

✎ Drive It Home

A. Fill in the blanks with depuis or pendant.

1. Nous habiterons à Paris _____ deux ans.

   (We will live in Paris for two years.)

2. Nous habitons à Paris _____ deux ans.

   (We've been living in Paris for two years.)

3. Nous avons habité à Paris _____ deux ans.

   (We lived in Paris for two years.)

4. Nous allons habiter à Paris _____ deux ans.

   (We're going to live in Paris for two years.)

The Imperfect Tense (*I Was Speaking*)   The Imperfect Tense vs. The Past Tense

Irregular Imperfect Tense

I Read, I Write, I Say

B. Give the correct present tense of the following verbs.

1. Je _____ (dormir)

2. Tu _____ (servir)

3. Elle _____ (sentir)

4. Il _____ (partir)

5. Nous _____ (sortir)

6. Vous _____ (dormir)

7. Ils _____ (sortir)

8. Elles _____ (partir)

ANSWER KEY:
A. 1. pendant; 2. depuis; 3. pendant; 4. pendant
B. 1. dors; 2. sers; 3. sent; 4. part; 5. sortons; 6. dormez; 7. sortent; 8. partent

⊕ Culture Note

School life in France begins with l'école (*f.*) maternelle, the equivalent of *nursery school* or *preschool*. It continues with l'école (*f.*) primaire (*elementary* or *primary school*). Le collège is the equivalent of the American *middle school* or *junior high school*, followed by le lycée (*high school*).

French children generally attend school on Monday, Tuesday, Thursday, Friday, and only sometimes Saturday morning. Wednesdays and Sundays are days off, although some schools require half days on Wednesdays. The school day begins around 8 or 8:30 a.m. and finishes around 4:30 or 5 p.m. with a two-hour break for lunch.

In the last grade, or la classe terminale, of high school, a student wishing to continue his or her education beyond high school must take a special exam called le baccalauréat (informally known as le bac). Successful completion of this rigorous exam is one of the key components of acceptance to a French university.

How Did You Do?

Let's see how you did! By now, you should be able to:

☐ Describe your work environment
(Still unsure? Jump back to page 120)

☐ Talk about duration
(Still unsure? Jump back to page 123)

☐ Talk about classes, tests, and activities at school
(Still unsure? Jump back to page 125)

☐ Say *I leave* and *I sleep*
(Still unsure? Jump back to page 128)

Lesson 8: Conversations

By the end of this lesson, you will be able to:

☐ Tell someone what you *see*

☐ Say what you *know* and whom you *know*

Ⓖ Conversation 1

Marie is a literature student at a university in Paris and her friend René is visiting her for the weekend. They're eating lunch at a Paris café that was frequented by two of their favorite écrivains: Jean-Paul Sartre and Simone de Beauvoir.

▶ 8A Lesson 8 Conversation 1 (CD 8, Track 5)

Marie :	Tu te souviens ? Ils étaient toujours assis à cette table.
René :	Qui donc ?
Marie :	Sartre et Beauvoir !

The Imperfect Tense (*I Was Speaking*) The Imperfect Tense vs. The Past Tense

Irregular Imperfect Tense *I Read, I Write, I Say*

René :	C'est vrai ! Ils buvaient du café toute la journée. Et ils parlaient de politique avec tous leurs amis.
Marie :	Il avait toujours une montagne de livres à côté de lui.
René :	Moi, je me souviens que tu commandais toujours le même sandwich.
Marie :	Un jambon-beurre !

Marie:	Do you remember? They were always sitting at this table.
Réné:	Who? (lit., Who then?)
Marie:	Sartre and de Beauvoir!
Réné:	That's true! They used to drink coffee all day. And they used to talk about politics with all of their friends.
Marie:	He always had a mountain of books next to him.
Réné:	Me, I remember that you always used to order the same sandwich.
Marie:	A ham and butter (sandwich)!

Take It Further

You've seen that both le jour and la journée mean *day*, and you know that both l'an (*m.*) and l'année (*f.*) mean *year*. So what's the difference?

Well, it's complicated, and there are many exceptions. However, in general, use the words that end in -ée if you want to emphasize the amount of time that has passed (as in *all day, all year, the whole year,* etc.), use an adjective or a possessive, or use the word in an exclamation.

Here are some examples:

J'ai travaillé toute l'année.
I worked all year.

Je parle de ma journée.
I'm talking about my day.

Bonne journée !
Have a good day!

However, don't use the -ée words if you want to talk about *every*:

tous les jours
every day

Other words like jour/journée and an/année include:

| evening, night | le soir, la soirée |
| morning | le matin, la matinée |

Finally, note the two new words in the dialogue:

| mountain | la montagne |
| politics | la politique |

✎ Conversation Practice 1

Translate the following phrases into English.

1. tu te souviens _____

2. toute la journée _____

3. parler de politique _____

The Imperfect Tense (*I Was Speaking*)   The Imperfect Tense vs. The Past Tense

Irregular Imperfect Tense   *I Read, I Write, I Say*

4. à côté de lui _____

5. le même sandwich _____

ANSWER KEY:
1. *you remember*; 2. *all day*; 3. *to talk about politics*; 4. *next to him*; 5. *the same sandwich*

✎ Word Recall

Quelle heure est-il ? Rewrite the following times using numbers. For example: **12h10, 4h37**, etc.

1. Il est deux heures et quart. _____

2. Il est quatre heures moins vingt. _____

3. Il est cinq heures dix. _____

4. Il est onze heures vingt-cinq. _____

5. Il est dix heures moins dix. _____

6. Il est sept heures et demie. _____

ANSWER KEY:
1. 2h15; 2. 3h40; 3. 5h10; 4. 11h25; 5. 9h50; 6. 7h30

Grammar Builder 1
TO SEE

▶ 8B Lesson 8 Grammar Builder 1 (CD 8, Track 6)

Another good irregular verb to know is **voir** (*to see*). Here are its forms in the present tense:

VOIR *(TO SEE)* - **PRESENT**			
je vois	*I see*	nous voyons	*we see*
tu vois	*you see*	vous voyez	*you see*

VOIR (TO SEE) - PRESENT			
il voit	he sees	ils voient	they see
elle voit	she sees	elles voient	they see

The past participle of voir is vu. The conditional and future tenses are formed with verr- + the endings.

Here are some examples:

Hier soir, j'ai vu un film extraordinaire.
Last night, I saw an extraordinary film.

Je te verrai demain.
I'll see you tomorrow.

✎ Work Out 1

Fill in the blanks with the correct form of voir in the present tense.

1. Nous _____ le patron. (*We see the boss.*)

2. Ils _____ beaucoup de personnes au bureau.

   (*They see a lot of people at the office.*)

3. Vous _____ le directeur du personnel.

   (*You see the human resources manager.*)

4. Elle _____ le pharmacien. (*She sees the pharmacist.*)

5. Je _____ une voiture rouge. (*I see a red car.*)

   ANSWER KEY:

   1. voyons; 2. voient; 3. voyez; 4. voit; 5. vois

The Imperfect Tense (*I Was Speaking*)   The Imperfect Tense vs. The Past Tense

Irregular Imperfect Tense   *I Read, I Write, I Say*

Conversation 2

Patrick is meeting his friend Karine at a party and he shows up very late. He begins to tell her the story of what happened.

▶ 8C Lesson 8 Conversation 2 (CD 8, Track 7)

Karine :	Nous t'attendons depuis deux heures ! Qu'est-ce qui t'est arrivé ?
Patrick :	Quelle histoire ! Je traversais la place de la Victoire quand soudain j'ai vu une foule de gens en blouse blanche.
Karine :	Un accident ?
Patrick :	Non, c'était une manifestation des étudiants en médecine.
Karine :	Pourquoi manifestaient-ils ?
Patrick :	Je ne sais pas vraiment.
Karine :	Qu'est-ce que tu as fait... ?

Karine:	*We've been waiting for you for two hours ! What happened to you?*
Patrick:	*What a story! I was crossing the Place de la Victoire when suddenly I saw a crowd of people in white coats (lit., in white coat).*
Karine:	*An accident?*
Patrick:	*No, it was a demonstration of medical students.*
Karine:	*Why were they demonstrating?*
Patrick:	*I don't really know.*
Karine:	*What did you do ... ?*

Take It Further

If you spend any time in France, chances are you will encounter une grève (*a strike*) or une manifestation (*a demonstration, a protest*) at some point.

They are pretty common, whether they're formed by des étudiants en médecine (*medical students*), des employés (*workers, employees*), or even des lycéens (*high schoolers, high school students*).

As a result, some good words to know include:

on strike	en grève
to strike	faire (la) grève
to demonstrate, to protest	manifester
demonstrator, protestor	le manifestant/la manifestante
to march	défiler

Finally, you know that arriver can mean *to arrive* or *to manage/be able to do something*. However, it can also mean *to happen*.

Arriver is used this way in the expression Qu'est-ce qui t'arrive ? which means *What's happening to you?* but can also carry the sense of *What's wrong with you?* or *What's up with you?* or *What's going on with you?* Note that the t' in the expression is the indirect object pronoun te (t') since you're talking about something happening *to you*.

You saw the expression in the past tense in Conversation 2:

Qu'est-ce qui t'est arrivé ?
What happened to you?

Of course, keep in mind that te (t') is informal. Use the indirect object pronoun vous instead of te if you want or need to be more formal:

Qu'est-ce qui vous est arrivé ?
What happened to you?

The Imperfect Tense (*I Was Speaking*)   The Imperfect Tense vs. The Past Tense

Irregular Imperfect Tense   *I Read, I Write, I Say*

So why do you use qu'est-ce qui... ? and not qu'est-ce que... ? to mean *what* ... ?
Don't worry about it for now. You'll learn all about it in Unit 3.

✎ Conversation Practice 2

Re-read Conversation 2. Then say whether each sentence below is vrai (*true*) or
faux (*false*). Next to each sentence, write down V for vrai or F for faux.

1. Karine attend depuis plus d'une heure. _____

2. Il y avait beaucoup de gens sur la place de la Victoire. _____

3. C'était un accident. _____

4. Les gens avaient des blouses blanches. _____

ANSWER KEY:
1. V (*She's been waiting for two hours, so she has been waiting for more than an hour.*) 2. V (*Yes, there were a lot of people in the place de la Victoire. He says there was a crowd.*) 3. F (*No, it wasn't an accident; it was a demonstration.*) 4. V (*Yes, they had white coats.*)

✎ Word Recall

Give the feminine form of the following adjectives.

1. cher _____

2. vieux _____

3. nouveau _____

4. inquiet _____

5. fier _____

6. heureux _____

7. gentil _____

8. national _____

ANSWER KEY:
1. chère (*dear, expensive*); 2. vieille (*old*); 3. nouvelle (*new*); 4. inquiète (*worried, anxious*); 5. fière (*proud*); 6. heureuse (*happy*); 7. gentille (*nice, kind*); 8. nationale (*national*)

Grammar Builder 2
TO KNOW

▶ 8D Lesson 8 Grammar Builder 2 (CD 8, Track 8)

The phrases je sais (*I know*) and je ne sais pas (*I don't know*) are very useful expressions to know. They're forms of the irregular verb savoir (*to know*).

Here is the full conjugation of savoir in the present tense:

SAVOIR (TO KNOW) - **PRESENT**			
je sais	*I know*	nous savons	*we know*
tu sais	*you know*	vous savez	*you know*
il sait	*he knows*	ils savent	*they know*
elle sait	*she knows*	elles savent	*they know*

The past participle of savoir is su.

Comment a-t-il su ?
How did he know?

Note that savoir is irregular in the conditional and future tenses. The conditional and future tenses of savoir are both formed with saur- + the endings.

The Imperfect Tense (*I Was Speaking*)   The Imperfect Tense vs. The Past Tense

Irregular Imperfect Tense   *I Read, I Write, I Say*

The irregular verb connaître also means *to know*. Here is its full conjugation in the present tense. Notice the î in the infinitive form and the il/elle form.

CONNAÎTRE *(TO KNOW)* - **PRESENT**			
je connais	*I know*	nous connaissons	*we know*
tu connais	*you know*	vous connaissez	*you know*
il connaît	*he knows*	ils connaissent	*they know*
elle connaît	*she knows*	elles connaissent	*they know*

The past participle of connaître is connu.

Est-ce que tu as connu cet homme ?
Did you know this man?

Although they both mean to know, savoir and connaître are actually **not** interchangeable. They are used in different ways.

Savoir refers to the possession of knowledge. It can also be translated as *to know how* and is placed in front of a verb, an adverb, or a question word.

Il sait nager.
He knows how to swim.

Je sais où il est.
I know where he is.

Je sais pourquoi j'ai raté.
I know why I failed.

On the other hand, connaître refers to familiarity with someone or something. It is sometimes translated as *to be familiar with* and is placed in front of a noun.

Duration | To See

Irregular **-IR** Verbs | To Know

Je connais les chansons d'Édith Piaf.
I know the songs of Edith Piaf. (I am familiar with the songs of Edith Piaf.)

Je connais bien Denise.
I know Denise well.

Elle connaît très bien ce nouveau restaurant.
She knows this new restaurant very well.

✎ Work Out 2

Fill in the blanks with either connaître or savoir in the present tense.

1. **Je ne** _____ **pas la sœur de Marie.** *(I don't know Marie's sister.)*

2. **Est-ce que tu** _____ **pourquoi il est en retard ?** *(Do you know why he's late?)*

3. **Ils** _____ **jouer au foot.** *(They know how to play soccer.)*

4. **Vous** _____ **l'histoire de Cendrillon ?**

(Do you know the story of Cinderella?)

ANSWER KEY:
1. connais ; 2. sais ; 3. savent ; 4. connaissez

✎ Drive It Home

A. Fill in the blanks with the present tense form of savoir.

1. **Quelle heure est-il ? Je ne** _____ **pas.** *(What time is it? I don't know.)*

2. **Quelle heure est-il ? Il ne** _____ **pas.** *(What time is it? He doesn't know.)*

3. **Quelle heure est-il ? Nous ne** _____ **pas.** *(What time is it? We don't know.)*

The Imperfect Tense (*I Was Speaking*)   The Imperfect Tense vs. The Past Tense

Irregular Imperfect Tense   *I Read, I Write, I Say*

4. Quelle heure est-il ? Elles ne _____ pas. (*What time is it? They don't know.*)

5. Quelle heure est-il ? Elle ne _____ pas. (*What time is it? She doesn't know.*)

6. Quelle heure est-il ? Ils ne _____ pas. (*What time is it? They don't know.*)

B. Now fill in the blanks with the present tense form of connaître.

1. Sophie ? Je ne la _____ pas. (*Sophie? I don't know her.*)

2. Sophie ? Elles ne la _____ pas. (*Sophie? They don't know her.*)

3. Sophie ? Ils ne la _____ pas. (*Sophie? They don't know her.*)

4. Sophie ? Vous ne la _____ pas. (*Sophie? You don't know her.*)

5. Sophie ? Nous ne la _____ pas. (*Sophie? We don't know her.*)

6. Sophie ? Il ne la _____ pas. (*Sophie? He doesn't know her.*)

ANSWER KEY:
A. 1. sais; 2. sait; 3. savons; 4. savent; 5. sait; 6. savent
B. 1. connais; 2. connaissent; 3. connaissent; 4. connaissez; 5. connaissons; 6. connaît

Tip

Now that you know how to talk about what you *know*, you should also know how to say what you *believe*. The irregular verb croire means *to believe* in French, and it's a good verb to know.

CROIRE *(TO BELIEVE)* - **PRESENT**			
je crois	*I believe*	nous croyons	*we believe*
tu crois	*you believe*	vous croyez	*you believe*
il croit	*he believes*	ils croient	*they believe*
elle croit	*she believes*	elles croient	*they believe*

Elle travaille dans un restaurant, je crois.
She works in a restaurant, I believe.

The past participle of croire is cru.

How Did You Do?

Let's see how you did! By now, you should be able to:

☐ Tell someone what you *see*
(Still unsure? Jump back to page 136)

☐ Say what you *know* and who you *know*
(Still unsure? Jump back to page 141)

Unit 2 Essentials

Remember that if the word has more than one translation, or different masculine and feminine forms, make sure to write them all down.

Don't forget to go to **www.livinglanguage.com/languagelab** to access your free online tools for this lesson: audiovisual flashcards, and interactive games and quizzes.

Vocabulary Essentials

PROFESSIONS

accountant		dentist	
bank clerk		nurse	
civil servant		actor/actress	
pharmacist		plumber	
homemaker		farmer	
construction worker		carpenter	
author		beautician	
writer		policeman/ policewoman	
computer programmer		businessman/ businesswoman	

[Pg. 91] (If you're stuck, visit this page to review!)

AT THE OFFICE

job, work		meeting	
factory		staff	
company		colleague	
computer		boss	
software		salary	

[Pg. 99]

DEPARTMENTS WITHIN A COMPANY

department	
accounting department	
computer science/IT department	
finance department	
sales department	
legal department	
marketing department	
public relations (PR) department	
shipping department, mail room	
customer service department	
management	

[Pg. 99]

APPLYING FOR A JOB

at the office		retired	
to earn money		unemployment	
human resources manager, personnel manager		to be unemployed	
to apply for a job		summer job	
to have an interview		to work hard	
full-time		to be busy	
part-time			

[Pg. 105]

AT SCHOOL

school		to teach	
middle school		diploma	
high school		academic year	
college		back-to-school	
classroom		report card	

[Pg. 111]

WORK EXPRESSIONS

I get along well with my boss.	
I'm on vacation.	
(I) can't wait for the end of the day!	
I work forty hours a week/per week.	

[Pg. 120]

Advanced French

SCHOOL EXPRESSIONS

I did my homework.	
I'm taking a class.	
I'm taking my calculus test.	
I did well on my test.	
I failed my test.	
I failed.	

[Pg. 125]

DURATION EXPRESSIONS

how long?/ for how long?		*since when?*	

[Pg. 124]

Grammar Essentials

THE IMPERFECT (L'IMPARFAIT)

To form the imperfect tense:

1. Take the nous form of the verb in the present tense and drop the -ons ending.

2. Next, add one of the following endings:

PRONOUN	ENDING	PRONOUN	ENDING
je	-ais	nous	-ions
tu	-ais	vous	-iez
il	-ait	ils	-aient
elle	-ait	elles	-aient

AVOIR *(TO HAVE)* **- IMPERFECT**

I had	j'avais	we had	nous avions
you had (infml.)	tu avais	you had (pl./fml.)	vous aviez
he had	il avait	they had (m.)	ils avaient
she had	elle avait	they had (f.)	elles avaient

COMMENCER *(TO BEGIN, TO START)* **- IMPERFECT**

I was beginning	je commençais	we were beginning	nous commencions
you were beginning (infml.)	tu commençais	you were beginning (pl./fml.)	vous commenciez
he was beginning	il commençait	they were beginning (m.)	ils commençaient
she was beginning	elle commençait	they were beginning (f.)	elles commençaient

ÊTRE *(TO BE)* **- IMPERFECT**

I was	j'étais	we were	nous étions
you were (infml.)	tu étais	you were (pl./fml.)	vous étiez
he was	il était	they were (m.)	ils étaient
she was	elle était	they were (f.)	elles étaient

MANGER *(TO EAT)* **- IMPERFECT**

I was eating	je mangeais	we were eating	nous mangions
you were eating (infml.)	tu mangeais	you were eating (pl./fml.)	vous mangiez

MANGER *(TO EAT)* - **IMPERFECT**			
he was eating	il mangeait	*they were eating (m.)*	ils mangeaient
she was eating	elle mangeait	*they were eating (f.)*	elles mangeaient

PARLER *(TO SPEAK, TO TALK)* - **IMPERFECT**			
I was speaking	je parlais	*we were speaking*	nous parlions
you were speaking (infml.)	tu parlais	*you were speaking (pl./fml.)*	vous parliez
he was speaking	il parlait	*they were speaking (m.)*	ils parlaient
she was speaking	elle parlait	*they were speaking (f.)*	elles parlaient

THE IMPERFECT VS THE PAST TENSE

TENSE	HOW IT'S USED
Imperfect (l'imparfait)	actions that are continuous, habitual, or repetitive; descriptions
Past Tense (le passé composé)	actions that have been completed

DURATION

1. To talk about the duration of a completed action in the past, use the past tense or the imperfect + pendant.

2. To talk about the duration of an action that started in the past and continues in the present, use the present tense + depuis.

3. To talk about the duration of an action that will take place in the future or near future, use the near future or future tense + pour or pendant.

SST VERBS

	DROP THE LAST *THREE* LETTERS OF THE INFINITIVE AND ADD ...		DROP THE LAST *TWO* LETTERS OF THE INFINITIVE AND ADD ...
je	-s	nous	-ons
tu	-s	vous	-ez
il	-t	ils	-ent
elle	-t	elles	-ent

PARTIR (TO LEAVE) - PRESENT			
I leave	je pars	*we leave*	nous partons
you leave (infml.)	tu pars	*you leave (pl./fml.)*	vous partez
he leaves	il part	*they leave (m.)*	ils partent
she leaves	elle part	*they leave (f.)*	elles partent
Past Participle: parti			

SAVOIR VS CONNAÎTRE

Savoir refers to the possession of knowledge. It can also be translated as *to know how.*

SAVOIR (TO KNOW, TO KNOW HOW) - PRESENT			
I know	je sais	*we know*	nous savons
you know (infml.)	tu sais	*you know (pl./fml.)*	vous savez
he knows	il sait	*they know (m.)*	ils savent
she knows	elle sait	*they know (f.)*	elles savent
Past Participle: su; Future and Conditional stem: saur-			

Connaître refers to familiarity with someone or something. It is sometimes translated as *to be familiar with*.

CONNAÎTRE *(TO KNOW, TO BE FAMILIAR WITH)* - **PRESENT**			
I know	je connais	*we know*	nous connaissons
you know (infml.)	tu connais	*you know (pl./fml.)*	vous connaissez
he knows	il connaît	*they know (m.)*	ils connaissent
she knows	elle connaît	*they know (f.)*	elles connaissent
Past Participle: connu			

OTHER VERBS

ÉCRIRE *(TO WRITE)* - **PRESENT**			
I write	j'écris	*we write*	nous écrivons
you write (infml.)	tu écris	*you write (pl./fml.)*	vous écrivez
he writes	il écrit	*they write (m.)*	ils écrivent
she writes	elle écrit	*they write (f.)*	elles écrivent
Past Participle: écrit			

LIRE *(TO READ)* - **PRESENT**			
I read	je lis	*we read*	nous lisons
you read (infml.)	tu lis	*you read (pl./fml.)*	vous lisez
he reads	il lit	*they read (m.)*	ils lisent
she reads	elle lit	*they read (f.)*	elles lisent
Past Participle: lu			

DIRE *(TO SAY, TO TELL)* - **PRESENT**			
I say	je dis	*we say*	nous disons
you say (infml.)	tu dis	*you say (pl./fml.)*	vous dites
he says	il dit	*they say (m.)*	ils disent
she says	elle dit	*they say (f.)*	elles disent

Past Participle: dit

VOIR *(TO SEE)* - **PRESENT**			
I see	je vois	*we see*	nous voyons
you see (infml.)	tu vois	*you see (pl./fml.)*	vous voyez
he sees	il voit	*they see (m.)*	ils voient
she sees	elle voit	*they see (f.)*	elles voient

Past Participle: vu; Future and Conditional stem: verr-

Unit 2 Quiz

Now let's see how you did in Unit 2!

In this section you'll find a short quiz testing what you learned in Unit 2. After you've answered all of the questions, don't forget to score your quiz to see how you did. If you find that you need to go back and review, please do so before continuing on to Unit 3.

A. Can you find the English equivalent for these professions?

1. le pharmacien/la pharmacienne	a. *nurse*
2. le fonctionnaire/la fonctionnaire	b. *bank clerk*
3. l'infirmier/l'infirmière	c. *civil servant*
4. l'employé de banque/ l'employée de banque	d. *businessman/businesswoman*
5. l'homme d'affaires/ la femme d'affaires	e. *pharmacist*

B. Translate the following expressions.

1. *I'm taking a class.* _____

2. *I did well on my test.* _____

3. *I failed my test.* _____

4. *I work forty hours a week.* _____

5. *I'm on vacation.* _____

C. Fill in the blanks with depuis or pendant.

1. **Je connais Sophie** _____ **dix ans.** (*I've known Sophie for ten years.*)

2. **Il va travailler en France** _____ **un an.** (*He's going to work in France for a year.*)

3. **Elle a joué au tennis** _____ **six mois.** (*She played tennis for six months.*)

4. **J'étudie le français** _____ **trois semaines.** (*I've been studying French for three weeks.*)

5. **Elle sera à l'école** _____ **sept ans.** (*She will be in school for seven years.*)

D. Give the imperfect form of each verb.

1. **Il y** _____ **(avoir) beaucoup de gens à la fête.**
   (There were a lot of people at the party.)

2. **Nous** _____ **(être) en retard.** *(We were late.)*

3. **Elle** _____ **(manger) toujours une salade pour le déjeuner.** *(She always used to eat a salad for lunch.)*

4. **Je** _____ **(parler) au prof.** *(I was speaking to the professor.)*

5. **Tu** _____ **(finir) tes devoirs.** *(You were finishing your homework.)*

ANSWER KEY:
A. 1. e; 2. c; 3. a; 4. b; 5. d
B. 1. J'assiste à un cours. 2. J'ai réussi à mon examen. 3. J'ai échoué à mon examen. (J'ai raté mon examen.) 4. Je travaille quarante heures par semaine. 5. Je suis en vacances.
C. 1. depuis; 2. pendant; 3. pendant; 4. depuis; 5. pendant
D. 1. avait; 2. étions; 3. mangeait; 4. parlais; 5. finissais

How Did You Do?

Give yourself a point for every correct answer, then use the following key to determine whether or not you're ready to move on:

0-7 points: It's probably best to go back and study the lessons again to make sure you understood everything completely. Take your time; it's not a race! Make sure you spend time reviewing the vocabulary and reading through each grammar note carefully.

8-16 points: If the questions you missed were in Section A or B, you may want to review the vocabulary again; if you missed answers mostly in Section C or D, check the Unit 2 Essentials to make sure you have your conjugations and other grammar basics down.

17-20 points: Feel free to move on to Unit 3! Great job!

Points

Unit 3:
Sports and Leisure

In this unit, we're going to talk about les sports *(m.) (sports)* and les loisirs *(m.)*
(leisure activities, recreation). We're also going to look at a few advanced tenses
and how to form more complex sentences using *who, that, what,* and *which.*

By the end of this unit, you should be able to:

☐ Name different sports

☐ Say *I will have spoken* or *I will have finished*

☐ Talk about hobbies and other leisure activities

☐ Say *I had spoken* or *I had finished*

☐ Discuss games and matches

☐ Say *I would have spoken* or *I would have finished*

☐ Discuss outdoor activities

☐ Explain where you *put* something

☐ Connect two sentences using *who* or *that*

☐ Tell someone that you understand *what* they are saying

☐ Say *with which* or *in which*

☐ Order someone to *Hurry up!*

☐ Say you *had a good time*

Lesson 9: Words

By the end of this lesson, you will be able to:

☐ Name different sports

☐ Say *I will have spoken* or *I will have finished*

☐ Talk about hobbies and other leisure activities

☐ Say *I had spoken* or *I had finished*

Word Builder 1

Let's get started with les sports *(m.)* *(sports)*.

▶ 9A Lesson 9 Word Builder 1 (CD 8, Track 9)

soccer	le foot(ball)
(American) football	le football américain
ice hockey (lit., hockey on ice)	le hockey sur glace
ice skating (lit., skating on ice)	le patinage sur glace (le patin à glace)
swimming	la natation
gymnastics	la gymnastique
track (and field)	l'athlétisme *(m.)*
horseback riding	l'équitation *(f.)*
(mountain) climbing	l'alpinisme *(m.)*
fishing	la pêche
bodybuilding, strength training (weight lifting)	la musculation
golf	le golf
cycling	le cyclisme

hunting	la chasse
skiing	le ski
water-skiing	le ski nautique
surfing	le surf
snowboarding (lit., surfing on snow)	le surf sur neige

Take It Further

You've seen jouer (*to play*) used many times before. However, let's look at how to use jouer when it's followed by the preposition à or the partitive.

Jouer à is used with sports and games:

Mon mari joue au golf.
My husband plays golf.

Jouer + partitive (du, de la, etc.), on the other hand, is used with musical instruments.

Elle joue du piano.
She plays the piano.

Following that thought, here are a few more sports, games, and musical instruments.

SPORTS AND GAMES	
baseball	le baseball
basketball	le basket(-ball)
volleyball	le volley(-ball)
tennis	le tennis

SPORTS AND GAMES	
wrestling	la lutte
boxing	la boxe
auto racing, car racing	la course automobile
card game	le jeu de cartes
(playing) cards	les cartes (f.) (à jouer)

MUSICAL INSTRUMENTS	
guitar	la guitare
violin	le violon
cello	le violoncelle
flute	la flûte
clarinet	la clarinette
drums	la batterie
saxophone	le saxophone

Tu joues au baseball.
You play baseball.

Je joue au tennis.
I play tennis.

Nous jouons aux cartes.
We're playing cards.

Jouez-vous de la guitare ?
Do you play the guitar?

Ma mère jouait du violon.
My mother used to play the violin.

✎ Word Practice 1

Translate the following words into English.

1. le patinage sur glace _____

2. la natation _____

3. la pêche _____

4. le surf sur neige _____

5. l'athlétisme _____

ANSWER KEY:

1. *ice skating*; 2. *swimming*; 3. *fishing*; 4. *snowboarding*; 5. *track (and field)*

✎ Word Recall

Now let's practice some of the activities you learned in *Essential French*. Match the French to the English below.

1. la moto	a. *sailing*
2. la voile	b. *weight lifting*
3. la course à pied	c. *running*
4. l'haltérophilie	d. *motorcycling*

ANSWER KEY:

1. d; 2. a; 3. c; 4. b

Grammar Builder 1

THE FUTURE PERFECT (*I WILL HAVE SPOKEN*)

Now that we're halfway through *Advanced French*, we're going to begin looking at some more advanced tenses.

To start, let's take a look at a tense known as the "future perfect." It's equivalent to *will have* + past participle in English, as in *I **will have sold** the house by then.*

The future perfect tense is formed in the following way:

future tense of avoir or être + past participle of the verb

The same verbs that use avoir in the past tense use avoir in the future perfect, and the same verbs that use être in the past tense use être in the future perfect.

Remember that être and avoir are irregular in the future tense. Let's review the future tense conjugation of avoir:

AVOIR *(TO HAVE)* - **FUTURE**	
j'aurai	nous aurons
tu auras	vous aurez
il aura	ils auront
elle aura	elles auront

And here is the future tense conjugation of être:

ÊTRE *(TO BE)* - **FUTURE**	
je serai	nous serons
tu seras	vous serez
il sera	ils seront
elle sera	elles seront

▶ 9B Lesson 9 Grammar Builder 1 (CD 8, Track 10)

Okay, now let's look at full conjugations of verbs in the future perfect. We'll first look at examples of verbs that use avoir.

Parler (*to speak, to talk*) is an example of a regular -er verb that uses **avoir**. So to form the future perfect of **parler**, take the future tense of **avoir** and add the past participle of **parler**, which is **parlé**.

PARLER (*TO SPEAK, TO TALK*) - **FUTURE PERFECT**			
j'aurai parlé	*I will have spoken*	nous aurons parlé	*we will have spoken*
tu auras parlé	*you will have spoken*	vous aurez parlé	*you will have spoken*
il aura parlé	*he will have spoken*	ils auront parlé	*they will have spoken*
elle aura parlé	*she will have spoken*	elles auront parlé	*they will have spoken*

Now here is an example of a regular -ir verb that uses **avoir**: **finir** (*to finish*).

FINIR (*TO FINISH*) - **FUTURE PERFECT**			
j'aurai fini	*I will have finished*	nous aurons fini	*we will have finished*
tu auras fini	*you will have finished*	vous aurez fini	*you will have finished*
il aura fini	*he will have finished*	ils auront fini	*they will have finished*
elle aura fini	*she will have finished*	elles auront fini	*they will have finished*

Here is an example of a regular -re verb that uses avoir: vendre (to sell).

VENDRE (TO SELL) - FUTURE PERFECT			
j'aurai vendu	I will have sold	nous aurons vendu	we will have sold
tu auras vendu	you will have sold	vous aurez vendu	you will have sold
il aura vendu	he will have sold	ils auront vendu	they will have sold
elle aura vendu	she will have sold	elles auront vendu	they will have sold

And here is an example of an irregular verb that uses avoir: faire (to do, to make). Notice that faire forms the future perfect normally.

FAIRE (TO DO, TO MAKE) - FUTURE PERFECT			
j'aurai fait	I will have made	nous aurons fait	we will have made
tu auras fait	you will have made	vous aurez fait	you will have made
il aura fait	he will have made	ils auront fait	they will have made
elle aura fait	she will have made	elles auront fait	they will have made

Now that you've seen examples of verbs that use avoir, let's look at an example of a verb that uses être. Keep in mind that the past participle of a verb that uses être must agree in gender and number with the subject.

Here is the full conjugation of aller (to go) in the future perfect:

ALLER (TO GO) - FUTURE PERFECT			
je serai allé(e)	I will have gone	nous serons allé(e)s	we will have gone
tu seras allé(e)	you will have gone	vous serez allé(e)(s)	you will have gone
il sera allé	he will have gone	ils seront allés	they will have gone
elle sera allée	she will have gone	elles seront allées	they will have gone

Remember that être itself actually uses avoir, so: j'aurai été (I will have been), etc.

In English, the future perfect is often followed by the present tense: He **will have eaten** all of the food when I **arrive**. However, in French, the future perfect is usually followed by the future tense in that type of sentence:

Tu auras mangé toute la nourriture quand j'arriverai.
You will have eaten all of the food when I arrive. (lit., You will have eaten all the food when I will arrive.)

Tu auras commencé la leçon quand j'entrerai dans la classe.
You will have begun the lesson when I enter the classroom. (lit., You will have begun the lesson when I will enter the class.)

Il sera parti quand la police sera là.
He will have left when the police get there. (lit., He will have left when the police will be there.)

When the future perfect is used with avant de (before), the verb that follows will be in the infinitive:

Nous aurons pris le livre avant de rentrer à la maison.
We will have taken the book before coming home.

Elles auront fini leurs devoirs avant de regarder la télévision.
They will have finished their homework before they watch television (before watching television).

The negative version of that sentence would be: Elles n'auront pas fini leurs devoirs avant de regarder la télévision. (*They will not have finished their homework before watching television.*) Notice that pas comes in between avoir and the past participle. The same is true for verbs that use être.

Finally, a good phrase to know when using the future perfect is d'ici. It literally means *from here,* but it can also mean *by* or *until* when combined with a time word or phrase:

d'ici demain	by tomorrow, until tomorrow
d'ici juin	by June, until June
d'ici la fin de la semaine	by the end of the week, until the end of the week

You can also say:

d'ici là	by then, from now on, from now until, until then (lit., from here there)

D'ici là, j'aurai vendu la maison.
By then, I will have sold the house.

✎ Work Out 1

Fill in the blanks with the correct future perfect form of the verbs in parentheses.

1. **Mes amis** _____ **(finir) avant six heures.**

   (My friends will have finished before 6:00.)

2. **D'ici demain, j'**_____ **(regarder) le film.**

   (By tomorrow, I will have watched the movie.)

3. **Nous n'** _____ **pas** _____ **(attendre) trois jours.**

   (We will not have waited three days.)

4. **Elle** _____ **(partir) quand mon père arrivera.**

   (She will have left when my father arrives.)

   ANSWER KEY:
   1. **auront fini**; 2. **aurai regardé**; 3. **aurons, attendu**; 4. **sera partie**

Word Builder 2

Here are some hobbies and other activities that you might do in your spare time.

▶ 9C Lesson 9 Word Builder 2 (CD 8, Track 11)

hobbies (pastimes)	les passe-temps (m.)
chess	les échecs (m.)
checkers	les dames (f.)
entertainment	le divertissement
play	la pièce
theater	le théâtre
ballet	le ballet

movies	le cinéma*
sewing	la couture
knitting	le tricot
vacation	les vacances (*f.*)
camping	le camping
yoga	le yoga
dance class	le cours de danse
reading	la lecture
painting	la peinture

* Remember that le cinéma also means *movie theater*.

Take It Further

When you're on vacation, you may want to visit some sites in the area. Use the verb visiter (*to visit*) when you want to talk about visiting places, cities, monuments, etc.

Je visite la Tour Eiffel.
I'm visiting the Eiffel Tower.

However, use rendre visite à (*to visit, to pay a visit*) when you want to talk about visiting a person.

Je rends visite à ma tante Nancy.
I'm visiting my aunt Nancy.

Word Practice 2

Let's talk about your passe-temps favori (*favorite hobby*). Fill in the blanks with the correct French translations.

1. **Mon passe-temps favori est** _____ (*knitting*).

2. **Mon passe-temps favori est** _____ (*reading*).

3. **Mon passe-temps favori est** _____ (*chess*).

4. **Mon passe-temps favori est** _____ (*yoga*).

5. **Mon passe-temps favori est** _____ (*painting*).

ANSWER KEY:
1. le tricot; 2. la lecture; 3. les échecs; 4. le yoga; 5. la peinture

✎ Word Recall

Fill in the blanks with the correct question word.

1. _____ **de sœurs avez-vous ?** (*How many sisters do you have?*)

2. _____ **est-elle toujours en retard ?** (*Why is she always late?*)

3. _____ **habitent-elles ?** (*Where do they live?*)

4. _____ **partez-vous?** (*When are you leaving?*)

5. _____ **vas-tu ?** (*How are you?*)

ANSWER KEY:
1. Combien; 2. Pourquoi; 3. Où; 4. Quand; 5. Comment

Grammar Builder 2
THE PAST PERFECT (*I HAD SPOKEN*)

If you want to talk about the past, another good tense to know is the "past perfect," also known as the "pluperfect." It's equivalent to *had* + past participle in English, as in *the train **had left** when we arrived.*

Forming the past perfect is similar to forming the future perfect. Here's what you do:

imperfect tense of avoir or être + past participle of the verb

Again, if a verb uses avoir in the past tense then it uses avoir in the past perfect. The same goes for être.

Before we look at verbs in the past perfect, let's review the imperfect tense of avoir:

AVOIR *(TO HAVE)* - **IMPERFECT**	
j'avais	nous avions
tu avais	vous aviez
il avait	ils avaient
elle avait	elles avaient

And être:

ÊTRE *(TO BE)* - **IMPERFECT**	
j'étais	nous étions
tu étais	vous étiez
il était	ils étaient
elle était	elles étaient

▶ 9D Lesson 9 Grammar Builder 2 (CD 8, Track 12)

Now let's look at some verbs in the past perfect. As we did with the future perfect, let's start with verbs that use avoir.

Parler *(to speak, to talk)* uses avoir, so to form the past perfect of parler, take the imperfect form of avoir and add the past participle of parler: parlé.

PARLER *(TO SPEAK, TO TALK)* - **PAST PERFECT**			
j'avais parlé	*I had spoken*	nous avions parlé	*we had spoken*
tu avais parlé	*you had spoken*	vous aviez parlé	*you had spoken*
il avait parlé	*he had spoken*	ils avaient parlé	*they had spoken*
elle avait parlé	*she had spoken*	elles avaient parlé	*they had spoken*

Now let's look at **finir** (*to finish*):

FINIR *(TO FINISH)* - **PAST PERFECT**			
j'avais fini	*I had finished*	nous avions fini	*we had finished*
tu avais fini	*you had finished*	vous aviez fini	*you had finished*
il avait fini	*he had finished*	ils avaient fini	*they had finished*
elle avait fini	*she had finished*	elles avaient fini	*they had finished*

Here is **vendre** (*to sell*):

VENDRE *(TO SELL)* - **PAST PERFECT**			
j'avais vendu	*I had sold*	nous avions vendu	*we had sold*
tu avais vendu	*you had sold*	vous aviez vendu	*you had sold*
il avait vendu	*he had sold*	ils avaient vendu	*they had sold*
elle avait vendu	*she had sold*	elles avaient vendu	*they had sold*

And **faire** (*to do, to make*):

FAIRE *(TO DO, TO MAKE)* - **PAST PERFECT**			
j'avais fait	*I had done*	nous avions fait	*we had done*
tu avais fait	*you had done*	vous aviez fait	*you had done*
il avait fait	*he had done*	ils avaient fait	*they had done*
elle avait fait	*she had done*	elles avaient fait	*they had done*

Now that we've looked at several examples of verbs that use avoir, let's look at an example of a verb that uses être. Don't forget that the past participle of a verb that uses être must agree in gender and number with the subject.

Here is aller *(to go)* in the past perfect:

ALLER *(TO GO)* - **PAST PERFECT**			
j'étais allé(e)	*I had gone*	nous étions allé(e)s	*we had gone*
tu étais allé(e)	*you had gone*	vous étiez allé(e)(s)	*you had gone*
il était allé	*he had gone*	ils étaient allés	*they had gone*
elle était allée	*she had gone*	elles étaient allées	*they had gone*

As in English, the past perfect in French is often followed by the past tense:

Le train était parti quand nous sommes arrivés à la gare.
The train had left when we arrived at the station.

Here are some more examples of sentences with the past perfect:

Elle était partie à midi.
She had left at noon.

Nous avions eu un rendez-vous.
We had had an appointment.

Aviez-vous pu le faire...
Had you been able to do it ...

Ⅱ

✎ Work Out 2

Fill in the blanks with the correct form of avoir or être to create the past perfect.

1. j' _____ pris *(I had taken)*

2. il _____ sorti *(he had gone out)*

3. vous _____ été *(you had been)*

4. ils _____ partis *(they had left)*

5. elle _____ bu *(she had drunk)*

ANSWER KEY:
1. avais; 2. était; 3. aviez; 4. étaient; 5. avait

✎ Drive It Home

A. Conjugate each verb in the future perfect.

1. Je/J' _____ (choisir). *(I will have chosen.)*

2. Je/J' _____ (aller). *(I will have gone.)*

3. Je/J' _____ (répondre). *(I will have responded.)*

4. Je/J' _____ (avoir). *(I will have had.)*

5. Je/J' _____ (danser). *(I will have danced.)*

6. Je/J' _____ (tomber). *(I will have fallen.)*

7. Je/J' _____ (lire). *(I will have read.)*

8. Je/J' _____ (savoir). *(I will have known.)*

B. Great! Now give each verb in the past perfect.

1. J' _____ (choisir). (*I had chosen.*)

2. J' _____ (aller). (*I had gone.*)

3. J' _____ (répondre). (*I had responded.*)

4. J' _____ (avoir). (*I had had.*)

5. J' _____ (danser). (*I had danced.*)

6. J' _____ (tomber). (*I had fallen.*)

7. J' _____ (lire). (*I had read.*)

8. J' _____ (savoir). (*I had known.*)

ANSWER KEY:
A. 1. aurai choisi; 2. serai allé(e); 3. aurai répondu; 4. aurai eu; 5. aurai dansé; 6. serai tombé(e); 7. aurai lu; 8. aurai su
B. 1. avais choisi; 2. étais allé(e); 3. avais répondu; 4. avais eu; 5. avais dansé; 6. étais tombé(e); 7. avais lu; 8. avais su

⊕ Culture Note

Speaking of visiter and vacances, here is some background information on Paris and the surrounding area with a few highlights of places to see.

Paris, known as Lutèce (*Lutetia*) around Roman times, gets its current name from an ancient Gaelic tribe called the Parisii who were early settlers of the area. They first settled on the Île de la Cité (lit., *city island*) around 2,000 years ago. L'Île de la Cité is a small island in the Seine that is now at the heart of the modern city of Paris (and home to Notre Dame cathedral).

Here's a sampling of some of the most popular tourist sites in modern Paris:

La Tour Eiffel (*Eiffel Tower*) was built out of steel by Alexandre Gustave Eiffel for the World's Fair of 1889. It is approximately 1,100 feet high and serves as a radio

and television transmitter. It is also a world-famous tourist site open to visitors all year round. You can climb the stairs or take the elevator to the top. There are three levels open to visitors and a high-end restaurant on the second level.

L'Arc de Triomphe (lit., *Arch of Triumph*), built to commemorate the victories of Napoléon, is located in the center of a busy traffic circle called la Place Charles de Gaulle. The circle used to be called la Place de l'Étoile (lit., *Place of the Star*) because twelve avenues converge there. The Arch stands around 160 feet tall. The Tomb of the Unknown Soldier lies beneath the Arch, with a flame that burns in honor of all departed soldiers.

Le Musée du Louvre (*Louvre Museum*) started out as a fortress and was built up and expanded over the centuries into a residence of the French kings. Today it is one of the largest museums in the world, with masterpieces such as La Joconde (*Mona Lisa*), La Vénus de Milo, and La Victoire de Samothrace (*Winged Victory of Samothrace*). In 1989, glass pyramids designed by the architect Ieoh Ming Pei were added in front of the museum. The largest one was built to serve as a new entrance to the always crowded museum.

Across the Seine river from the Louvre, Le Musée d'Orsay (*Orsay Museum*) is a former train station that was transformed into a museum in the 1980s. It houses many realist and impressionist works of famous artists, such as Manet, Degas, Van Gogh, and Monet.

Le Centre National d'Art et de Culture Georges-Pompidou (lit., *the National Center of Art and Culture Georges-Pompidou*) is a futuristic, industrial-style structure housing a museum of modern art, a large library, a center for industrial creation, and an institute for musical experimentation. It opened its doors in 1977 and is also known as Le Centre Pompidou or Beaubourg, after the district of Paris in which it is located.

When visiting Paris, don't miss la Cathédrale Notre-Dame (*Notre Dame Cathedral*) on L'Île de la Cité in the center of Paris. Construction of the cathedral began in the 12th century and took more than 100 years to complete. The cathedral is famous for its stained-glass rose windows and beautiful gothic architecture.

There are also numerous parks and gardens throughout Paris, including the two massive ones at the edges of Paris: Le Bois de Boulogne and Le Bois de Vincennes.

If you care to venture beyond Paris, you can take a short trip to Versailles, Louis XIV's extravagant palace and its grounds, or take a longer excursion to the Loire Valley, where you will find more than one hundred châteaux (*castles*) with beautiful views and gardens.

How Did You Do?

Let's see how you did! By now, you should be able to:

☐ Name different sports
(Still unsure? Jump back to page 160)

☐ Say *I will have spoken* or *I will have finished*
(Still unsure? Jump back to page 165)

☐ Talk about hobbies and other leisure activities
(Still unsure? Jump back to page 169)

☐ Say *I had spoken* or *I had finished*
(Still unsure? Jump back to page 173)

Lesson 10: Phrases

By the end of this lesson, you will be able to:

☐ Discuss games and matches

☐ Say *I would have spoken* or *I would have finished*

☐ Discuss outdoor activities

☐ Explain where you *put* something

Phrase Builder 1

10A Lesson 10 Phrase Builder 1 (CD 8, Track 13)

to play a sport (to do a sport)	faire du sport
to play a game (to play a match)	jouer un match
to win a game (to win a match)	gagner un match
to lose a game (to lose a match)	perdre un match
spectator	le spectateur/la spectatrice
end of the game (end of the match)	la fin du match
final score	le score final
to kick (lit., to give a kick)	donner un coup de pied
first/second/third base	la première/deuxième/troisième base
rugby team	l'équipe (f.) de rugby
to dive in(to) the pool	plonger dans la piscine
to run the marathon	courir le marathon
to jump a hurdle	sauter une haie
to go horseback riding (to ride a horse)	monter à cheval
skateboard	la planche à roulettes, le skateboard

Take It Further

Like jouer (to play), faire (to do, to make) is often used when talking about sports and other activities. It can mean *to do* or *to play* or *to go (do)* a sport or activity. Note that, when talking about activities, faire is frequently followed by the partitive (du, de la, etc.).

You should already be familiar with some of these examples:

to play a sport, to do a sport, to play sports, to do sports	faire du sport
to play soccer, to do soccer	faire du foot(ball)
to do horseback riding, to go horseback riding	faire de l'équitation
to swim, to go swimming	faire de la natation
to ski, to go skiing	faire du ski
to water-ski, to go water-skiing	faire du ski nautique
to camp, to go camping	faire du camping
to do yoga	faire du yoga

✎ Phrase Practice 1

Unscramble the sentences below based on Phrase Builder 1.

1. plonge / la / Elle / dans / piscine / . _____

2. allez / monter / à / Vous / cheval / . _____

3. j'ai / pied / coup / donné / de / un / . _____

4. marathon / Nous / courir / le / allons / . _____

ANSWER KEY:

1. Elle plonge dans la piscine. (*She dives in/into the pool.*) 2. Vous allez monter à cheval. (*You're going to go horseback riding./You're going to ride a horse.*) 3. J'ai donné un coup de pied. (*I kicked.*) 4. Nous allons courir le marathon. (*We're going to run the marathon.*)

Word Recall

Identify the following weather conditions by filling in the correct sentence in French.

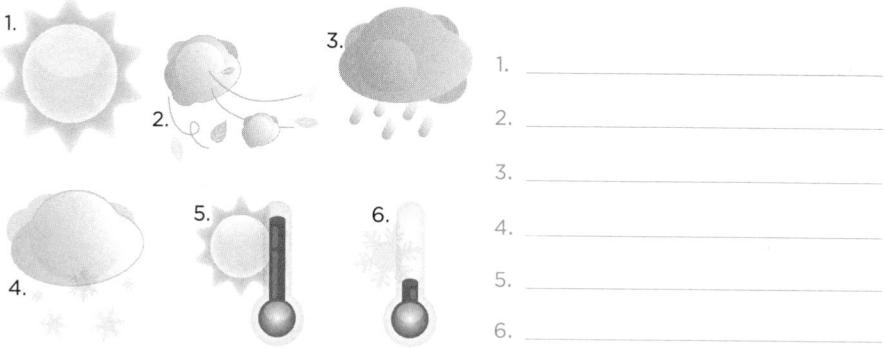

1. _____

2. _____

3. _____

4. _____

5. _____

6. _____

ANSWER KEY:

1. Il fait soleil./Il fait du soleil. 2. Il fait du vent. 3. Il pleut. 4. Il neige. 5. Il fait chaud. 6. Il fait froid.

Grammar Builder 1
THE PAST CONDITIONAL (*I WOULD HAVE SPOKEN*)

If you want to talk about what you *would have* done in French, then you need to use the "past conditional."

Fortunately, forming the past conditional is similar to forming both the future perfect and the past perfect. Here's what you do:

conditional of avoir or être + past participle of the verb

Once again, if a verb uses avoir in the past tense then it uses avoir in the past conditional. The same goes for être.

Before we look at verbs in the past conditional, let's review the conditional of avoir:

AVOIR *(TO HAVE)* - **CONDITIONAL**	
j'aurais	nous aurions
tu aurais	vous auriez
il aurait	ils auraient
elle aurait	elles auraient

And être:

ÊTRE *(TO BE)* - **CONDITIONAL**	
je serais	nous serions
tu serais	vous seriez
il serait	ils seraient
elle serait	elles seraient

▶ 10B Lesson 10 Grammar Builder 1 (CD 8, Track 14)

Now let's look at some examples of verbs in the past conditional. As we did with the future perfect and past perfect, let's start with verbs that use avoir.

Parler *(to speak)* uses avoir, so to form the past conditional, take the conditional form of avoir and add the past participle of parler: parlé.

PARLER *(TO SPEAK)* - **PAST CONDITIONAL**			
j'aurais parlé	*I would have spoken*	nous aurions parlé	*we would have spoken*
tu aurais parlé	*you would have spoken*	vous auriez parlé	*you would have spoken*

PARLER *(TO SPEAK)* - **PAST CONDITIONAL**			
il aurait parlé	*he would have spoken*	**ils auraient parlé**	*they would have spoken*
elle aurait parlé	*she would have spoken*	**elles auraient parlé**	*they would have spoken*

Now let's look at finir *(to finish)*:

FINIR *(TO FINISH)* - **PAST CONDITIONAL**			
j'aurais fini	*I would have finished*	**nous aurions fini**	*we would have finished*
tu aurais fini	*you would have finished*	**vous auriez fini**	*you would have finished*
il aurait fini	*he would have finished*	**ils auraient fini**	*they would have finished*
elle aurait fini	*she would have finished*	**elles auraient fini**	*they would have finished*

Here is vendre *(to sell)*:

VENDRE *(TO SELL)* - **PAST CONDITIONAL**			
j'aurais vendu	*I would have sold*	**nous aurions vendu**	*we would have sold*
tu aurais vendu	*you would have sold*	**vous auriez vendu**	*you would have sold*
il aurait vendu	*he would have sold*	**ils auraient vendu**	*they would have sold*
elle aurait vendu	*she would have sold*	**elles auraient vendu**	*they would have sold*

And here is faire (*to do, to make*):

FAIRE (*TO DO, TO MAKE*) - **PAST CONDITIONAL**			
j'aurais fait	*I would have done*	nous aurions fait	*we would have done*
tu aurais fait	*you would have done*	vous auriez fait	*you would have done*
il aurait fait	*he would have done*	ils auraient fait	*they would have done*
elle aurait fait	*she would have done*	elles auraient fait	*they would have done*

Also, it's important to mention that the past conditional of devoir (*to have to, must, should*) is usually translated as *should have*: tu aurais dû attendre (*you should have waited*). Notice that the verb following dû is in its infinitive form in French, even though it's in the past tense in English.

Similarly, the past conditional of pouvoir (*can, to be able to*) is usually translated as *could have*: Tu aurais pu attendre. (*You could have waited.*)

Now that we've looked at some examples of verbs that use avoir, let's look at an example of a verb that uses être. Again, remember that the past participle of a verb that uses être must agree in gender and number with the subject.

Here is aller (*to go*) in the past conditional:

ALLER (*TO GO*) - **PAST CONDITIONAL**			
je serais allé(e)	*I would have gone*	nous serions allé(e)s	*we would have gone*
tu serais allé(e)	*you would have gone*	vous seriez allé(e)(s)	*you would have gone*

ALLER *(TO GO)* - **PAST CONDITIONAL**			
il serait allé	he would have gone	ils seraient allés	they would have gone
elle serait allée	she would have gone	elles seraient allées	they would have gone

In both French and English, the past conditional is often used with the word si (*if*) plus the past perfect (which you already know how to form!).

J'aurais fait un gâteau pour son anniversaire si j'avais été à la maison.
I would have made a cake for his birthday if I had been (at) home.

Vous seriez resté à la maison si elle avait été là.
You would have stayed (at) home if she had been there.

✎ Work Out 1

Translate the following sentences into French.

1. *She would have gone* _____.

2. *We would have finished* _____.

3. *I should have studied* _____.

4. *You (infml.) would have waited* _____.

5. *They (m.) could have finished* _____.

ANSWER KEY:
1. Elle serait allée. 2. Nous aurions fini./On aurait fini. 3. J'aurais dû étudier. 4. Tu aurais attendu.
5. Ils auraient pu finir.

Phrase Builder 2

10C Lesson 10 Phrase Builder 2 (CD 8, Track 15)

outdoor activities	les activités (f.) de plein air
to go to the beach	aller à la plage
to sunbathe (lit., to take a bath of sun)	prendre un bain de soleil
to make a sandcastle	faire un château de sable
to go scuba diving	faire de la plongée sous-marine
to go jogging	faire du jogging
to ride a stationary bike (lit., to do stationary bike)	faire du vélo d'appartement
to stay in shape	rester en forme
to go on a picnic (lit., to do a picnic)	faire un pique-nique
to play hide and seek (lit., to play hide-hide)	jouer à cache-cache
to roll the dice	lancer les dés
TV series	le feuilleton (télévisé)
sitcom	la comédie de situation
to spend time with friends	passer du temps avec des amis

Take It Further

If you want to talk about hobbies and leisure activities, a good word to know is temps (time, weather).

Temps is used in a variety of French phrases and expressions dealing with time. Here are some examples:

to spend time	passer du temps
hobby, pastime (lit., the spend-time)	le passe-temps

free time	le temps libre
halftime (of a game)	la mi-temps
long time	longtemps
full-time	à plein temps
part-time	à temps partiel
for how long? (lit., since how much time?)	depuis combien de temps ?
from time to time	de temps en temps
to have (the) time	avoir le temps
to waste time (lit., to lose time)	perdre du temps
to waste your time	perdre votre/ton temps
It is time to .../Now is the time to ...	Il est temps de...

il y a longtemps
a long time ago

Avez-vous le temps d'aller avec moi ?
Do you have time to go with me?

J'ai le temps. Je n'ai pas le temps.
I have time. I don't have time.

Nous aurions joué au tennis si nous avions eu le temps.
We would have played tennis if we had had the time.

Il perd son temps.
He's wasting his time.

Il est temps de te reposer.
It's time for you to relax.

✎ Phrase Practice 2

Choose the correct translation of the following English words.

1. *beach*
   a. la plage
   b. le château de sable
   c. la plongée sous-marine
   d. le pique-nique

2. *scuba diving*
   a. le vélo d'appartement
   b. la plongée sous-marine
   c. le cache-cache
   d. le feuilleton

3. *TV series*
   a. les dés
   b. le feuilleton
   c. la comédie de situation
   d. le vélo d'appartement

4. *hide and seek*
   a. la comédie de situation
   b. les dés
   c. le cache-cache
   d. le vélo d'appartement

ANSWER KEY:
1. a; 2. b; 3. b; 4. c

✎ Word Recall

Replace each word with its opposite. For example, if one of the words was jour, you would write nuit.

1. droite_____

2. près_____

3. ici_____

4. toujours _____

ANSWER KEY:
1. gauche (*right and left*); 2. loin (*near and far*); 3. là (*here and there*); 4. jamais (ne... jamais) (*always and never*)

Grammar Builder 2
TO PUT

▶ 10D Lesson 10 Grammar Builder 2 (CD 8, Track 16)

Mettre (*to put, to put on*) is an irregular verb. Its conjugation in the present tense is actually very similar to the SST verbs:

METTRE (*TO PUT, TO PUT ON*) - **PRESENT**			
je mets	*I put*	nous mettons	*we put*
tu mets	*you put*	vous mettez	*you put*
il met	*he puts*	ils mettent	*they put*
elle met	*she puts*	elles mettent	*they put*

The past participle of mettre is mis.

Hier soir il faisait froid, alors j'ai mis mon manteau.
Last night it was cold, so I put on my coat.

⏸ The verb permettre (*to allow, to permit*) is conjugated in the same way as mettre.

✎ Work Out 2
Fill in the blanks with the correct present tense form of mettre.

1. Où _____ -vous vos livres ? (*Where are you putting your books?*)

2. Tu ne _____ pas ton pull. (*You're not putting on your sweater.*)

3. Est-ce qu'elle _____ l'écharpe ? (*Is she putting on the scarf?*)

4. Les enfants _____ leurs devoirs sur la table.

(The children put their homework on the table.)

5. Je _____ mon violon dans ma chambre.

(I'm putting my violin in my bedroom.)

ANSWER KEY:
1. mettez ; 2. mets ; 3. met ; 4. mettent ; 5. mets

✎ Drive It Home

Change each verb from the conditional to the past conditional.

1. elle finirait _____

2. elle irait _____

3. elle jouerait _____

4. elle arriverait _____

5. elle vendrait _____

6. elle serait _____

7. elle aurait _____

8. elle ferait _____

9. elle devrait _____

10. elle pourrait _____

ANSWER KEY:
1. elle aurait fini ; 2. elle serait allée ; 3. elle aurait joué ; 4. elle serait arrivée ; 5. elle aurait vendu ;
6. elle aurait été ; 7. elle aurait eu ; 8. elle aurait fait ; 9. elle aurait dû ; 10. elle aurait pu

How Did You Do?

Let's see how you did! By now, you should be able to:

☐ Discuss games and matches
(Still unsure? Jump back to page 179)

☐ Say *I would have spoken* or *I would have finished*
(Still unsure? Jump back to page 181)

☐ Discuss outdoor activities
(Still unsure? Jump back to page 186)

☐ Explain where you *put* something
(Still unsure? Jump back to page 189)

Lesson 11: Sentences

By the end of this lesson, you will be able to:

☐ Connect two sentences using *who* or *that*

☐ Tell someone that you understand *what* they are saying

Sentence Builder 1

▶ 11A Lesson 11 Sentence Builder 1 (CD 8, Track 17)

We're going to a ski resort (lit., winter sports resort).	Nous allons à une station de sports d'hiver.
I'm wearing my ice skates.	Je porte mes patins à glace.
I'm going to the bunny slope (lit., beginners' slope).	Je vais à la piste pour débutants.

The kids are making a snowman.	Les enfants font un bonhomme de neige.
I'm a fan. (sports)	Je suis un supporteur./Je suis une supportrice.
I like the commercials at halftime (lit., of halftime).	J'aime les publicités de la mi-temps.
This golf course is difficult.	Ce parcours de golf est difficile.
I'm looking for a partner.	Je cherche un partenaire.
I'm showing my horse in a competition. (lit., I'm presenting my horse at a competition.)	Je présente mon cheval à un concours.
Children must wear a helmet to go bike riding (to ride a bike).	Les enfants doivent porter un casque pour monter à bicyclette.
I'm having a good time. (I'm having fun.)	Je m'amuse.
You shouldn't cheat. (One shouldn't cheat.)	On ne doit pas tricher.

Take It Further

If you want to talk about sports in French, then you're going to need to know the word for *ball*. There are actually two words in French for *ball*: le ballon and la balle. Here's the difference:

la balle	smaller ball (tennis, table tennis, juggling, etc.)
le ballon	larger ball (basketball, volleyball, soccer, etc.)

You also saw a lot of new words in Sentence Builder 1. Let's take a look at some of them, along with some related words and phrases:

ski resort (lit., a resort of winter sports)	la station de sports d'hiver
ice skate	le patin à glace
trail, slope, track	la piste
beginner	le débutant/la débutante
bunny slope/hill, beginners' slope/hill	la piste pour débutants
snowman	le bonhomme de neige
fan (sports)	le supporteur/la supportrice
commercials	les publicités (*f.*), les pubs (*f.*)
golf course	le parcours de golf, le terrain de golf
partner	le partenaire/la partenaire
horse	le cheval
competition, contest	le concours, la compétition
helmet	le casque
to go bike riding, to ride a bike	monter à bicyclette
to cheat	tricher

Also remember that *halftime* is la mi-temps.

✎ Sentence Practice 1

Match the French translations on the left to the correct English phrases on the right.

1. un bonhomme de neige	a. *a fan*
2. un supporteur	b. *a competition*
3. un patin à glace	c. *a helmet*
4. un concours	d. *a snowman*
5. un casque	e. *an ice skate*

ANSWER KEY:
1. d; 2. a; 3. e; 4. b; 5. c

✎ Word Recall

Now match the food terms on the left to the correct French translations on the right.

1. *vegetable*	a. le citron
2. *lemon*	b. le repas
3. *apple*	c. le maïs
4. *corn*	d. le légume
5. *meal*	e. la pomme

ANSWER KEY:
1. d; 2. a; 3. e; 4. c; 5. b

Grammar Builder 1
WHO AND THAT

▶ 11B Lesson 11 Grammar Builder 1 (CD 8, Track 18)

English uses words like *who* and *that* to connect two sentences. For example:

There's the book. I read the book.

You can connect these two sentences with *that* to get:

*There's the book **that** I read.*

As you can see, *that* replaced *the book* from the second sentence: *I read **the book*** became ***that** I read.* In other words, when *that* connects two sentences, it replaces a person or thing from the second sentence. The same is true for *who*.

When they are used to connect two sentences, *who* and *that* are known as "relative pronouns."

The main relative pronouns in French are qui and que. They connect two sentences, just like in English. Here's how they're used:

1. Qui can mean *who* or *that*. It functions as the **subject** of the second sentence. It is usually followed by a verb **without** a subject (so it would be followed by aime, ai lu, a parlé, s'amuse, lui parlent, etc.).

2. Que (or qu') can mean *whom* or *that*. It functions as the **object** of the second sentence. It is usually followed by a verb **with** a subject (so it would be followed by Christine aime, j'ai lu, quelqu'un a parlé, elle s'amuse, ils lui parlent, etc.).

Keep in mind that both qui and que can refer to either people or things.

Let's first look at an example using que:

Voilà le livre. J'ai lu le livre.
There's the book. I read the book.

Voilà le livre que j'ai lu.
There's the book that I read.

In the sentence *I read the book*, *I* is the subject and *the book* is the object. *I* is the subject because it is doing the action of the verb *read*: *I read*. *The book* is the object because it is receiving the action, it is being read. So **que** is used here because it replaces the object of the second sentence: *the book*.

Also notice that **que** is followed by a verb with a subject pronoun (j'ai lu). This is true in English as well.

Now here's an example using **qui**:

Je vois le pain. Le pain est sur la table.
I see the bread. The bread is on the table.

Je vois le pain qui est sur la table.
I see the bread that is on the table.

Qui is used here because it replaces the subject of the second sentence: *the bread*. You can also see that in both French and English, **qui** (*who*) is followed by a verb without a subject: **est** (*is*).

This can definitely be a bit confusing at first, but it will get easier with practice. Keeping that in mind, here are some more examples:

C'est la voiture que je conduis.
That's the car that I drive.

Natalie est la fille qui chante bien.
Natalie is the girl who sings well.

In English, you don't always have to use relative pronouns in sentences like this. However, you **must** use them in French.

Tu manges le dessert que j'ai fait.
You're eating the dessert that I made.
(You're eating the dessert I made.)

Marie est la fille qu'il aime.
Marie is the girl that he loves.
(Marie is the girl he loves.)

Finally, **qui** can be preceded by a preposition when it refers to a person or people. In this case, it translates as *whom* or *whose*.

à qui	to whom
avec qui	with whom
chez qui	at whose house
de qui	from whom, of whom, about whom
pour qui	for whom

Note that a preposition + **qui** is usually followed by a verb **with** a subject, in both French and English.

C'est la femme pour qui je travaille.
She's (lit., It's) the woman for whom I work.

La dame à qui vous parlez s'appelle Sophie.
The woman (lit., lady) to whom you are speaking is named Sophie.

C'est le jeune homme avec qui elle sort.
It's the young man she goes out with.
(lit., It's the young man with whom she goes out.)

You can also use a preposition + **qui** as a question: **Avec qui ?** (*With whom?*),
Chez qui ? (*At whose house?*), etc.

✎ Work Out 1

Fill in the blanks with qui or que.

1. Voici le garçon _____ est tombé. (*Here is the boy that fell.*)

2. Voilà la jeune fille avec _____ Jean joue au tennis.

   (*There is the young girl with whom Jean plays tennis.*)

3. Je n'ai pas vu le livre _____ Christine cherche.

   (*I didn't see the book that Christine is looking for.*)

4. Donnez-moi le verre _____ est sur la table, s'il vous plaît.

   (*Give me the glass that is on the table, please.*)

5. Voici les cartes _____ j'ai. (*Here are the cards that I have.*)

   ANSWER KEY:
   1. qui; 2. qui; 3. que; 4. qui; 5. que

Sentence Builder 2

▶ 11C Lesson 11 Sentence Builder 2 (CD 8, Track 19)

We go to the opera from time to time.	Nous allons à l'opéra de temps en temps.
My nephew is a ballet dancer.	Mon neveu est danseur classique. (Mon neveu est danseur de ballet.)
I'm a lifeguard.	Je suis maître-nageur.
They like bus tours.	Ils aiment les excursions en autocar.
We visited the castles of the Loire (Valley).	Nous avons visité les châteaux de la Loire.
I (really) like to spend time with friends.	J'aime bien passer du temps avec des amis.

I (really) like to tinker. (I really like to fix things/fiddle with things.)	J'aime bien bricoler.
I collect butterflies.	Je collectionne les papillons.
I (really) like to relax.	J'aime bien me reposer.

Take It Further

Okay, now that you've been introduced to the relative pronouns qui and que, let's talk more about the question qu'est-ce que ? (*what?*).

The relative pronoun que is actually in qu'est-ce que? That question is composed of qu'est-ce, which literally means *what is this* or *what is it* and is simply a way of forming a question in French, plus que.

So qu'est-ce que literally translates as *what is this that* or *what is it that*:

Qu'est-ce que tu dis ?
What are you saying? (lit., What is this that you're saying?)

However, now you know that que is usually followed by a verb with a subject. So what do you do if you want to ask *what?* followed by a verb without a subject? In that case, you have to use qu'est-ce qui... ? For example, remember the phrase from Unit 2:

Qu'est-ce qui t'est arrivé ?
What happened to you?

Here's another common expression that uses qu'est-ce qui:

Qu'est-ce qui se passe ?
What's going on?/What's happening?

Unit 3 Lesson 11: Sentences   199

Finally, you saw a lot of new words for talking about hobbies and leisure activities in Sentence Builder 2. Let's review:

opera	l'opéra (m.)
ballet dancer	le danseur/la danseuse de ballet, le danseur/la danseuse classique, la ballerine
lifeguard	la maître-nageur, le sauveteur
bus tour	l'excursion (f.) en autocar
to tinker, to fiddle with things, to fix/ repair things	bricoler
to collect	collectionner
butterfly	le papillon

✎ Sentence Practice 2

Translate the following sentences into French.

1. *I like to go to the opera.* _____

2. *I like bus tours.* _____

3. *I like to visit the castles.* _____

4. *I like to go to a ski resort.* _____

5. *I like to go to the bunny slope.* _____

ANSWER KEY:
1. J'aime aller à l'opéra. 2. J'aime les excursions en autocar. 3. J'aime visiter les châteaux.
4. J'aime aller à une station de sports d'hiver. 5. J'aime aller à la piste pour débutants.

✎ Word Recall

Translate the following menu into English.

le potage _____

les coquilles Saint-Jacques _____

la purée de pommes de terre _____

la glace à la fraise _____

la tisane _____

ANSWER KEY:
soup
scallops
mashed potatoes
strawberry ice cream
herbal tea

Grammar Builder 2
WHAT AS RELATIVE PRONOUN

▶ 11D Lesson 11 Grammar Builder 2 (CD 8, Track 20)

In English, the word *what* can also be used as a relative pronoun, but in a different way from *who* and *that*. Here is an example:

I see what is on the table.

Notice that *what* is used as a way of referring to something without explicitly identifying or naming it. You don't know *what* is on the table—as opposed to a sentence like *I see the bread that is on the table,* where you know *bread* is on the table.

In French, the relative pronouns ce qui and ce que are the equivalent of *what* as a relative pronoun in English. Here's how they're used:

1. Ce qui acts as a subject (***what** is on the table*). As a result, it is usually followed by a verb without a subject (such as *is*).

2. Ce que (or ce qu') acts as a direct object (***what** you are saying*, or, in other words, *you are saying **what***). As a result, it is usually followed by a verb with a subject (such as *you are saying*).

Je vois ce qui est sur la table.
I see what is on the table.

Je comprends ce que tu dis.
I understand what you are saying.

Marc dit toujours ce qu'il pense.
Marc always says what he's thinking.

✎ Work Out 2

Insert ce qui or ce que in the sentences below.

1. Il n'aime pas _____ est arrivé à Paul. (*He doesn't like what happened to Paul.*)

2. Je ne sais pas _____ vous faites. (*I don't know what you're doing.*)

3. J'adore _____ Sophie chante. (*I love what Sophie is singing.*)

4. Apportez-moi _____ est dans la cuisine. (*Bring me what is in the kitchen.*)

ANSWER KEY:
1. ce qui; 2. ce que; 3. ce que; 4. ce qui

✎ Drive It Home

Although this may seem repetitive and easy, make sure to read through each
sentence carefully and then say it out loud.

A. Fill in the blanks with qui.

1. **Nous lisons un livre** _____ est très intéressant. (*We're reading a book that is
   very interesting.*)

2. **Denise a une jupe** _____ est très longue. (*Denise has a skirt that is very long.*)

3. **Voici un homme** _____ est très fier. (*Here is a man who is very proud.*)

4. **Elle aime le restaurant** _____ est très loin. (*She likes the restaurant that
   is very far.*)

5. **Nous allons à la piste** _____ est très difficile. (*We're going to the slope that is
   very difficult.*)

B. Now fill in the blanks with que.

1. **Nous lisons un livre** _____ tu aimes. (*We're reading a book that you like.*)

2. **Denise a une jupe** _____ tu aimes. (*Denise has a skirt that you like.*)

3. **Voici un homme** _____ tu aimes. (*Here is a man that you like.*)

4. **Elle aime le restaurant** _____ tu aimes. (*She likes the restaurant that you like.*)

5. **Nous allons à la piste** _____ tu aimes. (*We're going to the slope that you like.*)

ANSWER KEY:
A. all qui
B. all que

How Did You Do?

Let's see how you did! By now, you should be able to:

☐ Connect two sentences using *who* and *that*
(Still unsure? Jump back to page 194)

☐ Tell someone that you understand *what* they are saying
(Still unsure? Jump back to page 201)

Lesson 12: Conversations

By the end of this lesson, you will be able to:

☐ Say *with which* or *in which*

☐ Order someone to *Hurry up!*

☐ Say you had a good time

⒂ Conversation 1

Marc recently had a Super Bowl party at his house and he's upset that his friend Paul didn't come.

▶ 12A Lesson 12 Conversation 1 (CD 9, Track 1)

Marc :	Tu n'es pas venu regarder le match de football (américain), le plus important de l'année, le « Super Bowl ». Qu'est-ce qui est arrivé ?
Paul :	Je suis désolé. J'aurais voulu venir si j'avais eu le temps, mais j'ai dû finir du travail chez moi.
Marc :	Tu aurais dû voir le match. C'était extraordinaire, surtout quand ils ont marqué le premier but.
Paul :	J'ai vu seulement une moitié du match.

Marc :	Laquelle ?
Paul :	La deuxième moitié, quand le joueur a envoyé le ballon très loin et notre équipe a gagné !
Marc :	Est-ce que tu avais regardé les publicités à la mi-temps ? Elles étaient si drôles!
Paul :	Pendant que je travaillais, j'ai vu la publicité qui montrait tous les grands chevaux qui parlaient.
Marc :	De toute façon, il y a toujours le match de basket-ball dimanche prochain et cette fois, tout le monde vient chez toi !

Marc:	You didn't come watch the football game, the most important (one) of the year, the "Super Bowl." What happened?
Paul:	I'm sorry. I would have wanted to come if I had had the time, but I had to finish some work at home.
Marc:	You should have seen the game. It was extraordinary, especially when they scored the first goal.
Paul:	I only saw one half of the game.
Marc:	Which one?
Paul:	The second half, when the player threw the ball very far and our team won!
Marc:	Had you watched the commercials at halftime? They were so funny!
Paul:	While I was working, I saw the commercial that showed all the big horses who were talking.
Marc:	At any rate, there's always the basketball game next Sunday and this time, everybody's coming to your house!

(II)

Take It Further

Le but is a general term that means *goal* or *target*. Perhaps since American football isn't really a big sport in France, the word for *touchdown* is simply le touchdown.

And of course, since we're talking about goals, we have to mention another new word that you saw in the dialogue: marquer (*to score*).

Finally, note that si can mean both *if* and *so*, as in si drôle (*so funny*), and the phrase pendant que means *while*.

✎ Conversation Practice 1

Unscramble the following phrases from Conversation 1 and then translate them into English.

1. aurais / voir / dû / tu / match / le _____

   _____

2. les / avais / publicités / regardé / tu _____

   _____

3. avais / le / eu / temps / j' _____

   _____

4. j' / venir / voulu / aurais _____

   _____

5. qui / arrivé / qu'est-ce / est / ? _____

   _____

ANSWER KEY:
1. tu aurais dû voir le match (*you should have seen the game/match*); 2. tu avais regardé les publicités (*you had watched the commercials*); 3. j'avais eu le temps (*I had had the time*); 4. j'aurais voulu venir (*I would have wanted to come*); 5. Qu'est-ce qui est arrivé ? (*What happened?*)

Word Recall

Translate the following daily routine into French.

1. *I get up.* _____

2. *I wash up.* _____

3. *I get dressed.* _____

4. *I go to bed.* _____

ANSWER KEY:
1. Je me lève. 2. Je me lave. 3. Je m'habille. 4. Je me couche.

Grammar Builder 1
WHICH

▶ 12B Lesson 12 Grammar Builder 1 (CD 9, Track 2)

Another relative pronoun in French is lequel (*which*).

Lequel is used after a preposition (dans, avec, etc.) and acts as the *which* in the phrases *with which, for which, in which,* etc. in English.

Lequel must agree in gender and number with the noun it is referring to. Here are its forms:

	SINGULAR	PLURAL
Masculine	lequel	lesquels
Feminine	laquelle	lesquelles

Let's look at an example using le crayon (*pencil*) and the preposition avec (*with*):

Où est le crayon avec lequel j'écrivais ?
Where's the pencil with which I was writing?

In this case, *which* refers to the masculine noun crayon (the item *with which* you were writing), so you need to use the masculine singular form lequel.

Here is another example, this time using la maison (*the house*) and the preposition dans (*in*):

Voici la maison dans laquelle nous habitions.
Here's the house in which we used to live.

In this case, *which* refers to la maison (the place *in which* you used to live), so you need to use the feminine singular form laquelle.

Also note that sometimes où (*where*) can be used instead of dans lequel. The same is true in English.

Voici la maison dans laquelle nous habitions.
Here's the house in which we used to live.

Voici la maison où nous habitions.
Here's the house where we used to live.

Finally, as you saw in the dialogue, lequel can be used as a question. When used as a question, it can appear without a preposition. For instance, if someone says J'ai lu le livre. (*I read the book.*), you could ask Lequel ? (*Which one?*). Of course, it can also be used **with** a preposition in a question. If someone says J'écris avec le crayon. (*I'm writing with the pencil.*), you could ask Avec lequel ? (*With which one?*).

Another relative pronoun in French is dont. Dont is typically used to replace
de (*of*) or the partitive (du, de la, etc.) + noun (person or thing). As a result, it
literally translates as *of which* or *of whom*, although it doesn't always translate that
way when used.

For example, instead of saying Voici le stylo. J'ai besoin du stylo. (*Here is the pen.
I need the pen.*) you can say:

Voici le stylo dont j'ai besoin.
Here's the pen I need. (lit., Here's the pen of which I have need.)

In this case, dont replaced du stylo in the second sentence.

Note that dont can also be used to indicate possession, in which case it means
whose. Instead of saying, for example, C'est le mari. Sa femme est actrice. (*That's
the husband. His wife is an actress.*) you could say:

C'est le mari dont la femme est actrice.
That's the husband whose wife is an actress.

(II)

✎ Work Out 1

Choose the correct relative pronoun to complete the sentence. Pay close attention
to the English translations.

1. Marie est la petite fille _____ j'ai parlé.

   (*Marie is the little girl of whom I spoke.*)

2. Voici le papier sur _____ j'ai écrit. (*Here is the paper on which I wrote.*)

3. C'est le film _____ j'ai peur.

   (This is the movie of which I'm afraid.)

4. Où est la salle dans _____ j'ai dansé ?

   (Where is the room in which I danced?)

   ANSWER KEY:
   1. dont; 2. lequel; 3. dont; 4. laquelle

Conversation 2

Martine and Donna are discussing what they did during summer vacation.

▶ 12C Lesson 12 Conversation 2 (CD 9, Track 3)

Martine :	Dis-moi ce que tu as fait pendant les vacances cet été. Je sais bien que tu as fait quelque chose d'extraordinaire, comme toujours !
Donna :	Tu sais que j'adore voyager avec mes amis, mais ils avaient décidé d'aller faire du camping dans les montagnes. Je serais allée avec eux, mais franchement, je voulais aller à la plage.
Martine :	Alors, qu'est-ce que tu as fait ?
Donna :	J'ai fait ce qui me plaît. Je suis allée au Mexique.
Martine :	Avec qui as-tu voyagé ?
Donna :	J'y suis allée avec Claire et Dominique, les deux sœurs dont le père est le meilleur ami de mon père.
Martine :	Ah, oui, les filles qui sont dans tes photos de l'année dernière.
Donna :	Il y avait beaucoup à faire ; nous avons nagé et nous étions à la plage tous les jours, en train de jouer au volley-ball.
Martine :	Tu es toute bronzée, ma chère !
Donna :	Eh bien, qu'est-ce que tu as fait l'été dernier ?
Martine :	Mon mari et moi, nous avons préparé un beau séjour en France. Ce qui me rend heureuse, c'est d'être à Paris ! C'est la ville que j'adore.

Martine:	*Tell me what you did during vacation this summer. I definitely know that you did something extraordinary, as always!*
Donna:	*You know that I love to travel with my friends, but they had decided to go camping in the mountains. I would have gone with them, but frankly, I wanted to go to the beach.*
Martine:	*So, what did you do?*
Donna:	*I did what I want (lit., I did what pleases me). I went to Mexico.*
Martine:	*With whom did you travel?*
Donna:	*I went there with Claire and Dominique, the two sisters whose father is my father's best friend.*
Martine:	*Oh, yes, the girls who are in your photos from last year.*
Donna:	*There was a lot to do; we went swimming and we were at the beach every day, playing volleyball.*
Martine:	*You're all tan, my dear!*
Donna:	*Well, what did you do last summer?*
Martine:	*My husband and I prepared a beautiful trip to France. What makes me happy, it's to be in Paris! It's the city that I love.*

Take It Further

Être en train de is a very useful expression to know. It basically means *to be in the middle of* or *to be in the process of*. It can also be translated as *to be* + the *-ing* form of a verb (*to be playing, to be doing*, etc.).

To use it, simply say:

form of être + en train de + verb in the infinitive

For example:

Je suis en train de jouer au volley-ball.
I'm in the middle of playing volleyball.

Je ne peux pas venir, je suis en train de faire mes devoirs.
I can't come, I'm doing my homework.

Elle était en train de tricher.
She was cheating.

Note that en train de doesn't have to immediately follow être:

Nous étions à la plage tous les jours, en train de jouer au volley-ball.
We were at the beach every day, playing volleyball.

Il est là-bas, en train de faire du yoga.
He's over there, doing yoga.

In the dialogue, you also saw the reflexive verb se rendre. It means *to surrender*, but it can mean a variety of other things as well, depending on what follows the verb.

to make oneself happy	se rendre heureux/heureuse
to make oneself sick	se rendre malade
to realize, to notice (to make oneself aware)	se rendre compte (de)
to go to, to take oneself to (a place)	se rendre à (+ *location*)
to give in to, to yield to	se rendre à (+ *evidence, an argument, etc.*)

Finally, you saw some other new vocabulary in the dialogue:

frankly, honestly	franchement
trip, stay, sojourn	le séjour
tan, tanned (adjective)	bronzé/bronzée

A related verb is bronzer, which means *to tan* or *to get a tan*.

✎ Conversation Practice 2

Fill in the blanks in the following sentences based on Conversation 2.

1. les filles _____ sont dans tes photos. *(the girls who are in your photos)*

2. Dis-moi_____ tu as fait. *(Tell me what you did.)*

3. J'ai fait _____ me plaît. *(I did what I want.)*

4. Tu sais_____ j'adore voyager. *(You know that I love to travel.)*

5. Les deux sœurs _____ le père est le meilleur ami de mon père.

(The two sisters whose father is my father's best friend.)

ANSWER KEY:
1. qui; 2. ce que; 3. ce qui; 4. que; 5. dont

✎ Word Recall

Find the correct match for each French word.

1. le magasin	a. *shoe*
2. le chapeau	b. *hat*
3. la chemise	c. *sock*
4. la chaussure	d. *shirt*
5. la chaussette	e. *store*

ANSWER KEY:
1. e; 2. b; 3. d; 4. a; 5. c

Grammar Builder 2
THE IMPERATIVE AND PAST TENSE OF REFLEXIVE VERBS

▷ 12D Lesson 12 Grammar Builder 2 (CD 9, Track 4)

You first learned about reflexive verbs in *Essential French* and studied them more in-depth in Unit 2 of *Intermediate French*.

As a review, here is the full conjugation of the reflexive verb se laver (*to wash oneself, to wash up*) in the present tense:

SE LAVER *(TO WASH ONESELF, TO WASH UP)* - **PRESENT**			
je me lave	*I wash myself*	nous nous lavons	*we wash ourselves*
tu te laves	*you wash yourself*	vous vous lavez	*you wash yourselves* (or *you wash yourself, fml.*)
il se lave	*he washes himself* (or *it washes itself*)	ils se lavent	*they wash themselves*
elle se lave	*she washes herself* (or *it washes itself*)	elles se lavent	*they wash themselves*

And here are some example sentences with reflexive verbs in the present tense:

Je m'amuse.
I'm having a good time. (I'm having fun.)

Je ne me dépêche pas.
I do not hurry.

If you want to use a reflexive verb in the imperative—in other words, if you want to use the verb in a command or strong request—do the following:

verb in the imperative + hyphen (-) + reflexive pronoun

To review the imperative, see Lesson 17 in Unit 5 of *Intermediate French*.

Here are some examples:

Amusez-vous bien !
Have a (very) good time! (Have a lot of fun!)

Dépêchons-nous !
Let's hurry!

Note that, in the imperative, the te reflexive pronoun becomes toi.

Amuse-toi bien!
Have a (very) good time! (Have a lot of fun!)

Dépêche-toi !
Hurry up!

If you want to use a reflexive verb in the past tense, do the following:

reflexive pronoun + present tense of être + past participle of the verb

Note that **all** reflexive verbs form the past tense with être.

Let's look at an example.

Here's the full conjugation of se laver in the past tense. Remember that the past participles of verbs that use être must agree in gender and number with the subject.

SE LAVER *(TO WASH ONESELF, TO WASH UP)* - **PAST**			
je me suis lavé(e)	*I washed myself*	nous nous sommes lavé(e)s	*we washed ourselves*
tu t'es lavé(e)	*you washed yourself*	vous vous êtes lavé(e)(s)	*you washed yourselves (or you washed yourself, fml.)*
il s'est lavé	*he washed himself (or it washed itself)*	ils se sont lavés	*they washed themselves*
elle s'est lavée	*she washed herself (or it washed itself)*	elles se sont lavées	*they washed themselves*

Elle s'est lavée.
She washed herself.

Mes amis se sont amusés.
My friends had a good time. (My friends had fun.)

However, there are certain times when the past participle of a reflexive verb does **not** agree with the subject. If a reflexive verb's past participle is followed by a direct object, then the past participle does not agree with the subject:

Elle s'est lavé la figure.
She washed her face. (lit., She washed the face herself.)

Ils se sont brossé les dents.
They brushed their teeth. (lit., They brushed the teeth themselves.)

In these sentences, la figure (*the face*) and les dents (*f.*) (*the teeth*) are direct objects that follow the past participles lavé and brossé. As a result, lavé and brossé retain their original form and do not agree with the subject (elle or ils) in gender or number.

Also note that French uses le, la, or les instead of a possessive (ma, mes, ta, tes, etc.) when expressing an action with a part of the body: Elle s'est lavé la figure. Saying Elle s'est lavé sa figure would be incorrect. This applies to all verbs, not just reflexive ones: Je lève la main. (*I raise my hand.*)

Finally, keep in mind that since reflexive verbs use être in the past tense, they also use être in the future perfect, past perfect, and past conditional. (Note that the direct object exception regarding past participles applies to those tenses as well.)

For instance, here is se laver in the future perfect:

SE LAVER *(TO WASH ONESELF, TO WASH UP)* - **FUTURE PERFECT**			
je me serai lavé(e)	*I will have washed myself*	nous nous serons lavé(e)s	*we will have washed ourselves*
tu te seras lavé(e)	*you will have washed yourself*	vous vous serez lavé(e)(s)	*you will have washed yourselves* (or *you will have washed yourself, fml.*)
il se sera lavé	*he will have washed himself* (or *it will have washed itself*)	ils se seront lavés	*they will have washed themselves*
elle se sera lavée	*she will have washed herself* (or *it will have washed itself*)	elles se seront lavées	*they will have washed themselves*

To review the future perfect and past perfect, see Lesson 9 of Unit 3 in this book. To review the past conditional, see Lesson 10 of Unit 3.

✎ Work Out 2

Translate the following sentences into English.

1. Elle s'était levée. _____

2. Tu t'es habillé. _____

3. Ils se seraient couchés. _____

4. Levez-vous ! _____

ANSWER KEY:
1. *She had gotten up. (She had risen.)* 2. *You got dressed. (You dressed yourself.)* 3. *They would have gone to bed. (They would have lain down.)* 4. *Get up! (Rise!)*

✎ Drive It Home

A. Fill in the blanks with the correct form of lequel.

1. Où est la table sur _____ j'écrivais ?

   (Where is the table on which I was writing?)

2. Où est le stylo avec _____ j'écrivais ?

   (Where is the pen with which I was writing?)

3. 3. Où sont les cahiers (m.) dans _____ j'écrivais ?

   (Where are the notebooks in which I was writing?)

4. Où sont les choses (f.) avec _____ j'écrivais ?

   (Where are the things with which I was writing?)

B. Now fill in the blanks with dont.

1. **Voici l'ordinateur** _____ j'ai besoin. *(Here is the computer I need.)*

2. **Voici le footballeur** _____ j'ai peur. *(Here is the soccer player I'm afraid of.)*

3. **Voici la prof** _____ le mari est mon cousin. *(Here is the professor whose husband is my cousin.)*

4. **Voici le livre** _____ vous avez parlé. *(Here is the book of which you spoke.)*

C. Finally, change the following reflexive verbs to the past tense.

1. **Elle s'amuse.** _____

2. **Elle se couche.** _____

3. **Elle s'habille.** _____

4. **Elle se lève.** _____

5. **Elle se lave les mains.** _____

ANSWER KEY:
A. 1. laquelle; 2. lequel; 3. lesquels; 4. lesquelles
B. all dont
C. 1. Elle s'est amusée. 2. Elle s'est couchée. 3. Elle s'est habillée. 4. Elle s'est levée. 5. Elle s'est lavé les mains.

Tip

In one of the Tips in Unit 1, you saw how to use more than one pronoun in a sentence. Now let's look at how to use more than one pronoun in the imperative.

In the positive imperative, use the following order of pronouns:

ORDER OF PRONOUNS IN THE POSITIVE IMPERATIVE				
positive imperative form of verb	le la les	me (moi) te (toi) lui nous vous leur	y	en

Donnez-le-lui.

Give it to him.

Donnez-leur-en.

Give them some.

Remember that the direct and indirect object pronoun me becomes moi in the positive imperative. Also, the direct object, indirect object, and reflexive pronoun te becomes toi in the positive imperative.

Montrez-moi.

Show me.

However, when moi and toi are followed by en or y, they become m' and t'.

Montrez-m'en.

Show me some.

In the negative imperative, just use the same order for sentences that you learned in the Unit 1 Tip, bracketed by ne and pas.

Ne le lui donnez pas.
Don't give it to him.

Ne m'en montrez pas.
Don't show me any.

How Did You Do?

Let's see how you did! By now, you should be able to:

☐ Say *with which* or *in which*
(Still unsure? Jump back to page 207)

☐ Order someone to *Hurry up!*
(Still unsure? Jump back to page 214)

☐ Say you *had a good time*
(Still unsure? Jump back to page 214)

Unit 3 Essentials

Don't forget to go to **www.livinglanguage.com/languagelab** to access your free online tools for this lesson: audiovisual flashcards, and interactive games and quizzes.

Vocabulary Essentials

SPORTS

sports		horseback riding	
soccer		fishing	
(American) football		golf	
swimming		skiing	
gymnastics		snowboarding	
track, track and field			

[Pg. 160] (If you're stuck, visit this page to review!)

HOBBIES AND OTHER LEISURE ACTIVITIES

hobbies, pastimes		movies	
chess		vacation	
entertainment		dance class	
play (at a theater)		reading	
theater		painting	

[Pg. 169]

SPORTS PHRASES

to play a sport, to do a sport	
to play a game/match	
to win a game/match	
to lose a game/match	
spectator	
end of the game/match	
final score	
to kick (lit., to give a kick)	
rugby team	
to run the marathon	
to ride a horse, to go horseback riding	

[Pg. 179]

MORE LEISURE ACTIVITIES

outdoor activities	
to go to the beach	
to sunbathe	
to go scuba diving	
to go jogging	
to stay in shape	
to go on a picnic	
to play hide and seek	
to roll the dice	
TV series	
to spend time with friends	

[Pg. 186]

SPORTS EXPRESSIONS

We're going to a ski resort (lit., winter sports resort).	
I'm a fan. (sports)	
I like the commercials at halftime.	
I'm having a good time./I'm having fun.	
You shouldn't cheat./One shouldn't cheat.	

[Pg. 191]

ACTIVITIES EXPRESSIONS

I'm a lifeguard.	
They like bus tours.	
I really like to spend time with my friends.	
I really like to relax.	

[Pg. 198]

Grammar Essentials

FUTURE PERFECT

1. To form the future perfect, use the future tense of avoir or être + past participle of the verb.

2. The future perfect is equivalent to *will have* + past participle in English.

PARLER *(TO SPEAK, TO TALK)* - **FUTURE PERFECT**			
I will have spoken	j'aurai parlé	*we will have spoken*	nous aurons parlé
you will have spoken (infml.)	tu auras parlé	*you will have spoken (pl./fml.)*	vous aurez parlé
he will have spoken	il aura parlé	*they will have spoken (m.)*	ils auront parlé
she will have spoken	elle aura parlé	*they will have spoken (f.)*	elles auront parlé

PAST PERFECT

1. To form the past perfect, use the imperfect tense of avoir or être + past participle of the verb.

2. The past perfect is equivalent to *had* + past participle in English.

FINIR *(TO FINISH)* - **PAST PERFECT**			
I had finished	j'avais fini	*we had finished*	nous avions fini
you had finished (infml.)	tu avais fini	*you had finished (pl./fml.)*	vous aviez fini
he had finished	il avait fini	*they had finished (m.)*	ils avaient fini
she had finished	elle avait fini	*they had finished (f.)*	elles avaient fini

PAST CONDITIONAL

1. To form the past conditional, use the conditional of avoir or être + past participle of the verb.

2. The future perfect is equivalent to *would have* + verb in English.

3. The past conditional of devoir is usually translated as *should have*. The past conditional of pouvoir is usually translated as *could have*.

VENDRE *(TO SELL)* - **PAST CONDITIONAL**			
I would have sold	j'aurais vendu	*we would have sold*	nous aurions vendu
you would have sold (infml.)	tu aurais vendu	*you would have sold (pl./fml.)*	vous auriez vendu
he would have sold	il aurait vendu	*they would have sold (m.)*	ils auraient vendu
she would have sold	elle aurait vendu	*they would have sold (f.)*	elles auraient vendu

ALLER *(TO GO)* - **PAST CONDITIONAL**			
I would have gone	je serais allé(e)	*we would have gone*	nous serions allé(e)s
you would have gone (infml.)	tu serais allé(e)	*you would have gone (pl./fml.)*	vous seriez allé(e)(s)
he would have gone	il serait allé	*they would have gone (m.)*	ils seraient allés
she would have gone	elle serait allée	*they would have gone (f.)*	elles seraient allées

RELATIVE PRONOUN QUI

1. Qui can mean *who* or *that*.
2. Qui replaces the **subject** in the second sentence.
3. It is usually followed directly by a verb (qui is the subject).
4. Qui can be preceded by a preposition when it refers to a person or people. In this case, it translates as *whom* or *whose*. These phrases are usually followed by a verb **with** a subject.

to whom	à qui
with whom	avec qui
at whose house	chez qui
from whom, of whom, about whom	de qui
for whom	pour qui

RELATIVE PRONOUN QUE/QU'

1. Que (or qu') can mean *whom* or *that*.
2. Que (or qu') replaces the **object** of the second sentence.
3. It is usually followed by a verb **with** a subject.

RELATIVE PRONOUN CE QUI

1. Ce qui is the equivalent of *what* as a relative pronoun in English.
2. Ce qui acts as a subject.
3. It is usually followed by a verb without a subject.

RELATIVE PRONOUN CE QUE/CE QU'

1. Ce que/Ce qu' is the equivalent of *what* as a relative pronoun in English.
2. Ce que/Ce qu' acts as a direct object.
3. It is usually followed by a verb with a subject.

RELATIVE PRONOUN LEQUEL

1. **Lequel** means *which*.
2. It is used after a preposition.
Here are its forms:

	SINGULAR	PLURAL
Masculine	lequel	lesquels
Feminine	laquelle	lesquelles

RELATIVE PRONOUN DONT

1. **Dont** is typically used to replace **de** (*of*) or the partitive (**du, de la,** etc.) + noun (person or thing).
2. It literally translates as *of which* or *of whom*.
3. It can also be used to indicate possession, in which case it means *whose*.

IMPERATIVE OF REFLEXIVE VERBS

1. To form the imperative of reflexive verbs, use the verb in the imperative + hyphen (-) + reflexive pronoun
2. In the imperative, the reflexive pronoun **te** becomes **toi**.

PAST TENSE OF REFLEXIVE VERBS

1. To form a reflexive verb in the past tense, use reflexive pronoun + present tense of **être** + past participle of the verb.
2. All reflexive verbs use **être** in the past tense.

3. If the reflexive verb's past participle is followed by a direct object, then the past participle does not agree with the subject.

SE LAVER *(TO WASH ONESELF, TO WASH UP)* - **PAST**			
I washed myself	je me suis lavé(e)	*we washed ourselves*	nous nous sommes lavé(e)s
you washed yourself	tu t'es lavé(e)	*you washed yourselves (or you washed yourself, fml.)*	vous vous êtes lavé(e)(s)
he washed himself (or it washed itself)	il s'est lavé	*they washed themselves*	ils se sont lavés
she washed herself (or it washed itself)	elle s'est lavée	*they washed themselves*	elles se sont lavées

OTHER VERBS

METTRE *(TO PUT, TO PUT ON)* - **PRESENT**			
I put	je mets	*we put*	nous mettons
you put (infml.)	tu mets	*you put (pl./fml.)*	vous mettez
he puts	il met	*they put (m.)*	ils mettent
she puts	elle met	*they put (f.)*	elles mettent
Past Participle: mis			

Unit 3 Quiz

Now let's see how you did in Unit 3!

After you've answered all of the questions, don't forget to score your quiz to see how you did. If you find that you need to go back and review, please do so before continuing on to Unit 4.

A. Translate these sports into English.

1. la natation _____

2. l'athlétisme _____

3. l'équitation _____

4. le surf sur neige _____

5. la pêche _____

B. Now fill in the blanks with qui, que, or dont.

1. C'est la fille _____ est partie. (*It's the girl who left.*)

2. C'est la fille _____ tu as aimée. (*It's the girl that you loved.*)

3. C'est la fille _____ tu as parlé. (*It's the girl of whom you spoke.*)

4. C'est la fille avec _____ tu as parlé. (*It's the girl with whom you spoke.*)

5. C'est la fille _____ le père est acteur. (*It's the girl whose father is an actor.*)

C. Now translate these sentences into English.

1. Nous avons gagné le match.

   _____

2. C'est la fin du match.

   _____

3. Je voudrais monter à cheval.

   _____

4. Elle sera allée à la plage.

   _____

5. Tu serais resté en forme.

   _____

D. Fill in the blanks with the past perfect tense of the verbs in parentheses.

1. Nous _____ (parler) avec nos amis.
   (We had spoken with our friends.)

2. Il _____ (aller) à l'université. (He had gone to college.)

3. Tu _____ (lire) le livre. (You had read the book.)

4. Mon professeur _____ (écrire) ce livre.
   (My professor had written that book.)

5. Elles _____ (se réveiller) tôt.
   (They had woken up early.)

How Did You Do?

Give yourself a point for every correct answer, then use the following key to determine whether or not you're ready to move on:

0-7 points: It's probably best to go back and study the lessons again to make sure you understood everything completely. Take your time; it's not a race! Make sure you spend time reviewing the vocabulary and reading through each grammar note carefully.

8-16 points: If the questions you missed were in Section A or B, you may want to review the vocabulary again; if you missed answers mostly in Section C or D, check the Unit 3 Essentials to make sure you have your conjugations and other grammar basics down.

17-20 points: Feel free to move on to the next unit! You're doing a great job.

 **Points**

Unit 4:
Doctors and Health

You've made it to the very last unit of *Advanced French*. Congratulations!

In this last unit, we're going to look at vocabulary dealing with la santé (*health*) and le corps humain (*the human body*). We'll also tackle a final verb tense that deals with wishes, doubts, and necessities: the subjunctive.

By the end of this unit, you should be able to:

☐ Name different parts of the body

☐ Tell someone that you're hurt or in pain

☐ Say whether you have a *cold* or the *flu*

☐ Talk about *each other*

☐ Name different injuries and disabilities

☐ Tell someone to *follow* the instructions

☐ Talk about exercise

☐ Say *I saw her*

☐ Explain what's wrong to a doctor

☐ Understand what you hear in an emergency situation

☐ Express wishes, desires, doubts, and needs

☐ Talk about what you need to *buy*, *take*, or *see*

☐ Say what you have to *be* or what you doubt someone *can* do

Lesson 13: Words

By the end of this lesson, you will be able to:

☐ Name different parts of the body

☐ Tell someone that you're hurt or in pain

☐ Say whether you have a *cold* or the *flu*

☐ Talk about *each other*

Word Builder 1

Let's get started with **les parties** (*f.*) **du corps** (*parts of the body*).

▶ 13A Lesson 13 Word Builder 1 (CD 9, Track 5)

head	la tête
eye	l'œil (*m.*)
eyes	les yeux (*m.*)
nose	le nez
mouth	la bouche
ear	l'oreille (*f.*)
tooth	la dent
neck	le cou
shoulder	l'épaule (*f.*)
back	le dos
arm	le bras
hand	la main
leg	la jambe

| knee | le genou |
| foot | le pied |

Take It Further

Les parties du corps provide a good review of irregular plurals:

SINGULAR	PLURAL
l'œil *(eye)*	les yeux *(eyes)*
le nez *(nose)*	les nez *(noses)*
le dos *(back)*	les dos *(backs)*
le bras *(arm)*	les bras *(arms)*
le genou *(knee)*	les genoux *(knees)*

Note that cou *(neck)* becomes cous *(necks)* in the plural, not coux. Genoux vs. cous is a good example of the fact that only *some* words that end in -ou add -x in the plural.

To review the patterns of irregular plurals, see Lesson 5 of *Essential French* and Lesson 2 of *Intermediate French*. Of course, œil/yeux doesn't follow any particular rule, it's just entirely irregular.

Also don't forget that French uses le, la, or les instead of a possessive (ma, mes, ta, tes, etc.) when expressing an action with a part of the body:

Je me lave les mains.
I'm washing my hands. (lit., I'm washing up the hands.)

✎ Word Practice 1

Identify the following body parts in French. Make sure to include the appropriate definite article (le, la, l', les).

1. _____

2. _____

3. _____

4. _____

ANSWER KEY:
1. l'œil; 2. le nez; 3. l'oreille; 4. la bouche

✎ Word Recall

Now conjugate the verbs below in the present tense.

1. je _____ (mettre)

2. tu _____ (sortir)

3. il _____ (employer)

4. nous _____ (commencer)

5. vous _____ (savoir)

6. elles _____ (acheter)

ANSWER KEY:
1. mets; 2. sors; 3. emploie; 4. commençons; 5. savez; 6. achètent

Grammar Builder 1
TO HAVE PAIN OR *TO HURT*

▶ 13B Lesson 13 Grammar Builder 1 (CD 9, Track 6)

Hopefully you won't have to use these expressions very often, but just in case, it's good to know how to explain that you're hurt or in pain.

To express a hurt or pain in a certain part of your body, use avoir mal à (*to have pain in, to ache, to have an ache, to have a sore something*) + part of the body.

Il a mal aux pieds.
He has sore feet.

J'ai mal aux dents.
I have a toothache.

Note that avoir du mal à is very different from avoir mal à. Avoir du mal à means *to have trouble* (*doing something*). For example: j'ai du mal à choisir (*I'm having trouble choosing*).

If your pain is caused by someone or something, use an indirect object pronoun (me, te, lui, etc.) + faire mal (*to hurt*).

Tu me fais mal.
You're hurting me.

Mes chaussures me font mal.
My shoes hurt me.

Son dentiste ne lui fait jamais mal.
His dentist never hurts him.

You can also use faire mal à + indirect object: **Les chaussures font mal à Marie.** (*The shoes are hurting Marie.*)

Work Out 1

Translate the following sentences into French.

1. *He has a backache.* _____

2. *I have a headache.* _____

3. *My earring is hurting me.* _____

4. *I have a tooth that is hurting me.* _____

ANSWER KEY:
1. Il a mal au dos. **2.** J'ai mal à la tête. **3.** Ma boucle d'oreille me fait mal.
4. J'ai une dent qui me fait mal.

Word Builder 2

Now let's look at les maladies (*f.*) (*illnesses, diseases*) and other words you might need to know at the doctor's office.

▶ 13C Lesson 13 Word Builder 2 (CD 9, Track 7)

medical checkup	l'examen (*m.*) médical
doctor's office	le cabinet médical
doctor	le docteur/la doctoresse*
patient	le patient/la patiente
laboratory	le laboratoire
x-ray	la radiographie, la radio

* Docteur/doctoresse and médecin are synonyms. Remember, however, that médecin only has a masculine form.

diagnosis	le diagnostic
(common) cold	le rhume
fever	la fièvre
flu	la grippe
virus	le virus
allergy	l'allergie (f.)
infection	l'infection (f.)
care	le soin

Take It Further

Let's look at some more words related to la santé (health) that are good to know:

LE CORPS (BODY)	
finger	le doigt
fingernail	l'ongle (m.)
toe	l'orteil (m.), le doigt de pied
toenail	l'ongle (m.) de pied
ankle	la cheville
wrist	le poignet
elbow	le coude
skin	la peau
mole	le grain de beauté
heart	le cœur
heart attack	la crise cardiaque
brain	le cerveau
stroke	l'attaque (f.) cérébrale
throat	la gorge
lung	le poumon

LE CORPS **(BODY)**	
belly, stomach (general term)	le ventre
stomach	l'estomac *(m.)*
abdomen	l'abdomen *(m.)*

J'ai mal au ventre.
I have a bellyache.

LE MÉDECIN **(DOCTOR)**	
sick	malade
to be sick	être malade
to get sick	tomber malade
to cure, to get better	guérir
to examine	examiner
results	les résultats *(m.)*
instructions	les instructions *(f.)*
prescription	l'ordonnance *(f.)*
pill	la pilule, le comprimé
antibiotics	les antibiotiques *(m.)*
needle	l'aiguille *(f.)*
vaccine	le vaccin
shot, injection	la piqûre, l'injection *(f.)*
to get a shot	recevoir une piqûre
allergic	allergique

J'ai peur des aiguilles.
I'm afraid of needles.

Je suis allergique à la pénicilline.
I'm allergic to penicillin.

✎ Word Practice 2

Choose the correct translation of each French word.

1. le rhume

   a. *flu*
   b. *fever*
   c. *common cold*
   d. *virus*

2. la grippe

   a. *fever*
   b. *flu*
   c. *care*
   d. *infection*

3. le soin

   a. *allergy*
   b. *diagnosis*
   c. *x-ray*
   d. *care*

4. le cabinet médical

   a. *doctor's office*
   b. *medical checkup*
   c. *laboratory*
   d. *diagnosis*

ANSWER KEY:
1. c; 2. b; 3. d; 4. a

✎ Word Recall

Give the feminine form of the following words.

1. le docteur *(doctor)* _____

2. l'infirmier *(nurse)* _____

3. le dentiste *(dentist)* _____

4. le patient (*patient*) _____

5. l'esthéticien (*beautician*) _____

ANSWER KEY:
1. la doctoresse; 2. l'infirmière; 3. la dentiste; 4. la patiente; 5. l'esthéticienne

Grammar Builder 2
EACH OTHER

▶ 13D Lesson 13 Grammar Builder 2 (CD 9, Track 8)

You know that you use reflexive pronouns to talk about something that is happening to the *self*: je me lave (*I wash myself*), tu te blesses (*you hurt yourself*), etc.

However, you can also use reflexive pronouns to talk about *each other*. To do so, just use one of the plural reflexive pronouns—nous, vous, or se (s')—the same way you would normally use it.

Here are some examples using se:

Ils se regardent.
They look at each other. (They watch each other.)

Jennifer et Carol se voient de temps en temps.
Jennifer and Carol see each other from time to time.

Thomas et Nicole se marient dimanche.
Thomas and Nicole are getting married on Sunday. (Thomas and Nicole are marrying each other on Sunday.)

When a verb uses a plural reflexive pronoun to mean *each other*, it is known as a "reciprocal verb." As with reflexive verbs, there are some common reciprocal verbs, such as s'aimer (*to like/love each other*) and se dire (*to tell each other, to say to each other*). You will find a list of common reciprocal verbs in the Tip at the end of this lesson.

Of course, some verbs can have both reflexive and reciprocal meanings. Whether the reflexive pronoun means *self* or *each other* often depends simply on context. For example, se regarder could mean *to look at oneself* or *to look at each other*. You could say nous nous regardons and mean *we look at each other* or *we look at ourselves* depending on what you're talking about.

Also remember that only **plural** reflexive pronouns can mean *each other*. If it's a singular reflexive pronoun, it will never mean *each other*. For instance, you would never translate je me vois (*I see myself*) as *I see each other*. That wouldn't make sense in French or in English.

Ⓘ

✎ Work Out 2

Change the verbs in the following sentences to reciprocal verbs.

1. Ils parlent de temps en temps. (*They speak from time to time.*)

_____

2. Nous téléphonons tous les jours. (*We call every day.*)

_____

3. Mes parents comprennent. (*My parents understand.*)

_____

4. Est-ce que vous parlez souvent ? (*Do you speak often?*)

_____

ANSWER KEY:

1. Ils se parlent de temps en temps. (*They speak to each other from time to time.*) 2. Nous nous téléphonons tous les jours. (*We call each other every day.*) 3. Mes parents se comprennent. (*My parents understand each other.*) 4. Est-ce que vous vous parlez souvent ? (*Do you speak to each other often?*)

✎ Drive It Home

You've learned a lot in *Advanced French* so far, so let's go back a bit and review what you saw in *Intermediate French*. Change the following verbs to the past tense.

1. je bois _____

2. j'ai _____

3. je parle _____

4. je finis _____

5. je prends _____

6. je vois _____

7. je fais _____

8. je réponds _____

9. je suis _____

10. je dois _____

ANSWER KEY:

1. j'ai bu; 2. j'ai eu; 3. j'ai parlé; 4. j'ai fini; 5. j'ai pris; 6. j'ai vu; 7. j'ai fait; 8. j'ai répondu; 9. j'ai été; 10. j'ai dû

 Tip

Here are some common recriprocal verbs. Notice that, as with the *self* in reflexive verbs, sometimes the *each other* in reciprocal verbs isn't translated into English.

se parler	to speak to each other
se téléphoner	to call each other
se comprendre	to understand each other
se regarder	to look at each other, to watch each other
se voir	to see each other
se marier	to get married (to each other)
se fiancer	to get engaged (to each other)
s'aimer	to like/love each other
s'embrasser	to hug (each other), to kiss (each other)
se dire	to tell each other, to say to each other
se disputer	to argue (with each other)
se connaître	to know each other

Nous nous aimons.
We love each other.

Vous vous connaissez ?
You know each other?

How Did You Do?

Let's see how you did! By now, you should be able to:

☐ Name different parts of the body
  (Still unsure? Jump back to page 234)

☐ Tell someone that you're hurt or in pain
  (Still unsure? Jump back to page 237)

☐ Say whether you have a *cold* or the *flu*
  (Still unsure? Jump back to page 238)

☐ Talk about *each other*
  (Still unsure? Jump back to page 242)

Lesson 14: Phrases

By the end of this lesson, you will be able to:

☐ Name different injuries and disabilities

☐ Tell someone to *follow* the instructions

☐ Talk about exercise

☐ Say *I saw her*

Phrase Builder 1

▶ 14A Lesson 14 Phrase Builder 1 (CD 9, Track 9)

to break one's arm	se casser le bras
to sprain one's ankle	se fouler la cheville
to walk with a cane	marcher avec une canne
to walk with crutches	marcher avec des béquilles

wheelchair	la chaise roulante
to be disabled	être handicapé/handicapée
to have Alzheimer's disease	avoir la maladie d'Alzheimer
to have Parkinson's disease	avoir la maladie de Parkinson
to be deaf	être sourd/sourde
to use sign language	utiliser le langage des signes
to be paralyzed	être paralysé/paralysée
to wear contact lenses	porter des verres de contact (porter des lentilles de contact)
to be blind	être aveugle
to need a seeing-eye dog	avoir besoin d'un chien d'aveugle

Take It Further

You know that la langue means *language*, so why do you say le langage des signes (*sign language*)?

Well, la langue, which can also mean *tongue*, is generally only used to refer to the language of a country or a language that is spoken:

Marc parle trois langues.
Marc speaks three languages.

L'anglais est la langue des États-Unis.
English is the language of the United States.

By contrast, le langage (*language*) is commonly used to describe a way of talking or writing, such as using "formal language" or "inappropriate language," or the terminology of a specific field (computer language, legal language, etc.). It is also used to refer to a non-spoken language system, or, more abstractly, to the idea of language in general.

Here are some examples using le langage:

informal language, familiar language	le langage familier
formal language	le langage soutenu
everyday language	le langage courant
bad language	le langage grossier
body language	le langage du corps
baby talk (baby language)	le langage enfantin
sign language	le langage des signes
programming language	le langage informatique
legal language, legal terminology	le langage juridique

✎ Phrase Practice 1

Translate the following sentences into English.

1. Je me suis cassé le bras. _____

2. Il s'est foulé la cheville. _____

3. Elle marchait avec des béquilles. _____

_____

4. Est-ce que tu portes des verres de contact ? _____

_____

5. Mon père est aveugle. _____

ANSWER KEY:
1. *I broke my arm. 2. He sprained his ankle. 3. She was walking with crutches./She used to walk with crutches. 4. Do you wear contact lenses? 5. My father is blind.*

Word Recall

Match the French phrases on the left to the correct English translations on the right.

1. avoir peur de	a. *to be sleepy*
2. avoir besoin de	b. *to be afraid*
3. avoir honte	c. *to feel like*
4. avoir sommeil	d. *to be ashamed*
5. avoir envie de	e. *to need*

ANSWER KEY:
1. b; 2. e; 3. d; 4. a; 5. c

Grammar Builder 1
TO FOLLOW

▶ 14B Lesson 14 Grammar Builder 1 (CD 9, Track 10)

You already know how to conjugate a lot of verbs that are irregular in the present tense: avoir, être, aller, faire, vouloir, pouvoir, conduire, voir, savoir, connaître, etc.

Well, here's one more to add to your list. The verb suivre (*to follow*) is irregular in the present tense. Here are its forms:

SUIVRE (TO FOLLOW) - **PRESENT**			
je suis	*I follow*	nous suivons	*we follow*
tu suis	*you follow*	vous suivez	*you follow*
il suit	*he follows*	ils suivent	*they follow*
elle suit	*she follows*	elles suivent	*they follow*

Nous suivons la route vers la ville.
We follow the road to town.

Suivez les instructions.
Follow the instructions.

Suivez-moi au café du quartier.
Follow me to the neighborhood café.

Pour être en bonne santé, il faut suivre un bon régime.
To be in good health, you must follow a good diet.

S'il vous plaît, faites suivre mon courrier à la nouvelle adresse.
Please forward my mail to the new address.

Note that faire suivre means *to forward* or *to redirect*. Also note that suivre is used in education to mean *to take*: suivre un cours (*to take a class*).

The past participle of suivre is suivi: J'ai suivi les instructions. (*I followed the instructions.*)

✎ Work Out 1

Fill in the blanks with the correct form of suivre. Pay attention to the tense in the English translations.

1. Marc _____ la route de l'école. (*Marc followed the road to school.*)

2. _____-ils les instructions du médecin ?

   (*Are they following the doctor's instructions?*)

3. Nous _____ un régime pour maigrir.

   (*We're following a diet to lose weight.*)

4. Est-ce que vous _____ mes instructions ?

   (*Did you follow my instructions?*)

5. Tu ne _____ pas la route. (*You're not following the road.*)

ANSWER KEY:
1. a suivi; 2. Suivent; 3. suivons; 4. avez suivi; 5. suis

Phrase Builder 2

Now we're going to look at l'exercice (*m.*) (*exercise, exercising*). Remember from Unit 2 that *gym* is le gymnase.

▶ 14C Lesson 14 Phrase Builder 2 (CD 9, Track 11)

health club	le club de remise en forme (le club de forme/gym)
to train	s'entraîner
to do strength training, to lift weights (to do bodybuilding)	faire de la musculation
treadmill	le tapis de course, le tapis de jogging

sit-ups	les abdominaux (*m.*)
push-ups	les pompes (*f.*)
pull-ups	les tractions (*f.*)
to lift a dumbbell	soulever un haltère
stationary bike	le vélo d'appartement
workout	l'entraînement (*m.*)*
to be sweating	être en sueur (être en nage)
heartbeat	le battement de cœur
to pull a muscle	se faire une élongation
to be fit, to be in shape	être en forme

* **Entraînement** can also mean *training*.

Take It Further

Speaking of irregular verbs like suivre (*to follow*), let's review some of the other irregular verbs that you've seen in this program, focusing on verbs that deal with wishes, desires, and needs.

To start, here is the present tense conjugation of vouloir (*to want*):

VOULOIR (TO WANT) - **PRESENT**			
je veux	*I want*	nous voulons	*we want*
tu veux	*you want*	vous voulez	*you want*
il veut	*he wants*	ils veulent	*they want*
elle veut	*she wants*	elles veulent	*they want*

The past participle of vouloir is voulu. The future and conditional are formed with voudr-.

Here is the present tense of préférer (*to prefer*):

PRÉFÉRER (TO PREFER) - **PRESENT**			
je préfère	*I want*	nous préférons	*we want*
tu préfères	*you want*	vous préférez	*you want*
il préfère	*he wants*	ils préfèrent	*they want*
elle préfère	*she wants*	elles préfèrent	*they want*

The past participle of préférer is simply préféré. The future and conditional are formed with préférer-.

Don't forget that verbs like suggérer (*to suggest*) are conjugated in the same way as préférer.

Now let's look at permettre (*to allow, to permit*). Remember that permettre is formed in the same way as mettre (*to put, to put on*).

PERMETTRE (TO ALLOW, TO PERMIT) - **PRESENT**			
je permets	*I allow*	nous permettons	*we allow*
tu permets	*you allow*	vous permettez	*you allow*
il permet	*he allows*	ils permettent	*they allow*
elle permet	*she allows*	elles permettent	*they allow*

The past tense of permettre is permis. The future and conditional are formed with permettr-.

Finally, let's look at the important irregular verb falloir (*to be necessary*), which only has an il form. Here is its il form in a variety of tenses, some of which you've already seen and some you haven't:

FALLOIR (TO BE NECESSARY)		
Present Tense	il faut	*it is necessary to*
Past Tense	il a fallu	*it was necessary to*

FALLOIR *(TO BE NECESSARY)*		
Imperfect Tense	il fallait	it was necessary to, it used to be necessary to
Future Tense	il faudra	it will be necessary to
Conditional	il faudrait	it would be necessary to

Remember that il faut can also mean *you need to, one needs to, you have to, one has to, you must,* and *one must.* The same is true for the other tenses: il faudra can mean *you will need to, you will have to,* and so on.

✎ Phrase Practice 2

Translate this short conversation into English.

A: J'adore ce club de remise en forme !

_____

B: Moi aussi ! Qu'est-ce que tu veux faire ?

_____

A: Je veux faire de la musculation.

_____

B: Moi, je veux faire du vélo d'appartement.

_____

A: Nous serons en forme !

_____

ANSWER KEY:
A: *I love this health club!*
B: *Me too! What do you want to do?*

A: *I want to do strength training./I want to lift weights./I want to do bodybuilding.*
B: *Me, I want to ride a stationary bike.*
A: *We'll be in shape!*

✎ Word Recall

Let's review direct object pronouns. Fill in the blanks with the correct direct object pronouns in French.

me _____	*us* _____
you _____	*you* _____
him, it (m.) _____	*them (m.)* _____
her, it (f.) _____	*them (f.)* _____

ANSWER KEY:
me/m'; te/t'; le/l'; la/l'; nous; vous; les; les

Grammar Builder 2
DIRECT OBJECTS AND AVOIR

▶ 14D Lesson 14 Grammar Builder 2 (CD 9, Track 12)

You know that the past participles of verbs that use avoir do not need to agree in gender and number with the subject. For instance, you would say elle a parlé, not elle a parlée.

However, there is one case where the past participles of verbs that use avoir **do** need to agree in gender and number with a noun.

If a verb that uses avoir is **preceded** by a direct object noun or pronoun, then that verb's past participle must agree in gender and number with the direct object noun or pronoun. Keep in mind that this does not apply when the direct object noun or pronoun follows the verb.

As a review, here are the direct object pronouns in French:

DIRECT OBJECT PRONOUNS			
me (m')	*me*	nous	*us*
te (t')	*you*	vous	*you*
le (l')	*him, it (m.)*	les	*them (or plural it) (m.)*
la (l')	*her, it (f.)*	les	*them (or plural it) (f.)*

Remember that direct objects are nouns that receive the action of a verb. For example, in the phrase *I took a pill, a pill* is the direct object noun. Direct object pronouns replace direct object nouns: *I took **it**.*

Now take a look at the following sentence:

J'ai vu Christine.
I saw Christine.

In this sentence, **Christine** is the direct object noun. Notice that the past participle **vu** does not agree with **Christine** because **Christine** follows the verb; it does not precede it.

However:

Je l'ai vue.
I saw her.

In this case, **vu** must be changed to the feminine singular **vue** because the feminine singular pronoun **la (l')** (*her*) precedes it.

Now let's look at some examples of a direct object noun preceding the verb. Remember that **exercice** is a masculine noun.

Il a fait des exercices.
He did some exercises.

Voici les exercices qu'il a faits.
Here are the exercises that he did.

J'ai pris une pilule.
I took a pill.

Voici la pilule que j'ai prise.
Here's the pill that I took.

Note that this rule applies to any tense that uses **avoir**. For example, you would say: **J'aurais pris une pilule. Voici la pilule que j'aurais prise.** (*I would have taken a pill. Here is the pill I would have taken.*)

Also note that it does not apply to verbs that use **être**. Verbs that use **être** always agree with the subject, not the direct object or direct object pronoun.

To Have Pain or To Hurt		To Follow	
	Each Other		Direct Objects and **Avoir**

✎ Work Out 2

Decide whether the past participles in the following sentences are in the correct form. If they aren't, rewrite the past participles in the correct form.

1. Où sont les voitures que tu as acheté ? (*Where are the cars that you bought?*)

   _____

2. Il a acheté trois voitures. (*He bought three cars.*) _____

3. Voici les livres que Sophie a donné à Paul. (*Here are the books that Sophie gave

   to Paul.*) _____

4. Sophie a donné ces livres à Paul. (*Sophie gave these books to Paul.*)

   _____

ANSWER KEY:
1. achetées; 2. no change; 3. donnés; 4. no change

✎ Drive It Home

Fill in the blanks with the past tense of the verbs in parentheses.

1. C'est la doctoresse que j'_____ (voir).

   (*That's the doctor that I saw.*)

2. C'est le docteur que j'_____ (voir).

   (*That's the doctor that I saw.*)

3. Voici les doctoresses que j'_____ (voir).

   (*Here are the doctors that I saw.*)

4. Voici les docteurs que j'_____ (voir).

   (*Here are the doctors that I saw.*)

Advanced French

ANSWER KEY:
1. ai vue; 2. ai vu; 3. ai vues; 4. ai vus

How Did You Do?

Let's see how you did! By now, you should be able to:

☐ Name different injuries and disabilities
(Still unsure? Jump back to page 246)

☐ Tell someone to *follow* the instructions
(Still unsure? Jump back to page 249)

☐ Talk about exercise
(Still unsure? Jump back to page 251)

☐ Say *I saw her*
(Still unsure? Jump back to page 255)

Lesson 15: Sentences

By the end of this lesson, you will be able to:

☐ Explain what's wrong to a doctor

☐ Understand what you hear in an emergency situation

☐ Express wishes, desires, doubts, and needs

Sentence Builder 1

▶ 15A Lesson 15 Sentence Builder 1 (CD 9, Track 13)

I would like to make an appointment.	Je voudrais prendre rendez-vous.
What's the matter? (lit., What is there?)	Qu'est-ce qu'il y a ?
What happened to you? (pl./fml.)	Qu'est-ce qui vous est arrivé ?

Ouch!	Aïe !
What should I do?	Qu'est-ce que je dois faire ?
The doctor gives a prescription. (lit., The doctor makes a prescription.)	Le médecin fait une ordonnance.
I have trouble swallowing.	J'ai du mal à avaler.
I have a sore throat.	J'ai mal à la gorge.
You have a frog in your throat. (lit., You have a cat in your throat.)	Tu as un chat dans la gorge.
He has a headache.	Il a mal à la tête.
The child is going to catch a cold.	L'enfant va attraper un rhume.
My nose is stuffed up. (I have a stuffy nose.)	J'ai le nez bouché.
Because of his allergies, he coughs.	À cause de ses allergies, il tousse.
I'm not myself./I'm not feeling well. (lit., I'm not in my plate.)	Je ne suis pas dans mon assiette.

Take It Further

If you're talking about why something happened, two good phrases to know are:

thanks to ...	grâce à...
because of ... , as a result of ... , due to ... (in a negative way)	à cause de...

Grâce au médecin, je suis en bonne santé.
Thanks to the doctor, I'm in good health.

Il a mal à la gorge à cause de la grippe.
He has a sore throat because of the flu.

Earlier in this unit we looked at how to conjugate falloir in different tenses. However, it's also important to keep in mind how to use the verb in sentences. There are several different ways:

1. il + form of falloir + noun or verb in the infinitive

Use this construction to say *it is necessary,* or to make a general statement about what *people in general, one, they, we,* or *you* must or need to do.

Il faut prendre votre température.
It is necessary to take your temperature.

Pour être en bonne santé, il faut suivre un bon régime.
To be in good health, you must follow a good diet.

Il faudra un manteau pour aller dehors.
You will need a coat to go outside.

Il faut de la nourriture !
We need food!

2. il + indirect object pronoun + form of falloir + noun or verb in the infinitive

Use this construction to talk specifically about what *he must do, they must do, it needs, she needs,* etc.

Il nous faut dormir.
We must sleep.

Il lui fallait un plâtre.
He needed a cast.

3. il + form of falloir + que

You can use this construction to talk generally or specifically.

Il faut qu'on...
It is necessary that one ... /It is necessary that we ...

Il faut que Marie...
Marie needs to ... /Marie must ...

Il faut que must be followed by what's known as the "subjunctive" tense. You'll learn about the subjunctive in Grammar Builder 1.

Finally, note that falloir is also used in certain expressions, such as s'il le faut (*if necessary, if needed*).

Elle sera là, s'il le faut.
She'll be there, if necessary.

✎ Sentence Practice 1

Translate the following phrases into French.

1. *I have trouble swallowing.* _____

2. *I have a sore throat.* _____

3. *I have a stuffy nose.* _____

4. *I have a headache.* _____

5. *I'm not feeling well.* _____

ANSWER KEY:
1. J'ai du mal à avaler. 2. J'ai mal à la gorge. 3. J'ai le nez bouché. 4. J'ai mal à la tête. 5. Je ne suis pas dans mon assiette.

✎ Word Recall

Let's review indirect object pronouns. Fill in the blanks with the correct indirect object pronouns in French.

to me _____	*to us* _____
to you (infml.) _____	*to you (pl./fml.)* _____
to him/her/it _____	*to them* _____

ANSWER KEY:
me/m'; te/t'; lui; nous; vous; leur

Grammar Builder 1
FORMING THE SUBJUNCTIVE

▶ 15B Lesson 15 Grammar Builder 1 (CD 9, Track 14)

The subjunctive is the final tense that you'll learn in this course. It is used when expressing wishes, necessities, doubts, and other emotions.

We'll go into depth about when and how to use the subjunctive, and what it means, in Grammar Builder 2, but for now, let's just focus on forming it.

Here's how to form the subjunctive:

1. Drop the -ent from the ils/elles form of the verb in the present tense.

2. Add the following endings:

PRONOUN	ENDING	PRONOUN	ENDING
je	-e	nous	-ions
tu	-es	vous	-iez
il	-e	ils	-ent
elle	-e	elles	-ent

Notice that the ils/elles form drops and then adds -ent. In other words, it often doesn't change at all from the present tense into the subjunctive.

Let's look at an example from each verb group. The subjunctive usually follows the conjunction que (*that*)—not to be confused with the relative pronoun que— so all of the examples will follow that word.

PARLER (*TO SPEAK*)	FINIR (*TO FINISH*)	RÉPONDRE (*TO ANSWER*)
que je parle	que je finisse	que je réponde
que tu parles	que tu finisses	que tu répondes
qu'il parle	qu'il finisse	qu'il réponde
qu'elle parle	qu'elle finisse	qu'elle réponde
que nous parlions	que nous finissions	que nous répondions
que vous parliez	que vous finissiez	que vous répondiez
qu'ils parlent	qu'ils finissent	qu'ils répondent
qu'elles parlent	qu'elles finissent	qu'elles répondent

Note that all of these verbs are in the "present subjunctive." This form of the subjunctive is used for both the present tense and the future tense. For example, qu'elle parle can mean *that she speak* or *that she will speak*.

The subjunctive has four tenses: the present, imperfect, past, and past perfect. However, we will only be covering the present subjunctive in this course.

✎ Work Out 1

Conjugate the following verbs in the present subjunctive.

1. que tu _____ (danser)

2. qu'elle _____ (répondre)

3. que je _____ (vendre)

4. qu'ils _____ (choisir)

5. que nous _____ (parler)

6. que vous _____ (finir)

ANSWER KEY:

1. danses; 2. réponde; 3. vende; 4. choisissent; 5. parlions; 6. finissiez

Sentence Builder 2

If there is ever an emergency, it could be very helpful to know or be able to understand the following sentences.

▶ 15C Lesson 15 Sentence Builder 2 (CD 9, Track 15)

emergency situations	les cas (*m.*) d'urgence
It's necessary to have a first-aid kit.	Il faut avoir une trousse de secours.
to have an accident	avoir un accident
Call the emergency medical service.	Appelez le service d'assistance médicale d'urgence.
The ambulance is arriving.	L'ambulance arrive.
He needs a blood transfusion.	Il lui faut une transfusion de sang.
It's a superficial injury.	C'est une blessure superficielle.
It's not serious.	Ce n'est pas grave.

Each Other | Direct Objects and **Avoir**

Do you have insurance?	Est-ce que vous avez une assurance ?
Take a pill (a tablet/a capsule).	Prenez une pilule (un cachet/une capsule).*
Sometimes there are side effects.	Quelquefois il y a des effets secondaires.
It's a burn.	C'est une brûlure.
It's a cut.	C'est une coupure.
The dentist is going to replace the filling.	Le dentiste va remplacer le plombage.
It's necessary to have a tooth pulled. (We need to pull a tooth.)	Il faut arracher une dent.

* Remember that le comprimé is another term for *pill*. It can also mean *tablet*.

Take It Further

Speaking of quelquefois (*sometimes*), let's review what are known as the "adverbs of frequency":

sometimes	quelquefois, parfois
never	jamais
always, still	toujours
rarely	rarement
usually	normalement, d'habitude
occasionally	de temps en temps
frequently	fréquemment
often	souvent

However, if you want to say *how often?* (or *how many times?*), say combien de fois ? Note that fois (*f.*) means *time*:

once, one time	une fois
twice, two times	deux fois
last time, final time	la dernière fois

Finally, ce n'est pas grave (*it's not serious*) is a good expression to know. You can also use this expression casually to mean *It's not a problem, It's not a big deal,* or *Don't worry about it.*

Sentence Practice 2

Match the French words on the left to the correct English translations on the right.

1. la trousse de secours	a. *pill*
2. le cas d'urgence	b. *burn*
3. la pilule	c. *emergency situation*
4. la brûlure	d. *cut*
5. la coupure	e. *first-aid kit*

ANSWER KEY:
1. e; 2. c; 3. a; 4. b; 5. d

✎ Word Recall

Now match the following verbs to their correct French translations.

1. vouloir	a. *to suggest*
2. préférer	b. *to want*
3. permettre	c. *to believe*
4. suggérer	d. *to prefer*
5. croire	e. *to allow*

ANSWER KEY:
1. b; 2. d; 3. e; 4. a; 5. c

Grammar Builder 2
USING THE SUBJUNCTIVE

▶ 15D Lesson 15 Grammar Builder 2 (CD 9, Track 16)

The subjunctive is a tense that conveys specific moods. It expresses requests, commands, doubt, uncertainty, possibility, approval and disapproval, preference, wishing, want, desire, necessity, need, urgency, importance, and emotions like joy and fear.

If a verb or phrase expressing any of these moods is followed by the conjunction que (*that*), then the verb **after** que is usually in the subjunctive. Also, certain specific expressions are always followed by the subjunctive.

Let's look more in detail at when and how the subjunctive is used.

1. The subjunctive is used after verbs of command, request, permission, or other expressions imposing your will on someone else + que.

For example, the subjunctive would be used after these phrases:

demander que	to request that, to ask that
empêcher que	to prevent from, to keep from
exiger que	to demand that, to require that
ordonner que	to order that
permettre que	to allow that
suggérer que	to suggest that

Let's look at some examples:

Il exige que tu partes.
He demands that you leave.

Le professeur suggère que vous parliez français.
The teacher suggests that you speak French.

As you can see, tu partes and vous parliez are in the subjunctive because they follow the phrases exige que and suggère que.

Note that it doesn't matter what tense exiger que, suggérer que, etc. are in. They could be in the future, conditional, past, and so on, and they would still be followed by the subjunctive: il a exigé que tu partes (*he demanded that you leave*). This is true of all verbs and phrases that are followed by the subjunctive.

2. The subjunctive is used after verbs or expressions of doubt, denial, uncertainty, or possibility + que.

For example, you would use the subjunctive after douter que (*to doubt that*):

Je doute que vous m'écoutiez.
I doubt that you're listening to me.

You would also use the subjunctive after the expressions il semble que (*it seems that*) and il est possible que (*it is possible that*):

Il est possible que nous travaillions samedi.
It's possible that we will work on Saturday.

Remember that the present subjunctive is used to express both the present tense and the future tense, so nous travaillions can mean *we work* or *we will work*.

Note that you would **not** use the subjunctive after the expression il est probable que (*it is probable that*). You also wouldn't use it after expressions of certainty like il est vrai que (*it is true that*) or il est certain que (*it is certain that*).

3. After verbs or expressions of approval, disapproval, or preference + que.

For example, the subjunctive would be used after these phrases:

aimer mieux que	to prefer that (lit., to like better that)
préférer que	to prefer that
recommander que	to recommend that

Aimez-vous mieux que je vous attende ?
Do you prefer that I wait for you?

You would also use the subjunctive after the expression il est préférable que (*it is preferable that*): Il est préférable que vous attendiez. (*It is preferable that you wait.*)

4. After verbs or expressions of wishing, want, or desire + que.

désirer que	to desire that, to want that, to wish that
souhaiter que	to wish that
vouloir que	to want that, to wish that

Je veux qu'elle parte.
I want her to leave. (lit., I want that she leave.)

Sa femme désire qu'il finisse le travail autour de la maison.
His wife wants him to finish the work around the house. (lit., His wife wants that he finish the work around the house.)

Notice that the subjunctive is sometimes translated as the infinitive in English: *I want her **to leave**, His wife wants him **to finish**, etc.*

Also don't forget that vouloir que, souhaiter que, etc. don't have to be in the present tense. They could be in any other tense and they would still need to be followed by the subjunctive. So je voudrais que (*I would like that*), for instance, would be followed by the subjunctive because it's a conditional form of vouloir que: Je voudrais que tu partes. (*I would like you to leave.*)

5. After verbs of thinking or believing when they are negative or in the form of a question + que.

For instance, the phrases penser que (*to think that*), croire que (*to believe that*), and trouver que (*to find that, to think that*) are usually followed by the subjunctive when they are negative (such as je ne pense pas que) or in the form of a question (pensez-vous que... ?) and you want to emphasize a feeling of doubt.

Here is an example:

Je ne pense pas que vous m'écoutiez.
I don't think (that) you're listening to me.

However, make sure to keep in mind that you only use the subjunctive if penser que, croire que, and trouver que are negative or in the form of a question. If they aren't, don't use the subjunctive: Je pense que vous m'écoutez. (*I think that you're listening to me.*)

6. After verbs or expressions of necessity or need + que.

For example, you would use the subjunctive after the expressions il faut que (*it is necessary that, one has to, one needs to, one must*) and il est nécessaire que (*it is necessary that, one has to, one needs to, one must*).

Il faut que ma nièce vende sa maison.
My niece must sell her house. (It is necessary that my niece sell her house.)

Il est nécessaire que je finisse la lettre.
I have to finish the letter. (It is necessary that I finish the letter.)

You would also use the subjunctive after:

avoir besoin que	to need for

For instance: j'ai besoin que vous finissiez (*I need for you to finish*).

7. After expressions of urgency or importance + que.

Il est urgent que je finisse la lettre.
It is urgent that I finish the letter.

Il est important que tu arrives à l'heure.
It is important that you arrive on time.

Il est essentiel que vous arriviez à l'heure.
It is essential that you arrive on time.

8. After expressions of emotion, such as joy, fear, sorrow, or regret + que.

Je suis content que vous m'aidiez.
I'm happy that you are helping me.

Je regrette que tu partes si tôt.
I am sorry that you're leaving so soon. (I regret that you're leaving so soon/early.)

Nous avons peur qu'il ne parte.
We are afraid (that) he may leave. (lit., We're afraid that he leaves.)

Notice the ne in that last sentence? In French, expressions of fear often have ne before the verb in the subjunctive, even though the verb isn't negative. This doesn't translate into English; it's just something you have to remember to do in French. Of course, if there is also a pas after the verb, then the verb is negative: **Nous avons peur qu'il ne parte pas.** (*We're afraid that he may not leave.*)

9. After specific conjunctions with que.

afin que, pour que	in order that, so that
avant que	before
à moins que… ne	unless
bien que, quoique	although
sans que	without
jusqu'à ce que	until

Il travaille dur pour que sa famille réussisse.
He works hard so that his family succeeds.

10. The subjunctive is **only** used when the subject of the verb before que is different from the subject of the verb after que.

For example:

Je veux qu'il parte.
I want him to leave. (lit., I want that he leave.)

In this case, the subjunctive can be used because the subject of the verb before que is je, while the subject of the verb after que is il.

However, you couldn't say je veux que je parte (*I want that I leave/I want me to leave*). That is incorrect because the two subjects are the same; they are both je. Instead, you would say:

Je veux partir.
I want to leave.

Notice that the infinitive is used instead of the subjunctive, and the que is removed.

Here is another example:

Ils désirent que nous restions.
They want us to stay. (lit., They want that we stay.)

Ils désirent rester.
They want to stay.

And that's it on the subjunctive for this lesson! Got all that? The subjunctive can definitely be a lot to take in, so don't be afraid to review this section as many times as you need to.

Work Out 2

Conjugate the following verbs in the correct tense: either the present tense or the subjunctive.

1. Il est important que nous _____ (arriver) tôt.

   (It is important that we arrive early.)

2. Il faut que vous _____ (fermer) la porte. *(You need to close the door.)*

3. Il est vrai que nous _____ (vendre) la maison.

   (It's true that we're selling the house.)

4. Il est possible que vous _____ (parler) cinq langues.

   (It's possible that you speak five languages.)

5. Je crois qu'elle _____ (finir) la lettre. *(I believe she's finishing the letter.)*

   ANSWER KEY:
   1. arrivions; 2. fermiez; 3. vendons; 4. parliez; 5. finit

Drive It Home

A. Fill in the blanks with the subjunctive form of the regular -er verbs in parentheses.

1. Il faut que tu _____ (écouter). *(You need to listen.)*

2. Il faut que tu _____ (parler). *(You need to talk.)*

3. Il faut que tu _____ (danser). (*You need to dance.*)

4. Il faut que tu _____ (étudier). (*You need to study.*)

5. Il faut que tu _____ (rester). (*You need to stay.*)

B. Now fill in the blanks with the subjunctive form of the -ir verbs in parentheses. Note that SST verbs form the subjunctive normally.

1. Je suis content qu'elle _____ (partir). (*I'm happy that she's leaving.*)

2. Je suis content qu'elle _____ (dormir). (*I'm happy that she's sleeping.*)

3. Je suis content qu'elle _____ (choisir). (*I'm happy that she's choosing.*)

4. Je suis content qu'elle _____ (finir). (*I'm happy that she's finishing.*)

5. Je suis content qu'elle _____ (réussir). (*I'm happy that she's doing well.*)

C. Finally, fill in the blanks with the subjunctive form of the regular -re verbs in parentheses.

1. Il voudrait que vous _____ (répondre). (*He would like you to respond.*)

2. Il voudrait que vous _____ (attendre). (*He would like you to wait.*)

3. Il voudrait que vous _____ (descendre). (*He would like you to come down.*)

4. Il voudrait que vous _____ (perdre). (*He would like you to lose.*)

5. Il voudrait que vous _____ (entendre). (*He would like you to hear.*)

ANSWER KEY:
A. 1. écoutes; 2. parles; 3. danses; 4. étudies; 5. restes
B. 1. parte; 2. dorme; 3. choisisse; 4. finisse; 5. réussisse
C. 1. répondiez; 2. attendiez; 3. descendiez; 4. perdiez; 5. entendiez

 **Tip**

It can be a challenge to remember when to use the subjunctive. To help yourself remember, think of the word *wedding*. Each letter in *wedding* stands for a kind of verb or expression that is followed by the subjunctive.

W	Wishing and Wanting
E	Emotion
D	Doubt and Denial
D	Disapproval (and approval)
I	Imposing your will
N	Necessity, Need, and Negation (of verbs of thinking or believing)
G	Great importance (a bit of stretch, sure, but that's why you'll remember it!)

Obviously, this doesn't cover everything, but it will help you get started!

How Did You Do?

Let's see how you did! By now, you should be able to:

☐ Explain what's wrong to a doctor
(Still unsure? Jump back to page 259)

☐ Understand what you hear in an emergency situation
(Still unsure? Jump back to page 265)

☐ Express wishes, desires, doubts, and needs
(Still unsure? Jump back to page 268)

Lesson 16: Conversations

By the end of this lesson, you will be able to:

☐ Talk about what you need to *buy, take,* or *see*

☐ Say what you have to *be* or what you doubt someone *can* do

🎧 Conversation 1

Mme Laurent is chez le médecin/docteur (*at the doctor's*) to ask him about her leg.

▶ 16A Lesson 16 Conversation 1 (CD 9, Track 17)

Le docteur :	Qu'est-ce qui ne va pas ? Vous avez du mal à marcher.
Mme Laurent :	J'ai très mal à la jambe.
Le docteur :	Qu'est-ce qui vous est arrivé ? Vous êtes tombée ?
Mme Laurent :	Non, je ne suis pas tombée. Hier, j'étais au club de forme où j'ai fait beaucoup d'exercice. J'ai suivi un cours de danse moderne, j'ai couru, et j'ai nagé un peu.
Le docteur :	Allongez-vous. Je vais vous examiner.
Mme Laurent :	Aïe !!!
Le docteur :	Vous n'avez rien de cassé, mais vous avez une inflammation musculaire.
Mme Laurent :	Qu'est-ce que je dois faire ? C'est grave ?
Le docteur :	Non, mais il vaut mieux cesser toute forme d'exercice et prendre des comprimés anti-inflammatoires trois fois par jour. Voilà votre ordonnance.
Mme Laurent :	Merci, docteur.
Le docteur :	Revenez me voir dans une semaine si vous avez toujours des douleurs.

The doctor:	What's wrong? (lit., What isn't going?) You're having trouble walking.
Mrs. Laurent:	I have a lot of pain in my leg.
The doctor:	What happened to you? Did you fall?
Mrs. Laurent:	No, I didn't fall. Yesterday, I was at the health club where I did a lot of exercising. I took a modern dance class, I ran, and I swam a little.
The doctor:	Lie down. I'm going to examine you.
Mrs. Laurent:	Ouch!!!
The doctor:	You don't have anything broken, but you have a muscular inflammation.
Mrs. Laurent:	What should I do? Is it serious?
The doctor:	No, but it would be better to stop all forms of exercise and to take some anti-inflammatory pills three times per day. There is your prescription.
Mrs. Laurent:	Thank you, doctor.
The doctor:	Come back to see me in one week if you still have pain.

Take It Further

You saw some useful irregular verbs in that dialogue: courir (*to run*) and valoir (*to be worth*).

Here is the full conjugation of courir in the present tense:

COURIR (*TO RUN*) - **PRESENT**			
je cours	*I run*	nous courons	*we run*
tu cours	*you run*	vous courez	*you run*
il court	*he runs*	ils courent	*they run*
elle court	*she runs*	elles courent	*they run*

As you saw in the dialogue, the past participle of courir is couru.

J'ai couru le marathon.

I ran the marathon.

The future and conditional are formed with courr-. The subjunctive is formed the same way as any other verb (drop the -ent from courent and add the subjunctive endings).

Now here is the full conjugation of valoir (*to be worth*) in the present tense:

VALOIR *(TO BE WORTH)* - **PRESENT**			
je vaux	*I am worth*	nous valons	*we are worth*
tu vaux	*you are worth*	vous valez	*you are worth*
il vaut	*he is worth*	ils valent	*they are worth*
elle vaut	*she is worth*	elles valent	*they are worth*

Vous valez combien ?

How much are you worth?

When il vaut (*he is worth, it is worth*) is followed by mieux (*better*), it becomes a fixed expression that means *it is better* or *it would be better*.

Il vaut mieux cesser toute forme d'exercice.

It would be better to stop all forms of exercise.

Il vaut mieux le faire.

It is better to do it.

Note that il vaut mieux que (*it is better that, it would be better that*) is followed by the subjunctive:

Il vaut mieux que vous finissiez.
It would be better for you to finish. (lit., It would be better that you finish.)

Valoir is also used in expressions like **valoir la peine** (*to be worth the trouble*):

Ça ne vaut pas la peine.
It's not worth the trouble./This is not worth the trouble.

The past participle of **valoir** is **valu**. The future and conditional are formed with **vaudr-**. In fact, sometimes the conditional form is used instead of the present tense form:

Il vaudrait mieux...
It would be better ...

Valoir is actually irregular in the subjunctive as well, but you'll learn more about that later on in this lesson.

Regarding the other verbs you saw in the dialogue, remember that **allonger** (*to lay down, to lie down*) and **nager** (*to swim*) conjugate like **manger** (*to eat*) in the present tense. You also saw the verb **cesser** (*to stop, to cease*), which is a regular -er verb.

Finally, let's look at some of the new words you saw in the dialogue:

inflammation	**l'inflammation** (*f.*)
anti-inflammatory	**anti-inflammatoire**
muscular	**musculaire** (*medical*), **musclé/ musclée** (*person*)
form, shape, figure	**la forme**
pain, sorrow	**la douleur**

Note that forme is used in a variety of health-related phrases and expressions, such as le club de forme/le club de remise en forme (*health club*), être en forme (*to be fit, to be in shape*), rester en forme (*to stay in shape*), and être en pleine/ bonne forme (*to be in good shape*).

Conversation Practice 1

Re-read Conversation 1. Then say whether each sentence below is vrai (*true*) or faux (*false*). Next to each sentence, write down V for vrai or F for faux.

1. Mme Laurent a du mal à marcher. _____

2. Mme Laurent est tombée. _____

3. Au club de forme, Mme Laurent a fait de la natation. _____

4. Le docteur dit que Mme Laurent s'est cassé la jambe. _____

ANSWER KEY:
1. V (*Yes, she is having trouble walking.*) 2. F (*No, she didn't fall.*) 3. V (*Yes, she did go swimming at the health club.*) 4. F (*No, the doctor said she didn't break anything.*)

Word Recall

Let's practice quantities. Match the quantities on the left to the correct English translations on the right.

1. un peu de	a. *a lot of*
2. beaucoup de	b. *more of*
3. moins de	c. *less of, fewer of*
4. plus de	d. *a little of*

ANSWER KEY:
1. d; 2. a; 3. c; 4. b

Grammar Builder 1
IRREGULAR SUBJUNCTIVE

▶ 16B Lesson 16 Grammar Builder 1 (CD 9, Track 18)

To form the subjunctive, most verbs that are irregular in the present tense follow the same pattern as verbs that are regular in the present tense: they drop the -ent from the present tense ils/elles form and add the appropriate subjunctive ending.

For example, to form the subjunctive of the irregular verb écrire (*to write*), simply drop the -ent from the ils/elles form in the present tense (écrivent) and then add the endings.

ÉCRIRE (*TO WRITE*) - **SUBJUNCTIVE**	
que j'écrive	que nous écrivions
que tu écrives	que vous écriviez
qu'il écrive	qu'ils écrivent
qu'elle écrive	qu'elles écrivent

However, there are exceptions.

For instance, if a verb has a different spelling for its nous and vous forms than for the rest of its forms in the present tense (such as elle achète vs. nous achetons), then that verb is usually conjugated a little differently in the subjunctive.

Examples of verbs with nous and vous spelling variations include, but are not limited to:

acheter	to buy
appeler	to call
jeter	to throw, to throw out/away
préférer	to prefer

prendre	to take, to have
comprendre	to understand
venir	to come
boire	to drink
croire	to believe
devoir	to have to, must, should, to owe
envoyer	to send
payer	to pay, to pay for
voir	to see

For these verbs, the nous and vous forms in the subjunctive are based on the present tense nous form instead of the ils/elles form. The rest of the forms (je, tu, il/elle, ils/elles) conjugate normally.

In other words, to conjugate the nous and vous forms of these types of verbs in the subjunctive, drop the -ons from the present tense nous form and then add the appropriate subjunctive ending (-ions or -iez).

For example, in the present tense, the ils/elles form of the verb acheter is achètent. So to create the je form of acheter in the subjunctive, you would drop the -ent from achètent and then add the -e subjunctive ending.

que j'achète
that I buy

However, to create the nous form of acheter in the subjunctive, you would drop the -ons from the nous form of acheter in the present tense (achetons), and then add the -ions subjunctive ending.

que nous achetions
that we buy

Advanced French

Now let's take a look at some more examples of verbs with nous and vous spelling variations.

Here is the full conjugation of prendre (*to take*) in the subjunctive. Remember that the ils/elles form of prendre in the present tense is prennent, but the nous form is prenons.

PRENDRE *(TO TAKE)* - **SUBJUNCTIVE**	
que je prenne	que nous prenions
que tu prennes	que vous preniez
qu'il prenne	qu'ils prennent
qu'elle prenne	qu'elles prennent

Don't forget that there are other verbs that conjugate like prendre, such as comprendre (*to understand*). Verbs that conjugate like prendre form the subjunctive in the same way. This is true for all verbs with nous and vous spelling variations.

Nous doutons qu'elle comprenne.
We doubt (that) she understands.

Now here is the full conjugation of venir (*to come*) in the subjunctive. Remember that the ils/elles form of venir in the present tense is viennent, but the nous form is venons.

VENIR *(TO COME)* - **SUBJUNCTIVE**	
que je vienne	que nous venions
que tu viennes	que vous veniez
qu'il vienne	qu'ils viennent
qu'elle vienne	qu'elles viennent

BOIRE *(TO DRINK)* - SUBJUNCTIVE

que je boive	que nous buvions
que tu boives	que vous buviez
qu'il boive	qu'ils boivent
qu'elle boive	qu'elles boivent

CROIRE *(TO BELIEVE)* - SUBJUNCTIVE

que je croie	que nous croyions
que tu croies	que vous croyiez
qu'il croie	qu'ils croient
qu'elle croie	qu'elles croient

DEVOIR *(TO HAVE TO, MUST, SHOULD, TO OWE)* - SUBJUNCTIVE

que je doive	que nous devions
que tu doives	que vous deviez
qu'il doive	qu'ils doivent
qu'elle doive	qu'elles doivent

ENVOYER *(TO SEND)* - SUBJUNCTIVE

que j'envoie	que nous envoyions
que tu envoies	que vous envoyiez
qu'il envoie	qu'ils envoient
qu'elle envoie	qu'elles envoient

VOIR *(TO SEE)* - SUBJUNCTIVE

que je voie	que nous voyions
que tu voies	que vous voyiez

VOIR *(TO SEE)* - **SUBJUNCTIVE**	
qu'il voie	qu'ils voient
qu'elle voie	qu'elles voient

Note that manger *(to eat)* and commencer *(to start, to begin)* do not belong to this group of irregular verbs in the subjunctive; those two verbs, and any verbs that conjugate like them, form the subjunctive normally.

Finally, there are also verbs that are completely irregular in the subjunctive. We'll look at them in Grammar Builder 2.

Work Out 1

Translate the following sentences into English, with the subjunctive only expressing the present tense.

1. Je voudrais que tu envoies cette lettre. _____

2. Il faut que vous croyiez. _____

3. Il préfère qu'elle vienne au restaurant. _____

4. Ils ne pensent pas que je doive aller à l'université. _____

5. Je vais partir avant que vous appeliez Hélène. _____

ANSWER KEY:

1. *I would like you to send this/that letter.* 2. *It is necessary that you believe./You must/need to/have to believe.* 3. *He prefers (that) she come to the restaurant.* 4. *They don't think (that) I should/must/have to go to college.* 5. *I'm going to leave before you call Hélène.*

Conversation 2

In this dialogue, Anne and Nancy are discussing diets.

▶ 16C Lesson 16 Conversation 2 (CD 9, Track 19)

Anne :	Eh bien, mon mari et moi, nous sommes en train de suivre un régime.
Nancy :	Comment ? Tu suis un régime ? Pourquoi faut-il que tu perdes du poids? Tu ne grossis pas, ma chère.
Anne :	Merci, Anne. Grâce à Dieu, je suis en bonne forme après tout le chocolat que je mange, mais il est nécessaire que mon mari perde cinq kilos.
Nancy :	Je doute que ce soit facile. Tu sais bien que les hommes n'aiment pas manger tout ce qui est bon pour eux.
Anne :	Il est important que je fasse des repas plus légers car il faut que mon mari maigrisse. C'est plus facile de le faire ensemble, tu sais.
Nancy :	Mon docteur voudrait aussi que nous perdions quelques kilos. Mais moi, j'adore les desserts.
Anne :	Il est possible que tu puisses manger des desserts s'ils sont faits avec de bons ingrédients, comme les fruits, par exemple.

Anne:	*Well, my husband and I, we are in the middle of following a diet.*
Nancy:	*What did you say? You're following a diet? Why do you need to lose some weight? You're not gaining weight, my dear.*
Anne:	*Thanks, Anne. Thank God (lit., Thanks to God), I am in good shape after all the chocolate that I eat, but my husband needs to lose five kilos (~eleven pounds).*

Nancy:	*I doubt that it will be easy. You know well that men don't like eating everything that is good for them (lit., all what is good for them).*
Anne:	*It's important that I make lighter meals because my husband needs to lose weight. It's easier to do it together, you know.*
Nancy:	*My doctor would also like us to lose some kilos. But me, I love desserts.*
Anne:	*Maybe (lit., It is possible that) you can eat desserts if they are made with good ingredients, like fruit, for example.*

Take It Further

There are a few more cases where the subjunctive is used. Unfortunately, they are a little more complicated than the ones you learned earlier. We will cover some of them briefly here.

1. The subjunctive is used after a relative pronoun (que or qui) if there is doubt or denial.

For example:

Nous cherchons une personne qui vende sa maison.
We're looking for a person who's selling his/her house.

There is doubt—this person may not be found—so the subjunctive is used. Now take a look at the following sentence:

Nous avons un ami qui vend sa maison.
We have a friend who's selling his house.

In this case, you don't use the subjunctive because there is no doubt. The person clearly exists.

2. The subjunctive is also used after a relative pronoun (que or qui) if it's preceded by a superlative (*the most, the best, the tallest*, etc.), unless you're stating a fact.

For instance, you would use the subjunctive here because you're expressing your opinion:

Paris est la plus belle ville que nous visitions.
Paris is the most beautiful city that we're visiting.

But you wouldn't use the subjunctive in this sentence because you're stating a fact:

Paris est la plus grande ville que nous visitons.
Paris is the biggest city that we're visiting.

3. Sometimes the subjunctive is used in certain exclamations or commands.

Qu'elle entre !
Let her enter!/Let her come in! (lit., That she enter!)

Vive la France !
Long live France! (lit., Live France!)

✎ Conversation Practice 2
Translate the following sentences into English.

1. Tu suis un régime. _____

2. Je suis en bonne forme. _____

3. Tu ne grossis pas. _____

4. C'est plus facile de le faire ensemble. _____

_____

ANSWER KEY:
1. *You're following a diet./You follow a diet.* 2. *I'm in good shape.* 3. *You're not gaining weight./You don't gain weight.* 4. *It's easier to do it together.*

✎ Word Recall

Remember greetings from *Essential* and *Intermediate French*? They're important to know, so let's review.

1. *How are you? (polite)* _____

2. *How are you? (familiar)* _____

3. *What's your name? (familiar)* _____

4. *What's your name? (polite)* _____

5. *Nice to meet you.* _____

ANSWER KEY:
1. Comment allez-vous ? 2. Comment vas-tu ? 3. Comment t'appelles-tu ? 4. Comment vous appelez-vous ? 5. Enchanté/Enchantée (de faire votre connaissance).

Grammar Builder 2
MORE IRREGULAR SUBJUNCTIVE

▶ 16D Lesson 16 Grammar Builder 2 (CD 9, Track 20)

As you know, there are some verbs that are completely irregular in the subjunctive. Unfortunately, they simply need to be memorized.

FAIRE *(TO DO, TO MAKE)* - **SUBJUNCTIVE**	
que je fasse	que nous fassions
que tu fasses	que vous fassiez

FAIRE *(TO DO, TO MAKE)* - **SUBJUNCTIVE**	
qu'il fasse	qu'ils fassent
qu'elle fasse	qu'elles fassent

POUVOIR *(CAN, TO BE ABLE TO)* - **SUBJUNCTIVE**	
que je puisse	que nous puissions
que tu puisses	que vous puissiez
qu'il puisse	qu'ils puissent
qu'elle puisse	qu'elles puissent

SAVOIR *(TO KNOW)* - **SUBJUNCTIVE**	
que je sache	que nous sachions
que tu saches	que vous sachiez
qu'il sache	qu'ils sachent
qu'elle sache	qu'elles sachent

For the following verbs, notice that the **nous** and **vous** forms are different from the rest of the forms.

VOULOIR *(TO WANT, TO WISH)* - **SUBJUNCTIVE**	
que je veuille	que nous voulions
que tu veuilles	que vous vouliez
qu'il veuille	qu'ils veuillent
qu'elle veuille	qu'elles veuillent

ALLER *(TO GO)* - **SUBJUNCTIVE**	
que j'aille	que nous allions
que tu ailles	que vous alliez
qu'il aille	qu'ils aillent

ALLER *(TO GO)* - **SUBJUNCTIVE**	
qu'elle aille	qu'elles aillent

Remember valoir *(to be worth)* from Take It Further? It's also irregular in the subjunctive, and it's formed in a similar way to aller: que je vaille, que tu vailles, qu'il/elle vaille, que nous valions, que vous valiez, qu'ils/elles vaillent.

Not surprisingly, être *(to be)* and avoir *(to have)* are completely irregular as well. However, they also have different endings from the normal subjunctive endings. Fortunately, they are the only verbs that have different endings in the subjunctive.

Here are avoir and être in the subjunctive:

AVOIR *(TO HAVE)* - **SUBJUNCTIVE**	
que j'aie	que nous ayons
que tu aies	que vous ayez
qu'il ait	qu'ils aient
qu'elle ait	qu'elles aient

ÊTRE *(TO BE)* - **SUBJUNCTIVE**	
que je sois	que nous soyons
que tu sois	que vous soyez
qu'il soit	qu'ils soient
qu'elle soit	qu'elles soient

Finally, let's look at some example sentences using irregular verbs in the subjunctive:

Il faut que tu sois à l'heure.
You have to be on time. (It is necessary that you be on time.)

Je ne crois pas qu'il puisse le faire.
I don't believe (that) he can do it.

J'ai peur qu'il ne sache pas la vérité.
I'm afraid (that) he doesn't know the truth.

✎ Work Out 2

Translate the following sentences into English, with the subjunctive only expressing the present tense.

1. Nous doutons qu'elle ait le livre. _____

2. Il faut que nous écrivions beaucoup. _____

3. Je suis heureux que tu puisses venir avec nous. _____

4. Bien qu'elle soit gentille, il n'est pas gentil. _____

5. Je ne veux pas que vous fassiez du jogging. _____

ANSWER KEY:
1. *We doubt (that) she has the book.* 2. *It is necessary that we write a lot./We must/need to/have to write a lot.* 3. *I am happy that you can come with us.* 4. *Although she is nice/kind, he is not nice/kind.* 5. *I don't want you to go jogging.*

✎ Drive It Home

A. Fill in the blanks with the subjunctive of être.

1. Je veux que tu _____ heureux. (*I want you to be happy.*)

2. Je veux qu'il _____ heureux. (*I want him to be happy.*)

3. Je veux que vous_____ heureux. (*I want you to be happy.*)

4. Je veux qu'elle_____ heureuse. (*I want her to be happy.*)

B. Now fill in the blanks with the subjunctive of aller.

1. Il faut que nous _____ au cabinet médical.

   (We need to go to the doctor's office.)

2. Il faut qu'ils _____ au cabinet médical.

   (They need to go to the doctor's office.)

3. Il faut que j'_____ au cabinet médical.

   (I need to go to the doctor's office.)

4. Il faut que tu _____ au cabinet médical.

   (You need to go to the doctor's office.)

C. Finally, fill in the blanks with the subjunctive of avoir.

1. Je ne pense pas que vous _____ le verre. *(I don't think you have the glass.)*

2. Je ne pense pas qu'elle _____ le verre. *(I don't think she has the glass.)*

3. Je ne pense pas qu'elles _____ le verre. *(I don't think they have the glass.)*

4. Je ne pense pas que tu _____ le verre. *(I don't think you have the glass.)*

ANSWER KEY:
A. 1. sois; 2. soit; 3. soyez; 4. soit
B. 1. allions; 2. aillent; 3. aille; 4. ailles
C. 1. ayez; 2. ait; 3. aient; 4. aies

⚡ Tip

Of course, the best way to learn when to use the subjunctive is simply by practicing as much as possible. Here are some more example sentences with the subjunctive:

Il faut qu'on aille au gymnase cet après-midi.
We need to go to the gym this afternoon.

Il faut que je fasse beaucoup d'exercice.
I need to do a lot of exercising.

Pour que je puisse être en forme, je vais au club de remise en forme.
So that I can be in shape, I go to the health club.

Il est nécessaire de bien manger pour que tu puisses être en bonne santé.
It is necessary to eat well so that you can be in good health.

Je voudrais bien que vous veniez avec nous.
I'd really like you to come with us.

Nous regrettons que vous ne puissiez pas venir.
We're sorry (that) you can't come.

Je doute que j'y aille.
I doubt that I'll go there.

Croyez-vous que ce soit possible ?
Do you believe it's possible?

Elles sont contentes que vous soyez ici.
They are happy (that) you're here.

Nous cherchons quelqu'un qui puisse voyager.
We're looking for someone who can travel.

Qu'ils viennent !
Let them come! (lit., That they come!)

Votre société fait les meilleurs produits que je connaisse.
Your company makes the best products (that) I know.

How Did You Do?

Let's see how you did! By now, you should be able to:

☐ Talk about what you need to *buy*, *take*, or *see*
(Still unsure? Jump back to page 283)

☐ Say what you have to *be* or what you doubt someone *can* do
(Still unsure? Jump back to page 291)

Unit 4 Essentials

Don't forget to go to **www.livinglanguage.com/languagelab** to access your free online tools for this lesson: audiovisual flashcards, and interactive games and quizzes.

Vocabulary Essentials

PARTS OF THE BODY

body		neck	
head		shoulder	
eye		back	
eyes		arm	
nose		hand	
mouth		leg	
ear		knee	
tooth		foot	

[Pg. 234] (If you're stuck, visit this page to review!)

TO HAVE PAIN OR TO HURT

to have pain in, to ache, to have an ache, to have a sore something	
to have trouble (doing something)	
to hurt	

[Pg. 237]

HEALTH

illness, disease		common cold	
medical checkup		fever	
doctor's office		flu	
doctor		virus	
patient		allergy	
x-ray		infection	
diagnosis		care	

[Pg. 238]

INJURIES AND DISABILITIES

to break one's arm/leg	
to sprain one's ankle	
to walk with a cane	
to walk with crutches	
wheelchair	
to be disabled	
to have Alzheimer's disease	
to have Parkinson's disease	
to be deaf	
to use sign language	
to be paralyzed	
to wear contact lenses	
to be blind	
to need a seeing-eye dog	

[Pg. 246]

EXERCISE

exercise		stationary bike	
gym		workout, training	
health club		to be sweating	
to train		heartbeat	
treadmill		to be fit, to be in shape	

[Pg. 251]

AT THE DOCTOR'S OFFICE

I would like to make an appointment.	
What's the matter? (lit., What is there?)	
What happened to you? (pl./fml.)	
What should I do?	
The doctor gives a prescription. (lit., The doctor makes a prescription.)	
I have trouble swallowing.	
I have a sore throat.	
He has a headache.	
My nose is stuffed up./I have a stuffy nose.	

[Pg. 259]

Advanced French

EMERGENCIES

emergency situations	
It's necessary to have a first-aid kit.	
to have an accident	
Call the emergency medical service.	
The ambulance is arriving.	
He needs a blood transfusion.	
It's a superficial injury.	
It's not serious.	
Do you have insurance?	
Take a pill/a tablet/a capsule.	
Sometimes there are side effects.	
It's a burn.	
It's a cut.	
The dentist is going to replace the filling.	
It's necessary to have a tooth pulled.	

[Pg. 265]

Grammar Essentials

RECIPROCAL VERBS

When a verb uses a plural reflexive pronoun to mean *each other*, it is known as a reciprocal verb, such as s'aimer (*to like/love each other*) and se dire (*to tell each other, to say to each other*).

DIRECT OBJECTS AND AVOIR

If a verb that uses avoir is *preceded* by a direct object noun or pronoun, then that verb's past participle must agree in gender and number with the direct object noun or pronoun.

FORMING THE SUBJUNCTIVE

1. Drop the -ent from the ils/elles form of the verb in the present tense.
2. Add the following endings:

PRONOUN	ENDING	PRONOUN	ENDING
je	-e	nous	-ions
tu	-es	vous	-iez
il	-e	ils	-ent
elle	-e	elles	-ent

3. The subjunctive usually follows the conjunction que (*that*).
4. This form of the subjunctive, known as the "present subjunctive," is used for both the present tense and the future tense.

PARLER (TO SPEAK) - SUBJUNCTIVE			
that I speak	que je parle	*that we speak*	que nous parlions
that you speak (infml.)	que tu parles	*that you speak (pl./fml.)*	que vous parliez
that he speak	qu'il parle	*that they speak (m.)*	qu'ils parlent
that she speak	qu'elle parle	*that they speak (f.)*	qu'elles parlent

FINIR *(TO FINISH)* - **SUBJUNCTIVE**

that I finish	que je finisse	*that we finish*	que nous finissions
that you finish (infml.)	que tu finisses	*that you finish (pl./fml.)*	que vous finissiez
that he finish	qu'il finisse	*that they finish (m.)*	qu'ils finissent
that she finish	qu'elle finisse	*that they finish (f.)*	qu'elles finissent

RÉPONDRE *(TO ANSWER, TO RESPOND)* - **SUBJUNCTIVE**

that I answer	que je réponde	*that we answer*	que nous répondions
that you answer (infml.)	que tu répondes	*that you answer (pl./fml.)*	que vous répondiez
that he answer	qu'il réponde	*that they answer (m.)*	qu'ils répondent
that she answer	qu'elle réponde	*that they answer (f.)*	qu'elles répondent

5. Some verbs that are irregular in the present tense, such as écrire *(to write)*, still form the subjunctive regularly.

ÉCRIRE *(TO WRITE)* - **SUBJUNCTIVE**

that I write	que j'écrive	*that we write*	que nous écrivions
that you write (infml.)	que tu écrives	*that you write (pl./fml.)*	que vous écriviez
that he write	qu'il écrive	*that they write (m.)*	qu'ils écrivent
that she write	qu'elle écrive	*that they write (f.)*	qu'elles écrivent

THE SUBJUNCTIVE OF VERBS WITH SPELLING VARIATIONS

Verbs that have a different spelling for their nous and vous forms than for the rest of their forms in the present tense conjugate the subjunctive differently. To conjugate the nous and vous forms of these types of verbs in the subjunctive, drop the -ons from the present tense nous form and then add the appropriate subjunctive ending.

ACHETER (TO BUY) - SUBJUNCTIVE			
that I buy	que j'achète	that we buy	que nous achetions
that you buy (infml.)	que tu achètes	that you buy (pl./fml.)	que vous achetiez
that he buy	qu'il achète	that they buy (m.)	qu'ils achètent
that she buy	qu'elle achète	that they buy (f.)	qu'elles achètent

PRENDRE (TO TAKE) - SUBJUNCTIVE			
that I take	que je prenne	that we take	que nous prenions
that you take (infml.)	que tu prennes	that you take (pl./fml.)	que vous preniez
that he take	qu'il prenne	that they take (m.)	qu'ils prennent
that she take	qu'elle prenne	that they take (f.)	qu'elles prennent

Other verbs with these spelling variations include: appeler (to call), jeter (to throw, to throw out/away), préférer (to prefer), comprendre (to understand), venir (to come), boire (to drink), croire (to believe), devoir (to have to, must, should, to owe), payer (to pay, to pay for), and voir (to see).

MORE IRREGULAR VERBS IN THE SUBJUNCTIVE

ALLER *(TO GO)* - **SUBJUNCTIVE**			
that I go	que j'aille	*that we go*	que nous allions
that you go (infml.)	que tu ailles	*that you go (pl./fml.)*	que vous alliez
that he go	qu'il aille	*that they go (m.)*	qu'ils aillent
that she go	qu'elle aille	*that they go (f.)*	qu'elles aillent

AVOIR *(TO HAVE)* - **SUBJUNCTIVE**			
that I have	que j'aie	*that we have*	que nous ayons
that you have (infml.)	que tu aies	*that you have (pl./fml.)*	que vous ayez
that he have	qu'il ait	*that they have (m.)*	qu'ils aient
that she have	qu'elle ait	*that they have (f.)*	qu'elles aient

ÊTRE *(TO BE)* - **SUBJUNCTIVE**			
that I be	que je sois	*that we be*	que nous soyons
that you be (infml.)	que tu sois	*that you be (pl./fml.)*	que vous soyez
that he be	qu'il soit	*that they be (m.)*	qu'ils soient
that she is	qu'elle soit	*that they be (f.)*	qu'elles soient

FAIRE *(TO DO, TO MAKE)* - **SUBJUNCTIVE**			
that I make	que je fasse	*that we make*	que nous fassions
that you make (infml.)	que tu fasses	*that you make (pl./fml.)*	que vous fassiez
that he make	qu'il fasse	*that they make (m.)*	qu'ils fassent

FAIRE *(TO DO, TO MAKE)* - **SUBJUNCTIVE**			
that she make	qu'elle fasse	*that they make (f.)*	qu'elles fassent

POUVOIR *(CAN, TO BE ABLE TO)* - **SUBJUNCTIVE**			
that I can	que je puisse	*that we can*	que nous puissions
that you can (infml.)	que tu puisses	*that you can (pl./fml.)*	que vous puissiez
that he can	qu'il puisse	*that they can (m.)*	qu'ils puissent
that she can	qu'elle puisse	*that they can (f.)*	qu'elles puissent

SAVOIR *(TO KNOW)* - **SUBJUNCTIVE**			
that I know	que je sache	*that we know*	que nous sachions
that you know (infml.)	que tu saches	*that you know (pl./fml.)*	que vous sachiez
that he know	qu'il sache	*that they know (m.)*	qu'ils sachent
that she know	qu'elle sache	*that they know (f.)*	qu'elles sachent

VOULOIR *(TO WANT)* - **SUBJUNCTIVE**			
that I want	que je veuille	*that we want*	que nous voulions
that you want (infml.)	que tu veuilles	*that you want (pl./fml.)*	que vous vouliez
that he want	qu'il veuille	*that they want (m.)*	qu'ils veuillent
that she want	qu'elle veuille	*that they want (f.)*	qu'elles veuillent

USING THE SUBJUNCTIVE

The subjunctive is used after:

1. verbs of command, request, permission, or other expressions imposing your will on someone else + que

to request that, to ask that	demander que	to order that	ordonner que
to prevent from, to keep from	empêcher que	to allow that	permettre que
to demand that, to require that	exiger que	to suggest that	suggérer que

2. verbs or expressions of doubt, denial, uncertainty, or possibility + que

to doubt that	douter que
it seems that	il semble que
it is possible that	il est probable que

3. verbs or expressions of approval, disapproval, or preference + que

to prefer that (lit., to like better that)	aimer mieux que
to recommend that	recommander que
to prefer that	préférer que
it is preferable that	il est préférable que

4. verbs or expressions of wishing, want, or desire + que

to desire that, to want that, to wish that	désirer que
to want that, to wish that	vouloir que
to wish that	souhaiter que

5. verbs of thinking or believing when they are negative or in the form of a question + que.

to think that	penser que
to believe that	croire que
to find that, to think that	trouver que

6. verbs or expressions of necessity or need + que

it is necessary that	il faut que
to need for	avoir besoin que

7. expressions of urgency or importance + que

it is urgent that	il est urgent que
it is important that	il est important que
it is essential that	il est essentiel que

8. expressions of emotion, such as joy, fear, sorrow, or regret + que

9. specific conjunctions with que

in order that, so that	afin que, pour que	*although*	bien que, quoique
before	avant que	*without*	sans que
unless	à moins que... ne	*until*	jusqu'à ce que

10. The subjunctive is **only** used when the subject of the verb before que is different from the subject of the verb after que.

OTHER VERBS

SUIVRE *(TO FOLLOW)* - **PRESENT**			
I follow	je suis	*we follow*	nous suivons
you follow (infml.)	tu suis	*you follow (pl./fml.)*	vous suivez
he follows	il suit	*they follow (m.)*	ils suivent
she follows	elle suit	*they follow (f.)*	elles suivent
Past Participle: suivi			

Unit 4 Quiz

You've made it to the very last quiz! Félicitations !

Once you successfully complete this quiz, you'll be done with the entire program and ready to go out and speak French naturally and conversationally.

Ready?

A. Match English words on the left to the correct French translations on the right.

1. *eye*	a. **la tête**
2. *head*	b. **la bouche**
3. *nose*	c. **l'œil**
4. *mouth*	d. **le dos**
5. *back*	e. **le nez**

B. Translate the following sentences into English.

1. J'ai un rhume. _____

2. J'ai la grippe. _____

3. J'ai mal à la tête. _____

4. J'ai mal à la gorge. _____

5. J'ai mal aux dents. _____

C. Conjugate the following verbs in the subjunctive.

1. que j' _____ (aller)

2. que tu _____ (être)

3. qu'il _____ (avoir)

4. que nous _____ (acheter)

5. qu'elles _____ (vendre)

D. Translate the following sentences into English. Only translate the subjunctive in the present tense.

1. 1. J'ai suggéré qu'elle fasse ses devoirs. _____

_____

2. Nous doutons qu'elle puisse le faire. _____

_____

3. Elle voudrait que vous leur répondiez. _____

_____

4. Pensez-vous qu'il veuille venir au restaurant ? _____

_____

5. J'ai peur que vous ne compreniez pas. _____

_____

How Did You Do?

Give yourself a point for every correct answer, then use the following key to determine whether or not you're ready to move on:

0-7 points: It's probably best to go back and study the lessons again to make sure you understood everything completely. Take your time; it's not a race! Make sure you spend time reviewing the vocabulary and reading through each grammar note carefully.

8-16 points: If the questions you missed were in Section A or B, you may want to review the vocabulary again; if you missed answers mostly in Section C or D, check the Unit 4 Essentials to make sure you have your conjugations and other grammar basics down.

17-20 points: Wow, congratulations! You made it through the entire program successfully! However, don't forget to come back and review as much as you can. This is one of the keys to learning a new language—not just holding it temporarily in your short-term memory, but making it stick in your long-term memory. Go back over old lists and example sentences. Test yourself with flashcards. Listen to the audio from previous lessons. Just practice, practice, practice.

Bonne chance ! (Good luck!)

Points

Pronunciation Guide

Consonants

Note that the letter **h** can act as either a vowel or a consonant. See the end of the Pronunciation Guide for more information.

FRENCH	APPROXIMATE SOUND	PHONETIC SYMBOL	EXAMPLES
b, d, f, k, m, n, p, t, v, z	same as in English	same as in English	
ç	*s*	[s]	**français** [frah(n)-seh] (*French*)
c before a, o, u	*k*	[k]	**cave** [kahv] (*cellar*)
c before e, i, y	*s*	[s]	**cinéma** [see-nay-mah] (*movie theater*)
ch	*sh*	[sh]	**chaud** [shoh] (*hot*)
g before a, o, u	*g* in *game*	[g]	**gâteau** [gah-toh] (*cake*)
g before e, i, y	*s* in *measure*	[zh]	**âge** [ahzh] (*age*)
gn	*ni* in *onion*	[ny]	**agneau** [ah-nyoh] (*lamb*)
j	*s* in *measure*	[zh]	**jeu** [zhuh] (*game*)
l	*l*	[l]	**lent** [lah(n)] (*slow*)
l when it's at the end of the word and follows i	*y* in *yes*	[y]	**fauteuil** [foh-tuhy] (*armchair*)
ll	*ll* in *ill*	[l]	**elle** [ehl] (*she*), **ville** [veel] (*town*)
ll between i and another vowel	*y* in *yes*	[y]	**fille** [feey] (*girl, daughter*), **papillon** [pah-pee-yoh(n)] (*butterfly*)

FRENCH	APPROXIMATE SOUND	PHONETIC SYMBOL	EXAMPLES
qu, final q	k	[k]	qui [kee] (who), cinq [sa(n)k] (five)
r	pronounced in the back of the mouth, like a light gargling sound	[r]	Paris [pah-ree] (Paris)
s between vowels	z in zebra	[z]	maison [meh-zoh(n)] (house)
s at the beginning of a word or before/after a consonant	s	[s]	salle [sahl] (hall, room), course [koors] (errand)
ss	s	[s]	tasse [tahs] (cup)
th	t	[t]	thé [tay] (tea)
w	v	[v]	wagon-lit [vah-goh(n)-lee] (sleeping car)
x usually before a vowel	x in exact	[gz]	exact [ehgz-ahkt] (exact)
x before a consonant or final e	x in exterior	[ks]	extérieur [ehks-tay-ree-uhr] (outside)

Keep in mind that most final consonants are silent in French, as with the -s in Paris [pah-ree] (Paris). However, there are five letters that are often (but not always) pronounced when final: c, f, l, q, and r.

French speakers also pronounce some final consonants when the next word begins with a vowel or silent h (see the end of the Pronunciation Guide for more information on the "silent h"). This is known as liaison [lyeh-zoh(n)] (*link*).

For example, the -s in nous [noo] (*we*) normally isn't pronounced. However, if it's followed by a word that begins with a vowel, such as allons [ah-loh(n)], then you do pronounce it: nous allons [noo zah-loh(n)] (*we go*). Notice that, in liaison, the s or x is pronounced *z* and it is "linked" to the following word: [zah-loh(n)]. Here's another example of liaison: un grand arbre [uh(n) grah(n) tahr-bruh] (*a big tree*). Normally, the -d in grand [grah(n)] is not pronounced, but, in liaison, it is pronounced *t* and linked to the following word.

Vowels

FRENCH	APPROXIMATE SOUND	PHONETIC SYMBOL	EXAMPLES
a, à, â	*a* in *father*	[ah]	laver [lah-vay] (*to wash*), à [ah] (*in, to, at*)
é, er, ez (end of a word), et	*ay* in *lay*	[ay]	été [ay-tay] (*summer*), aller [ah-lay] (*to go*), ballet [bah-lay] (*ballet*)
è, ê, ei, ai, aî	*e* in *bed*, with relaxed lips	[eh]	père [pehr] (*father*), forêt [foh-reh] (*forest*), faire [fehr] (*to do*)

FRENCH	APPROXIMATE SOUND	PHONETIC SYMBOL	EXAMPLES
e without an accent (and not combined with another vowel or r, z, t)	a in *above*, or e in *bed* with relaxed lips, or silent	[uh] *or* [eh] or silent at end of word	le [luh] (*the*), belle [behl] (*beautiful*), danse [dah(n)s] (*dance*)
eu, œu followed by a consonant sound	u in *fur* with lips very rounded and loose	[uh]	cœur [kuhr] (*heart*)
eu, œu not followed by any sound	u in *fur* with lips very rounded and tight	[uh]	feu [fuh] (*fire*)
eille, ey	ey in *hey*	[ehy]	bouteille [boo-tehy] (*bottle*)
euille, œil	a in *above* + y in *yesterday*	[uhy]	œil [uhy] (*eye*)
i	ee in *beet*	[ee]	ici [ee-see] (*here*)
i plus vowel	ee in *beet* + y in *yesterday*	[y]	violon [vyoh-loh(n)] (*violin*)
o, au, eau, ô	o in *both*	[oh]	mot [moh] (*word*), eau [oh] (*water*), hôtel [oh-tehl] (*hotel*)
oi	wa in *watt*	[wah]	moi [mwah] (*me*)
ou	oo in *boot*	[oo]	vous [voo] (*you*)
ou *before a vowel*	w in *week*	[w]	ouest [wehst] (*west*), oui [wee] (*yes*)
oy	wa in *watt* + y in *yesterday*	[wahy]	foyer [fwahy-ay] (*home*)

FRENCH	APPROXIMATE SOUND	PHONETIC SYMBOL	EXAMPLES
u	keep your lips rounded as you pronounce *ee* in *beet*	[ew]	tu [tew] (*you*)
ui	*wee* in *week*	[wee]	lui [lwee] (*he, him, her*)

Nasal Vowels

FRENCH	APPROXIMATE SOUND	PHONETIC SYMBOL	EXAMPLES
an/en or am/em	*a* in *balm*, pronounced through both the mouth and the nose	[ah(n)] or [ah(m)]	France [frah(n)s] (*France*), entrer [ah(n)-tray] (*to enter*), emmener [ah(m)-muh-nay] (*to take along*)
in/yn/ain/ein or im/ym/aim/eim	*a* in *mad*, pronounced through both the mouth and the nose	[a(n)] or [a(m)]	vin [va(n)] (*wine*), vain [va(n)] (*vain*), sympa [sa(m)-pah] (*cool, nice, good*), faim [fa(m)] (*hunger*)
ien	*ee* in *beet* + *y* in *yesterday* + nasal *a* in *mad*	[ya(n)]	rien [rya(n)] (*nothing*)
oin	*w* + nasal *a* in *mad*	[wa(n)]	loin [lwa(n)] (*far*)

FRENCH	APPROXIMATE SOUND	PHONETIC SYMBOL	EXAMPLES
on or om	o in *song*, pronounced through both the mouth and the nose	[oh(n)] or [oh(m)]	bon [boh(n)] (*good*), tomber [toh(m)-bay] (*to fall*)
ion	*ee* in *beet* + *y* in *yesterday* + nasal *o* in *song*	[yoh(n)]	station [stah-syoh(n)] (*station*)
un or um	*u* in *lung*, pronounced through both the mouth and the nose	[uh(n)] or [uh(m)]	un [uh(n)] (*one, a/an*), parfum [pahr-fuh(m)] (*perfume*)

The Letter H

In French, the letter h is not pronounced. For example, huit (*eight*) would be pronounced [weet].

However, there are actually two different types of h in French: the silent or mute h and the aspirated h. While you wouldn't pronounce either one, they behave differently.

The silent h acts like a vowel. For example, words like le, la, se, de, and so on become "contracted" (l', s', d', etc.) before a silent h:

l'homme (le + homme)	*the man*
s'habiller (se + habiller)	*to get dressed*

Also, you usually use liaison with a silent h. For instance, les hommes would be pronounced [lay zohm].

However, the aspirated h acts like a consonant. Words like le, la, se, de, etc. do **not** become l', s', d', and so on before an aspirated h:

le homard	the lobster
se hâter	to rush

Also, you do not use liaison with an aspirated h: les homards would be pronounced [lay oh-mahr].

Most h are silent, not aspirated. Still, there are many words that begin with an aspirated h. Unfortunately, there isn't an easy way to tell which are which. Just start by learning the common ones, and then continue memorizing others that you come across.

Apart from homme and habiller, here are some other examples of common words that begin with a silent h: habiter (*to live*), heure (*hour*), heureux/heureuse (*happy*), hier (*yesterday*), hôpital (*hospital*), horaire (*schedule*), and huile (*oil*). Apart from homard and hâter, here are some other examples of common words that begin with an aspirated h: huit (*eight*), héros (*hero*), haine (*hatred*), hasard (*chance*), hâte (*haste*), haut (*high*), honte (*shame*), and hors (*outside*).

Grammar Summary

Here is a brief snapshot of French grammar from *Essential* and *Intermediate French*. Keep in mind that there are exceptions to many grammar rules. For a more comprehensive grammar summary, please visit www.livinglanguage.com.

1. NUMBERS

CARDINAL		ORDINAL	
un/une	one	premier/première	first
deux	two	deuxième, second/seconde	second
trois	three	troisième	third
quatre	four	quatrième	fourth
cinq	five	cinquième	fifth
six	six	sixième	sixth
sept	seven	septième	seventh
huit	eight	huitième	eighth
neuf	nine	neuvième	ninth
dix	ten	dixième	tenth

2. ARTICLES

	DEFINITE		INDEFINITE	
	Singular	Plural	Singular	Plural
Masculine	le	les	un	des
Feminine	la	les	une	des

Note that l' is used instead of le and la before words beginning with a vowel or silent h.

3. CONTRACTIONS

de + le = du (*some/of the, masculine*)

de + les = des (*some/of the, plural*)

à + le = au (*to/at/in the, masculine*)

à + les = aux (*to/at/in the, plural*)

There is no contraction with la or l'. In a negative sentence, de la, de l', du, and des change to de/d'.

4. PLURALS

Most nouns add -s to form the plural. If a noun ends in -s, -x, or -z in the singular, there is no change in the plural.

Nouns ending in -eau or -eu, and some nouns ending in -ou, add -x instead of -s to form the plural. Many nouns ending in -al and -ail change to -aux in the plural.

5. ADJECTIVES

Adjectives agree with the nouns they modify in gender and number; that is, they are masculine if the noun is masculine, plural if the noun is plural, etc.

a. The feminine of an adjective is normally formed by adding -e to the masculine singular.

b. If the masculine singular already ends in -e, the adjective has the same form in the feminine.

c. Some adjectives double the final consonant of the masculine singular form and then add -e to form the feminine.

d. If the masculine singular ends in -x, change the ending to -se to form the feminine.

e. If the masculine singular ends in -f, change the ending to -ve to form the feminine.

f. If the masculine singular ends in -er, change the ending to -ère to form the feminine.

g. If the masculine singular ends in -et, change the ending to -ète or -ette to form the feminine.

h. The plural of adjectives is usually formed by adding -s to the masculine or feminine singular form. But if the adjective ends in -s or -x in the masculine singular, the masculine plural stays the same.

i. Most masculine adjectives ending in -al in the masculine singular, change the ending to -aux in the masculine plural.

Adjectives usually come after the noun. However, adjectives of beauty, age, goodness, and size (B-A-G-S adjectives) usually come before the noun.

6. POSSESSIVE ADJECTIVES

Possessive adjectives agree in gender and number with the possession.

BEFORE SINGULAR NOUNS		BEFORE PLURAL NOUNS	
Masculine	Feminine	Masculine and Feminine	
mon	ma	mes	*my*
ton	ta	tes	*your (familiar)*
son	sa	ses	*his, her, its*
notre	notre	nos	*our*
votre	votre	vos	*your (polite/plural)*
leur	leur	leurs	*their*

Before feminine singular nouns beginning with a vowel or silent h, use mon, ton, and son.

7. COMPARISONS

Most adjectives form the comparative with plus (*more*) and moins (*less*), using que where English uses *than*. To express *as ... as*, use aussi and que.

To express the superlative of something, use le/la/les + plus + adjective to express superiority (*the most, -est*) and le/la/les + moins + adjective to express inferiority (*the least*).

8. PRONOUNS

	SUBJECT	DIRECT OBJECT	INDIRECT OBJECT	STRESSED	REFLEXIVE
1st singular	je/j'	me/m'	me/m'	moi	me/m'
2nd singular	tu	te/t'	te/t'	toi	te/t'
3rd masculine singular	il	le/l'	lui	lui	se/s'
3rd feminine singular	elle	la/l'	lui	elle	se/s'
1st plural	nous	nous	nous	nous	nous
2nd plural	vous	vous	vous	vous	vous
3rd masculine plural	ils	les	leur	eux	se/s'

	SUBJECT	DIRECT OBJECT	INDIRECT OBJECT	STRESSED	REFLEXIVE
3rd feminine plural	elles	les	leur	elles	se/s'

On is an indefinite subject pronoun that means *we, one,* or *people/you/they in general.*

Stressed pronouns are generally used after prepositions (avec moi, etc.) or for emphasis (moi, j'ai vingt ans).

9. ORDER OF PRONOUNS

In sentences or negative commands, place pronouns in the following order:

subject pronouns	me/m' te/t' se/s' nous vous	le la l' les	lui leur	y	en	verb

In the positive imperative, place pronouns in the following order:

positive imperative form of verb	le la les	m' moi t' toi lui nous vous leur	y	en

10. QUESTION WORDS

où	where	de quel/quelle/ quels/quelles + noun	what/of what + noun
qu'est-ce que	what	combien (de)	how much, how many
quel/quelle, quels/quelles	which, what	à quelle heure	at what time
qui	who	pourquoi	why
comment	how	quand	when

11. DEMONSTRATIVES ADJECTIVES

Masculine Singular	ce	this, that
Masculine Singular (before a vowel or silent h)	cet	this, that
Feminine Singular	cette	this, that
Masculine Plural	ces	these, those
Feminine Plural	ces	these, those

When it is necessary to distinguish between *this* and *that*, -ci and -là are added to the noun: Donnez-moi ce livre-ci. (*Give me this book.*)

12. NEGATION

A sentence is made negative by placing ne before the verb and pas after it. When placed before a vowel or silent h, ne becomes n'.

To form the negative of the past tense, place ne (n') and pas around the present tense form of avoir or être. To form a negative statement with a reflexive verb, place ne after the subject pronoun but before the reflexive pronoun, and then place pas immediately after the verb.

13. ADVERBS

Adverbs are usually placed after the verb. In the past tense, they're placed after the past participle. However, adverbs of quality (bien, mal), quantity (beaucoup) and frequency (toujours), along with some other adverbs, come before the past participle.

Most adverbs are formed from their corresponding adjectives. If the adjective ends in -e in the masculine singular, just add -ment to the masculine singular form. If the adjective ends in a consonant in the masculine singular, add -ment to the feminine singular form.

14. THE SUBJUNCTIVE

The subjunctive is used after:

a. verbs of command, request, permission, or other expressions imposing your will on someone else + que

b. verbs or expressions of doubt, denial, uncertainty, or possibility + que

c. verbs or expressions of approval, disapproval, or preference + que

d. verbs or expressions of wishing, want, or desire + que

e. verbs of thinking or believing when they are negative or in the form of a question + que

f. verbs or expressions of necessity or need + que

g. expressions of urgency or importance + que

h. expressions of emotion, such as joy, fear, sorrow, or regret + que

i. specific conjunctions with que

j. a relative pronoun (que or qui) if there is doubt or denial

k. a relative pronoun (que or qui) if it's preceded by a superlative, unless you're stating a fact

Sometimes the subjunctive is used in certain exclamations or commands: Vive la France ! (*Long live France!*).

15. REGULAR VERBS

There are three types of regular French verbs:

TYPE	EXAMPLE
verbs ending in -er	parler (*to speak*)
verbs ending in -re	vendre (*to sell*)
verbs ending in -ir	finir (*to finish*)

Here are the full conjugations of each example.

parler
to speak, to talk

je	nous
tu	vous
il/elle/on	ils/elles

Present		Imperative	
parle	parlons		Parlons !
parles	parlez	Parle !	Parlez !
parle	parlent		

Past		Imperfect	
ai parlé	avons parlé	parlais	parlions
as parlé	avez parlé	parlais	parliez
a parlé	ont parlé	parlait	parlaient

Future		Conditional	
parlerai	parlerons	parlerais	parlerions
parleras	parlerez	parlerais	parleriez
parlera	parleront	parlerait	parleraient

Future Perfect		Past Conditional	
aurai parlé	aurons parlé	aurais parlé	aurions parlé
auras parlé	aurez parlé	aurais parlé	auriez parlé
aura parlé	auront parlé	aurait parlé	auraient parlé

Past Perfect		Subjunctive	
avais parlé	avions parlé	parle	parlions
avais parlé	aviez parlé	parles	parliez
avait parlé	avaient parlé	parle	parlent

vendre
to sell

je	nous
tu	vous
il/elle/on	ils/elles

Present		Imperative	
vends	vendons		Vendons !
vends	vendez	Vends !	Vendez !
vend	vendent		

Past		Imperfect	
ai vendu	avons vendu	vendais	vendions
as vendu	avez vendu	vendais	vendiez
a vendu	ont vendu	vendait	vendaient

Future		Conditional	
vendrai	vendrons	vendrais	vendrions
vendras	vendrez	vendrais	vendriez
vendra	vendront	vendrait	vendraient

Future Perfect		Past Conditional	
aurai vendu	aurons vendu	aurais vendu	aurions vendu
auras vendu	aurez vendu	aurais vendu	auriez vendu
aura vendu	auront vendu	aurait vendu	auraient vendu

Past Perfect		Subjunctive	
avais vendu	avions vendu	vende	vendions
avais vendu	aviez vendu	vendes	vendiez
avait vendu	avaient vendu	vende	vendent

finir
to finish

je	nous
tu	vous
il/elle/on	ils/elles

Present			Imperative	
finis	finissons			Finissons !
finis	finissez		Finis !	Finissez !
finit	finissent			

Past			Imperfect	
ai fini	avons fini		finissais	finissions
as fini	avez fini		finissais	finissiez
a fini	ont fini		finissait	finissaient

Future			Conditional	
finirai	finirons		finirais	finirions
finiras	finirez		finirais	finiriez
finira	finiront		finirait	finiraient

Future Perfect			Past Conditional	
aurai fini	aurons fini		aurais fini	aurions fini
auras fini	aurez fini		aurais fini	auriez fini
aura fini	auront fini		aurait fini	auraient fini

Past Perfect			Subjunctive	
avais fini	avions fini		finisse	finissions
avais fini	aviez fini		finisses	finissiez
avait fini	avaient fini		finisse	finissent

16. COMMON IRREGULAR VERBS

aller
to go

je	nous
tu	vous
il/elle/on	ils/elles

Present		Imperative	
vais	allons		Allons !
vas	allez	Va !	Allez !
va	vont		

Past		Imperfect	
suis allé(e)	sommes allé(e)s	allais	allions
es allé(e)	êtes allé(e)(s)	allais	alliez
est allé(e)	sont allé(e)s	allait	allaient

Future		Conditional	
irai	irons	irais	irions
iras	irez	irais	iriez
ira	iront	irait	iraient

Future Perfect		Past Conditional	
serai allé(e)	serons allé(e)s	serais allé(e)	serions allé(e)s
seras allé(e)	serez allé(e)(s)	serais allé(e)	seriez allé(e)(s)
sera allé(e)	seront allé(e)s	serait allé(e)	seraient allé(e)s

Past Perfect		Subjunctive	
étais allé(e)	étions allé(e)s	aille	allions
étais allé(e)	étiez allé(e)(s)	ailles	alliez
était allé(e)	étaient allé(e)s	aille	aillent

avoir
to have

je	nous
tu	vous
il/elle/on	ils/elles

Present		Imperative	
ai	avons		Ayons !
as	avez	Aie !	Ayez !
a	ont		

Past		Imperfect	
ai eu	avons eu	avais	avions
as eu	avez eu	avais	aviez
a eu	ont eu	avait	avaient

Future		Conditional	
aurai	aurons	aurais	aurions
auras	aurez	aurais	auriez
aura	auront	aurait	auraient

Future Perfect		Past Conditional	
aurai eu	aurons eu	aurais eu	aurions eu
auras eu	aurez eu	aurais eu	auriez eu
aura eu	auront eu	aurait eu	auraient eu

Past Perfect		Subjunctive	
avais eu	avions eu	aie	ayons
avais eu	aviez eu	aies	ayez
avait eu	avaient eu	ait	aient

être
to be

je	nous
tu	vous
il/elle/on	ils/elles

Present		Imperative	
suis	sommes		Soyons !
es	êtes	Sois !	Soyez !
est	sont		

Past		Imperfect	
ai été	avons été	étais	étions
as été	avez été	étais	étiez
a été	ont été	était	étaient

Future		Conditional	
serai	serons	serais	serions
seras	serez	serais	seriez
sera	seront	serais	seraient

Future Perfect		Past Conditional	
aurai été	aurons été	aurais été	aurions été
auras été	aurez été	aurais été	auriez été
aura été	auront été	aurait été	auraient été

Past Perfect		Subjunctive	
avais été	avions été	sois	soyons
avais été	aviez été	sois	soyez
avait été	avaient été	soit	soient

faire
to do, to make

je	nous
tu	vous
il/elle/ on	ils/elles

Present		Imperative	
fais	faisons		Faisons !
fais	faites	Fais !	Faites !
fait	font		

Past		Imperfect	
ai fait	avons fait	faisais	faisions
as fait	avez fait	faisais	faisiez
a fait	ont fait	faisait	faisaient

Future		Conditional	
ferai	ferons	ferais	ferions
feras	ferez	ferais	feriez
fera	feront	ferait	feraient

Future Perfect		Past Conditional	
aurai fait	aurons fait	aurais fait	aurions fait
auras fait	aurez fait	aurais fait	auriez fait
aura fait	auront fait	aurait fait	auraient fait

Past Perfect		Subjunctive	
avais fait	avions fait	fasse	fassions
avais fait	aviez fait	fasses	fassiez
avait fait	avaient fait	fasse	fassent

Glossary

Note that the following abbreviations will be used in this glossary: (m.) = masculine, (f.) = feminine, (sg.) = singular, (pl.) = plural, (fml.) = formal/polite, (infml.) = informal/familiar. If a word has two grammatical genders, (m./f.) or (f./m.) is used.

French-English

A

à *in, at, to*
  à la / à l' / au / aux (f./m. or f. before a vowel or silent h/m./pl.) *in/at/to the*
  à cause de *because of, as a result of, due to (in a negative way)*
  à côté de *next to*
  à côté *at the side, on the side, to the side*
  à plein temps *full-time*
  à temps partiel *part-time*
  à la retraite *retired*
  à quelle heure ? *at what time?*
  à gauche *on the left, to the left, at the left*
  à droite *on the right, to the right, at the right*
  à moins que... ne *unless*
  à mon avis *in my opinion*
  à travers *through, across*
  à l'heure *on time*
  à la maison *at the house, at home*
  à pied *on foot, by foot*
  À votre santé ! *To your health!*
  À la prochaine ! *See you later!*
  À plus tard ! *See you later!*
  À plus ! *See you later!* (infml.)
  À tout à l'heure ! *See you later!*
  À bientôt ! *See you soon!*
  À table ! *Dinner's ready!/The food is ready! (lit., To the table!)*
abdomen (m.) *abdomen*
abdominaux (m. pl.) *sit-ups*
Absolument ! *Absolutely!*
accessoires (m. pl.) *accessories*
accident (m.) *accident*
accompagner *to accompany*
  plat (m.) d'accompagnement *side dish*

accord (m.) *agreement*
  D'accord. *Okay./All right.*
acheter *to buy*
acteur / actrice (m./f.) *actor/actress*
actif / active (m./f.) *active*
action (f.) *action*
  film (m.) d'action *action film*
activement *actively*
activité (f.) *activity*
  activités de plein air *outdoor activities*
  activités extra-scolaires / parascolaires *extracurricular activities*
addition (f.) *check, bill*
admirer *to admire*
adolescent / adolescente (m./f.) *adolescent, teenager*
adorer *to love, to adore*
adulte (m./f.) *adult, grown-up*
aéroport (m.) *airport*
affaires (f. pl.) *business, belongings*
  homme / femme (m./f.) d'affaires *businessman/woman*
afin que *in order that, so that*
âge (m.) *age*
  personne (f.) âgée *elderly person*
agent / agente de police (m./f.) *policeman/policewoman*
agir *to act (to behave)*
agneau (m.) *lamb*
  carré (m.) d'agneau rôti *roast rack of lamb*
agréable *pleasant, enjoyable*
Ah bon... *Oh really .../Oh okay ...*
aider *to help*
  Pouvez-vous m'aider, s'il vous plaît ? *Can you help me, please?*
aigre *sour*
aiguille (f.) *needle*
ailleurs *elsewhere*

aimable *kind (nice)*
aimer *to like, to love*
  J'aime (bien)... *I (do) like ...*
  J'aime ça. *I like that./I love that.*
  Je n'aime pas... *I do not like ...*
  aimer mieux *to prefer*
aîné / aînée (m./f.) *oldest child*
alcool (m.) *alcohol*
Algérie (f.) *Algeria*
algérien / algérienne (m./f.) *Algerian*
Allemagne (f.) *Germany*
allemand / allemande (m./f.) *German*
aller *to go*
  aller visiter *to go sightseeing*
  aller à ravir à quelqu'un *to look great on someone, to suit someone well*
  Allons-y. *Let's go.*
  On y va. *Let's go.* (infml.)
  Comment allez-vous ? *How are you?* (pl./fml.)
  Comment vas-tu ? *How are you?* (infml.)
  Je vais très bien. *I'm very well.*
  Va ! *Go!* (infml.)
  Allez ! *Go!* (pl./fml.)
  Vas-y ! *Go there!/Go on!/Go ahead!* (infml.)
aller simple (m.) *one-way*
allergie (f.) *allergy*
allergique *allergic*
aller-retour (m.) *round-trip*
  Je voudrais un billet aller-retour. *I would like a round-trip ticket.*
alliance (f.) *wedding ring*
Allô. *Hello.* (only on the phone)
allonger *to lay down, to lie down*
Alors... *Well .../So .../Then ...*
  Alors là... *So then ... , Well, well, well!*
alpinisme (m.) *(mountain) climbing*
amande (f.) *almond*
ambulance (f.) *ambulance*
américain / américaine (m./f.) *American*
ami / amie (m./f.) *friend*
  petit ami / petite amie (m./f.) *boyfriend/ girlfriend*
amical / amicale (m./f.) *friendly*
amusant / amusante (m./f.) *amusing, funny*
amuser *to entertain*
  s'amuser *to have a good time, to enjoy oneself, to have fun*
  Je m'amuse. *I'm having a good time./I'm having fun.*
an (m.) *year*
  jour (m.) de l'An *New Year's Day*
  Nouvel An *New Year*
  avoir... ans *to be ... years old*
ancien / ancienne (m./f.) *old, former, ancient*
anglais (m.) *English language*
  en anglais *in English*
anglais / anglaise (m./f.) *English*
Angleterre (f.) *England*
animal (m.) *animal*
anneau (m.) *ring*
année (f.) *year*
  mois (m. pl.) de l'année *months of the year*
  Bonne Année ! *Happy New Year!*
  année dernière *last year*
  année scolaire *academic year*
anniversaire (m.) *birthday, anniversary*
  Joyeux / Bon anniversaire ! *Happy birthday!/Happy anniversary!*
annoncer *to announce*
antibiotiques (m. pl.) *antibiotics*
anti-inflammatoire *anti-inflammatory*
août *August*
apéritif *drink served before the meal*
appareil (m.) *device, telephone*
  Qui est à l'appareil ? *Who is it?/Who's calling?* (on the phone)
  appareil photo *camera*
appartement (m.) *apartment*
appeler *to call*
  s'appeler *to be called (to call oneself)*
appétit (m.) *appetite*
  Bon appétit ! *Enjoy your meal! (lit., Good appetite!)*
apporter *to bring*
apprendre *to learn*
  apprendre par cœur *to learn by heart*
  J'apprends le français. *I'm learning French.*
après *after, afterwards*
après-demain *the day after tomorrow*
après-midi (m./f.) *afternoon*
arbre (m.) *tree*
Arc (m.) de Triomphe *Arc de Triomphe (Arch of Triumph)*
architecte (m./f.) *architect*
argent (m.) *money, cash, silver*
armoire (f.) *wardrobe, cabinet*

Glossary

armoire à pharmacie *medicine cabinet*
arracher (une dent) *to pull (a tooth)*
arrêt (m.) *stop*
  arrêt de bus / d'autobus *bus stop*
arriver *to arrive, to get somewhere, to reach, to happen*
  arriver à (+ verb) *to be able to (do something), to manage to (do something)*
  arriver à (+ destination) *to arrive (somewhere), to get to (a destination)*
  heure (f.) d'arrivée *arrival time*
art (m.) *art*
artiste (m./f.) *artist*
assez *quite, enough*
assiette (f.) *plate*
assis / assise (m./f.) *sitting (down), seated*
assistant / assistante (m./f.) *assistant*
assister à (un cours) *to attend (a class), to take (a class)*
assurance (f.) *insurance*
athlétisme (m.) *track (and field)*
attaque (f.) cérébrale *stroke*
attendre *to wait (for), to expect*
au *to/at/in the* (m.)
  Au revoir. *Good-bye.*
  au bout de *at the end of*
  au pied de *at the foot of*
  au bord de *at the edge of (at the border of)*
  au milieu de *in the middle of*
  au bureau *at the office*
  au travail *at work*
  au collège *in middle school*
  au lycée *in high school*
auberge (f.) *inn*
  auberge de jeunesse *youth hostel*
aujourd'hui *today*
auparavant *before*
  deux mois auparavant *two months before*
aussi *also, too, as, just as*
  aussi... que *as ... as*
  moins... que *not as ... as*
Australie (f.) *Australia*
australien / australienne (m./f.) *Australian*
autant *as much, as many*
  autant de *as many as*
auteur / auteure (m./f.) *author*
auto(mobile) (f.) *car, automobile*
autobus (m.) *bus*

arrêt (m.) d'autobus *bus stop*
autocar (m.) *bus*
automne (m.) *fall, autumn*
  en automne *in (the) fall, in autumn*
autour de *around*
autre *other, else*
  d'autre *else*
  un / une autre (m./f.) *another*
  de l'autre côté de *on the other side of*
  autre chose *something else, anything else*
  ne... rien d'autre *nothing else, anything else*
  quelqu'un d'autre *someone else*
autrefois *formerly, in the past*
aux *to/at/in the* (pl.)
  aux États-Unis *to the United States*
avancer *to advance*
avant *before*
  deux mois avant *two months before*
  d'avant *before last*
  semaine (f.) d'avant *the week before last*
  avant que *before*
avant-hier *the day before yesterday*
avec *with*
  Avec plaisir. *With pleasure.*
  sortir avec *to go out with (to date)*
avenue (f.) *avenue*
aveugle *blind*
  être aveugle *to be blind*
avion (m.) *airplane*
avis (m.) *opinion*
  à mon avis *in my opinion*
avocat / avocate (m./f.) *lawyer*
avoir *to have*
  avoir besoin de *to need*
  avoir besoin que *to need for*
  avoir envie de *to feel like*
  avoir chaud *to be hot/warm*
  avoir froid *to be cold*
  avoir faim *to be hungry*
  avoir soif *to be thirsty*
  avoir hâte *to look forward to (can't wait)*
  avoir honte *to be ashamed*
  avoir lieu *to take place, to be held*
  avoir peur *to be afraid*
  avoir raison *to be right*
  avoir tort *to be wrong*
  avoir sommeil *to be sleepy*
  avoir... ans *to be ... years old*

avoir le temps *to have (the) time*

avoir du mal à *to have trouble (doing something)*

avoir mal à *to ache, to have pain in, to have a sore (something)*

avoir un accident *to have an accident*

avoir une entrevue *to have an interview*

avril *April*

B

baccalauréat / bac (m.) *baccalauréat (an exam for students wishing to continue their education beyond high school)*

bague (f.) *ring*

  bague de fiançailles *engagement ring*

  bague en diamant *diamond ring*

baguette (f.) *baguette (French bread), chopstick*

baignoire (f.) *bathtub*

balai (m.) *broom*

balle (f.) *ball (small – tennis, etc.)*

ballet (m.) *ballet*

ballon (m.) *ball (large – basketball, etc.)*

banane (f.) *banana*

bandage (m.) *bandage*

banlieue (f.) *suburbs*

  de banlieue *suburban*

banque (f.) *bank*

  employé de banque / employée de banque (m./f.) *bank clerk*

banquier / banquière (m./f.) *banker*

bar (m.) *counter*

bas (m.) *stocking (hose)*

bas / basse (m./f.) *low*

  en bas *downstairs, down below*

baseball (m.) *baseball*

basket (f.) *sneaker, tennis shoe*

basket(-ball) (m.) *basketball*

bateau (m.) *boat, ship*

bâtiment (m.) *building*

  ouvrier en bâtiment / ouvrière en bâtiment (m./f.) *construction worker*

bâtir *to build*

battement (m.) de cœur *heartbeat*

batterie (f.) *drums*

beau / bel / belle (m./m. before a vowel or silent h/f.) *beautiful, handsome, nice*

  Il fait beau. *It's beautiful (outside).*

Beaubourg *Beaubourg (area in Paris and another name for the Pompidou Center)*

beaucoup *many, a lot, much*

  beaucoup de *a lot of, many*

beau-fils (m.) *stepson, son-in-law*

beau-père (m.) *father-in-law, stepfather*

beauté (f.) *beauty*

  institut (m.) de beauté *beauty parlor, beauty salon*

bébé (m.) *baby*

beige *beige, tan (color)*

belge *Belgian*

Belgique (f.) *Belgium*

belle / beau / bel (f./m./m. before a vowel or silent h) *beautiful, handsome, nice*

belle-fille (f.) *stepdaughter, daughter-in-law*

belle-mère (f.) *mother-in-law, stepmother*

Ben... *Oh well ... / Well ...*(infml.)

béquilles (f. pl.) *crutches*

  marcher avec des béquilles *walk with crutches (to)*

besoin (m.) *need*

  avoir besoin de *to need (lit., to have need of)*

beurre (m.) *butter*

  livre (f.) de beurre *pound of butter*

  radis (m. pl.) au beurre *rosette-cut radishes served with butter on top (lit., radishes in butter)*

bibliothèque (f.) *library, bookshelf*

bicyclette (f.) *bicycle*

  monter à bicyclette *to go bike riding, to ride a bike*

bidet (m.) *bidet*

bien *well, good, fine, really, very*

  Ça va bien. *It's going well.*

  très bien *very good, very well*

  Bien sûr. *Of course.*

  Eh bien... *Oh well ... / Well ...*

  J'aime bien... *I like ...*

  Je veux bien... *I want ... / I do want ...*

  Je voudrais bien... *I would like ...*

  J'ai bien... *I do have ...*

  Merci bien. *Thank you very much.*

  Bien entendu. *I do understand. / Completely understood. / Of course.*

ou bien *or even, or else, either, or*

et bien plus *and even more, and much more*

bien au contraire *quite the opposite, quite the contrary*

bien habillé / habillée (m./f.) *well-dressed*
bien que *although*
bientôt *soon*
  À bientôt ! *See you soon!*
Bienvenue. *Welcome.*
bière (f.) *beer*
bijou (m.) *jewel*
  bijoux (m. pl.) *jewelry*
billard (m.) *pool, billiards*
billet (m.) *ticket, banknote, bill (currency)*
  distributeur (m.) de billets *ATM*
biologie (f.) *biology*
bisque (f.) *bisque (creamy soup)*
  bisque de homard *lobster bisque*
bizarre *strange, bizarre*
  C'est bizarre. *It's strange.*
blanc / blanche (m./f.) *white*
  vin (m.) blanc *white wine*
  blouse (f.) blanche *white coat (doctor's coat)*
blancs (m. pl.) (d'œufs) *egg whites*
blessé / blessée (m./f.) *wounded*
blesser *to hurt*
  se blesser *to hurt oneself*
blessure (f.) *injury*
  blessure superficielle *superficial injury*
bleu / bleue (m./f.) *blue*
  truite (f.) au bleu *trout cooked in wine and vinegar*
blond / blonde (m./f.) *blonde*
blouse (f.) *blouse, coat*
  blouse blanche *white coat (doctor's coat)*
bœuf (m.) *beef*
  rôti (m.) de bœuf *roast beef*
boire *to drink*
bois (m.) *wood*
  en bois *wooden*
  Bois de Vincennes *Bois de Vincennes (Vincennes Wood – a large park in Paris)*
  Bois de Boulogne *Bois de Boulogne (Boulogne Wood – a large park in Paris)*
boisson (f.) *drink*
  boisson gazeuse *soft drink*
boîte (f.) *club, nightclub, box*
  boîte de nuit *nightclub*
  sortir en boîte *to go out to clubs, to go out clubbing*
  boîte de conserve (f.) *can*
  boîte (en carton) *carton, can (food)*

bon / bonne (m./f.) *good*
  très bon / bonne (m./f.) *very good*
  Bon appétit. *Bon appetit.*
  Bonne chance. *Good luck.*
  Bon anniversaire ! *Happy birthday!/Happy anniversary!*
  Bonne Année ! *Happy New Year!*
  Bonne nuit ! *Good night!*
  Bonnes Fêtes ! *Happy Holidays!*
  Ah bon... *Oh really .../Oh okay ...*
  moins bon / bonne *not as good*
  bon marché *inexpensive, a good buy*
bonbons (m. pl.) *(pieces of) candy*
bonhomme (m.) de neige *snowman*
Bonjour. *Hello./Good day.*
Bonsoir. *Good evening.*
bord (m.) *border, edge*
  au bord de *at the edge of (at the border of)*
botte (f.) *bundle, bunch*
  botte d'asperges *bunch of asparagus*
bouche (f.) *mouth*
boucherie (f.) *butcher shop*
boucle (f.) d'oreille *earring*
boulangerie (f.) *bakery*
boulevard (m.) *boulevard*
bouquet (m.) *bouquet*
boulot (m.) *job, work*
bout (m.) *end*
  au bout de *at the end of*
bouteille (f.) *bottle*
  bouteille de champagne *bottle of champagne*
boutique (f.) *boutique*
boxe (f.) *boxing*
bracelet (m.) *bracelet*
bras (m.) *arm*
brave *good, courageous, brave*
Bravo. *Well done.*
Brésil (m.) *Brazil*
brésilien / brésilienne (m./f.) *Brazilian*
bricoler *to tinker, to fiddle with things, to fix/ repair things*
brioche *sweet bun*
brique (f.) *carton (for milk/juice), brick (construction)*
brochure (f.) *brochure*
bronzé / bronzée (m./f.) *tan/tanned (from the sun)*
bronzer *to tan, to get a tan*

brosser *to brush*
  se brosser *to brush oneself (hair, teeth, etc.)*
brouillard (m.) *fog*
brouiller *to scramble*
  œufs (m. pl.) **brouillés** *scrambled eggs*
brûlure (f.) *burn*
brun / brune (m./f.) *brown*
brut / brute (m./f.) *dry (alcohol)*
bulletin (m.) **scolaire** *report card*
bureau (m.) *office, desk*
  bureau de poste *post office*
  bureau de change *currency exchange office*
bus (m.) *bus*
  arrêt (m.) **de bus** *bus stop*
but (m.) *goal*

C

c'est *this is, that is, it is*
  C'est nuageux. *It's cloudy.*
  C'est tout ? *Is that all?*
  C'est tout. *That's all.*
  Qu'est-ce que c'est ? *What is this/that?*
  C'est délicieux ! *It's delicious!*
  C'est ennuyeux. *It's boring.*
  C'est bizarre. *It's strange.*
  C'est étrange. *It's strange.*
  C'est parfait. *It's perfect.*
  C'est mauvais. *That's bad.*
ça / c' *this, that, it*
  (Comment) ça va ? *How's it going?/How are you?*
  Ça va. *I'm fine./It's going fine.*
  Ça va bien. *It's going well.*
  Ça va mal. *It's not going well./It's going badly.*
  Ça fait... *That makes .../That is ...*
  Ça coûte... *That costs ...*
  J'aime ça. *I like that./I love that.*
  Ça suffit. *That's enough.*
cabines (f. pl.) **d'essayage** *dressing rooms*
cabinet (m.) **médical** *doctor's office*
câble (m.) *cable*
cache-cache (m.) *hide and seek*
  jouer à cache-cache *to play hide and seek*
cachet (m.) *tablet*
cadet / cadette (m./f.) *youngest child*
café (m.) *café, coffee shop, coffee*
  café-crème (m.) *coffee with cream*
cafétéria (f.) *cafeteria (general)*

cafetière (f.) *coffeemaker*
cahier (m.) *notebook*
caisse (f.) *cash register*
calcul (m.) *calculus*
caleçon (m.) *underpants*
calme *quiet, calm*
camion (m.) *truck*
camper *to go camping*
camping (m.) *camping*
Canada (m.) *Canada*
canadien / canadienne (m./f.) *Canadian*
canapé (m.) *sofa, couch*
canard (m.) *duck*
  canard à l'orange *duck à l'orange, duck with orange sauce*
canne (f.) *cane*
cantine (f.) *school cafeteria*
capsule (f.) *capsule*
carafe (f.) *pitcher*
  carafe d'eau *pitcher of water*
  carafe de vin *pitcher of wine*
caramel (m.) *caramel*
  crème (f.) **caramel** *creamy dessert made with caramel*
carotte (f.) *carrot*
carré (m.) *square, rack (of meat)*
  carré d'agneau (rôti) *(roast) rack of lamb*
carte (f.) *menu, card, map*
  carte des vins *wine list*
  carte de la ville *map of the city*
  carte du métro *map of the subway*
  cartes (pl.) **à jouer** *playing cards*
  La carte, s'il vous plaît. *The menu, please.*
carton (m.) *carton*
cas (m. pl.) **d'urgence** *emergency situations*
casque (m.) *helmet*
casquette (f.) *cap*
casser *to break*
  se casser le bras / la jambe *to break one's arm/leg*
cassis (m.) *black currant*
cathédrale (f.) *cathedral*
  Cathédrale Notre-Dame *Notre Dame Cathedral*
cause (f.) *cause*
  à cause de *because of, as a result of, due to (in a negative way)*
cave (f.) *cellar*

CD-ROM (m.) *CD-ROM*

ce / cet / cette (m./m. before a vowel or silent h/f.) *this, that*

ce soir *tonight, this evening*

ceinture (f.) *belt*

célèbre *famous*

célébrer *to celebrate*

céleri (m.) *celery*

célibataire *single*

celui-ci / celle-ci (m./f.) *this one, this one here*

celui-là / celle-là (m./f.) *that one, that one there*

ceux-ci / celles-ci (m. pl./f. pl.) *these ones, these ones here*

ceux-là / celles-là (m. pl./f. pl.) *those ones, those ones there*

cent *hundred*

cent (m.) *cent*

centre (m.) *center*

centre d'informations *information center*

centre commercial *mall*

Centre National d'Art et de Culture Georges-Pompidou (Centre Pompidou) *National Center of Art and Culture Georges-Pompidou (Pompidou Center)*

cercle (m.) *club*

cerise (f.) *cherry*

certain / certaine (m./f.) *certain*

il est certain que *it is certain that*

certainement *certainly*

cerveau (m.) *brain*

ces *these, those*

cesser *to stop, to cease*

cette / ce / cet (f./m./m. before a vowel or silent h) *this, that*

chacun / chacune (m./f.) *each, each one*

chaîne (f.) hi-fi *sound system*

chaise (f.) *chair*

chaise roulante *wheelchair*

chambre (f.) (à coucher) *bedroom*

champ (m.) *field*

champagne (m.) *champagne*

bouteille (f.) de champagne *bottle of champagne*

champignon (m.) *mushroom*

champion / championne (m./f.) *champion*

chance (f.) *luck*

Pas de chance ! *No luck!*

Bonne chance ! *Good luck!*

changer *to change, to exchange*

changer de chaîne *to change channels*

bureau (m.) de change *currency exchange office*

chanson (f.) *song*

chanter *to sing*

chanteur / chanteuse (m./f.) *singer*

chapeau (m.) *hat*

chaque *each, every*

charcuterie (f.) *delicatessen (store that sells prepared meats)*

charmant / charmante (m./f.) *charming*

charpentier (m.) *carpenter*

chasse (f.) *hunting*

château (m.) *castle*

château de sable *sandcastle*

faire un château de sable *to make/build a sandcastle*

chaud / chaude (m./f.) *hot, warm*

Il fait chaud. *It's hot./It's warm.*

avoir chaud *to be hot/warm (person)*

chocolat (m.) chaud *hot chocolate*

chauffeur (m.) de taxi *taxi driver*

chaussette (f.) *sock*

chaussure (f.) *shoe*

chaussure de basket / tennis *sneaker, tennis shoe*

chef (m.) *boss*

chemin (m.) *path, way*

chemise (f.) *shirt*

chemisier (m.) *blouse*

chèque (m.) *check*

chèque de voyage *traveler's check*

cher / chère (m./f.) *dear, expensive*

chercher *to look for*

chéri / chérie (m./f.) *honey, dear, darling*

cheval (m.) *horse*

monter à cheval *to ride a horse, to go horseback riding*

cheveux (m. pl.) *hair*

cheveu (m.) *hair (single strand)*

avoir les cheveux bruns / blonds / roux / noirs *to have brown/blond/red/black hair*

cheville (f.) *ankle*

chez *at someone's house/place*

chez moi *at my house, at home*

chien (m.) *dog*

chien d'aveugle *seeing-eye dog*
chimie (f.) *chemistry*
Chine (f.) *China*
chinois (m.) *Chinese language*
chinois / chinoise (m./f.) *Chinese*
chocolat (m.) *chocolate*
   gâteau (m.) au chocolat *chocolate cake*
   mousse (f.) au chocolat *chocolate mousse*
   glace (f.) au chocolat *chocolate ice cream*
   chocolat (m.) chaud *hot chocolate*
choisir *to choose*
choix (m.) *choice*
chômage (m.) *unemployment*
   au chômage *unemployed*
chose (f.) *thing*
   Pas grand-chose. *Not a lot.*
   autre chose *something else, anything else*
ci *this, here*
cidre (m.) *cider*
ciel (m.) *sky*
cil (m.) *eyelash*
cinéma (m.) *movie theater, the movies*
cinq *five*
cinquante *fifty*
cinquième *fifth*
circuit (m.) en bus *bus tour*
circulation (f.) *traffic*
cirque (m.) *circus*
citron (m.) *lemon*
   citron vert *lime*
citrouille (f.) *pumpkin*
   tarte (f.) à la citrouille *pumpkin pie*
clam (m.) *clam*
clarinette (f.) *clarinet*
classe (f.) *class, grade, classroom*
   classe terminale *final year of high school*
clavier (m.) *keyboard*
client / cliente (m./f.) *client*
club (m.) *club (organization)*
   centre/club de remise en forme *health club*
cochon (m.) *pig*
code (m.) vestimentaire *dress code*
cœur (m.) *heart*
   battement (m.) de cœur *heartbeat*
   apprendre par cœur *to learn by heart*
coin (m.) *neighborhood, corner*
coïncidence (f.) *coincidence*
   Quelle coïncidence ! *What a coincidence!*

collection (f.) *collection*
collectionner *to collect*
collège (m.) *secondary school, junior high school,
   middle school*
collègue / collègue (m./f.) *colleague*
collier (m.) *necklace*
colline (f.) *hill*
combien *how many, how much*
   C'est combien, s'il vous plaît ? *That's how
   much, please?/It's how much, please?*
comédie (f.) *comedy*
   comédie romantique *romantic comedy*
   comédie musicale *musical*
   comédie de situation *sitcom*
commander *to order*
comme *like, as, how*
   Comme ci, comme ça. *So-so.*
commencer *to begin, to start*
comment *how*
   Comment ? *Pardon?/What did you say?/How?*
   (Comment) ça va ? *How's it going?/How are
   you?*
   Comment allez-vous ? *How are you?* (pl./fml.)
   Comment vas-tu ? *How are you?* (infml.)
   Comment vous appelez-vous ? *What's your
   name?* (pl./fml.)
   Comment t'appelles-tu ? *What's your name?*
   (infml.)
commercial / commerciale (m./f.) *commercial*
   centre (m.) commercial *mall*
compétition (f.) *competition, contest*
complet (m., fml.) *man's suit*
   complet-veston *three-piece suit*
compléter *to complete*
compliqué / compliquée (m./f.) *complicated*
comprendre *to understand*
   Je ne comprends pas. *I don't understand.*
comprimé (m.) *tablet, pill*
comptabilité (f.) *accounting*
   service (m.) de comptabilité *accounting
   department*
comptable / comptable (m./f.) *accountant*
comptoir (m.) *counter*
concert (m.) *concert*
concombre (m.) *cucumber*
concours (m.) *competititon, contest*
conduire *to drive*
confiserie (f.) *candy store*

pâtisserie-confiserie (f.) *pastry and candy store*

confiture (f.) *jelly, jam, marmalade*

confortable *comfortable*

connaissance (f.) *acquaintance*

Enchanté / Enchantée (de faire votre connaissance). *Pleased to meet you./Nice to meet you.*

Je suis ravi / ravie de faire votre connaissance. *I'm delighted to make your acquaintance.*

connaître *to know, to be familiar with*

consommé (m.) *consommé (clear soup made from stock)*

consommé aux vermicelles *noodle soup (vermicelli pasta consommé)*

construire *to construct*

consulter *to consult*

consulter l'annuaire *to consult a phone book*

contraire *opposite, contrary*

bien au contraire *quite the opposite, quite the contrary*

cool *cool (great)*

copain / copine (m./f.) *boyfriend/girlfriend*

coq (m.) *rooster*

coq au vin *chicken/rooster cooked in wine*

coque (f.) *shell*

œuf (m.) à la coque *soft-boiled egg*

coquilles (f. pl.) Saint-Jacques *scallops*

corps (m.) *body*

corps humain *human body*

parties (f. pl.) du corps *body parts*

costume (m.) *suit*

côte (f.) *chop, rib, coast*

côte de porc *pork chop*

côté (m.) *side*

à côté *at the side, on the side, to the side*

à côté de *next to*

de l'autre côté de *on the other side of*

coton (m.) *cotton*

cou (m.) *neck (necks)*

coucher *to lay down, to put someone to bed*

se coucher *to go to bed, to lie down (to lie oneself down)*

chambre (f.) (à coucher) *bedroom*

coude (m.) *elbow*

couloir (m.) *hallway, corridor/hall*

coupure (f.) *cut*

cour (f.) de récréation *schoolyard, playground*

courir *to run*

courir le marathon *to run the marathon*

courriel (m.) *e-mail*

courrier (m.) électronique *e-mail*

cours (m.) *course, class*

cours de français *French class*

cours de danse *dance class*

réussir à un cours *to pass a class, to do well in a class*

course (f.) *errand, run, race*

course à pied *running*

faire des / les courses *to shop*

course automobile *auto racing, car racing*

court / courte (m./f.) *short*

cousin / cousine (m./f.) *cousin*

couteau (m.) *knife*

coûter *to cost*

Combien ça coûte, s'il vous plaît ? *How much does that cost, please?*

couture (f.) *sewing*

haute couture *high fashion*

couturier (m.) *fashion designer*

couvert (m.) *table setting*

cravate (f.) *tie*

crémant (m.) *type of French sparkling wine*

crème (f.) *cream, creamy dessert*

crème à raser *shaving cream*

crème caramel *creamy dessert made with caramel*

crème chantilly *whipped cream (that is flavored and sweetened)*

crème de marrons *chestnut paste*

crêpe (f.) *crêpe (tissue-thin pancake)*

crêpe Suzette *Crêpe suzette (crêpe with sugar, orange, and liqueur)*

crevettes (f. pl.) *shrimp*

crise (f.) cardiaque *heart attack*

croire *to believe*

croissant *croissant*

croque-madame (m.) *grilled ham and cheese sandwich with an egg on top*

croque-monsieur (m.) *grilled ham and cheese sandwich*

cru / crue (m./f.) *raw*

crudités (f. pl.) *crudités (French appetizer of raw, mixed vegetables)*

cruel / cruelle (m./f.) *cruel*

cuiller / cuillère (f.) *spoon*
cuir (m.) *leather*
cuisine (f.) *kitchen, cooking*
   faire la cuisine *to cook, to do the cooking*
cuisiner *to cook*
cuisinier / cuisinière (m./f.) *cook*
cuisinière (f.) *stove, cook*
cyclisme (m.) *cycling*

D

dame (f.) *lady*
dames (f. pl.) *checkers*
dans *in, into*
   dans un mois *next month, in one month*
   dans une semaine *next week, in one week*
   dans deux semaines *the week after next, in two weeks*
danse (f.) *dancing, dance*
danser *to dance*
danseur / danseuse (m./f.) *dancer*
   danseur / danseuse de ballet, ballerine *ballet dancer*
date (f.) *date*
de / d' *of, for, from*
   de la / de l' / du / des (f./m. or f. before a vowel or silent h/m./pl.) *of the, some*
   d'ici *from here, by, until*
   d'ici là *by then, from now on, from now until, until then*
   D'accord. *Okay./All right.*
   D'abord... *First ...*
   De rien. *You're welcome./It's nothing.*
   de l'autre côté de *on the other side of*
   de ma part *on my behalf, from me, on my part*
   de la part de *on behalf of, from (someone)*
   C'est de la part de qui ? *Who's calling? (on the phone)*
   de quel / quelle ? (m./f.) *what?/of what?*
   de temps en temps *from time to time, occasionally*
   de toute façon *at any rate, in any case, anyhow*
debout *standing (up)*
débutant / débutante (m./f.) *beginner*
décembre *December*
décider *to decide*
   se décider *to make up one's mind, to be decided, to be resolved (to do something)*

décontracté / décontractée (m./f.) *casual*
décrocher *to pick up (the phone)*
défendre *to defend*
défiler *to march*
degré (m.) *degree*
dehors *outside*
déjà *already*
déjeuner *to have lunch*
déjeuner (m.) *lunch*
   petit déjeuner (m.) *breakfast (lit., little lunch)*
délicieux / délicieuse (m./f.) *delicious*
demain *tomorrow*
   après-demain *the day after tomorrow*
demander *to ask, to ask for*
   se demander *to wonder, to ask oneself*
déménager *to move out*
demi / demie (m./f.) *half*
   ... et demie *half past ...*
demi-heure (f.) *half hour*
dent (f.) *tooth*
dentiste (m./f.) *dentist*
déodorant (m.) *deodorant*
départ (m.) *departure*
   heure (f.) du départ *departure time*
dépêcher *to dispatch*
   se dépêcher *to hurry*
depuis *since, for*
   depuis quand ? *since when?*
   depuis combien de temps ? *(for) how long?*
dernier / dernière (m./f.) *last, final, latest*
   lundi dernier *last Monday*
   mois (m.) dernier *last month*
   été (m.) dernier *last summer*
   nuit (f.) dernière *last night*
   année (f.) dernière *last year*
   la dernière fois *the last time, the final time*
derrière *behind*
des *some (pl.), of the (pl.), plural of un / une*
descendre *to go down, to come down, to descend*
   Où dois-je descendre ? *Where do I have to get off?/Where should I get off?*
description (f.) *description*
désert (m.) *desert*
désirer *to want, to wish*
désobéir *to disobey*
désolé / désolée (m./f.) *sorry*
   Je suis désolé / désolée. *I am sorry.*
dessert (m.) *dessert*

dessin (m.) *drawing*
dessin animé *animated movie*
dessous *underneath*
dessus *on top*
détester *to hate, to detest*
deux *two*
 deux fois *twice, two times*
deuxième *second*
 deuxième base (f.) *second base*
devant *in front (of), ahead, before*
devenir *to become*
devoir *to have to, must, should, to owe*
devoirs (m. pl.) *homework*
diagnostic (m.) *diagnosis*
diamant (m.) *diamond*
 bague (f.) en diamant *diamond ring*
d'ici *from here, by, until*
 d'ici demain *by tomorrow, until tomorrow*
 d'ici la fin de la semaine *by the end of the week, until the end of the week*
 d'ici là *by then, from now on, from now until, until then*
dieu (m.) *god*
 Mon dieu ! *My god!*
différent / différente (m./f.) *different*
difficile *difficult*
dimanche *Sunday*
dîner *to dine, to have dinner*
dîner (m.) *dinner*
diplôme (m.) *diploma*
 diplôme universitaire *college degree*
dire *to say, to tell*
 Dis donc ! *Man!/You don't say!/Say! (lit., Say so!)*
directeur / directrice (m./f.) *director, manager*
 directeur / directrice du personnel *human resources manager, personnel manager*
direction (f.) *direction, way, management*
discothèque (f.) *(night)club*
distributeur (m.) de billets *ATM*
divertissement (m.) *entertainment*
divorce (m.) *divorce*
divorcer *to get a divorce*
dix *ten*
dix-huit *eighteen*
dixième *tenth*
dix-neuf *nineteen*
dix-sept *seventeen*

docteur / doctoresse (m./f.) *doctor*
document (m.) *document*
documentaire (m.) *documentary*
doigt (m.) *finger*
 doigt de pied *toe*
donc *so, then, therefore*
 Dis donc ! *Man!/You don't say!/Say! (lit., Say so!)*
donner *to give, to show*
 donner un coup de fil *to make a phone call (lit., to give/pass a hit of the wire) (infml.)*
 donner un coup de pied *to kick (lit., to give a kick)*
dont *whom, whose, of which, of whom*
dos (m.) *back*
doublé / doublée (m./f.) *dubbed*
doucement *gently, softly, sweetly*
douche (f.) *shower*
 gel (m.) douche *shower gel*
douleur (f.) *pain, sorrow*
douter que *to doubt that*
doux / douce (m./f.) *sweet, gentle, soft*
douzaine (f.) *dozen*
 douzaine d'œufs *dozen eggs*
douze *twelve*
drame (m.) *drama*
 drame d'époque *period drama*
drapeau (m.) *flag*
droit *straight*
 tout droit *straight ahead*
 Il faut aller tout droit. *You must go straight ahead.*
droite (f.) *right (opposite of left)*
 à droite *on the right, to the right, at the right*
 rive (f.) droite *right bank*
drôle *funny*
 si drôle *so funny*
du / de l' / de la / des (m./m. or f. before a vowel or silent h/f./pl.) *some, of the*
dur / dure (m./f.) *hard*
 œuf (m.) dur *hard-boiled egg (lit., hard egg)*

E

eau (f.) *water*
 eau de cologne *cologne*
 eau de Javel *bleach*
 eau minérale *mineral water*
 carafe (f.) d'eau *pitcher of water*

écharpe (f.) *scarf (long)*
échecs (m. pl.) *chess*
échouer à (un examen / cours) *to fail (a test/ class)*
éclair (m.) *lightning, éclair (type of cream-filled pastry)*
école (f.) *school*
   école maternelle *nursery school, preschool*
   école primaire *elementary school, primary school*
écossais / écossaise (m./f.) *Scottish*
Écosse (f.) *Scotland*
écouter *to listen (to)*
écran (m.) *monitor, screen*
écrire *to write*
écrivain (m.) (sometimes: écrivaine, f.) *writer*
effet (m.) secondaire *side effect*
effrayant / effrayante (m./f.) *scary*
égal / égale (m./f.) *equal*
église (f.) *church*
électricien (m.) *electrician*
élégant / élégante (m./f.) *elegant*
éléphant (m.) *elephant*
élève (m./f.) *student, pupil*
elle *she, it* (f.), *her*
elles *they* (f.), *it* (f. pl.), *them* (f.)
e-mail (m.) *e-mail*
émission (f.) *television program*
emmener *to take (someone) along*
emploi (m.) *employment, job*
   emploi régulier *steady job*
   emploi saisonnier *summer job*
   sans emploi *unemployed*
employé / employée (m./f.) *employee, worker*
   employé de banque / employée de banque *bank clerk*
employer *to use, to employ*
en *in, into, to, some, of it, of them*
   en effet *really, indeed*
   en avance *early*
   en face de *across from, facing*
   en général *in general, generally, usually*
   en haut *upstairs, up above*
   en bas *downstairs, down below*
   en retard *late*
   en solde *on sale*
   en grève *on strike*
   en tenue de soirée *formal, in formal dress/*

   attire
Enchanté. / Enchantée. (m./f.) *Pleased to meet you./Nice to meet you.*
encore *again, still, more*
   ne... pas encore *not yet*
enfant (m./f.) *child*
enfin *finally*
enlever *to remove, to take off*
ennuyer *to annoy, to bore (someone)*
   s'ennuyer *to get bored, to be bored*
   C'est ennuyeux. *It's boring.*
énorme *enormous*
enseignant / enseignante (m./f.) *teacher*
enseigner *to teach*
ensemble *together*
ensemble (m.) *outfit*
ensuite *then, next*
entendre *to understand, to hear*
   Entendu. *All right./Understood.*
   s'entendre avec *get along with (to)*
   s'entendre bien avec *get along well with (to)*
entraînement (m.) *workout, training*
entraîneur (m.) *coach*
entre *between*
entrée (f.) *appetizer, entrance*
entrer *to enter, to come in*
   Entre ! / Entrez ! *Come in! (infml./pl., fml.)*
entrevue (f.) *interview*
envie (f.) *desire*
   avoir envie de *to feel like (lit., to have desire for)*
envoyer *to send, to throw*
   envoyer en pièce jointe *to attach a file*
   envoyer un fichier *to send a file*
   envoyer un mail / mèl / e-mail / courriel / courrier électronique *to send an e-mail*
épaule (f.) *shoulder*
épicerie (f.) *grocery store*
épinards (m. pl.) *spinach*
éponger *to mop, to soak up*
épouser (quelqu'un) *to marry (someone)*
équipe (f.) *team*
   équipe de rugby *rugby team*
équitation (f.) *horseback riding*
   faire de l'équitation *to go horseback riding*
erreur (f.) *mistake*
escaliers (m. pl.) *stairs*
escargots (m. pl.) *snails, escargots*

Espagne (f.) *Spain*
espagnol (m.) *Spanish language*
espagnol / espagnole (m./f.) *Spanish*
espérer *to hope*
essai (m.) *touchdown*
essayer *to try, to try on/out*
essentiel / essentielle (m./f.) *essential*
  il est essentiel que *it is essential that*
est (m.) *east*
est-ce...? *is it ...?*
esthéticien / esthéticienne (m./f.) *beautician*
estomac (m.) *stomach, abdomen*
et *and*
étage (m.) *floor (as in, second floor, third floor, etc.)*
  premier étage *first floor (one floor above the ground floor)*
étagère (f.) *shelf, bookshelf*
étang (m.) *pond*
état (m.) *state*
  États-Unis (m. pl.) *United States*
été (m.) *summer*
  en été *in (the) summer*
  été dernier *last summer*
étoile (f.) *star*
étrange *strange*
  C'est étrange. *It's strange.*
être *to be*
  peut-être *maybe, possibly*
  être fiancé / fiancée (à) (m./f.) *to be engaged (to)*
  être aveugle *to be blind*
  être en forme *to be fit, to be in shape*
  être en pleine / bonne forme *to be in good shape*
  être en pleine expansion *to be growing (business)*
  être en sueur *to be sweating*
  être en nage *to be sweating*
  être en train de *to be in the middle of, to be in the process of*
  être handicapé / handicapée (m./f.) *to be disabled*
  être malade *to be sick*
  être occupé / occupée (m./f.) *to be busy*
  être paralysé / paralysée (m./f.) *to be paralyzed*
  être sans emploi, être sans travail *to be unemployed*
  être sourd / sourde (m./f.) *to be deaf*
  être membre de *to be a member of*
être (m.) humain *human being*
étudiant / étudiante (m./f.) *student*
  étudiant / étudiante en médecine *medical student*
étudier *to study*
euro (m.) *euro*
européen / européenne (m./f.) *European*
  Union (f.) européenne *European Union*
eux *them* (m.)
évier (m.) *sink*
  évier de la cuisine *kitchen sink*
exact / exacte (m./f.) *exact, correct*
examen (m.) *test, exam, examination*
  rater un examen *to fail a test*
  échouer à un examen *to fail a test*
  réussir à un examen *to pass a test*
  examen médical *medical checkup*
examiner *to examine*
excellent / excellente (m./f.) *excellent*
excursion (f.) *tour, excursion*
  excursion en autocar *bus tour*
excuser *to excuse*
  Excusez-moi. *Excuse me.*
exiger que *to demand that*
expression (f.) *expression*
extérieur (m.) *outside, exterior*
extra *great*
extra-scolaire *extracurricular*
  activités (f. pl.) extra-scolaires *extracurricular activities*

F

face (f.) *face, side*
  en face de *across from, facing*
facile *easy*
facilement *easily*
façon (f.) *way, manner, fashion*
  de toute façon *at any rate, in any case, anyhow*
faible *weak*
faim (f.) *hunger*
  avoir faim *to be hungry*
faire *to do, to make*
  faire la cuisine *to do the cooking, to cook*
  faire la lessive *to do the laundry*

faire la vaisselle *to do the dishes*
faire le ménage *to do the house cleaning, to clean the house*
faire les / des courses *to do the shopping, to go shopping, to shop*
faire des achats *to run errands*
faire la queue *to wait in line*
faire un tour *to take/do a tour*
faire du sport *to play a sport, to do a sport*
faire du foot(ball) *to play soccer, to do soccer*
faire match nul *to tie (in a game/match)*
faire de la natation *to go swimming, to swim*
faire du ski *to ski, to go skiing*
faire du ski nautique *to water-ski, to go water-skiing*
faire de la plongée sous-marine *to go scuba diving*
faire une promenade *to take a walk*
faire une réservation *to make a reservation*
faire des réservations *to make reservations*
faire de l'équitation *to do horseback riding, to go horseback riding*
faire de la musculation *to do strength training, to lift weights, to do bodybuilding*
faire du camping *to camp, to go camping*
faire de la marche *to go hiking*
faire du jogging *to go jogging*
faire du vélo d'appartement *to ride a stationary bike*
faire du yoga *to do yoga*
faire mal *to hurt*
faire partie de *to be a member of*
faire un château de sable *to make/build a sandcastle*
faire un pique-nique *to go on a picnic*
faire (la) grève *to strike*
faire une demande d'emploi *to apply for a job*
faire une faute / erreur *to make a mistake*
faire suivre *to forward*
Ça fait... *That makes ... /That is ...*
Il fait beau. *It's beautiful (outside).*
Il fait chaud. *It's hot./It's warm.*
Il fait froid. *It's cold.*
Il fait (du) soleil. *It's sunny.*
Il fait du vent. *It's windy.*
falloir *to be necessary*
il faut *it's necessary to, you have/need to, you must*

il faut que *it is necessary that*
s'il le faut *if necessary, if needed*
famille (f.) *family*
faute (f.) *mistake*
faute d'orthographe *spelling mistake*
fauteuil (m.) *armchair*
faux / fausse (m./f.) *false, wrong*
favori / favorite (m./f.) *favorite*
Félicitations. *Congratulations.*
femme (f.) *woman, wife*
femme d'affaires *businesswoman*
femme au foyer *homemaker* (f.)
fenêtre (f.) *window*
fer (m.) à repasser *iron*
fermer *to close*
fermer un fichier *to close a file*
fermier / fermière (m./f.) *farmer*
fête (f.) *party, festival, holiday*
fête nationale *national holiday*
Bonnes / Joyeuses Fêtes ! *Happy Holidays!*
feu (m.) *fire*
feuilleton (m.) (télévisé) *TV series*
février *February*
fiancé / fiancée (m./f.) *fiancé/fiancée*
être fiancé / fiancée (à) *to be engaged (to)*
bague (f.) de fiançailles *engagement ring*
fichier (m.) *file*
fier / fière (m./f.) *proud*
fièvre (f.) *fever*
figure (f.) *face*
fille (f.) *girl, daughter*
fille unique *only child* (f.)
film (m.) *movie, film*
film d'action *action film*
film policier *crime drama/film, detective drama/film*
film à suspense *thriller*
film d'épouvante *horror movie*
fils (m.) *son*
fils unique *only child* (m.)
fin (f.) *end*
fin du match *end of the game, end of the match*
Vivement la fin de la journée ! *Can't wait for the end of the day!*
finir *to finish*
firme (f.) *company, firm*
fleur (f.) *flower*

flûte (f.) *flute*
fois (f.) *time*
 une fois *once, one time*
 la dernière fois *the last time, the final time*
fonctionnaire / fonctionnaire (m./f.) *civil servant*
foot(ball) (m.) *soccer*
football (m.) américain *(American) football*
footballeur / footballeuse (m./f.) *soccer player*
forêt (f.) *forest*
forme (f.) *form, shape, figure*
Formidable. *Fantastic.*
fort / forte (m./f.) *strong*
foulard (m.) *scarf (fashion)*
foule (f.) *crowd*
four (m.) *oven*
fourchette (f.) *fork*
foyer (m.) *home*
 homme au foyer / femme au foyer (m./ f.) *homemaker*
fraise (f.) *strawberry*
 glace (f.) à la fraise *strawberry ice cream*
 tarte (f.) aux fraises *strawberry pie*
français (m.) *French language*
 en français *in French*
français / française (m./f.) *French*
France (f.) *France*
franchement *frankly, honestly*
fréquemment *frequently*
frère (m.) *brother*
frites (f. pl.) *french fries*
 moules (f. pl.) frites *mussels and fries*
 poulet (m.) frites *chicken and fries*
 steak (m.) frites *steak and fries*
froid / froide (m./f.) *cold*
 Il fait froid. *It's cold.*
 avoir froid *to be cold (person)*
fromage (m.) *cheese*
 sandwich (m.) au fromage *cheese sandwich*
 sandwich (m.) jambon-fromage *ham and cheese sandwich*
 tranche (f.) de fromage *slice of cheese*
front (m.) *forehead*
fruit (m.) *fruit*
 salade (f.) de fruits *fruit salad*

G

gagner *to win, to earn*
 gagner de l'argent *to earn money*
 gagner un match *to win a game, to win a match*
galerie (f.) *gallery*
gant (m.) *glove*
garage (m.) *garage*
garçon (m.) *boy*
gare (f.) *train station*
gastronomie (f.) *gastronomy*
gâteau (m.) *cake*
 gâteau au chocolat *chocolate cake*
gauche (f.) *left*
 à gauche *on the left, to the left, at the left*
 rive (f.) gauche *left bank*
gaufre (f.) *waffle*
gel (m.) douche *shower gel*
général / générale (m./f.) *general*
généralement *generally*
généreux / généreuse (m./f.) *generous*
genou (m.) *knee*
genre *kind, type, genre*
gens (m. pl.) *people*
gentil / gentille (m./f.) *nice, kind*
géométrie (f.) *geometry*
gérant / gérante (m./f.) *manager*
glace (f.) *ice cream, ice*
 glace à la vanille *vanilla ice cream*
 glace à la fraise *strawberry ice cream*
 glace au chocolat *chocolate ice cream*
 hockey (m.) sur glace *ice hockey*
 patin (m.) à glace *ice skating, ice skate*
 patinage (m.) sur glace *ice skating*
golf (m.) *golf*
gorge (f.) *throat*
gourmand (m.) *lover of food, gourmand*
gourmet (m.) *gourmet, lover of fine food*
goût (m.) *taste*
grâce à... *thanks to ...*
grain (m.) de beauté *mole*
grammaire (f.) *grammar*
gramme (m.) *gram*
grand / grande (m./f.) *big, large, tall*
 grand magasin (m.) *department store*
 grandes vacances (f. pl.) *summer vacation*
 Pas grand-chose. *Not a lot.*

grandir *to grow*
grand-mère (f.) *grandmother*
grand-parent (m.) *grandparent*
grand-père (m.) *grandfather*
gratiné / gratinée (m./f.) *topped with browned cheese (and possibly also breadcrumbs)*
grave *serious*
  Ce n'est pas grave. *It's not serious./It's not a problem./It's not a big deal./Don't worry about it.*
grec / grecque (m./f.) *Greek*
Grèce (f.) *Greece*
grêle (f.) *hail*
  Il grêle. *It's hailing.*
grève (m.) *strike*
  en grève *on strike*
  faire (la) grève *to strike*
grippe (f.) *flu*
gros / grosse (m./f.) *fat*
grossir *to gain weight*
groupe (m.) de musique *band*
guérir *to cure, to get better*
guichet (m.) *ticket window, counter, window, box office*
  guichet automatique *ATM*
guichetier (m.) *clerk (at the window/counter), teller*
guide (m.) *guide*
guitare (f.) *guitar*
gym / gymnastique (f.) *gym (physical education), gymnastics*
gymnase (m.) *gym (place)*

H

habillé / habillée (m./f.) *dressed*
  bien habillé / habillée (m./f.) *well-dressed*
habiller *to dress*
  s'habiller *to dress oneself, to get dressed*
habiter *to live*
habitude (f.) *habit*
  d'habitude *usually*
haie (f.) *hurdle*
haine (f.) *hatred*
haltérophilie (f.) *weight lifting*
handicapé / handicapée (m./f.) *disabled*
Hanoukka / Hanoucca (f.) *Hanukkah*
haricot (m.) *bean*
  haricot vert *green bean*

hasard (m.) *chance*
hâte (f.) *haste*
  avoir hâte *to look forward to (can't wait)*
hâter *to hasten*
  se hâter *to rush*
haut / haute (m./f.) *high*
  en haut *upstairs, up above*
  haute couture *high fashion*
hériter *to inherit*
héros / héroïne (m./f.) *hero/heroine*
heure (f.) *hour*
  Quelle heure est-il ? *What time is it?*
  heure du départ *departure time*
  heure de l'arrivée *arrival time*
  à l'heure *on time*
  à quelle heure ? *at what time?*
  À tout à l'heure ! *See you later!*
heureusement *happily, fortunately*
heureux / heureuse (m./f.) *happy*
hier *yesterday*
  avant-hier *the day before yesterday*
  hier soir *last night*
histoire (f.) *story, history, tale*
hiver (m.) *winter*
  en hiver *in (the) winter*
hockey (m.) *hockey*
  hockey sur glace *ice hockey*
homard (m.) *lobster*
  bisque (f.) de homard *lobster bisque*
homme (m.) *man*
  homme d'affaires *businessman*
  homme au foyer *homemaker (m.)*
honte (f.) *shame*
  avoir honte *to be ashamed*
hôpital (m.) *hospital*
horaire (m.) *schedule*
horrible *horrible*
hors *outside*
hors-d'œuvre (m.) *appetizer*
hôtel (m.) *hotel*
  hôtel de ville *city hall, town hall, municipal building*
huile (f.) *oil*
huit *eight*
huitième *eighth*
huître (f.) *oyster*
humain / humaine (m./f.) *human, humane*
  être (m.) humain *human being*

I

ici *here*
 d'ici *from here, by, until*
 d'ici là *by then, from now on, from now until, until then*
 par ici *this way*
idée (f.) *idea*
 Quelle bonne idée ! *What a good idea!*
il *he, it* (m.)
 Il fait beau. *It's beautiful (outside).*
 Il fait chaud. *It's hot./It's warm.*
 Il fait froid. *It's cold.*
 Il fait (du) soleil. *It's sunny.*
 Il fait du vent. *It's windy.*
 Il grêle. *It's hailing.*
 Il neige. *It's snowing.*
 Il pleut. *It's raining./It rains.*
 Il est temps de... *It is time to .../Now is the time to ...*
 il faut *it's necessary to, you have/need to, you must*
 il faut que *it is necessary that*
 il vaut mieux *it is better, it would be better*
 il vaut mieux que *it is better that, it would be better that*
 il est certain que *it is certain that*
 il est vrai que *it is true that*
 il est possible que *it is possible that*
 il est probable que *it is probable that*
 il semble que *it seems that*
 il est urgent que *it is urgent that*
 il est essentiel que *it is essential that*
 il est important que *it is important that*
 il est nécessaire que *it is necessary that*
 il est préférable que *it is preferable that*
il y a *there is/are, ago*
 il y avait *there was/were*
 Il n'y a pas de quoi. *You're welcome.*
 Il y a du soleil. *It's sunny.*
 Il y a du vent. *It's windy.*
Île (f.) de la Cité *Île de la Cité (City Island)*
ils *they (m./mixed), it (m. pl.)*
immeuble (m.) *apartment building, office building*
imperméable (m.) *raincoat*
important / importante (m./f.) *important*
 il est important que *it is important that*

importer *to matter*
 n'importe quoi / qui / où *whatever/whoever/ wherever, anything/anyone/anywhere*
imprimante (f.) *printer*
Inde (f.) *India*
indien / indienne (m./f.) *Indian*
individu (m.) *individual*
infection (f.) *infection*
infirmier / infirmière (m./f.) *nurse*
inflammation (f.) *inflammation*
informaticien / informaticienne (m./f.) *computer programmer*
informatique (f.) *IT, computer science*
 service (m.) d'informatique *IT department*
ingénieur (m.) *engineer*
injection (f.) *shot, injection*
inquiet / inquiète (m./f.) *worried (anxious)*
institut (m.) de beauté *beauty parlor, beauty salon*
instructions (f. pl.) *instructions*
intelligent / intelligente (m./f.) *intelligent*
intéressant / intéressante (m./f.) *interesting*
intéresser *to interest*
 s'intéresser à *to be interested in*
 Ça m'intéresse. *That interests me.*
 Ça ne m'intéresse pas. *That doesn't interest me.*
Internet (m.) *internet*
interrompre *to interrupt*
intersection (f.) *intersection*
inviter *to invite*
irlandais / irlandaise (m./f.) *Irish*
Irlande (f.) *Ireland*
Italie (f.) *Italy*
italien / italienne (m./f.) *Italian*

J

jamais *ever, never*
 ne... jamais *never*
jambe (f.) *leg*
jambon (m.) *ham*
 sandwich (m.) au jambon *ham sandwich*
 sandwich (m.) jambon-fromage *ham and cheese sandwich*
janvier *January*
Japon (m.) *Japan*
japonais / japonaise (m./f.) *Japanese*
jardin (m.) *garden*

jaune *yellow*
je / j' *I*
   Je m'appelle... *My name is .../I am called ...*
   Je ne comprends pas. *I don't understand.*
   Je vais très bien. *I'm very well.*
   Je veux... *I want ...*
   Je voudrais... *I would like ...*
   Je te présente... / Je vous présente... *Let me introduce ... (infml./pl., fml.)*
   Je vous en prie. *You're welcome. (fml.)*
   Je suis ravi / ravie de faire votre connaissance. *I'm delighted to make your acquaintance.*
jean (m.) *jeans*
jeter *to throw, to throw out/away*
jeu (m.) *game*
   jeu électronique *electronic game*
   jeu vidéo *video game*
   jeu de cartes *card game*
jeudi *Thursday*
jeune *young*
Joconde (f.) *Mona Lisa*
joli / jolie (m./f.) *nice, pretty*
joue (f.) *cheek*
jouer *to play, to perform, to act*
   jouer à cache-cache *to play hide and seek*
   jouer un match *to play a game, to play a match*
   cartes (f. pl.) **à jouer** *playing cards*
joueur / joueuse (m./f.) *player (games, sports, etc.)*
jour (m.) *day*
   jour de l'An *New Year's Day*
   jours (pl.) **de la semaine** *days of the week*
journal (m.) *newspaper*
journaliste (m./f.) *journalist*
journée (f.) *day*
   Vivement la fin de la journée ! *Can't wait for the end of the day!*
joyeux / joyeuse (m./f.) *joyful, cheerful*
   Joyeuses Fêtes ! *Happy Holidays!*
   Joyeux anniversaire ! *Happy birthday!/ Happy anniversary!*
   Joyeux Noël ! *Merry Christmas!*
juillet *july*
   14 (Quatorze) Juillet *Bastille Day, July 14th (France's national holiday)*
juin *June*

jupe (f.) *skirt*
juridique *legal (related to the law)*
   service (m.) **juridique** *legal department*
   langage (m.) **juridique** *legal language, legal terminology*
jus (m.) *juice*
   brique (f.) **de jus d'orange** *carton of orange juice*
jusqu'à *to, until, up to, up until*
   jusqu'à ce que *until*
juste *just, only*

K

kilo (m.) *kilo*
kilomètre (m.) *kilometer*
kir (m.) *white wine with black currant liqueur*
   kir royal *champagne with black currant liqueur*

L

là *there*
   là-bas *over there, there*
la / l' / le / les (f./m. or f. before a vowel or silent h/m./pl.) *the*
   la / le / les moins... *the least ...*
   la / le / les plus... *the most ...*
la / l' *her, it (f. direct object pronoun)*
laboratoire (m.) *laboratory*
lac (m.) *lake*
laid / laide (m./f.) *ugly*
laisser *to leave, to let (someone do something), to let go*
   Je voudrais laisser un message. *I would like to leave a message.*
lait (m.) *milk*
   verre (m.) **de lait** *glass of milk*
laitue (f.) *lettuce*
lampadaire (m.) *streetlight*
lampe (f.) *lamp*
lancer les dés *to roll the dice*
langage (m.) *language*
   langage des signes *sign language*
   langage courant *everyday language*
   langage du corps *body language*
   langage enfantin *baby talk (baby language)*
   langage familier *informal language, familiar language*
   langage soutenu *formal language*

langage grossier *bad language*
langage juridique *legal language, legal terminology,*
langage de programmation informatique *programming language*
langue (f.) *language, tongue*
langue étrangère *foreign language*
laquelle / lequel (f./m.) *which*
large *wide*
lavabo (m.) *sink*
lave-linge (m.) *washing machine*
laver *to wash*
se laver *to wash up, to wash oneself*
lave-vaisselle (m.) *dishwasher*
le / l' / la / les (m./m. or f. before a vowel or silent h/f./pl.) *the*
le / la / les moins... *the least ...*
le / la / les plus... *the most ...*
le / l' *him, it* (m. direct object pronoun)
leçon (f.) *lesson*
lecteur (m.) *player (CDs, DVDs, etc.), drive (computer)*
lecteur de CD *CD player*
lecteur de DVD *DVD player*
lecteur de CD-ROM *CD-ROM drive*
lecture *reading*
léger / légère (m./f.) *light*
légèrement *lightly*
légume (m.) *vegetable*
lent / lente (m./f.) *slow*
lentement *slowly*
Parlez plus lentement, s'il vous plaît. *Speak slower/more slowly, please.*
lentille (f.) *lens*
lentilles (pl.) de contact *contact lenses*
lequel / laquelle (m./f.) *which*
les *the* (pl.)
les moins... *the least ...* (pl.)
les plus... *the most ...* (pl.)
les *them, it* (pl. direct object pronoun)
lessive (f.) *laundry detergent*
lettre (f.) *letter*
leur *their, to them/it* (pl.) (indirect object pronoun)
leurs *their* (pl.)
lever *to lift, to raise, to pick up*
se lever *to get up, to rise (to get oneself up)*
liaison (f.) *link*
librairie (f.) *bookstore*

libre *free*
licence (f.) *bachelor's degree*
lieu (m.) *place*
avoir lieu *to take place, to be held (lit., to have place)*
liquide (m.) vaisselle *dishwashing detergent*
lire *to read*
lit (m.) *bed*
littérature (f.) *literature*
littérature anglaise *English literature*
livre (f.) *pound*
livre de beurre *pound of butter*
livre (m.) *book*
livre scolaire *textbook*
logiciel (m.) *software*
loin *far*
loin d'ici *far from here*
plus loin *farther*
loisirs (m. pl.) *leisure activities, recreation*
long / longue (m./f.) *long*
le long de *along, alongside*
longtemps *long time, for a long time, long*
il y a longtemps *a long time ago*
loup (f.) *wolf*
Louvre (m.) *Louvre*
musée (m.) du Louvre *Louvre museum*
lui *him, to him/her/it* (indirect object pronoun)
lundi *Monday*
lundi dernier *last Monday*
lune (f.) *moon*
lunettes (f. pl.) *(eye)glasses*
lunettes de soleil *sunglasses*
lustre (m.) *chandelier*
Lutèce (f.) *Lutetia (old name for Paris)*
lutte (f.) *wrestling*
lycée (m.) *high school*
lycéen / lycéenne (m./f.) *high school student*

M

M. *Mr.*
ma / mon / mes (f./m./pl.) *my*
macaron (m.) *meringue cookie*
machine (f.) à laver *washing machine*
madame *ma'am, Mrs., Ms., madam*
mesdames *ladies*
mademoiselle *miss*
mesdemoiselles *misses*
magasin (m.) *store*

grand magasin *department store*
magasin d'électronique *electronics store*
magasin de chaussures *shoe store*
magasin de vêtements *clothing store*
magazine (m.) *magazine*
magnifique *magnificent*
mai *May*
maigrir *to lose weight*
mail (m.) *e-mail*
maillot (m.) (de bain) *bathing suit, bathing trunks*
maillot (m.) de corps *undershirt*
main (f.) *hand*
maintenant *now*
maire (m.) *mayor*
mairie (f.) *city hall, municipal building*
mais *but*
maïs (m.) *corn*
maison *homemade*
maison (f.) *house, home*
  à la maison *at the house, at home*
maître-nageur (f.) *lifeguard*
maîtrise (f.) *master's degree*
mal *badly, bad, wrong*
  Ça va mal. *It's going badly./It's not going well.*
malade *sick*
maladie (f.) *illness, disease*
  maladie d'Alzheimer *Alzheimer's disease*
  maladie de Parkinson *Parkinson's disease*
malheureusement *unfortunately, unhappily*
malheureux / malheureuse (m./f.) *unfortunate, unhappy*
maman *Mom, Mommy*
manger *to eat*
  salle (f.) à manger *dining room*
manifestant / manifestante (m./f.) *demonstrator, protestor*
manifestation (f.) *demonstration, protest*
manifester *to demonstrate, to protest*
manteau (m.) *coat*
marchand / marchande (m./f.) *merchant, vendor, dealer*
marché (m.) *market*
  bon marché *inexpensive, a good buy*
marcher *to walk*
  marcher avec des béquilles *to walk with crutches*
  marcher avec une canne *to walk with a cane*

mardi *Tuesday*
mare (f.) *pond*
mari (m.) *husband*
marié / mariée (m./f.) *married*
Maroc (m.) *Morocco*
marocain / marocaine (m./f.) *Moroccan*
marquer *to score*
marron *brown*
marron (m.) *chestnut*
  crème (f.) de marrons *chestnut paste*
  marrons (pl.) glacés *sugar-coated chestnuts*
mars *March*
master (m.) *master's degree*
match (m.) *match, game*
mathématiques (f. pl.) *math*
maths (f. pl.) *math*
matière (f.) *subject*
  matière difficile *difficult subject*
matin (m.) *morning*
matinée (f.) *morning*
mauvais / mauvaise (m./f.) *bad*
  C'est mauvais. *That's bad.*
  plus mauvais / mauvaise *worse*
  le / la plus mauvais / mauvaise *the worst*
  moins mauvais / mauvaise *not as bad*
me / m' *myself* (reflexive pronoun), *me* (direct object pronoun), *to me* (indirect object pronoun)
  Je m'appelle... *My name is .../I am called...*
médecin (m.) *doctor*
médecine (f.) *medicine*
meilleur / meilleure (m./f.) *better, best*
  le / la meilleur / meilleure *the best*
mèl (m.) *e-mail*
melon (m.) *melon, cantaloupe*
membre (m.) *member*
même *same, even*
mémoire (f.) *memory*
menacer *to threaten*
ménage (m.) *house cleaning*
  faire le ménage *to clean the house, to do the house cleaning*
mener *to lead*
menthe (f.) *mint*
  menthe à l'eau *water with mint syrup*
menton (m.) *chin*
menu (m.) *menu*
  Le menu, s'il vous plaît. *The menu, please.*
mer (f.) *sea*

merci *thank you*
  Merci bien. *Thank you very much.*
mercredi *Wednesday*
mère (f.) *mother*
mes / mon / ma (pl./m./f.) *my*
mesdames *ladies*
mesdemoiselles *misses*
message (m.) instantané *instant message*
messieurs *gentlemen*
métro (m.) *subway, metro*
  station (f.) de métro *subway station*
  plan (m.) du métro *map of the subway*
  carte (f.) du métro *map of the subway*
mettre *to put, to put on*
  mettre à la poste *to mail, to put in the mail*
meubles (m. pl.) *furniture (in general)*
  meuble (m.) *a piece of furniture*
mexicain / mexicaine (m./f.) *Mexican*
Mexique (m.) *Mexico*
micro-ondes (m.) *microwave (oven)*
midi (m.) *noon*
  Il est midi. *It is noon.*
miel (m.) *honey*
mieux *better*
  il vaut mieux (que) *it is better (that), it would
    be better (that)*
milieu (m.) *middle*
  au milieu de *in the middle of*
mille *thousand*
milliard *billion*
milliardaire (m./f.) *billionaire*
million *million*
millionnaire (m./f.) *millionaire*
mince *thin*
minéral / minérale (m./f.) *mineral*
  eau (f.) minérale *mineral water*
minuit (m.) *midnight*
  Il est minuit. *It is midnight.*
miroir (m.) *mirror*
mi-temps (f.) *halftime*
mixer (m.) *blender*
Mlle *Miss*
Mme *Mrs., Ms.*
modem (m.) *modem*
moi *me*
moins *less, minus, fewer, not as*
  ... moins le quart *quarter to ...*
  moins de *less*

moins... que *less ... than, not as ... as*
  le / la moins... *the least ...*
  moins bon / bonne (m./f.) *not as good*
  moins mauvais / mauvaise (m./f.) *not as bad*
  à moins que... ne *unless*
mois (m.) *month*
  dans un mois *next month, in one month*
  mois prochain *next month*
  mois dernier *last month*
  deux mois auparavant *two months before*
  deux mois avant *two months before*
  mois (pl.) de l'année *months of the year*
moment (m.) *moment*
mon / ma / mes (m./f./pl.) *my*
monde (m.) *world, people*
  tout le monde *everyone*
monnaie (f.) *change, coins, currency*
monsieur *sir, Mr.*
  messieurs *gentlemen*
montagne (f.) *mountain*
monter *to go up, to come up, to rise*
  monter à bicyclette *to go bike riding, to ride
    a bike*
  monter à cheval *to go horseback riding, to
    ride a horse*
montre (f.) *watch*
montrer *to show*
monument (m.) *monument*
moquette (f.) *carpet*
morceau (m.) *piece, bite*
mosquée (f.) *mosque*
mot (m.) *word*
moto (f.) *motorcycle, motorcycling*
motocyclette (f.) *motorcycle*
mouchoir (m.) *handkerchief, tissue*
moule (f.) *mussel*
  moules (pl.) frites *mussels and fries*
mourir *to die*
mousse (f.) *mousse*
  mousse au chocolat *chocolate mousse*
moutarde (f.) *mustard*
  moutarde de Dijon *Dijon mustard*
mur (m.) *wall*
muscle (m.) *muscle*
musclé / musclée (m./f.) *muscular (person)*
musculaire *muscular (medical term)*
musculation (f.) *bodybuilding, strength training,
  weight lifting*

faire de la musculation *to do strength training, to lift weights, to do bodybuilding*
musée (m.) *museum*
  Musée du Louvre *Louvre Museum*
  Musée d'Orsay *Orsay Museum*
musicien / musicienne (m./f.) *musician*
musique (f.) *music*
mystérieux / mystérieuse (m./f.) *mysterious*

N

nager *to swim*
naître *to be born*
nappe (f.) *tablecloth*
natation (f.) *swimming*
  faire de la natation *to go swimming*
nation (f.) *nation*
national / nationale (m./f.) *national*
  fête (f.) nationale *national holiday*
nationalité (f.) *nationality*
naturel / naturelle (m./f.) *natural*
naturellement *naturally*
ne / n'... pas *not*
  n'est-ce pas ? *isn't it?, isn't that so?, right?*
  ne... jamais *never*
  ne... plus *no longer, no more, any more, anymore*
  ne... pas encore *not yet*
  ne... rien *nothing, anything*
  ne... rien d'autre *nothing else, anything else*
  il est nécessaire que *it is necessary that*
nécessaire *necessary*
neige (f.) *snow*
  vacances (f. pl.) de neige *winter vacation*
neiger *to snow*
  Il neige. *It's snowing.*
nettoyer *to clean*
neuf *nine*
neuf (m.) *new*
  Rien de neuf. *Nothing new.*
  Quoi de neuf ? *What's up?/What's new?*
neuvième *ninth*
neveu (m.) *nephew*
nez (m.) *nose*
nièce (f.) *niece*
Noël (m.) *Christmas*
  Joyeux Noël ! *Merry Christmas!*
  réveillon (m.) de Noël *Christmas Eve*
  veille (f.) de Noël *Christmas Eve*

noir / noire (m./f.) *black*
noisette (f.) *hazelnut*
nom (m.) *name*
  sous quel nom ? *under what name?*
nombre (m.) *number*
non *no*
nord (m.) *north*
normalement *usually*
note (f.) *grade, note*
notre / nos (m. or f./pl.) *our*
nourrir *to feed*
nourriture (f.) *food*
nous *we, us, ourselves* (reflexive pronoun), *to us* (indirect object pronoun), *each other*
nouveau / nouvel / nouvelle (m./m. before a vowel or silent h/f.) *new*
  Nouvel An (m.) *New Year*
nouveau-né (m.) *newborn*
nouvelles (f. pl.) *news (the news)*
novembre *November*
nuage (m.) *cloud*
nuageux / nuageuse (m./f.) *cloudy*
  C'est nuageux. *It's cloudy.*
nuit (f.) *night*
  Bonne nuit ! *Good night!*
  nuit dernière *last night*
nul / nulle (m./f.) *no, nil, null*
  nulle part *nowhere, anywhere*
numéro (m.) de téléphone *phone number*

O

obéir *to obey*
occupé / occupée (m./f.) *busy*
océan (m.) *ocean*
octobre *October*
œil (m.) (yeux, pl.) *eye (eyes)*
œuf (m.) *egg*
  œuf poché *poached egg*
  œuf au plat, œuf sur le plat *fried egg (over easy egg)*
  œuf à la coque *soft-boiled egg*
  œuf dur *hard-boiled egg (lit., hard egg)*
  œufs (pl.) brouillés *scrambled eggs*
  blancs (m. pl.) (d'œufs) *egg whites*
  douzaine (f.) d'œufs *dozen eggs*
Oh là là ! *Wow!/Oh dear!*
oignon (m.) *onion*
  soupe (f.) à l'oignon *onion soup*

omelette (f.) *omelette*
  omelette aux champignons *mushroom omelette*
on *we* (infml.), *people in general, one* (pronoun), *you* (general), *they* (general)
  On y va. *Let's go.* (infml.)
oncle (m.) *uncle*
ongle (m.) *fingernail*
  ongle de pied *toenail*
onze *eleven*
onzième *eleventh*
opéra (m.) *opera*
or (m.) *gold*
orage (m.) *storm*
orange *orange (color)*
orange (f.) *orange (fruit)*
  brique (f.) **de jus d'orange** *carton of orange juice*
  canard (m.) **à l'orange** *duck à l'orange, duck with orange sauce*
ordinateur (m.) *computer*
ordonnance (f.) *prescription*
oreille (f.) *ear*
  boucle (f.) **d'oreille** *earring*
organiser *to organize*
  organiser une fête *to have a party*
original / originale (m./f.) *original*
origine (f.) *origin*
orteil (m.) *toe*
orthographe (f.) *spelling*
os (m.) *bone*
ou *or*
  ou bien *or even, or else, either, or*
où *where*
  Où sont les toilettes ? *Where is the restroom?*
  Où se trouve… ? / Où est… ? *Where is … ?*
  n'importe où *wherever, anywhere*
ouest (m.) *west*
oui *yes*
ouragan (m.) *hurricane*
ouvrier / ouvrière (m./f.) *worker*
  ouvrier / ouvrière en bâtiment *construction worker*
ouvrir *to open*
  ouvrir un fichier *to open a file*

P

page (f.) **web** *webpage*
pain (m.) *bread*
paire (f.) *pair*
  Ça coûte trois euros la paire. *That's three euros per pair.*
palourde (f.) *clam*
panier (m.) *basket*
  panier de fraises *basket of strawberries*
pansement (m.) *bandage*
pantalon (m.) *pants*
papa *Dad, Daddy*
papier (m.) *paper*
  papier hygiénique *toilet paper*
papillon (m.) *butterfly*
paquebot (m.) *cruise ship, ocean liner*
par *by, through, per*
  par ici *this way*
  par là *that way*
  par cœur *by heart*
paralysé / paralysée (m./f.) *paralyzed*
parapluie (m.) *umbrella*
parascolaire *extracurricular*
  activités (f. pl.) **parascolaires** *extracurricular activities*
parc (m.) *park*
parce que *because*
parcours (m.) **de golf** *golf course*
pardon *pardon (me), excuse me*
parent (m.) *relative, parent*
parfait / parfaite (m./f.) *perfect*
  C'est parfait. *It's perfect.*
parfois *sometimes*
parfum (m.) *flavor, fragrance, perfume*
Paris *Paris*
parisien / parisienne (m./f.) *Parisian*
parler *to speak, to talk*
  Parlez plus lentement, s'il vous plaît. *Speak slower/more slowly, please.*
  Je parle un peu français. *I speak a little French.*
part (f.) *part, share, slice (cake, pie, pizza)*
  de la part de *on behalf of, from (someone)*
  de ma part *on my behalf, from me, on my part*
  nulle part *nowhere, anywhere*
partenaire / partenaire (m./f.) *partner*
partie (f.) *party*

partiel / partielle *partial*
  à temps partiel *part-time*
partir *to leave, to go away*
partout *everywhere*
pas *not*
  ne... pas *not*
  pas du tout *not at all*
  Pas mal. *Not bad.*
  Pas grand-chose. *Not a lot.*
passeport (m.) *passport*
passer *to pass, to go past, to spend (time)*
  Je vous le / la passe. *I'm getting him/her for you. (lit., I'm passing him/her to you.)*
  passer un coup de fil *to make a phone call (lit., to pass a hit of the wire)* (infml.)
  passer (un examen) *to take (a test)*
  passer du temps *to spend time*
passe-temps (m.) *hobby, pastime*
passionnant / passionnante (m./f.) *exciting*
pâté (m.) *pâté (spreadable purée of meat)*
  pâté de foie gras *goose liver pâté*
patient / patiente (m./f.) *patient*
  Sois patient. *Be patient.* (infml.)
  Soyez patient. *Be patient.* (pl./fml.)
patin (m.) *skating, skate*
  patin à glace *ice skating, ice skate*
patinage (m.) **sur glace** *ice skating*
pâtisserie (f.) *pastry shop, pastry*
  pâtisserie-confiserie (f.) *pastry and candy store*
patron / patronne (m./f.) *boss*
pauvre *unfortunate, poor, impoverished*
payer *to pay, to pay for*
peau (f.) *skin*
pêche (f.) *peach, fishing*
  pêche Melba *peaches with ice cream*
peindre *to paint*
peinture (f.) *painting*
pendant *during*
  pendant que *while*
pendule (f.) *grandfather clock*
penser *to think*
perdre *to lose*
  perdre du temps *to waste time*
  perdre votre / ton temps *to waste your time*
  perdre un match *to lose a game, to lose a match*
perdu / perdue (m./f.) *lost*

  Je suis perdu / perdue. *I'm lost.*
père (m.) *father*
permettre *to allow, to permit*
personne (f.) *person, no one, nobody*
  personne âgée *elderly person*
  ne / n'... personne *no one, anyone, nobody, anybody*
  pour quatre personnes *for four people, for a party of four*
personnel (m.) *staff*
peser *to weigh*
petit / petite (m./f.) *small, little, short*
  petit ami / petite amie (m./f.) *boyfriend/girlfriend*
  petit déjeuner (m.) *breakfast*
  prendre le petit déjeuner *to have breakfast*
  petits pois (m. pl.) *(green) peas (lit., little peas)*
peu *little, bit*
  peu de *little, few*
  un peu *a little*
  peu amical / peu amicale (m./f.) *unfriendly*
peur (f.) *fear*
  avoir peur *to be afraid (lit, to have fear)*
peut-être *maybe, possibly*
pharmacie (f.) *pharmacy, drugstore*
pharmacien / pharmacienne (m./f.) *pharmacist*
photo (f.) *photo*
  Pourriez-vous nous prendre en photo, s'il vous plaît ? *Can you take our picture (photo)?*
phrase (f.) *phrase*
physique (f.) *physics*
pièce (f.) *room, play (theater), piece, coin*
  pièce jointe *attachment*
pied (m.) *foot*
  à pied *on foot, by foot*
  au pied de *at the foot of*
  doigt (m.) **de pied** *toe*
  ongle (m.) **de pied** *toenail*
pilule (f.) *pill*
pique-nique (m.) *picnic*
piqûre (f.) *shot, injection*
pire *worse*
  le / la pire *the worst*
piste (f.) *trail, ski slope, track*
  piste pour débutants *bunny slope/hill, beginners' slope/hill*
placard (m.) *cupboard, closet*

place (f.) *place, seat, ticket, room*
plafond (m.) *ceiling*
plage (f.) *beach*
plaire *to please*
  s'il te plaît *please* (infml.)
  s'il vous plaît *please* (pl./fml.)
plaisir (m.) *pleasure*
  Avec plaisir. *With pleasure.*
plan (m.) *map, plan*
  plan de la ville *map of the city*
  plan du métro *map of the subway*
planche (f.) *board*
  planche à repasser *ironing board*
  planche à roulettes *skateboard*
plante (f.) *plant*
plastique (m.) *plastic*
  en plastique *made of plastic*
plat (m.) *dish*
  plat principal *main dish/course*
  plat d'accompagnement *side dish*
plein / pleine (m./f.) *full, solid*
  à plein temps *full-time*
  activités (f. pl.) de plein air *outdoor activities*
  être en pleine expansion *to be growing (business)*
  être en pleine forme *to be in good shape*
pleuvoir *to rain*
  Il pleut. *It's raining./It rains.*
plombage (m.) *filling (tooth)*
plombier (m.) *plumber*
plongée (f.) sous-marine *scuba diving*
  faire de la plongée sous-marine *to go scuba diving*
plonger *to dive*
  plonger dans la piscine *to dive in(to) the pool*
pluie (f.) *rain*
plus *more*
  plus loin *farther*
  le / la plus proche *the nearest, the closest*
  À plus tard ! *See you later!*
  À plus ! *See you later!* (infml.)
  et bien plus *and even more, and much more*
  ne... plus *no longer, no more, any more, anymore*
  plus de *more*
  plus... que *more ... than*
  plus mauvais / mauvaise (m./f.) *worse*
  le / la plus... *the most ...*

plusieurs *several*
pneu (m.) *tire*
pocher *to poach*
  œuf (m.) poché *poached egg*
poème (m.) *poem*
poignet (m.) *wrist*
pointure (f.) *shoe size*
poire (f.) *pear*
poireau (m.) *leek*
pois (m. pl.) *peas*
  petits pois *(green) peas (lit., little peas)*
poisson (m.) *fish*
poitrine (f.) *chest*
poivre (m.) *pepper (condiment)*
poivron (m.) *pepper (vegetable)*
poli / polie (m./f.) *polite*
policier / femme policier (m./f.) *policeman/woman*
policier / policière (m./f.) *police, detective (adjective)*
  film (m.) policier *detective drama/film, crime drama/film*
poliment *politely*
politique (f.) *politics*
pomme (f.) *apple*
  pomme de terre *potato*
  tarte (f.) aux pommes *apple pie*
  purée (f.) de pommes de terre *mashed potatoes*
  pommes (pl.) de terre en robe des champs *boiled potatoes in their skins, baked potatoes*
pompes (f. pl.) *push-ups*
pont (m.) *bridge*
porc (m.) *pork, pig*
  côte (f.) de porc *pork chop*
portable (m.) *cell phone*
porte (f.) *door*
porter *to carry, to wear*
portugais / portugaise (m./f.) *Portuguese*
Portugal (m.) *Portugal*
posséder *to own*
possible *possible*
  il est possible que *it is possible that*
  Ce n'est pas possible ! *I don't believe it!/ Oh man!/It's not possible! (disappointment, anger)*
poste (f.) *post office, mail*

bureau (m.) de poste *post office*
poste (m.) *telephone extension*
poste (m.) de police *police station*
pot (m.) *drink* (infml.)
potage (m.) *soup*
poubelle (f.) *garbage, trash can*
poudre (f.) *powder*
poulet (m.) *chicken*
  poulet frites *chicken and fries*
poumon (m.) *lung*
pour *for, to*
  pour que *in order that, so that*
pourquoi *why*
pouvoir *to be able to, can*
  Puis-je vous aider ? *Can I help you?*
praliné / pralinée (m./f.) *filled with hazelnut or almond ganache*
pratiquer *to practice*
précédent / précédente (m./f.) *before last*
  semaine (f.) précédente *the week before last*
précis / précise (m./f.) *sharp, exact, precise*
  à midi précis *exactly at noon (at noon sharp)*
préférable *preferable*
  il est préférable que *it is preferable that*
préféré / préférée (m./f.) *favorite*
préférer *to prefer*
  préférer que *to prefer that*
premier / première (m./f.) *first*
  premier étage (m.) *first floor (one floor above the ground floor)*
  première base (f.) *first base*
prendre *to take, to have (food/drink)*
  prendre un bain *to take a bath*
  prendre une douche *to take a shower*
  prendre un verre *to have a drink*
  prendre le petit déjeuner *to have breakfast*
  prendre une chambre *to check in*
  prendre rendez-vous *to make an appointment*
  prendre un bain de soleil *to sunbathe (lit., to take a bath of sun)*
  prendre une photo *to take a picture (photo)*
  Pourriez-vous nous prendre en photo, s'il vous plaît ? *Can you take our picture please?*
préparer *to prepare, to make, to cook*
près *close, near*
  tout près *very close, very near*

près d'ici *nearby, near here, close to here*
présenter *to introduce, to show, to present*
  Je te présente… / Je vous présente… *Let me introduce …* (infml./pl., fml.)
prêt / prête (m./f.) *ready*
prier *to ask, to beg, to pray*
  Je vous en prie. *You're welcome.* (fml.)
principal / principale (m./f.) *principal (main)*
  plat (m.) principal *main course*
printemps (m.) *spring*
  au printemps *in (the) spring*
probable *probable*
  il est probable que *it is probable that*
probablement *probably*
prochain / prochaine (m./f.) *next*
  mois (m.) prochain *next month*
  semaine (f.) prochaine *next week*
  À la prochaine ! *See you later! (Until next time!)*
proche *near, nearby, close*
  le / la plus proche *the nearest, the closest*
produire *to produce*
prof (m./f.) *professor, teacher* (infml.)
professeur / professeure (m./f.) *professor, teacher*
profession (f.) *profession*
progrès (m.) *progress*
projeter *to plan*
promenade (f.) *walk*
  faire une promenade *to take a walk*
promener *to take someone or something for a walk*
  se promener *to take a walk*
propre *clean, own*
protéger *to protect*
prune (f.) *plum*
pubs / publicités (f. pl.) *commercials*
puis *then*
pull(-over) (m.) *sweater*
punir *to punish*
purée (f.) *purée*
  purée de pommes de terre *mashed potatoes*
pyjama (m.) *pajamas*

Q

qu'est-ce qui/que… *what …*
quai (m.) *platform, quay, bank (of a river)*
quand *when*

quarante *forty*

quart (m.) *quarter*

  ... et quart *quarter after/past ...*

  ... moins le quart *quarter to ...*

quartier (m.) *neighborhood, quarter, area*

quatorze *fourteen*

quatre *four*

quatre-vingt-dix *ninety*

quatre-vingts *eighty*

quatrième *fourth*

que *what, that, which, whom, than*

  qu'est-ce que ? *what?*

  Qu'est-ce que c'est ? *What is this/that?*

  plus... que *more ... than*

  moins... que *less ... than, not as ... as*

  aussi... que *as ... as*

quel / quelle (m./f.) *which, what*

  à quelle heure ? *at what time?*

  de quel / quelle ? (m./f.) *what?/of what?*

  Quel temps fait-il aujourd'hui ? *What is the weather today?*

  Quelle heure est-il ? *What time is it?*

  Quel soulagement ! *What a relief!*

  Quelle coïncidence ! *What a coincidence!*

  Quelle bonne idée ! *What a good idea!*

quelque *some, any*

  quelqu'un *someone, somebody*

  quelqu'un d'autre *someone else*

  quelque chose *something*

quelquefois *sometimes*

question (f.) *question*

queue (m.) *line, tail*

  faire la queue *to wait in line*

qui *who, that*

  Qui est à l'appareil ? *Who is it?/Who's calling? (on the phone)*

  Qui est-ce ? *Who is it?*

  à qui *to whom*

  avec qui *with whom*

  chez qui *at whose house*

  de qui *from whom, of whom, about whom*

  pour qui *for whom*

  n'importe qui *whoever, anyone*

quiche (f.) *quiche (baked dish made with eggs and cream)*

  quiche lorraine *type of quiche made with bacon*

quincaillerie (f.) *hardware store*

quinze *fifteen*

quinzième *fifteenth*

quitter *to leave, to depart, to quit*

  Ne quittez pas, s'il vous plaît. *Hold on, please. (lit., Don't leave, please.)*

quoi *what*

  Quoi de neuf ? *What's up?/What's new?*

  n'importe quoi *whatever, anything*

quoique *although*

quotidien / quotidienne (m./f.) *everyday, daily*

R

raccrocher *to hang up*

radio(graphie) (f.) *x-ray*

radis (m.) *radish*

  radis au beurre *rosette-cut radishes served with butter on top (lit., radishes in butter)*

raisin (m.) *grape(s)*

raison (f.) *reason*

  avoir raison *to be right (lit., to have reason)*

Ramadan (m.) *Ramadan*

ranger *to put away*

rapide *quick*

rappeler *to call back*

rarement *rarely*

rasoir (m.) *razor*

rater (un examen) *to fail (a test)*

ravi / ravie (m./f.) *delighted, charmed*

  Je suis ravi / ravie de faire votre connaissance. *I'm delighted to make your acquaintance.*

réception (f.) *reception desk*

recette (f.) *recipe*

recevoir une piqûre *to get a shot*

recommander *to recommend*

  recommander que *to recommend that*

récré(ation) (f.) *recess, break*

réfléchir *to think, to reflect*

réfrigérateur (m.) *refrigerator*

regarder *to watch, to look at*

régler sa note *to check out*

rejeter *to reject*

remise (f.) *discount*

remplir *to fill (in)*

rencontrer (une personne/quelqu'un) *to meet (a person/someone)*

rendez-vous (m.) *meeting, appointment, date*

  prendre rendez-vous *to make an*

appointment

rendre *to return*

  rendre visite à *to visit, to pay a visit (to a person)*

rentrée (f.) *back-to-school*

rentrer *to go home, to come home, to return, to come back (in), to go in*

repas (m.) *meal*

répéter *to repeat*

  Répétez, s'il vous plaît. *Repeat (that), please.*

répondre *to answer, to respond, to reply*

  répondre au téléphone *to answer the phone*

reposer *to rest*

  se reposer *to rest (oneself), to relax*

réservation (f.) *reservation*

  faire une réservation *to make a reservation*

  faire des réservations *to make reservations*

réserver *to reserve*

restaurant (m.) *restaurant*

reste (f.) *rest (what's left)*

rester *to stay*

  rester en forme *to stay in shape*

résultats (m. pl.) *results*

retard (m.) *delay*

  en retard *late*

retourner *to return*

retraite (f.) *retirement*

  à la retraite *retired*

réunion (f.) *meeting, reunion*

réussir *to succeed, to do well*

  réussir à (un examen / cours) *to pass (a test/a class), to do well in (a test/a class)*

réveiller *to wake (someone)*

  se réveiller *to wake up (to wake oneself up)*

réveillon (m.) **(du jour de l'An)** *New Year's Eve*

réveillon (m.) **de Noël** *Christmas Eve*

revenir *to come back, to return*

réverbère (m.) *lamppost*

revue (f.) *magazine*

rez-de-chaussée (m.) *ground floor*

rhume (m.) *(common) cold*

riche *rich*

rideau (m.) *curtain*

rien *nothing, anything*

  ne... rien *nothing, anything*

  De rien. *You're welcome./It's nothing.*

  Rien de neuf. *Nothing new.*

  Rien de particulier. *Nothing much.*

  ne... rien d'autre *nothing else, anything else*

rive (f.) **droite** *right bank*

rive (f.) **gauche** *left bank*

rivière (f.) *river*

riz (m.) *rice*

robe (f.) *dress*

rocher (m.) *rock*

rôle (m.) *role, part (in a play, movie, etc.)*

romantique *romantic*

rompre *to break*

rondelle (f.) *(round) slice of (cucumber, banana, sausage, etc.)*

rose *pink*

rosé *rosé*

  vin (m.) **rosé** *rosé wine*

rose (f.) *rose*

rôti (m.) *roast, joint (of meat)*

  rôti de bœuf *roast beef*

rôti / rôtie (m./f.) *roast(ed)*

  carré (m.) **d'agneau rôti** *roast rack of lamb*

rouge *red*

  vin (m.) **rouge** *red wine*

rougir *to blush, to redden*

rue (f.) *street*

rural / rurale (m./f.) *rural*

russe *Russian*

Russie (f.) *Russia*

S

s'aimer *to like/love each other*

s'amuser *to have a good time, to enjoy oneself, to have fun*

s'appeler *to be called, to call oneself*

  Comment vous appelez-vous ? *What's your name?* (pl./fml.)

  Comment t'appelles-tu ? *What's your name?* (infml.)

  Je m'appelle... *My name is ... /I am called ...*

s'embrasser *to hug (each other), to kiss (each other)*

s'ennuyer *to get bored, to be bored*

s'entraîner *to train*

s'habiller *to get dressed, to dress oneself*

s'il le faut *if necessary, if needed*

s'il te plaît / s'il vous plaît *please (infml./pl., fml.) (lit., if it pleases you)*

sa / son / ses (f./m./pl.) *his, her, its*

sable (m.) *sand*

château (m.) de sable *sandcastle*
faire un château de sable *to make/build a sandcastle*
sac (m.) *purse, bag*
Sacré-Cœur (m.) *Sacré Cœur (Sacred Heart)*
Saint-Sylvestre (f.) *New Year's Eve*
salade (f.) *salad*
  salade de fruits *fruit salad*
  salade verte *green salad*
  salade niçoise *niçoise salad*
saladier (m.) *bowl*
salaire (m.) *salary*
sale *dirty*
salé / salée (m./f.) *savory, salty*
salle (f.) *room, hall*
  salle à manger *dining room*
  salle de bains *bathroom, washroom*
  salle de classe *classroom*
  salle de réunion *meeting room*
salon (m.) *parlor, living room*
Salut. *Hello./Hi./Bye./See you later!*
samedi *Saturday*
sandwich (m.) *sandwich*
  sandwich au jambon *ham sandwich*
  sandwich au fromage *cheese sandwich*
  sandwich jambon-fromage *ham and cheese sandwich*
sang (m.) *blood*
sans *without*
  sans que *without*
santé (f.) *health*
  À votre santé ! *To your health!*
  en bonne santé *healthy*
sardines (f. pl.) *sardines*
  sardines sauce tomate *sardines in tomato sauce*
sarrasin (m.) *buckwheat*
sauce (f.) *sauce*
  sardines (f. pl.) sauce tomate *sardines in tomato sauce*
saucisse (f.) *sausage*
sauter *to jump, to sauté*
  sauter une haie *to jump a hurdle*
sauvegarder un document *to save a document*
sauveteur (m.) *lifeguard*
savoir *to know*
  Je ne sais pas. *I don't know.*
savon (m.) *soap*

saxophone (m.) *saxophone*
science (f.) *science*
score (m.) *score*
  score final *final score*
sculpture (f.) *sculpture*
se / s' *himself, herself, themselves, oneself, each other* (reflexive pronoun)
  s'amuser *to have a good time, to enjoy oneself, to have fun*
  s'appeler *to be called, to call oneself*
  s'ennuyer *to get bored, to be bored*
  s'habiller *to get dressed, to dress oneself*
  se blesser *to hurt oneself*
  se brosser *to brush oneself (hair, teeth, etc.)*
  se casser le bras / la jambe *to break one's arm/leg*
  se coucher *to go to bed, to lie down (to lie oneself down)*
  se décider *to make up one's mind, to be decided, to be resolved (to do something)*
  se demander *to wonder, to ask oneself*
  se dépêcher *to hurry*
  se faire une élongation *to pull a muscle*
  se fouler la cheville *to sprain one's ankle*
  se hâter *to rush*
  se laver *to wash up, to wash oneself*
  se lever *to get up, to rise (to get oneself up)*
  se promener *to take a walk*
  se raser *to shave*
  se rendre *to surrender*
  se rendre à (+ evidence, an argument, etc.) *to give in to, to yield to*
  se rendre à (+ location) *to take oneself to (a place), to go to (a place)*
  se rendre compte (de) *to notice, to realize, to make oneself aware*
  se rendre heureux / heureuse (m./f.) *to make oneself happy*
  se rendre malade *to make oneself sick*
  se reposer *to rest (oneself), to relax*
  se réveiller *to wake up (to wake oneself up)*
  se souvenir *to remember*
  se tromper *to be mistaken, to make a mistake*
  se trouver *to find oneself (somewhere), to be situated*
  se comprendre *to understand each other*
  se connaître *to know each other*
  se dire *to tell each other, to say to each other*

se disputer *to argue (with each other)*
se fiancer *to get engaged (to each other)*
se marier *to get married (to each other)*
se parler *to speak to each other*
se regarder *to look at each other, to watch each other*
se téléphoner *to call each other*
se voir *to see each other*
sèche-linge (m.) *dryer*
second / seconde (m./f.) *second*
secrétaire (m./f.) *secretary*
seize *sixteen*
séjour (m.) *trip, stay, sojourn*
sel (m.) *salt*
semaine (f.) *week*
  dans une semaine *next week, in one week*
  semaine prochaine *next week*
  semaine précédente *the week before last*
  semaine suivante *the week after next*
  semaine d'avant *the week before last*
  semaine d'après *the week after next*
  jours (m. pl.) de la semaine *days of the week*
sembler *seem (to)*
  il semble que *it seems that*
sept *seven*
septembre *September*
septième *seventh*
sérieux / sérieuse (m./f.) *serious*
serveur / serveuse (m./f.) *waiter/waitress, server*
service (m.) *department*
  service de comptabilité *accounting department*
  service d'informatique *IT department*
  service financier *finance department*
  service des ventes *sales department*
  service juridique *legal department*
  service de marketing *marketing department*
  service des relations publiques *public relations (PR) department*
  service du courrier *shipping department, mail room*
  service clientèle / client *customer service department*
serviette (f.) *napkin, towel, briefcase*
  serviette de bain *bath towel*
ses / son / sa (pl./m./f.) *his, her, its*
seul / seule (m./f.) *alone*

seulement *only*
shampooing (m.) *shampoo*
si *if, yes (negative)*
  s'il te plaît / s'il vous plaît *please* (infml./pl., fml.) *(lit., if it pleases you)*
simple *simple*
  aller simple *one-way*
sincère *sincere*
sirop (m.) de cassis *black currant syrup*
site (m.) web *website*
six *six*
sixième *sixth*
skateboard (m.) *skateboard*
ski (m.) *skiing*
  faire du ski *to ski, to go skiing*
  ski nautique *water-skiing*
skier *to ski*
social / sociale (m./f.) *social*
société (f.) *company, firm*
sœur (f.) *sister*
soie (f.) *silk*
soif (f.) *thirst*
  avoir soif *to be thirsty*
soin (m.) *care*
soir (m.) *evening, night*
  ce soir *tonight, this evening*
  hier soir *last night*
  Bonsoir ! *Good evening!*
soirée (f.) *party, evening, night*
soixante *sixty*
soixante-dix *seventy*
sol (m.) *floor (of a room)*
sole (f.) *sole (fish)*
  sole meunière *sole covered in flour and sautéed in butter*
soleil (m.) *sun*
  Il fait (du) soleil. / Il y a du soleil. *It's sunny.*
  lunettes (f. pl.) de soleil *sunglasses*
solex (m.) *moped*
sommeil (m.) *sleep*
  avoir sommeil *to be sleepy (lit., to have sleep)*
son / sa / ses (m./f./pl.) *his, her, its*
sonner *to ring*
sortie (f.) *exit*
sortir *to go out, to leave, to come out*
  sortir avec *to go out with, to date*
  sortir en boîte *to go out to clubs, to go out clubbing*

soudain *suddenly*

  tout à coup, tout d'un coup *all of a sudden*

souhaiter *to wish*

soulagement (m.) *relief*

  Quel soulagement ! *What a relief!*

soulever un haltère *to lift a dumbbell*

soupe (f.) *soup*

  soupe à l'oignon *onion soup*

souper *to have a late dinner*

souper (m.) *late dinner*

sourcil (m.) *eyebrow*

sourd / sourde (m./f.) *deaf*

sourire (m.) *smile*

souris (f.) *mouse*

sous *under*

  sous quel nom ? *under what name?*

sous-titre (m.) *subtitle*

sous-vêtements (m. pl.) *underwear*

souvenir (m.) *souvenir, memory*

souvent *often*

spécialité (f.) *specialty*

spectateur / spectatrice (m./f.) *spectator*

sport (m.) *sport*

  faire du sport *to play sports, to do sports*

sportif / sportive (m./f.) *athletic*

stade (m.) *stadium*

  stade de foot *soccer stadium*

station (f.) *station*

  station de métro *subway station, metro station*

  station de sports d'hiver *ski resort*

statue (f.) *statue*

steak (m.) *steak*

  steak frites *steak and fries*

sucre (m.) *sugar*

sucré / sucrée (m./f.) *sweet*

sud (m.) *south*

sueur (f.) *sweat*

suggérer *to suggest*

suisse *Swiss*

Suisse (f.) *Switzerland*

suite (f.) *rest, next part, what happens next*

  Vivement la suite ! *Can't wait for the rest!/ Can't wait for what happens next!*

suivant / suivante (m./f.) *following, after next*

  semaine (f.) suivante *the week after next*

suivre *to follow*

  suivre un cours *to take a class*

sujet (m.) *subject*

super *super, great*

  Super ! *Great!*

supermarché (m.) *supermarket*

supporteur / supportrice (m./f.) *fan (sports)*

supprimer *to delete*

sur *on*

sûr / sûre (m./f.) *sure, certain*

  Bien sûr ! *Of course!*

surf (m.) *surfing*

  surf sur neige *snowboarding (lit., surfing on snow)*

surprendre *to surprise*

surtout *mostly, above all, especially*

sympa *cool, nice, good*

  très sympa *very cool/nice/good*

sympathique *friendly (nice)*

synagogue (f.) *synagogue*

T

ta / ton / tes (f./m./pl.) *your* (infml.)

table (f.) *table*

  table pour deux *table for two*

  À table ! *Dinner's ready! (lit., To the table!)*

tableau (m.) *painting*

taille (f.) *size (clothing)*

tailleur (m.) *suit (woman's)*

talc (m.) *powder*

talentueux / talentueuse (m./f.) *talented*

tante (f.) *aunt*

tapis (m.) *rug*

  tapis de course, tapis de jogging *treadmill*

tard *late*

  À plus tard ! *See you later!*

tarte (f.) *pie, tart*

  tarte aux fraises *strawberry pie*

  tarte aux pommes *apple pie*

  tarte à la citrouille *pumpkin pie*

tartine (f.) *bread with various spreads*

tasse (f.) *cup*

  tasse de thé *cup of tea*

taxi (m.) *taxi, cab*

te / t' *yourself* (infml., reflexive pronoun), *you* (infml., direct object pronoun), *to you* (infml., indirect object pronoun)

télé(vision) (f.) *television, TV*

télécopieur (m.) *fax machine*

téléphone (m.) *telephone*

(téléphone) portable *cell phone*

répondre au téléphone *to answer the phone*

numéro (m.) de téléphone *phone number*

téléphoner *to phone, to call, to make a phone call*

télévision (f.) *television*

température (f.) *temperature*

temple (m.) *temple*

temps (m.) *time, weather*

Quel temps fait-il aujourd'hui ? *What's the weather today?*

Je n'ai pas le temps. *I don't have (the) time.*

à plein temps *full-time*

à temps partiel *part-time*

temps libre *free time*

perdre du temps *waste time (to)*

perdre votre / ton temps *waste your time (to)*

tendon (m.) *tendon*

tenir *to hold*

tennis (m.) *tennis*

tenue (f.) *outfit*

en tenue de soirée *formal, in formal dress/attire*

terminer *to finish, to end*

terrain (m.) de golf *golf course*

terre (f.) *land, earth*

tes / ton / ta (pl./m./f.) *your* (infml.)

tête (f.) *head*

thé (m.) *tea*

tasse (f.) de thé *cup of tea*

théâtre (m.) *theater*

théière (f.) *teakettle, teapot*

thriller (m.) *thriller*

Tiens ! *Say!/Hey! (surprise)*

timbre (m.) *stamp*

tiroir (m.) *drawer*

tisane (f.) *herbal tea*

toi *you* (infml.)

toilettes (f. pl.) *toilet, restroom*

Où sont les toilettes ? *Where is the restroom?*

tomate (f.) *tomato*

sardines (f. pl.) sauce tomate *sardines in tomato sauce*

tomber *to fall*

tomber malade *to get sick*

ton / ta / tes (m./f./pl.) *your* (infml.)

tonnerre (m.) *thunder*

tort (m.) *wrong*

avoir tort *to be wrong (lit., to have wrong)*

tôt *early*

touchdown (m.) *touchdown*

toujours *always, still*

tour (f.) *tower*

Tour Eiffel *Eiffel Tower*

tour (m.) *tour, turn*

touriste (m./f.) *tourist*

tourner *to turn*

tout / toute / tous / toutes (m./f./m. pl./f. pl.) *all, every*

tout le monde *everyone*

tout droit *straight ahead*

pas du tout *not at all*

C'est tout ? *Is that all?*

C'est tout. *That's all.*

À tout à l'heure ! *See you later!*

tractions (f. pl.) *pull-ups*

train (m.) *train*

train à grande vitesse (TGV) *high-speed train*

tranche (f.) *slice (bread, cheese)*

tranche de fromage *slice of cheese*

transfusion (f.) de sang *blood transfusion*

transport (m.) *transportation*

travail (m.) *work*

travailler *to work*

travailler dur *to work hard*

travers (m.) *beam, quirk*

à travers *through, across*

traverser *to cross, to go across*

treize *thirteen*

trente *thirty*

très *very*

très bien *very good, very well*

très bon / bonne (m./f.) *very good*

tricher *to cheat*

tricot (m.) *knitting, sweater*

trillion *trillion*

triste *sad*

trois *three*

troisième *third*

troisième base (f.) *third base*

tromper *to deceive*

se tromper *to be mistaken, to make a mistake*

trop *too, too much*

trop de *too much*

trottoir (m.) *sidewalk*

trousse (f.) de secours *first-aid kit*

trouver *to find*
  se trouver *to find oneself (somewhere), to be situated*
  trouver que *to find that, to think that*
  Où se trouve... ? *Where is ... ?*
truite (f.) *trout*
  truite au bleu *trout cooked in wine and vinegar*
T-shirt (m.) *t-shirt*
tu *you* (infml.)

U

un / une (m./f.) (plural of un / une is des) *a, an, one*
  un peu *a little*
  une fois *once, one time*
Union (f.) européenne *European Union*
université (f.) *university, college*
urbain / urbaine (m./f.) *urban*
urgent / urgente (m./f.) *urgent*
  il est urgent que *it is urgent that*
usine (f.) *factory*
utiliser *to use*
  utiliser le langage des signes *to use sign language*

V

vacances (f. pl.) *vacation*
  grandes vacances *summer vacation*
  vacances d'hiver *winter vacation*
vaccin (m.) *vaccine*
vain / vaine (m./f.) *vain*
valoir *to be worth*
  valoir la peine *to be worth the trouble*
  il vaut mieux (que) *it would be better (that), it is better (that)*
vanille (f.) *vanilla*
  glace (f.) à la vanille *vanilla ice cream*
Vas-y ! (infml.) *Go there!/Go on!/Go ahead!*
veau (m.) *veal*
veille (f.) de *the day before*
  veille de Noël *Christmas Eve*
vélo (m.) *bike*
  vélo d'appartement *stationary bike*
vélomoteur (m.) *moped*
vendeur / vendeuse (m./f.) *salesman/woman*
vendre *to sell*
vendredi *Friday*

venir *to come*
vent (m.) *wind*
  Il fait du vent. / Il y a du vent. *It's windy.*
ventre (m.) *belly, stomach (general term)*
vermicelle (m.) *vermicelli pasta*
  consommé (m.) aux vermicelles *noodle soup (vermicelli pasta consommé)*
verre (m.) *glass, lens*
  prendre un verre *to have a drink*
  verre de lait *glass of milk*
  verres (pl.) de contact *contact lenses*
vers *around, about*
version (f.) *version*
  version française (v.f.) *French version of a film (dubbed into French)*
  version originale (v.o.) *original version of a film (not dubbed into French)*
vert / verte (m./f.) *green*
  citron (m.) vert *lime*
  haricots (m. pl.) verts *green beans*
  salade (f.) verte *green salad*
veste (f.) *jacket*
veston (m.) *jacket*
vêtements (m. pl.) *clothes, clothing*
vétérinaire (m.) *veterinarian*
viande (f.) *meat*
vie (f.) *life*
vietnamien / vietnamienne (m./f.) *Vietnamese*
vieux / vieil / vieille (m./m. before a vowel or silent h/f.) *old, elderly, outdated*
village (m.) *village*
ville (f.) *town, city*
  plan (m.) de la ville *map of the city*
  carte (f.) de la ville *map of the city*
  hôtel (m.) de ville *city hall, town hall, municipal building*
vin (m.) *wine*
  vin rouge / blanc / rosé / mousseux *red/white/rosé/sparkling wine*
  carafe (f.) de vin *pitcher of wine*
  coq (m.) au vin *chicken/rooster cooked in wine*
vingt *twenty*
vingtième *twentieth*
violet / violette (m./f.) *violet, purple*
violon (m.) *violin*
violoncelle (m.) *cello*
virus (m.) *virus*
visage (m.) *face*

visite (f.) guidée *guided tour*
visiter *to visit (a place)*
vite *quickly*
vivement *strongly*
  Vivement la fin de la journée ! *Can't wait for the end of the day!*
  Vivement la suite ! *Can't wait for the rest!/ Can't wait for what happens next!*
vocabulaire (m.) *vocabulary*
voici *here is/are, here it is/they are*
voie (f.) *track, lane*
voilà *there is/are, here is/are, there it is/they are, here it is/they are*
voile (f.) *sail/sailing*
  faire de la voile *sailing*
voir *to see*
voiture (f.) *car*
volaille (f.) *poultry*
volley(-ball) (m.) *volleyball*
votre / vos (m. or f./pl.) *your (pl./fml.)*
vouloir *to want, to wish*
  Je veux (bien)... *I (do) want ...*
  Je voudrais (bien)... *I would like ...*
  Que voulez-vous ? *What do you want?*
vous *you (pl./fml.), yourself (fml., reflexive pronoun), yourselves (reflexive pronoun), to you (pl./fml., indirect object pronoun), each other*
voyage (m.) *voyage, trip, travel*
  chèque (m.) de voyage *traveler's check*
voyager *to travel*
vrai / vraie (m./f.) *true, real*
  il est vrai que *it is true that*
vraiment *truly, really*

W

wagon (m.) *car (on a train)*
  wagon-lit (m.) *sleeping/sleeper car*
week-end (m.) *weekend*
western (m.) *western*

Y

y *there*
  il y a *there is/are, ago*
  il y avait *there was/were*
yeux (m. pl.) (œil, sg.) *eyes (eye)*
  avoir les yeux bleus / bruns / verts *to have blue/brown/green eyes*
yoga (m.) *yoga*

Z

zéro *zero*
zoo (m.) *zoo*

English-French

A

a, an *un / une (m./f.) (plural of un / une is des)*
  a little *un peu*
  a lot *beaucoup*
  a lot of *beaucoup de*
abdomen *ventre (m.), abdomen (m.)*
able to (to be) *pouvoir, arriver à (+ verb)*
above all *surtout*
Absolutely! *Absolument !*
academic year *année (f.) scolaire*
accessories *accessoires (m. pl.)*
accident *accident (m.)*
accompany (to) *accompagner*
accountant *comptable / comptable (m./f.)*
accounting *comptabilité (f.)*
  accounting department *service (m.) de comptabilité*
ache (to) *avoir mal à*
across *à travers*
  across from *en face de*
act (to) *agir, jouer*
action *action (f.)*
  action film/movie *film (m.) d'action*
active *actif / active (m./f.)*
actively *activement*
actor/actress *acteur / actrice (m./f.)*
admire (to) *admirer*
adolescent *adolescent / adolescente (m./f.)*
adore (to) *adorer*
adult *adulte (m./f.)*
advance (to) *avancer*
afraid (to be) *avoir peur*
after *après*
  after next *suivant / suivante (m./f.), d'après*
afternoon *après-midi (m./f.)*
afterwards *après*
again *encore*
age *âge (m.)*
ago *il y a*
ahead *devant*
airplane *avion (m.)*

Glossary   **369**

airport *aéroport* (m.)
alcohol *alcool* (m.)
Algeria *Algérie* (f.)
Algerian *algérien / algérienne* (m./f.)
all *tout / toute / tous / toutes* (m./f./m. pl./f. pl.)
  Is that all? *C'est tout ?*
  That's all. *C'est tout.*
  All right. *D'accord. / Entendu.*
allergic *allergique*
allergy *allergie* (f.)
allow (to) *permettre*
almond *amande* (f.)
  filled with hazelnut or almond ganache *praliné / pralinée* (m./f.)
alone *seul / seule* (m./f.)
along(side) *le long de*
already *déjà*
also *aussi*
although *bien que, quoique*
always *toujours*
ambulance *ambulance* (f.)
American *américain / américaine* (m./f.)
amusing *amusant / amusante* (m./f.)
and *et*
animal *animal* (m.)
animated movie *film* (m.) *dessin animé*
ankle *cheville* (f.)
  to sprain one's ankle *se fouler la cheville*
anniversary *anniversaire* (m.)
  Happy anniversary! *Joyeux / Bon anniversaire !*
announce (to) *annoncer*
annoy (to) *ennuyer*
another *un / une autre* (m./f.)
answer (to) *répondre*
  answer the phone (to) *répondre au téléphone*
antibiotics *antibiotiques* (m. pl.)
anti-inflammatory *anti-inflammatoire*
anxious *inquiet / inquiète* (m./f.)
any *quelque, du*
  in any case, at any rate *de toute façon*
anybody, anyone *personne, ne... personne, n'importe qui*
anyhow *de toute façon*
anymore, any more *ne... plus*
anything *rien, ne... rien, n'importe quoi*
  anything else *autre chose, ne... rien d'autre*
anywhere *nulle part, n'importe où*

apartment *appartement* (m.)
  apartment building *immeuble* (m.)
appetizer *entrée* (f.), *hors-d'œuvre* (m.)
apple *pomme* (f.)
  apple pie *tarte* (f.) *aux pommes*
apply for a job (to) *faire une demande d'emploi*
appointment *rendez-vous* (m.)
April *avril*
Arc de Triomphe (Arch of Triumph) *Arc* (m.) *de Triomphe*
architect *architecte* (m./f.)
area *quartier* (m.)
argue (with each other) (to) *se disputer*
arm *bras* (m.)
armchair *fauteuil* (m.)
around *autour de, vers*
arrive (to) *arriver*
  arrive (somewhere) (to) *arriver à (+ destination)*
  arrival time *heure* (f.) *de l'arrivée, d'arriveé*
art *art* (m.)
artist *artiste* (m./f.)
as *comme, aussi*
  as a result of ... (in a negative way) *à cause de...*
  as ... as *aussi... que*
  not as ... as *moins... que*
ashamed (to be) *avoir honte*
ask (for) (to) *demander*
  ask oneself (to) *se demander*
assistant *assistant / assistante* (m./f.)
at *à*
  at the *au / à la / à l' / aux* (m./f./m. or f. before a vowel or silent h/pl.)
  at someone's house/place *chez*
  at home *chez moi, à la maison*
  at what time? *à quelle heure ?*
  at any rate *de toute façon*
  at school *à l'école*
  at the office *au bureau*
  at work *au travail*
athletic *sportif / sportive* (m./f.)
ATM *guichet* (m.) *automatique, distributeur* (m.) *de billets*
attach a file (to) *envoyer un fichier en pièce jointe*
attachment *pièce* (f.) *jointe*
attend (a class) (to) *assister à (un cours)*
August *août*

aunt *tante* (f.)
Australia *Australie* (f.)
Australian *australien / australienne* (m./f.)
author *auteur / auteure* (m./f.)
auto racing *course* (f.) *automobile*
automobile *automobile* (f.)
autumn *automne* (m.)
 in autumn *en automne*
avenue *avenue* (f.)

B

baccalauréat (an exam for students wishing
 to continue their education beyond high
 school) *baccalauréat / bac* (m.)
baby *bébé* (m.)
 baby talk (baby language) *langage* (m.)
 enfantin
bachelor's degree *licence* (f.)
back *dos* (m.)
back-to-school *rentrée* (f.)
bad *mauvais / mauvaise* (m./f.), *mal*
 bad language *langage* (m.) *grossier*
badly *mal*
 It's going badly. *Ça va mal.*
bag *sac* (m.)
bakery *boulangerie* (f.)
ball *ballon (large – basketball, etc.)* (m.), *balle*
 (small – tennis, etc.) (f.)
ballet *ballet* (m.)
 ballet dancer *danseur / danseuse* (m./f.) *de*
 ballet, ballerine (f.)
banana *banane* (f.)
band *groupe* (m.) *de musique*
bandage *bandage* (m.), *pansement* (m.)
bank *banque* (f.), *quai (of a river)* (m.)
 bank clerk *employé / employée de banque*
 (m./f.)
banker *banquier / banquière* (m./f.)
banknote *billet* (m.)
baseball *baseball* (m.)
basket *panier* (m.)
 basket of strawberries *panier de fraises*
basketball *basket(-ball)* (m.)
bath towel *serviette* (f.) *de bain*
bathing suit/trunks *maillot* (m.) *de bain*
bathroom *salle* (f.) *de bains*
bathtub *baignoire* (f.)
be (to) *être*

be able to (to) *pouvoir*
be bored (to) *s'ennuyer*
be born (to) *naître*
be busy (to) *être occupé / occupée* (m./f.)
be called (to) *s'appeler*
be deaf (to) *être sourd / sourde* (m./f.)
be decided (to) *se décider*
be resolved (to do something) (to) *se décider*
be disabled (to) *être handicapé / handicapée*
 (m./f.)
be engaged (to) (to) *être fiancé / fiancée (à)*
 (m./f.)
be familiar with (to) *connaître*
be held (to) *avoir lieu*
be mistaken (to) *se tromper*
be necessary (to) *falloir*
be paralyzed (to) *être paralysé / paralysée*
 (m./f.)
be sick (to) *être malade*
be situated (to) *se trouver*
be sweating (to) *être en sueur, être en nage*
be unemployed (to) *être sans emploi, être*
 sans travail, chômeur, chômeuse
be afraid (to) *avoir peur*
be ashamed (to) *avoir honte*
be cold (to) *avoir froid*
be hot/warm (to) *avoir chaud*
be hungry (to) *avoir faim*
be thirsty (to) *avoir soif*
be sleepy (to) *avoir sommeil*
be right (to) *avoir raison*
be wrong (to) *avoir tort*
be … years old (to) *avoir… ans*
be in the middle of (to), be in the process of
 (to) *être en train de*
beach *plage* (f.)
bean *haricot* (m.)
 green bean *haricot vert*
beautician *esthéticien / esthéticienne* (m./f.)
beautiful *beau / bel / belle* (m./m. before a vowel
 or silent h/f.)
 It's beautiful (outside). *Il fait beau.*
beauty parlor (beauty salon) *institut* (m.) *de*
 beauté
because *parce que*
 because of … (in a negative way) *à cause de…*
become (to) *devenir*
bed *lit* (m.)

bedroom *chambre* (f.) *(à coucher)*
beef *bœuf* (m.)
beer *bière* (f.)
before *devant, avant (que), auparavant*
  the day before *veille* (f.) *de*
    before last *précédent / précédente* (m./f.),
    d'avant
beg (to) *prier*
begin (to) *commencer*
beginner *débutant / débutante* (m./f.)
  beginners' slope/hill *piste* (f.) *pour débutants*
behave (to) *agir*
behind *derrière*
beige *beige*
Belgian *belge*
Belgium *Belgique* (f.)
believe (to) *croire*
  I don't believe it! *Ce n'est pas possible !*
belly *ventre* (m.)
belongings *affaires* (f. pl.)
belt *ceinture* (f.)
best *meilleur / meilleure* (m./f.), *mieux*
  the best *le / la meilleur / meilleure*
better *meilleur / meilleure* (m./f.), *mieux*
  it is better (that), it would be better (that) *il*
  vaut mieux (que)
between *entre*
bicycle *bicyclette* (f.)
  go bike riding (to), ride a bike (to) *monter à*
  bicyclette
bidet *bidet* (m.)
big *grand / grande* (m./f.)
bike *vélo* (m.)
  go bike riding (to), ride a bike (to) *monter à*
  bicyclette
bill *billet* (currency) (m.), *addition* (restaurant,
  café, etc.) (f.)
  The bill, please. *L'addition, s'il vous plaît.*
billiards *billard* (m.)
billion *milliard*
billionaire *milliardaire* (m./f.)
biology *biologie* (f.)
birthday *anniversaire* (m.)
  Happy birthday! *Joyeux / Bon anniversaire !*
bisque (creamy soup) *bisque* (f.)
  lobster bisque *bisque de homard*
bite *morceau* (m.)
black *noir / noire* (m./f.)

black currant *cassis* (m.)
  black currant syrup *sirop* (m.) *de cassis*
bleach *eau* (f.) *de Javel*
blender *mixer* (m.)
blind *aveugle*
  be blind (to) *être aveugle*
blonde *blond / blonde* (m./f.)
blood *sang* (m.)
  blood transfusion *transfusion* (f.) *de sang*
blouse *chemisier* (m.), *blouse* (f.)
blue *bleu / bleue* (m./f.)
blush (to) *rougir*
boat *bateau* (m.)
body *corps* (m.)
  human body *corps humain*
  body parts *parties* (f. pl.) *du corps*
  body language *langage* (m.) *du corps*
bodybuilding *musculation* (f.)
  to do bodybuilding *faire de la musculation*
bone *os* (m.)
book *livre* (m.)
bookshelf *étagère* (f.), *bibliothèque* (f.)
bookstore *librairie* (f.)
border *bord* (m.)
  at the border of *au bord de*
bore (someone) (to) *ennuyer*
  be bored (to), get bored (to) *s'ennuyer*
  It's boring. *C'est ennuyeux.*
born (to be) *naître*
boss *patron / patronne* (m./f.), *chef* (m.)
bottle *bouteille* (f.)
  bottle of champagne *bouteille de*
  champagne
boulevard *boulevard* (m.)
boutique *boutique* (f.)
bowl *saladier* (m.), *bol* (m.)
box *boîte* (f.)
box office *guichet* (m.)
boxing *boxe* (f.)
boy *garçon* (m.)
boyfriend *copain* (m.), *petit ami* (m.)
bracelet *bracelet* (m.)
brain *cerveau* (m.)
brave *brave*
Brazil *Brésil* (m.)
Brazilian *brésilien / brésilienne* (m./f.)
bread *pain* (m.)
break (recess) *récré(ation)* (f.)

break (to) *casser, rompre*
  break one's arm/leg (to) *se casser le bras / la jambe*
breakfast *petit déjeuner* (m.)
  have breakfast (to) *prendre le petit déjeuner*
bridge *pont* (m.)
briefcase *serviette* (f.)
bring (to) *apporter*
brochure *brochure* (f.)
broom *balai* (m.)
brother *frère* (m.)
brown *brun / brune* (m./f.), *marron*
brush (to) *brosser*
  brush oneself (hair, teeth, etc.) (to) *se brosser*
buckwheat *sarrasin* (m.)
build (to) *bâtir*
  build a sandcastle (to) *faire un château de sable*
building *bâtiment* (m.), *immeuble (apartment, office)* (m.)
bundle, bunch *botte* (f.)
  bunch of asparagus *botte d'asperges*
bunny slope/hill *piste* (f.) *pour débutants*
burn *brûlure* (f.)
bus *bus* (m.), *autobus* (m.), *autocar* (m.)
  bus stop *arrêt* (m.) *de bus / d'autobus*
  bus tour *circuit* (m.) *en bus, excursion* (f.) *en autocar*
business *affaires* (f. pl.)
  businessman/woman *homme / femme d'affaires* (m./f.)
busy *occupé / occupée* (m./f.)
  be busy (to) *être occupé / occupée* (m./f.)
  The line is busy. *La ligne est occupée.*
but *mais*
butcher shop *boucherie* (f.)
butter *beurre* (m.)
butterfly *papillon* (m.)
buy (to) *acheter*
  a good buy (inexpensive) *bon marché*
by *par, d'ici*
  by foot *à pied*
  by heart *par cœur*
  by then *d'ici là*
  by the end of the week *d'ici la fin de la semaine*
Bye. *Salut.*

C

cab *taxi* (m.)
cabinet *armoire* (f.)
  medicine cabinet *armoire à pharmacie*
cable *câble* (m.)
café *café* (m.)
cafeteria *cafétéria (general term)* (f.), *cantine (school)* (f.)
cake *gâteau* (m.)
  chocolate cake *gâteau au chocolat*
calculus *calcul* (m.)
call (to) *appeler, téléphoner, donner / passer un coup de fil* (infml.)
  call back (to) *rappeler*
  Who's calling? (on the phone) *C'est de la part de qui ? / Qui est à l'appareil ?*
  call each other (to) *se téléphoner*
called (to be) *s'appeler*
calm *calme*
camera *appareil* (m.) *photo*
camp (to) *faire du camping*
camping *camping* (m.)
can (container) *boîte* (f.) *de conserve*
can (verb) *pouvoir*
  Can I help you? *Puis-je vous aider ?*
  can't wait (to look forward to) *avoir hâte*
  (I) can't wait for the end of the day! *Vivement la fin de la journée !*
Canada *Canada* (m.)
Canadian *canadien / canadienne* (m./f.)
candy *bonbons* (m. pl.)
  candy store *confiserie* (f.)
  pastry and candy store *pâtisserie-confiserie* (f.)
cane *canne* (f.)
  walk with a cane (to) *marcher avec une canne*
cantaloupe *melon* (m.)
cap *casquette* (f.)
capsule *capsule* (f.)
car *voiture* (f.), *automobile* (f.), *auto* (f.), *wagon (on a train)* (m.)
  car racing *course* (f.) *automobile*
caramel *caramel* (m.)
card *carte* (f.)
  playing cards *cartes* (pl.) *à jouer*
  card game *jeu* (m.) *de cartes*
care *soin* (m.)

carpenter *charpentier* (m.)

carpet *moquette* (f.)

carrot *carotte* (f.)

carry (to) *porter*

carton *boîte* (f.) *(en carton), carton* (m.), *brique* (f.)

   carton of orange juice *brique* (f.) *de jus d'orange*

cash *argent* (m.)

   cash register *caisse* (f.)

castle *château* (m.)

   sandcastle *château de sable*

casual *décontracté / décontractée* (m./f.)

cathedral *cathédrale* (f.)

   Notre Dame Cathedral *Cathédrale Notre-Dame*

CD player *lecteur* (m.) *de CD*

CD-ROM *CD-ROM* (m.)

   CD-ROM drive *lecteur* (m.) *de CD-ROM*

cease (to) *cesser*

ceiling *plafond* (m.)

celebrate (to) *célébrer*

celery *céleri* (m.)

cell phone *(téléphone) portable* (m.)

cellar *cave* (f.)

cello *violoncelle* (m.)

cent *cent* (m.)

center *centre* (m.)

   information center *centre d'informations*

   National Center of Art and Culture Georges-Pompidou (Pompidou Center) *Centre National d'Art et de Culture Georges-Pompidou (Centre Pompidou)*

certain *certain / certaine* (m./f.)

   it is certain that *il est certain que*

certainly *certainement*

chair *chaise* (f.)

champagne *champagne* (m.)

   bottle of champagne *bouteille* (f.) *de champagne*

   champagne with black currant liqueur *kir* (m.) *royal*

champion *champion / championne* (m./f.)

chance *hasard* (m.)

chandelier *lustre* (m.)

change *monnaie* (f.)

change (to) *changer*

   change channels (to) *changer de chaîne*

charming *charmant / charmante* (m./f.)

cheat (to) *tricher*

check *chèque* (m.), *addition (restaurant, café, etc.)* (f.)

   The check, please. *L'addition, s'il vous plaît.*

check in (to) *prendre une chambre*

check out (to) *régler sa note*

checkers *dames* (f. pl.)

checkup (medical) *examen* (m.) *médical*

cheek *joue* (f.)

cheese *fromage* (m.)

   slice of cheese *tranche* (f.) *de fromage*

   cheese sandwich *sandwich* (m.) *au fromage*

   ham and cheese sandwich *sandwich* (m.) *jambon-fromage*

   grilled ham and cheese sandwich *croque-monsieur* (m.)

   grilled ham and cheese sandwich with an egg on top *croque-madame* (m.)

chemistry *chimie* (f.)

cherry *cerise* (f.)

chess *échecs* (m. pl.)

chest *poitrine* (f.)

chestnut *marron* (m.)

   chestnut paste *crème* (f.) *de marrons*

   sugar-coated chestnuts *marrons* (pl.) *glacés*

chicken *poulet* (m.)

   chicken and fries *poulet frites*

   chicken/rooster cooked in wine *coq* (m.) *au vin*

child *enfant* (m./f.)

chin *menton* (m.)

China *Chine* (f.)

Chinese *chinois / chinoise* (m./f.)

   Chinese language *chinois* (m.)

chocolate *chocolat* (m.)

   chocolate cake *gâteau* (m.) *au chocolat*

   chocolate ice cream *glace* (f.) *au chocolat*

   chocolate mousse *mousse* (f.) *au chocolat*

   hot chocolate *chocolat* (m.) *chaud*

choice *choix* (m.)

choose (to) *choisir*

chop *côte* (f.)

   pork chop *côte de porc*

chopstick *baguette* (f.)

Christmas *Noël* (m.)

   Merry Christmas! *Joyeux Noël !*

Christmas Eve *réveillon* (m.) *de Noël, veille* (f.)

de Noël

church *église* (f.)

cider *cidre* (m.)

circus *cirque* (m.)

city *ville* (f.)

  city hall *mairie* (f.), *hôtel* (m.) *de ville*

civil servant *fonctionnaire / fonctionnaire* (m./f.)

clam *palourde* (f.), *clam* (m.)

clarinet *clarinette* (f.)

class *cours* (m.), *classe* (f.)

  French class *cours de français*

  dance class *cours de danse*

  to pass a class, to do well in a class *réussir à un cours*

classroom *salle* (f.) *de classe, classe* (f.)

clean *propre*

clean (to) *nettoyer*

  clean the house (to) *faire le ménage*

clerk *guichetier (at the window/counter)* (m.)

client *client / cliente* (m./f.)

climbing *alpinisme* (m.)

close *près*

  very close *tout près*

  close to here *près d'ici*

  the closest *le / la plus proche*

close (to) *fermer*

  close a file (to) *fermer un fichier*

closet *placard* (m.)

clothing/clothes *vêtements* (m. pl.)

  clothing store *magasin* (m.) *de vêtements*

  clothing size *taille* (f.)

cloud *nuage* (m.)

cloudy *nuageux / nuageuse* (m./f.)

  It's cloudy. *C'est nuageux.*

club (nightclub) *boîte* (f.) *(de nuit), discothèque* (f.), *centre* (m.)

  go out to clubs (to), go out clubbing (to) *sortir en boîte*

club (organization) *club* (m.), *cercle* (m.)

coach *entraîneur* (m.)

coast *côte* (f.)

coat *manteau* (m.), *blouse* (f.)

  white coat (doctor's coat) *blouse blanche*

coffee *café* (m.)

  coffee with cream *café-crème* (m.)

  coffee shop *café* (m.)

coffeemaker *cafétière* (f.)

coin *pièce* (f.)

coins *pièces* (pl.), *monnaie* (f.)

coincidence *coïncidence* (f.)

  What a coincidence! *Quelle coïncidence !*

cold *froid / froide* (m./f.)

  It's cold. *Il fait froid.*

  be cold (to) *avoir froid (person)*

cold (common cold) *rhume* (m.)

colleague *collègue / collègue* (m./f.)

collect (to) *collectionner*

collection *collection* (f.)

college *université* (f.)

  college degree *diplôme* (m.) *universitaire*

cologne *eau* (f.) *de cologne*

come (to) *venir*

  come back (to) *revenir*

  come back (in) (to), come home (to) *rentrer*

  come in (to) *entrer*

  come up (to) *monter*

  come down (to) *descendre*

  come out (to) *sortir*

comedy *comédie* (f.)

  romantic comedy *comédie romantique*

comfortable *confortable*

commercials *publicités* (f. pl.), *pubs* (f. pl.)

company *société* (f.), *firme* (f.)

competition *concours* (m.), *compétition* (f.)

complete (to) *compléter*

complicated *compliqué / compliquée* (m./f.)

computer *ordinateur* (m.)

  computer programmer *informaticien / informaticienne* (m./f.)

  computer science *informatique* (f.)

concert *concert* (m.)

Congratulations. *Félicitations.*

consommé (clear soup made from stock) *consommé* (m.)

  vermicelli pasta consommé (noodle soup) *consommé aux vermicelles*

construct (to) *construire*

construction worker *ouvrier / ouvrière en bâtiment* (m./f.)

consult (to) *consulter*

  consult a phone book (to) *consulter l'annuaire*

contest *concours* (m.), *compétition* (f.)

cook *cuisinier / cuisinière* (m./f.)

cook (to) *cuisiner, préparer, faire la cuisine*

cooking *cuisine* (f.)

do the cooking (to) *faire la cuisine*
cool (great) *sympa, cool*
corn *maïs* (m.)
corner *coin* (m.)
correct *exact / exacte* (m./f.)
cost (to) *coûter*
   That costs ... *Ça coûte...*
cotton *coton* (m.)
couch *canapé* (m.)
counter *bar* (m.), *comptoir* (m.), *guichet* (m.)
courageous *brave*
course *cours* (m.)
cousin *cousin / cousine* (m./f.)
cream, creamy dessert *crème* (f.)
   creamy dessert made with caramel *crème caramel*
   whipped cream (that is flavored and sweetened) *crème chantilly*
   shaving cream *crème à raser*
crêpe (tissue-thin pancake) *crêpe* (f.)
   crêpe Suzette (crêpe with sugar, orange, and liqueur) *Crêpe Suzette*
crime drama/film *film* (m.) *policier*
croissant *croissant*
cross (to) *traverser*
crowd *foule* (f.)
cruel *cruel, cruelle* (m./f.)
cruise ship *paquebot* (m.)
crutches *béquilles* (f. pl.)
   walk with crutches (to) *marcher avec des béquilles*
cucumber *concombre* (m.)
cup *tasse* (f.)
   cup of tea *tasse de thé*
cupboard *placard* (m.)
cure (to) *guérir*
currency *monnaie* (f.)
   currency exchange office *bureau* (m.) *de change*
curtain *rideau* (m.)
customer service department *service* (m.) *clientèle, service* (m.) *client*
cut *coupure* (f.)
cycling *cyclisme* (m.)

D

Dad/Daddy *papa*
daily *quotidien / quotidienne* (m./f.)
dance (to) *danser*
dance class *cours* (m.) *de danse*
dance/dancing *danse* (f.)
darling *chéri / chérie* (m./f.)
date (to) *sortir avec*
date *date* (f.), *rendez-vous* (m.)
daughter *fille* (f.)
daughter-in-law *belle-fille* (f.)
day *jour* (m.), *journée* (f.)
   the day after tomorrow *après-demain*
   the day before yesterday *avant-hier*
deaf *sourd / sourde* (m./f.)
dealer *marchand / marchande* (m./f.)
dear (adjective) *cher / chère* (m./f.)
dear (term of endearment) *chéri / chérie* (m./f.)
deceive (to) *tromper*
December *décembre*
decide (to) *décider*
decided (to be) *se décider*
defend (to) *défendre*
degree *degré* (m.)
degree (college) *diplôme* (m.) *universitaire*
delete (to) *supprimer*
delicatessen *charcuterie* (f.)
delicious *délicieux / délicieuse* (m./f.)
delighted *ravi / ravie* (m./f.)
demand (to) *exiger*
demonstrate (to) *manifester*
demonstration *manifestation* (f.)
demonstrator *manifestant / manifestante* (m./f.)
dentist *dentiste* (m./f.)
deodorant *déodorant* (m.)
depart (to) *quitter*
department *service* (m.)
   accounting department *service de comptabilité*
   IT department *service d'informatique*
   finance department *service financier*
   sales department *service des ventes*
   legal department *service juridique*
   marketing department *service de marketing*
   public relations (PR) department *service des relations publiques*
   shipping department (mail room) *service du*

courrier

customer service department *service clientèle, service client*

department store *grand magasin* (m.)

departure time *heure* (f.) *du départ*

descend (to) *descendre*

description *description* (f.)

desert *désert* (m.)

designer (fashion) *couturier* (m.)

desire *envie* (f.)

desire (to) *désirer*

desk *bureau* (m.)

dessert *dessert* (m.)

detective (adjective) *inspecteur/inspecteurice de police*

detective drama/film *film* (m.) *policier*

detest (to) *détester*

device *appareil* (m.)

diagnosis *diagnostic* (m.)

diamond *diamant* (m.)

diamond ring *bague* (f.) *en diamant*

die (to) *mourir*

different *différent / différente* (m./f.)

difficult *difficile*

difficult subject *matière* (f.) *difficile*

Dijon mustard *moutarde* (f.) *de Dijon*

dine (to) *dîner*

dining room *salle* (f.) *à manger*

dinner *dîner* (m.)

have dinner (to) *dîner*

Dinner's ready! *À table !*

late dinner *souper* (m.)

diploma *diplôme* (m.)

direction *direction* (f.)

director *directeur / directrice* (m./f.)

dirty *sale*

disabled *handicapé / handicapée* (m./f.)

discount *remise* (f.)

disease *maladie* (f.)

Alzheimer's disease *maladie d'Alzheimer*

Parkinson's disease *maladie de Parkinson*

dish *plat* (m.)

side dish *plat d'accompagnement*

dishwasher *lave-vaisselle* (m.)

dishwashing detergent *liquide* (m.) *vaisselle*

disobey (to) *désobéir*

dispatch (to) *dépêcher*

dive (to) *plonger*

dive in(to) the pool (to) *plonger dans la piscine*

divorce *divorce* (m.)

get a divorce (to) *divorcer*

do (to) *faire*

do well (to) *réussir*

do well on a test/in a class (to) *réussir à un examen / cours*

do the cooking (to) *faire la cuisine*

do the dishes (to) *faire la vaisselle*

do the house cleaning (to) *faire le ménage*

do the laundry (to) *faire la lessive*

do the shopping (to) *faire les / des courses*

do bodybuilding (to) *faire de la musculation*

do strength training (to) *faire de la musculation*

do horseback riding (to) *faire de l'équitation*

do sports (to) *faire du sport*

do yoga (to) *faire du yoga*

do a tour (to) *faire un tour*

doctor *médecin* (m.), *docteur / doctoresse* (m./f.)

doctor's office *cabinet* (m.) *médical*

white coat (doctor's coat) *blouse* (f.) *blanche*

document *document* (m.)

documentary *documentaire* (m.)

dog *chien* (m.)

seeing-eye dog *chien d'aveugle*

door *porte* (f.)

doubt (to) *douter*

downstairs, down below *en bas*

dozen *douzaine* (f.)

dozen eggs *douzaine d'œufs*

drama *drame* (m.)

period drama *drame d'époque*

drawer *tiroir* (m.)

drawing *dessin* (m.)

dress *robe* (f.)

dress (to) *habiller*

get dressed (to), dress oneself (to) *s'habiller*

dress code *code* (m.) *vestimentaire*

dressing rooms *cabines* (f. pl.) *d'essayage*

drink (to) *boire*

drive (computer) *lecteur* (m.)

CD-ROM drive *lecteur de CD-ROM*

drive (to) *conduire*

drugstore *pharmacie* (f.)

drums *batterie* (f.)

dry (alcohol) *brut / brute* (m./f.)

dryer *sèche-linge* (m.)
dubbed *doublé / doublée* (m./f.)
duck *canard* (m.)
  duck à l'orange, duck with orange
    sauce *canard à l'orange*
due to … (in a negative way) *à cause de…*
during *pendant*
DVD player *lecteur* (m.) *de DVD*

E

each *chaque, chacun / chacune* (m./f.)
ear *oreille* (f.)
early *en avance, tôt*
earn (to) *gagner*
  earn money (to) *gagner de l'argent*
earring *boucle* (f.) *d'oreille*
easily *facilement*
east *est* (m.)
easy *facile*
eat (to) *manger*
éclair (type of cream-filled pastry) *éclair* (m.)
edge *bord* (m.)
  at the edge of *au bord de*
egg *œuf* (m.)
  egg whites *blancs* (m. pl.) *(d'œufs)*
  fried egg (over easy egg) *œuf au plat, œuf sur le plat*
  hard-boiled egg *œuf dur*
  poached egg *œuf poché*
  scrambled eggs *œufs* (pl.) *brouillés*
  soft-boiled egg *œuf à la coque*
Eiffel Tower *Tour* (f.) *Eiffel*
eight *huit*
eighteen *dix-huit*
eighth *huitième*
eighty *quatre-vingts*
either *ou bien*
elbow *coude* (m.)
elderly person *personne* (f.) *âgée*
electrician *électricien* (m.)
electronic game *jeu* (m.) *électronique*
electronics store *magasin* (m.) *d'électronique*
elegant *élégant / élégante* (m./f.)
elementary school *école* (f.) *primaire*
elephant *éléphant* (m.)
eleven *onze*
eleventh *onzième*
else *autre, d'autre*

elsewhere *ailleurs*
e-mail *mail* (m.), *mèl* (m.), *e-mail* (m.), *courriel* (m.), *courrier* (m.) *électronique*
emergency *urgence* (f.)
  emergency medical service *service* (m.) *d'assistance médicale d'urgence*
  emergency situations *cas* (m. pl.) *d'urgence*
employ (to) *employer*
employee *employé / employée* (m./f.)
employment *emploi* (m.)
end (to) *terminer*
  at the end of *au bout de*
end *fin* (f.)
  end of the game, end of the match *fin du match*
engaged (to) (to be) *être fiancé / fiancée (à)*
  get engaged (to each other) (to) *se fiancer*
engagement ring *bague* (f.) *de fiançailles*
engineer *ingénieur* (m.)
England *Angleterre* (f.)
English *anglais / anglaise* (m./f.)
  English language *anglais* (m.)
  in English *en anglais*
  English literature *littérature anglaise*
enjoy oneself (to) *s'amuser*
Enjoy your meal! *Bon appétit !*
enjoyable *agréable*
enormous *énorme*
enough *assez*
  That's enough. *Ça suffit.*
enter (to) *entrer*
entertain (to) *amuser*
entertainment *divertissement* (m.)
entrance *entrée* (f.)
equal *égal / égale* (m./f.)
errand *course* (f.)
escargots *escargots* (m. pl.)
especially *surtout*
essential *essentiel / essentielle* (m./f.)
  it is essential that *il est essentiel que*
euro *euro* (m.)
European *européen / européenne* (m./f.)
  European Union *Union* (f.) *européenne*
even *même*
  even more *bien plus*
evening *soir* (m.), *soirée* (f.)
  this evening *ce soir*
ever *jamais*

every *tout / toute / tous / toutes* (m./f./m. pl./f. pl.), *chaque*

everyday *quotidien / quotidienne* (m./f.)
  everyday language *langage* (m.) *courant*

everyone *tout le monde*

everywhere *partout*

exact *exact / exacte* (m./f.), *précis / précise* (m./f.)

exam *examen* (m.)
  baccalauréat (an exam for students wishing to continue their education beyond high school) *baccalauréat / bac* (m.)
  examine (to) *examiner*

excellent *excellent / excellente* (m./f.)

exchange (to) *changer (banking), échanger (store-bought items)*

exciting *passionnant / passionnante* (m./f.)

excuse (to) *excuser*
  Excuse me. *Pardon. / Excusez-moi.*

exit *sortie* (f.)

expect (to) *attendre*

expensive *cher / chère* (m./f.)

expression *expression* (f.)

extension (telephone) *poste* (m.)

exterior *extérieur* (m.)

extracurricular activities *activités* (f. pl.) *extra-scolaires / parascolaires*

eye (eyes) *œil* (m.) (*yeux*, pl.)
  blue/brown/green eyes *les yeux bleus / bruns / verts*

eyebrow *sourcil* (m.)

eyeglasses *lunettes* (f. pl.)

eyelash *cil* (m.)

F

face *visage* (m.), *figure* (f.)

facing *en face de*

factory *usine* (f.)

fail (a test/class) (to) *échouer à (un examen / cours), rater (un examen / cours)*

fall (season) *automne* (m.)
  in (the) fall *en automne*

fall (to) *tomber*

false *faux / fausse* (m./f.)

familiar language *langage* (m.) *familier*

familiar with (to be) *connaître*

family *famille* (f.)

famous *célèbre*

fan (sports) *supporteur / supportrice* (m./f.)

Fantastic. *Formidable.*

far *loin*
  far from here *loin d'ici*
  farther *plus loin*

farmer *fermier / fermière* (m./f.)

fashion *mode* (f.), *façon* (f.)
  high fashion *haute couture* (f.)
  fashion designer *couturier* (m.)

fat *gros / grosse* (m./f.)

father *père* (m.)

father-in-law *beau-père* (m.)

favorite *préféré / préférée* (m./f.), *favori / favorite* (m./f.)

fax machine *télécopieur* (m.)

fear *peur* (f.)

February *février*

feed (to) *nourrir*

feel like (to) *avoir envie de*

festival *fête* (f.)

fever *fièvre* (f.)

fewer *moins*

fiancé/fiancée *fiancé / fiancée* (m./f.)

fiddle with things (to) *bricoler*

field *champ* (m.)

fifteen *quinze*

fifteenth *quinzième*

fifth *cinquième*

fifty *cinquante*

figure *forme* (f.)

file *fichier* (m.)

fill (in) (to) *remplir*

filling (tooth) *plombage* (m.)

film *film* (m.)
  action film *film d'action*
  crime/detective film, crime/detective drama *film policier*
  original version of a film (not dubbed into French) *version* (f.) *originale (v.o.)*
  French version of a film (dubbed into French) *version* (f.) *française (v.f.)*

final *dernier / dernière* (m./f.)
  final score *score* (m.) *final*
  final year of high school *classe* (f.) *terminale*

finally *enfin, finalement*

finance department *service* (m.) *financier*

find (to) *trouver*

find oneself (somewhere) (to) *se trouver*
find that (to) *trouver que*
fine *bien*
finger *doigt* (m.)
fingernail *ongle* (m.)
finish (to) *finir, terminer*
fire *feu* (m.)
firm (company) *firme* (f.)
First ... *D'abord...*
first *premier / première (number)* (m./f.)
   first floor (one floor above ground
      floor) *premier étage* (m.)
   first base *première base* (f.)
first-aid kit *trousse* (f.) *de secours*
fish *poisson* (m.)
fishing *pêche* (f.)
fit (to be) *être en forme*
five *cinq*
fix things (to) *bricoler*
flag *drapeau* (m.)
flavor *parfum* (m.)
floor *étage (as in, second floor, third floor, etc.)*
(m.), *sol (of a room)* (m.)
   ground floor *rez-de-chaussée* (m.)
flower *fleur* (f.)
flu *grippe* (f.)
flute *flûte* (f.)
fog *brouillard* (m.)
follow (to) *suivre*
food *nourriture* (f.)
foot *pied* (m.)
   on foot, by foot *à pied*
   at the foot of *au pied de*
football (American) *football* (m.) *américain*
for *pour, de / d', depuis, pendant*
   for a party of four, for four people *pour*
      quatre personnes
   for me *pour moi*
   for how long? *depuis combien de temps ?*
forehead *front* (m.)
foreign language *langue* (f.) *étrangère*
forest *forêt* (f.)
fork *fourchette* (f.)
form *forme* (f.)
formal language *langage* (m.) *soutenu*
formal (in formal dress/attire) *en tenue de
soirée*
former *ancien / ancienne* (m./f.)

formerly *autrefois*
fortunately *heureusement*
forty *quarante*
forward (to) *faire suivre*
four *quatre*
fourteen *quatorze*
fourth *quatrième*
fragrance *parfum* (m.)
France *France* (f.)
frankly *franchement*
free *libre*
   free time *temps* (m.) *libre*
French *français / française* (m./f.)
   French language *français* (m.)
   French version of a film (dubbed into
      French) *version* (f.) *française (v.f.)*
   in French *en français*
french fries *frites* (f. pl.)
frequently *fréquemment*
Friday *vendredi*
friend *ami / amie* (m./f.)
friendly *amical / amicale* (m./f.), *sympathique*
fries *frites* (f. pl.)
   chicken and fries *poulet* (m.) *frites*
   mussels and fries *moules* (f. pl.) *frites*
   steak and fries *steak* (m. pl.) *frites*
from *de / d'*
   from here *d'ici*
   from (someone) *de la part de*
   from me *de ma part*
   from time to time *de temps en temps*
front *devant*
   in front (of) *devant*
fruit *fruit* (m.)
   fruit salad *salade* (f.) *de fruits*
full-time *à plein temps*
funny *amusant / amusante* (m./f.), *drôle*
   so funny *si drôle*
furniture *meubles* (m. pl.)
   a piece of furniture *meuble* (m.)

G

gain weight (to) *grossir*
gallery *galerie* (f.)
game *jeu* (m.), *match* (m.)
garage *garage* (m.)
garbage *poubelle* (f.)
garden *jardin* (m.)

gastronomy *gastronomie* (f.)
general *général / générale* (m./f.)
generally *généralement, en général*
generous *généreux / généreuse* (m./f.)
genre *genre*
gentle *doux / douce* (m./f.)
gentlemen *messieurs*
gently *doucement*
geometry *géométrie* (f.)
German *allemand / allemande* (m./f.)
Germany *Allemagne* (f.)
get a divorce (to) *divorcer*
get a shot (to) *recevoir une piqûre*
get a tan (to) *bronzer*
get along with (to) *s'entendre bien avec*
get better (to) *guérir*
get bored (to) *s'ennuyer*
get dressed (to) *s'habiller*
get engaged (to each other) (to) *se fiancer*
get married (to each other) (to) *se marier*
get sick (to) *tomber malade*
get somewhere (to) *arriver*
  get to (a destination) (to) *arriver à (+
    destination)*
get up (to) *se lever*
girl *fille* (f.)
girlfriend *copine* (f.), *petite amie* (f.)
give (to) *donner*
  give in to (to) *se rendre à (+ evidence, an
    argument, etc.)*
glass *verre* (m.)
  glass of milk *verre de lait*
glasses *lunettes* (f. pl.)
glove *gant* (m.)
go (to) *aller*
  Let's go. *Allons-y. / On y va.* (infml.)
  Go on!/Go ahead!/Go there! *Vas-y !* (infml.)
  go across (to) *traverser*
  go away (to) *partir*
  go out (to) *partir, sortir*
  go out clubbing (to), go out to clubs
    (to) *sortir en boîte*
  go out with (to) (to date) *sortir avec*
  go down (to) *descendre*
  go up (to) *monter*
  go home (to), go in (to) *rentrer*
  go (past) (to) *passer*
  go to (to) *se rendre à (+ location)*

go shopping (to) *faire des / les courses*
go sightseeing (to) *aller visiter*
go to bed (to) *se coucher*
go swimming (to) *faire de la natation*
go hiking (to) *faire de la marche*
go camping (to) *camper, faire du camping*
go bike riding (to) *monter à bicyclette*
go horseback riding (to) *faire de l'équitation,
  monter à cheval*
go jogging (to) *faire du jogging*
go on a picnic (to) *faire un pique-nique*
go scuba diving (to) *faire de la plongée sous-
  marine*
go skiing (to) *faire du ski*
go water-skiing (to) *faire du ski nautique*
goal *but* (m.)
god *dieu* (m.)
  My god! *Mon dieu !*
gold *or* (m.)
golf *golf* (m.)
  golf course *parcours* (m.) *de golf, terrain* (m.)
    de golf
good *bon / bonne* (m./f.), *bien, sympa, brave*
  very good *très bien, très bon / bonne* (m./f.),
    très sympa
  Good luck. *Bonne chance.*
  Good day. *Bonjour.*
  Good evening. *Bonsoir.*
  Good night. *Bonne nuit.*
  Good-bye. *Au revoir.*
  I'm having a good time. *Je m'amuse.*
  a good buy (inexpensive) *bon marché*
grade *note (score)* (f.), *classe (year)* (f.)
gram *gramme* (m.)
grammar *grammaire* (f.)
grandfather *grand-père* (m.)
  grandfather clock *pendule* (f.)
grandmother *grand-mère* (f.)
grandparent *grand-parent* (m.)
grape(s) *raisin* (m.)
great *formidable, extra, super*
  Great! *Super !*
  It's great. *C'est extra.*
Greece *Grèce* (f.)
Greek *grec / grecque* (m./f.)
green *vert / verte* (m./f.)
  green bean *haricot* (m.) *vert*
  green salad *salade* (f.) *verte*

grocery store *épicerie* (f.)
grow (to) *grandir, pousser*
growing (to be) *être en pleine expansion* (business)
grown-up *adulte* (m./f.)
guide *guide* (m.)
guided tour *visite* (f.) *guidée*
guitar *guitare* (f.)
gym *gym(nastique)* (physical education) (f.), *gymnase* (place) (m.)
gymnastics *gymnastique* (f.)

H

hail *grêle* (f.)
  It's hailing. *Il grêle.*
hair *cheveux* (m. pl.)
  hair (single strand) *cheveu* (m.)
  brown/blond/red/black hair *les cheveux bruns / blonds / roux / noirs*
half *demi / demie* (m./f.)
  half past ... *... et demie*
  half hour *demi-heure* (f.)
halftime *mi-temps* (f.)
hall *salle* (f.) (for public events), *entrée* (f.) (foyer of a house)
hallway *couloir* (m.)
ham *jambon* (m.)
  ham and cheese sandwich *sandwich* (m.) *jambon-fromage*
  ham sandwich *sandwich* (m.) *au jambon*
  grilled ham and cheese sandwich *croque-monsieur* (m.)
  grilled ham and cheese sandwich with an egg on top *croque-madame* (m.)
hand *main* (f.)
handkerchief *mouchoir* (m.)
handsome *beau / bel / belle* (m./m. before a vowel or silent h/f.)
hang up (to) *raccrocher*
Hanukkah *Hanoukka* (f.), *Hanoucca* (f.)
happen (to) *arriver*
happily *heureusement*
happy *heureux / heureuse* (m./f.)
  to make oneself happy *se rendre heureux / heureuse*
  Happy birthday!/Happy anniversary! *Joyeux / Bon anniversaire !*

Happy Holidays! *Joyeuses / Bonnes Fêtes !*
Happy New Year! *Bonne Année !*
hard *dur / dure* (m./f.), *difficile*
  hard-boiled egg *œuf* (m.) *dur*
hardware store *quincaillerie* (f.)
haste *hâte* (f.)
hasten (to) *hâter*
hat *chapeau* (m.)
hate (to) *détester*
hatred *haine* (f.)
have (to) *avoir*
  have (food/drink) (to) *prendre*
  have a drink (to) *prendre un verre*
  have breakfast (to) *prendre le petit déjeuner*
  have lunch (to) *déjeuner*
  have dinner (to) *dîner*
  have a late dinner (to) *souper*
  have a good time (to) *s'amuser*
  have fun (to) *s'amuser*
  have a party (to) *organiser une fête*
  have (the) time (to) *avoir le temps*
  have to (to) *devoir*
  have a sore (something) (to) *avoir mal à*
  have pain in (to) *avoir mal à*
  have trouble (doing something) (to) *avoir du mal à*
  have an accident (to) *avoir un accident*
  have an interview (to) *avoir une entrevue*
hazelnut *noisette* (f.)
he *il*
head *tête* (f.)
health *santé* (f.)
  To your health! *À votre santé !*
  health club *club/centre* (m.) *de remise (en forme), club* (m.) *de forme*
  healthy *en bonne santé*
hear (to) *entendre*
heart *cœur* (m.)
  heart attack *crise* (f.) *cardiaque*
heartbeat *battement* (m.) *de cœur*
held (to be) *avoir lieu*
Hello. *Bonjour. / Salut.*
  Hello. (on the phone) *Allô.*
helmet *casque* (m.)
help (to) *aider*
her *son / sa / ses* (m./f./pl.), *elle, la / l'* (direct object pronoun)

to her *lui* (indirect object pronoun)
herbal tea *tisane* (f.)
here *ici, ci*
    from here *d'ici*
    here is/are, here it is/they are *voici, voilà*
hero/heroine *héros / héroïne* (m./f.)
herself *se / s'* (reflexive pronoun)
Hey! *Tiens ! (surprise)*
Hi. *Salut.*
hide and seek *cache-cache* (f.)
    to play hide and seek *jouer à cache-cache*
high *haut / haute* (m./f.)
    high fashion *haute couture*
    high-speed train *train* (m.) *à grande vitesse*
        (TGV)
    high school *lycée* (m.)
    high school student *lycéen / lycéenne* (m./f.)
hill *colline* (f.)
him *lui, le / l'* (direct object pronoun)
    to him *lui* (indirect object pronoun)
himself *se / s'* (reflexive pronoun)
his *son / sa / ses* (m./f./pl.)
history *histoire* (f.)
hobby *passe-temps* (m.)
hockey *hockey* (m.)
    ice hockey *hockey sur glace*
hold (to) *tenir*
    Hold on, please. *Ne quittez pas, s'il vous plaît.*
holiday *fête* (f.)
home *maison* (f.), *foyer* (m.)
homemade *maison*
homemaker *homme / femme au foyer* (m./f.)
homework *devoirs* (m. pl.)
honestly *franchement*
honey *miel* (m.)
honey (term of endearment) *chéri / chérie*
    (m./f.)
hope (to) *espérer*
horrible *horrible*
horror movie *film* (m.) *d'épouvante*
horse *cheval* (m.)
horseback riding *équitation* (f.)
    go horseback riding (to) *faire de l'équitation,*
        monter à cheval
hose (stocking) *bas* (m.)
hospital *hôpital* (m.)
hot *chaud / chaude* (m./f.)
    It's hot./It's warm. *Il fait chaud.*

be hot/warm (to) *avoir chaud (person)*
hot chocolate *chocolat* (m.) *chaud*
hotel *hôtel* (m.)
hour *heure* (f.)
house *maison* (f.)
    at someone's house/place *chez*
    house cleaning *ménage* (m.)
    do the house cleaning (to), clean the house
        (to) *faire le ménage*
how *comment, comme*
    how many, how much *combien*
    How? *Comment ?*
    How's it going?/How are you? *(Comment)*
        ça va ?
    How are you? *Comment vas-tu ?* (infml.) /
        Comment allez-vous ? (pl./fml.)
    (for) how long? *depuis combien de temps ?*
hug (each other) (to) *s'embrasser*
human being *être* (m.) *humain*
human body *corps* (m.) *humain*
human resources *personnel* (m.)
    human resources manager *directeur* (m.) *du*
        personnel
hundred *cent*
hunger *faim* (f.)
    hungry (to be) *avoir faim*
hunting *chasse* (f.)
hurdle *haie* (f.)
hurricane *ouragan* (m.)
hurry (to) *se dépêcher*
hurt (to) *blesser, faire mal*
    hurt oneself (to) *se blesser*
husband *mari* (m.)

I

I *je / j'*
    I am called ... (My name is ...) *Je m'appelle...*
    I don't understand. *Je ne comprends pas.*
    I'm fine. *Ça va.*
    I'm very well. *Je vais très bien.*
    I want ... *Je veux...*
    I would like ... *Je voudrais...*
ice *glace* (f.)
    ice hockey *hockey* (m.) *sur glace*
    ice skate, ice skating *patin* (m.) *à glace*
    ice skating *patinage* (m.) *sur glace*
ice cream *glace* (f.)
    chocolate ice cream *glace au chocolat*

strawberry ice cream *glace à la fraise*
vanilla ice cream *glace à la vanille*
idea *idée* (f.)
if *si*
  if necessary, if needed *s'il le faut*
Île de la Cité (City Island) *Île* (f.) *de la Cité*
illness *maladie* (f.)
important *important / importante* (m./f.)
  it is important that *il est important que*
impoverished *pauvre*
in *à, dans, en*
  in the *au / à la / à l' / aux* (m./f./m. or f. before a
    vowel or silent h/pl.)
  in front (of) *devant*
  in general *en général*
  in the middle of *au milieu de*
  be in the middle of (to), be in the process of
    (to) *être en train de*
  in college *à l'université*
  in high school *au lycée*
  in middle school *au collège*
  in my opinion *à mon avis*
  in order that *afin que, pour que*
indeed *en effet*
India *Inde* (f.)
Indian *indien / indienne* (m./f.)
individual *individu* (m.)
inexpensive *bon marché*
infection *infection* (f.)
inflammation *inflammation* (f.)
informal language *langage* (m.) *familier*
information center *centre* (m.) *d'informations*
information technology (IT) *informatique* (f.)
  IT department *service* (m.) *d'informatique*
inherit (to) *hériter*
injection *piqûre* (f.), *injection* (f.)
inn *auberge* (f.)
instant message *message* (m.) *instantané*
instructions *instructions* (f. pl.)
insurance *assurance* (f.)
intelligent *intelligent / intelligente* (m./f.)
interesting *intéressant / intéressante* (m./f.)
Internet *Internet* (m.)
interrupt (to) *interrompre*
intersection *intersection* (f.)
interview *entrevue* (f.)
into *dans, en*
introduce (to) *présenter*

Let me introduce ... *Je te présente...* (infml.) /
  Je vous présente... (pl./fml.)
invite (to) *inviter*
Ireland *Irlande* (f.)
Irish *irlandais / irlandaise* (m./f.)
  an Irishman *un Irlandais*
iron *fer* (m.) *à repasser*
ironing board *planche* (f.) *à repasser*
Is that all? *C'est tout ?*
isn't it?/isn't that so? *... n'est-ce pas ?*
it *ça / c', il / elle / ils / elles* (m./f./m. pl./f. pl.), *le
  / la / l' / les* (direct object pronoun) (m./f./m. or f.
  before a vowel or silent h/pl.)
  to it *lui* (indirect object pronoun)
  It rains. *Il pleut.*
it is *c'est*
  isn't it? *n'est-ce pas ?*
  It's going well. *Ça va bien.*
  It's not going well./It's going badly. *Ça va
    mal.*
  It's beautiful (outside). *Il fait beau.*
  It's hot./It's warm. *Il fait chaud.*
  It's cold. *Il fait froid.*
  It's sunny. *Il fait (du) soleil. / Il y a du soleil.*
  It's windy. *Il fait du vent. / Il y a du vent.*
  It's hailing. *Il grêle.*
  It's snowing. *Il neige.*
  It is time to .../Now is the time to ... *Il est
    temps de...*
  It's not serious./It's not a problem./It's not a
    big deal. *Ce n'est pas grave.*
  it's necessary to *il faut*
  it's necessary that *il faut que*
  it is better *il vaut mieux*
  it is better that *il vaut mieux que*
  it is certain that *il est certain que*
  it is true that *il est vrai que*
  it is possible that *il est possible que*
  it is probable that *il est probable que*
  it seems that *il semble que*
  it is urgent that *il est urgent que*
  it is essential that *il est essentiel que*
  it is important that *il est important que*
  it is necessary that *il est nécessaire que*
  it is preferable that *il est préférable que*
Italian *italien / italienne* (m./f.)
Italy *Italie* (f.)
its *son / sa / ses* (m./f./pl.)

itself *se / s'* (reflexive pronoun)

J

jacket *veste* (f.), *veston* (m.)
jam *confiture* (f.)
January *janvier*
Japan *Japon* (m.)
Japanese *japonais / japonaise* (m./f.)
jeans *jean* (m.)
jelly *confiture* (f.)
jewel *bijou* (m.)
   jewelry *bijoux* (m. pl.)
job *boulot* (m.), *emploi* (m.), *travail* (m.)
joint (of meat) *rôti* (m.)
journalist *journaliste* (m./f.)
juice *jus* (m.)
July *juillet*
jump (to) *sauter*
June *juin*
junior high school *collège* (m.)
just *juste*
   just as ... *aussi...*

K

keyboard *clavier* (m.)
kick (to) *donner un coup de pied*
kilo *kilo* (m.)
kind (nice) *gentil / gentille* (m./f.), *aimable*
kind (type) *genre*
kiss (each other) (to) *s'embrasser*
kitchen *cuisine* (f.)
   kitchen sink *évier* (m.) *de la cuisine*
knee *genou* (m.)
knife *couteau* (m.)
knitting *tricot* (m.)
know (to) *savoir, connaître*
   I don't know. *Je ne sais pas.*
   know each other (to) *se connaître*

L

laboratory *laboratoire* (m.)
lady
   ladies *dame* (f.), *mesdames*
lake *lac* (m.)
lamb *agneau* (m.)
lamp *lampe* (f.)
lamppost *réverbère* (m.)
land *terre* (f.)

lane *voie* (f.)
language *langue* (f.), *langage* (m.)
   informal language, familiar
     language *langage familier*
   formal language *langage soutenu*
   everyday language *langage courant*
   bad language *langage grossier*
   body language *langage du corps*
   baby talk (baby language) *langage enfantin*
   sign language *langage des signes*
   programming language *langage de*
     programmation
   legal language, legal terminology *langage*
     juridique
   foreign language *langue étrangère*
large *grand / grande* (m./f.)
last *dernier / dernière* (m./f.)
   last Monday *lundi dernier*
   last month *mois* (m.) *dernier*
   last summer *été* (m.) *dernier*
   last night *hier soir, nuit* (f.) *dernière*
   last year *année* (f.) *dernière*
   the last time *la dernière fois*
late *en retard, tard*
   late dinner *souper* (m.)
latest *dernier / dernière* (m./f.)
laundry detergent *lessive* (f.)
lawyer *avocat / avocate* (m./f.)
lay down (to) *coucher, allonger*
lead (to) *mener*
learn (to) *apprendre*
   learn by heart (to) *apprendre par cœur*
   I'm learning French. *J'apprends le français.*
the least ... *le / la moins...*
leather *cuir* (m.)
leave (to) *partir, sortir, laisser*
leek *poireau* (m.)
left *gauche* (f.)
   on the left, to the left, at the left *à gauche*
   left bank *rive* (f.) *gauche*
leg *jambe* (f.)
legal (related to the law) *juridique*
   legal department *service* (m.) *juridique*
   legal language, legal terminology *langage*
     (m.) *juridique*
leisure activities *loisirs* (m. pl.)
lemon *citron* (m.)
lens *verre* (m.), *lentille* (f.)

contact lenses *verres / lentilles* (pl.) *de contact*
less *moins*
   less ... than *moins... que*
lesson *leçon* (f.)
let (someone do something) (to) *laisser*
let go (to) *laisser*
Let me introduce ... *Je te présente...* (infml.) / *Je vous présente...* (pl./fml.)
Let's go. *Allons-y. / On y va.* (infml.)
letter *lettre* (f.)
lettuce *laitue* (f.)
library *bibliothèque* (f.)
lie down (to) *se coucher, allonger*
life *vie* (f.)
lifeguard *maître-nageur* (f.), *sauveteur* (m.)
lift (to) *lever*
   lift a dumbbell (to) *soulever un haltère*
   lift weights (to) *faire de la musculation*
light *léger / légère* (m./f.)
lightly *légèrement*
lightning *éclair* (m.)
like *comme*
like (to) *aimer*
   like each other (to) *s'aimer*
   I like ... *J'aime...*
   I do not like ... *Je n'aime pas...*
lime *citron vert* (m.)
line *queue* (f.)
   wait in line (to) *faire la queue*
link *liaison* (f.)
listen (to) (to) *écouter*
literature *littérature* (f.)
little *petit / petite* (m./f.)
   a little *un peu*
live (to) *habiter*
living room *salon* (m.)
lobster *homard* (m.)
   lobster bisque *bisque* (f.) *de homard*
lonely *seul / seule* (m./f.)
long *long / longue* (m./f.), *longtemps*
   a long time ago *il y a longtemps*
look at (to) *regarder*
   look at each other (to) *se regarder*
look for (to) *chercher*
look forward to (to) (can't wait) *avoir hâte*
look great on someone (to) *aller à ravir à quelqu'un*
lose (to) *perdre*

lose weight (to) *maigrir*
lose a game/match (to) *perdre un match*
lost *perdu / perdue* (m./f.)
   I'm lost. *Je suis perdu / perdue.*
Louvre *Louvre* (m.)
   Louvre museum *musée* (m.) *du Louvre*
love (to) *aimer, adorer*
   love each other (to) *s'aimer*
low *bas / basse* (m./f.)
luck *chance* (f.)
   No luck! *Pas de chance !*
   Good luck! *Bonne chance !*
lunch *déjeuner* (m.)
   have lunch (to) *déjeuner*
lung *poumon* (m.)
Lutetia (old name for Paris) *Lutèce* (f.)

M

ma'am/madam *madame*
magazine *magazine* (m.), *revue* (f.)
magnificent *magnifique*
mail *poste* (f.)
   mail room *service* (m.) *du courrier*
mail (to) *mettre à la poste*
main *principal / principale* (m./f.)
   main course/dish *plat* (m.) *principal*
make (to) *faire, préparer*
   make a phone call (to) *téléphoner, donner (or passer) un coup de fil* (infml.)
   make a mistake (to) *se tromper, faire une faute / erreur*
   make a reservation (to) *faire une réservation*
   make an appointment (to) *prendre rendez-vous*
   make up one's mind (to) *se décider*
   to make oneself happy (to) *se rendre heureux / heureuse* (m./f.)
   to make oneself sick (to) *se rendre malade*
   to make oneself aware (to) *se rendre compte (de)*
   make a sandcastle (to) *faire un château de sable*
   That makes ... *Ça fait...*
mall *centre commercial* (m.)
man *homme* (m.)
   Oh man! (disappointment, anger) *Ce n'est pas possible !*
   Man! (lit., Say so!) *Dis donc !*

manage to (do something) (to) *arriver à (+ verb)*

management *direction* (f.)

manager *gérant / gérante* (m./f.), *directeur / directrice* (m./f.)

  personnel manager, human resources manager *directeur / directrice* (m./f.) *du personnel*

many *beaucoup de, beaucoup*

  as many as *autant de*

map *plan* (m.), *carte* (f.)

  map of the city *plan* (m.) *de la ville, carte* (f.) *de la ville*

  map of the subway *plan* (m.) *du métro, carte* (f.) *du métro*

March *mars*

march (to) *défiler*

market *marché* (m.)

marketing department *service* (m.) *de marketing*

marmalade *confiture* (f.)

married *marié / mariée* (m./f.)

  get married (to each other) (to) *se marier*

marry (someone) (to) *épouser (quelqu'un)*

master's degree *maîtrise* (f.), *master* (m.)

match (in sports) *match* (m.)

math *maths* (f. pl.), *mathématiques* (f. pl.)

matter (to) *importer*

May *mai*

maybe *peut-être*

mayor *maire* (m.)

me *moi, me / m'* (direct object pronoun)

  to me *me / m'* (indirect object pronoun)

meal *repas* (m.)

meat *viande* (f.)

medical checkup *examen* (m.) *médical*

medical student *étudiant / étudiante* (m./f.) *en médecine*

medicine *médecine* (f.)

  medicine cabinet *armoire* (f.) *à pharmacie*

meet (a person/someone) (to) *rencontrer (une personne/quelqu'un), faire connaissance*

meeting *rendez-vous* (m.), *réunion* (f.)

  meeting room *salle* (f.) *de réunion*

melon *melon* (m.)

member *membre* (m.)

  be a member of (to) *faire partie de, être membre de*

memory *mémoire* (f.)

menu *menu* (m.), *carte* (f.)

  The menu, please. *Le menu / La carte, s'il vous plaît.*

merchant *marchand / marchande* (m./f.)

meringue cookie *macaron* (m.)

metro *métro* (m.)

  metro station *station* (f.) *de métro*

Mexican *mexicain / mexicaine* (m./f.)

Mexico *Mexique* (m.)

microwave (oven) *micro-ondes* (m.)

middle *milieu* (m.)

  in the middle of *au milieu de*

  be in the middle of (to) *en train de*

  middle school *collège* (m.)

midnight *minuit* (m.)

milk *lait* (m.)

million *million*

millionaire *millionnaire* (m./f.)

mineral water *eau* (f.) *minérale*

mint *menthe* (f.)

minus *moins*

mirror *miroir* (m.)

miss *mademoiselle (Mlle)*

  misses *mesdemoiselles*

mistake *faute* (f.), *erreur* (f.)

  spelling mistake *faute d'orthographe*

mistaken (to be) *se tromper*

modem *modem* (m.)

mole *grain* (m.) *de beauté*

Mom/Mommy *maman*

moment *moment* (m.)

Mona Lisa *Joconde* (f.)

Monday *lundi*

money *argent* (m.)

monitor *écran* (m.)

month *mois* (m.)

  next month, in one month *dans un mois*

  next month *mois prochain*

  last month *mois dernier*

  two months before *deux mois auparavant*

  two months before *deux mois avant*

  months of the year *mois* (pl.) *de l'année*

monument *monument* (m.)

moon *lune* (f.)

mop (to) *éponger*

moped *solex* (m.), *vélomoteur* (m.)

more *plus, encore*

even more, much more *bien plus*
more ... than *plus... que*
morning *matin* (m.), *matinée* (f.)
Moroccan *marocain / marocaine* (m./f.)
Morocco *Maroc* (m.)
mosque *mosquée* (f.)
the most ... *le / la plus...*
mostly *surtout*
mother *mère* (f.)
mother-in-law *belle-mère* (f.)
motorcycle *motocyclette* (f.), *moto* (f.)
mountain *montagne* (f.)
  mountain climbing *alpinisme* (m.)
mouse *souris* (f.)
mousse *mousse* (f.)
  chocolate mousse *mousse au chocolat*
mouth *bouche* (f.)
move out (to) *déménager*
movie *film* (m.)
  movie theater, the movies *cinéma* (m.)
Mr. *M. (Monsieur)*
Mrs. *Mme (Madame)*
Ms. *Mme (Madame)*
much *beaucoup*
  much more *bien plus*
municipal building *mairie* (f.), *hôtel* (m.) *de ville*
muscle *muscle* (m.)
muscular *musculaire* (medical), *musclé / musclée* (m./f.) *(person)*
museum *musée* (m.)
  Louvre museum *musée du Louvre*
  Orsay museum *musée d'Orsay*
mushroom *champignon* (m.)
music *musique* (f.)
musical *comédie* (f.) *musicale*
musician *musicien / musicienne* (m./f.)
mussel *moule* (f.)
  mussels and fries *moules* (pl.) *frites*
must *devoir*
mustard *moutarde* (f.)
  Dijon mustard *moutarde de Dijon*
my *mon / ma / mes* (m./f./pl.)
  My name is ... *Je m'appelle...*
myself *me / m'* (reflexive pronoun)
mysterious *mystérieux / mystérieuse* (m./f.)

N

name *nom* (m.)

under what name? *sous quel nom ?*
napkin *serviette* (f.)
nation *nation* (f.)
national *national / nationale* (m./f.)
  national holiday *fête nationale* (f.)
nationality *nationalité* (f.)
natural *naturel / naturelle* (m./f.)
naturally *naturellement*
near *près*
  very near *tout près*
  nearby, near here *près d'ici*
  the nearest *le / la plus proche*
necessary *nécessaire*
necessary (to be) *falloir*
  it's necessary to *il faut*
  it's necessary that *il faut que, il est nécessaire que*
neck *cou* (m.)
necklace *collier* (m.)
need *besoin* (m.)
need (to) *avoir besoin de, avoir besoin que*
  need for (to) *avoir besoin de*
needle *aiguille* (f.)
neighborhood *quartier* (m.), *coin* (m.)
nephew *neveu* (m.)
never *jamais, ne... jamais*
new *nouveau / nouvel / nouvelle* (m./m. before a vowel or silent h/f.)
  New Year *Nouvel An* (m.)
  New Year's Day *jour* (m.) *de l'An*
  New Year's Eve *Saint-Sylvestre* (f.), *réveillon* (m.) *(du jour de l'An)*
newborn *nouveau-né* (m.)
news (the news) *nouvelles* (f. pl.)
newspaper *journal* (m.)
next *prochain / prochaine* (m./f.), *ensuite*
  next part, what happens next *suite* (f.)
  Can't wait for what happens next! *Vivement la suite !*
  next to *à côté de*
  next month *dans un mois, mois prochain*
  next week *dans une semaine, semaine prochaine*
nice *gentil / gentille* (m./f.), *sympa, joli / jolie* (m./f.), *beau / bel / belle* (m./m. before a vowel or silent h/f.), *sympathique, aimable*
  Nice to meet you. *Enchanté. / Enchantée.* (m./f.)

niece *nièce* (f.)

night *nuit* (f.), *soir* (m.), *soirée* (f.)

nightclub *boîte* (f.) *de nuit, discothèque* (f.)

   go out to clubs (to), go out clubbing

     (to) *sortir en boîte*

nine *neuf*

nineteen *dix-neuf*

ninety *quatre-vingt-dix*

ninth *neuvième*

no *non*

   no longer, no more *ne... plus*

   No way! *Oh là là !*

   no one, nobody *ne... personne*

noodle soup (vermicelli pasta

   consommé) *consommé* (m.) *aux vermicelles*

noon *midi* (m.)

north *nord* (m.)

nose *nez* (m.)

not *ne / n'... pas, pas*

   not at all *pas du tout*

   not yet *ne... pas encore*

   Not bad. *Pas mal.*

   Not a lot. *Pas grand-chose.*

   not as good *moins bon / bonne* (m./f.)

   not as bad *moins mauvais / mauvaise* (m./f.)

note *note* (f.)

notebook *cahier* (m.)

nothing *rien, ne... rien*

   nothing else *ne... rien d'autre*

   It's nothing. *De rien.*

   Nothing much. *Rien de particulier.*

   Nothing new. *Rien de neuf.*

notice (to) *se rendre compte (de)*

November *novembre*

now *maintenant*

nowhere *nulle part*

number *nombre* (m.), *numéro* (m.)

   phone number *numéro de téléphone*

nurse *infirmier / infirmière* (m./f.)

nursery school *école* (f.) *maternelle*

O

obey (to) *obéir*

occasionally *de temps en temps*

ocean *océan* (m.)

  ocean liner *paquebot* (m.)

October *octobre*

of *de / d'*

of it, of them *en*

of which, of whom *dont*

of the *du / de la / de l' / des* (m./f./m. or f. before

   a vowel or silent h/pl.)

Of course. *Bien sûr. / Bien entendu.*

office *bureau* (m.)

  office building *immeuble* (m.)

often *souvent*

Oh okay ... *Ah bon...*

Oh really ... *Ah bon...*

Oh well ... *Eh bien..., Ben...* (infml.)

oil *huile* (f.)

Okay. *D'accord.*

  Oh okay ... *Ah bon...*

old *vieux / vieil / vieille* (m./m. before a vowel or

   silent h/f.), *ancien / ancienne* (m./f.)

  oldest child *aîné / aînée* (m./f.)

omelet *omelette* (f.)

  mushroom omelet *omelette aux champignons*

on *sur*

  on top *dessus*

  on behalf of *de la part de*

  on my behalf *de ma part*

  on foot *à pied*

  on one's own *seul / seule* (m./f.)

  on the left/on the right *à gauche / à droite*

  on the other side of *de l'autre côté de*

  on time *à l'heure*

  on strike *en grève*

once *une fois*

one (number) *un / une* (m./f.)

one (pronoun) *on*

oneself *se / s'* (reflexive pronoun)

one-way *aller simple* (m.)

onion *oignon* (m.)

  onion soup *soupe* (f.) *à l'oignon*

only *juste, seul / seule* (m./f.), *seulement*

  only child *fils / fille unique* (m./f.)

open (to) *ouvrir*

  open a file (to) *ouvrir un fichier*

opera *opéra* (m.)

or *ou*

  or even, or else *ou bien*

orange *orange, orange* (f.)

order (to) *commander*

organize (to) *organiser*

origin *origine* (f.)

original *original / originale* (m./f.)

Glossary

original version of a film (not dubbed into French) *version* (f.) *originale (v.o.)*
other *autre*
our *notre / nos* (m. or f./pl.)
ourselves *nous* (reflexive pronoun)
outdoor activities *activités* (f. pl.) *de plein air*
outfit *ensemble* (m.), *tenue* (f.)
outside *hors, dehors, extérieur* (m.)
oven *four* (m.)
over there *là-bas*
owe (to) *devoir*
own *propre*
own (to) *posséder*
oyster *huître* (f.)

P

pain *douleur* (f.)
paint (to) *peindre*
painting *tableau* (m.), *peinture* (f.)
pair *paire* (f.)
   That's three euros per pair. *Ça coûte trois euros la paire.*
pajamas *pyjama* (m.)
pants *pantalon* (m.)
paper *papier* (m.)
paralyzed *paralysé / paralysée* (m./f.)
Pardon (me). *Pardon.*
parent *parent* (m.)
Paris *Paris*
Parisian *parisien / parisienne* (m./f.)
park *parc* (m.)
parlor *salon* (m.)
part (in a play, movie, etc.) *rôle* (m.)
partner *partenaire / partenaire* (m./f.)
part-time *à temps partiel*
party *soirée* (f.), *fête* (f.), *partie* (f.)
pass (to) *passer*
   pass a test/class (to) *réussir à un examen / cours*
passport *passeport* (m.)
past *passé* (m.)
   in the past *autrefois*
pastry *pâtisserie* (f.)
   pastry shop *pâtisserie* (f.)
   pastry and candy store *pâtisserie-confiserie* (f.)
pastime *passe-temps* (m.)
path *chemin* (m.)

patient *patient / patiente* (m./f.)
pay (to) *payer*
peach *pêche* (f.)
   peaches with ice cream *pêche Melba*
pear *poire* (f.)
peas (green) *petits pois* (m. pl.)
people *gens* (m. pl.)
   people in general *on* (pronoun)
pepper *poivre (condiment)* (m.), *poivron (vegetable)* (m.)
per *par*
perfect *parfait / parfaite* (m./f.)
   It's perfect. *C'est parfait.*
perform (to) *jouer*
perfume *parfum* (m.)
permit (to) *permettre*
person *personne* (f.)
personnel manager *directeur / directrice du personnel* (m./f.)
pharmacist *pharmacien / pharmacienne* (m./f.)
pharmacy *pharmacie* (f.)
phone *téléphone* (m.)
   cell phone *portable* (m.)
   phone number *numéro* (m.) *de téléphone*
   answer the phone (to) *répondre au téléphone*
   telephone extension *poste* (m.)
phone (to) *téléphoner*
photo *photo* (f.)
   Can you take our picture (photo)? *Pourriez-vous nous prendre en photo, s'il vous plaît ?*
phrase *phrase* (f.)
physical education *gym(nastique)* (f.), *éducation physique*
physics *physique* (f.)
pick up (the phone) (to) *décrocher, ramasser (object), prende (passenger)*
pie *tarte* (f.)
   apple pie *tarte aux pommes*
   pumpkin pie *tarte à la citrouille*
   strawberry pie *tarte aux fraises*
piece *pièce* (f.), *morceau* (m.)
pig *porc* (m.), *cochon* (m.)
pill *pilule* (f.), *comprimé* (m.)
pink *rose*
pitcher *carafe* (f.)
   pitcher of wine *carafe de vin*
   pitcher of water *carafe d'eau*
place *place* (f.), *lieu* (m.), *endroit* (m.)

take place (to) *avoir lieu*
plan *plan* (m.)
plan (to) *projeter*
plant *plante* (f.)
plastic *plastique* (m.)
  made of plastic *en plastique*
plate *assiette* (f.)
platform *quai* (m.)
play (theater) *pièce* (f.) *(de théâtre)*
play (to) *jouer*
  play a sport (to) *faire du sport*
  play a game/match (to) *jouer un match*
  play hide and seek (to) *jouer à cache-cache*
  play soccer (to) *faire du foot(ball)*
player *joueur / joueuse (games, sports, etc.)*
  (m./f.), *lecteur (CDs, DVDs, etc.)* (m.)
  soccer player *footballeur / footballeuse* (m./f.)
  CD player *lecteur de CD*
  DVD player *lecteur de DVD*
playground *cour* (f.) *de récréation*
playing cards *cartes* (f. pl.) *à jouer*
pleasant *agréable*
please *s'il te plaît* (infml.) */ s'il vous plaît* (pl./fml.)
  Pleased to meet you. *Enchanté. / Enchantée.*
  (m./f.)
pleasure *plaisir* (m.)
  With pleasure. *Avec plaisir.*
plum *prune* (f.)
plumber *plombier* (m.)
poem *poème* (m.)
police (adjective) *policier / policière* (m./f.)
  police station *poste* (m.) *de police,*
  commissariat (m.)
policeman/woman *policier / femme policier*
  (m./f.), *agent / agente de police* (m./f.)
polite *poli*
politely *poliment*
politics *politique* (f.)
Pompidou Center *Centre* (m.) *Pompidou*
pond *étang* (m.), *mare* (f.)
pool *piscine (swimming)* (f.), *billard (billiards)*
  (m.)
poor *pauvre*
pork *porc* (m.)
  pork chop *côte* (f.) *de porc*
Portugal *Portugal* (m.)
Portuguese *portugais / portugaise* (m./f.)
possible *possible*

it is possible that *il est possible que*
  It's not possible! (disappointment,
  anger) *Ce n'est pas possible !*
possibly *peut-être*
post office *poste* (f.), *bureau* (m.) *de poste*
potato *pomme* (f.) *de terre*
  boiled potatoes in their skins, baked
  potatoes *pommes* (pl.) *de terre en robe des*
  champs
  mashed potatoes *purée* (f.) *de pommes de*
  terre
poultry *volaille* (f.)
pound *livre* (f.)
  pound of butter *livre de beurre*
powder *poudre* (f.), *talc* (m.)
practice (to) *pratiquer*
precise *précis / précise* (m./f.)
prefer (to) *préférer, aimer mieux*
preferable *préférable*
  it is preferable that *il est préférable que*
prepare (to) *préparer*
preschool *école* (f.) *maternelle*
prescription *ordonnance* (f.)
present (to) *présenter*
pretty *joli / jolie* (m./f.)
primary school *école* (f.) *primaire*
principal *principal / principale* (m./f.)
printer *imprimante* (f.)
probable *probable*
  it is probable that *il est probable que*
probably *probablement*
produce (to) *produire*
profession *profession* (f.)
professor *professeur / professeure* (m./f.), *prof*
  (m./f.) (infml.)
programmer (computer) *informaticien /*
  informaticienne (m./f.)
programming language *langage* (m.) *de*
  programmation/informatique
progress *progrès* (m.)
protect (to) *protéger*
protest *manifestation* (f.)
protest (to) *manifester*
protestor *manifestant / manifestante* (m./f.)
proud *fier / fière* (m./f.)
public relations (PR) department *service* (m.)
  des relations publiques
pull (a tooth) (to) *arracher (une dent)*

pull a muscle (to) *se faire une élongation*
pull-ups *tractions* (f. pl.)
pumpkin *citrouille* (f.)
   pumpkin pie *tarte* (f.) *à la citrouille*
punish (to) *punir*
pupil *élève* (m./f.)
purée *purée* (f.)
purple *violet / violette* (m./f.)
purse *sac* (m.)
push-ups *pompes* (f. pl.)
put (to) *mettre*
   put in the mail (to) *mettre à la poste*
   put away (to) *ranger*
   put someone to bed (to) *coucher*

Q

quarter *quart* (m.), *quartier* (m.)
   quarter after/past ... *... et quart*
   quarter to ... *... moins le quart*
quay *quai* (m.)
question *question* (f.)
quiche *quiche* (f.)
quick *rapide*
quickly *vite, rapide*
quiet *calme*
quit (to) *quitter*
quite *assez, bien*
   quite the opposite, quite the contrary *bien au contraire*

R

race *course* (f.)
rack (of meat) *carré* (m.)
   rack of lamb *carré d'agneau*
radish *radis* (m.)
   rosette-cut radishes served with butter on top (lit., radishes in butter) *radis* (m. pl.) *au beurre*
rain *pluie* (f.)
rain (to) *pleuvoir*
   It's raining./It rains. *Il pleut.*
raincoat *imperméable* (m.)
raise (to) *lever*
Ramadan *Ramadan* (m.)
rarely *rarement*
raw *cru / crue* (m./f.)
   crudités (French appetizer of raw, mixed vegetables) *crudités* (f. pl.)

razor *rasoir* (m.)
reach (to) *arriver*
read (to) *lire*
reading *lecture*
ready *prêt / prête* (m./f.)
real *vrai / vraie* (m./f.)
realize (to) *se rendre compte (de)*
really *vraiment, en effet, bien*
   I (do) like ... *J'aime bien...*
   I (do) want ... *Je veux bien...*
reason *raison*
recent *dernier / dernière* (m./f.)
reception desk *réception* (f.)
recess *récré(ation)* (f.)
recipe *recette* (f.)
recommend that (to) *recommander que*
recreation *loisirs* (m. pl.)
red *rouge*
   red wine *vin* (m.) *rouge*
redden (to) *rougir*
reflect (to) *réfléchir*
refrigerator *réfrigérateur* (m.)
reject (to) *rejeter*
relative *parent* (m.)
relax (to) *se reposer*
relief *soulagement* (m.)
   What a relief! *Quel soulagement !*
remember (to) *se souvenir*
remove (to) *enlever*
repair things (to) *bricoler, réparer (around the house)*
repeat (to) *répéter*
   Repeat (that), please. *Répétez, s'il vous plaît.*
reply (to) *répondre*
report card *bulletin* (m.) *scolaire*
reservation *réservation* (f.)
   to make a reservation *faire une réservation*
   to make reservations *faire des réservations*
reserve (to) *réserver*
resolved (to do something) (to be) *se décider*
respond (to) *répondre*
rest (what's left) *reste* (f.), *suite* (f.)
   Can't wait for the rest! *Vivement la suite !*
rest (to) *reposer*
   rest (oneself) (to) *se reposer*
restaurant *restaurant* (m.)
restroom *toilettes* (f. pl.)
   Where is the restroom? *Où sont les toilettes ?*

results *résultats* (m. pl.)
retired *à la retraite*
retirement *retraite* (f.)
return (to) *revenir, rentrer, rendre, retourner*
reunion *réunion* (f.)
rib (meat) *côte* (f.)
rice *riz* (m.)
rich *riche*
ride a bike (to) *monter à bicyclette*
ride a horse (to) *monter à cheval*
ride a stationary bike (to) *faire du vélo d'appartement*
right (opposite of left) *droite* (f.)
  be right (to) *avoir raison*
  right? *n'est-ce pas ?*
  right bank *rive* (f.) *droite*
ring *bague* (f.), *anneau* (m.)
  engagement ring *bague de fiançailles*
  diamond ring *bague en diamant*
  wedding ring *alliance* (f.)
ring (to) *sonner*
rise (to) *monter, se lever*
river *rivière* (f.)
roast (of meat) *rôti* (m.)
  roast beef *rôti de bœuf*
roast(ed) *rôti / rôtie* (m./f.)
  roast rack of lamb *carré* (m.) *d'agneau rôti*
rock *rocher* (m.)
role *rôle* (m.)
roll the dice (to) *lancer les dés*
romantic *romantique*
  romantic comedy *comédie* (f.) *romantique*
room *pièce* (f.), *salle* (f.), *place* (f.)
rooster *coq* (m.)
rose *rose* (f.)
rosé (wine) *vin* (m.) *rosé*
round-trip *aller-retour* (m.)
  I would like a round-trip ticket. *Je voudrais un billet aller-retour.*
rug *tapis* (m.)
rugby *rugby* (m.)
  rugby team *équipe* (f.) *de rugby*
run *course* (f.)
run (to) *courir*
  run errands (to) *faire des achats*
  run the marathon (to) *courir le marathon*
running *course* (f.) *à pied*
rural *rural / rurale* (m./f.)

rush (to) *se hâter*
Russia *Russie* (f.)
Russian *russe*

S

sad *triste*
sailing *voile* (f.)
salad *salade* (f.)
  fruit salad *salade de fruits*
green salad *salade verte*
salary *salaire* (m.)
sales department *service* (m.) *des ventes*
salesman/woman *vendeur / vendeuse* (m./f.)
salt *sel* (m.)
same *même*
sand *sable* (m.)
  sandcastle *château* (m.) *de sable*
  make/build a sandcastle (to) *faire un château de sable*
sandwich *sandwich* (m.)
  ham sandwich *sandwich au jambon*
  ham and cheese sandwich *sandwich jambon-fromage*
  grilled ham and cheese sandwich *croque-monsieur* (m.)
  grilled ham and cheese sandwich with an egg on top *croque-madame* (m.)
sardines *sardines* (f. pl.)
  sardines in tomato sauce *sardines sauce tomate*
Saturday *samedi*
sauce *sauce* (f.)
sausage *saucisse* (f.)
sauté (to) *sauter*
save a document (to) *sauvegarder un document*
savory *salé / salée* (m./f.)
saxophone *saxophone* (m.)
say (to) *dire*
  Say! *Tiens !* (surprise)
You don't say!/Say! (lit., Say so!) *Dis donc !*
say to each other (to) *se dire*
scallops *coquilles* (f. pl.) *Saint-Jacques*
scarf *foulard* (fashion) (m.), *écharpe* (long) (f.)
scary *effrayant / effrayante* (m./f.)
schedule *horaire* (m.)
school *école* (f.)
  at school *à l'école*
  high school *lycée* (m.)

in high school *au lycée*
high school student *lycéen / lycéenne* (m./f.)
final year of high school *classe* (f.) *terminale*
secondary school, junior high school,
  middle school *collège* (m.)
in middle school *au collège*
elementary school, primary school *école primaire*
nursery school, preschool *école maternelle*
school cafeteria *cantine* (f.)
back-to-school *rentrée* (f.)
schoolyard *cour* (f.) *de récréation*
science *science* (f.)
score *score* (m.)
  final score *score final*
score (to) *marquer*
Scotland *Écosse* (f.)
Scottish *écossais / écossaise* (m./f.)
screen *écran* (m.)
sculpture *sculpture* (f.)
sea *mer* (f.)
seat *place* (f.)
seated *assis / assise* (m./f.)
second *deuxième, second / seconde* (m./f.)
  second base *deuxième base* (f.)
secondary school *collège* (m.)
secretary *secrétaire* (m./f.)
see (to) *voir*
  See you later! *À tout à l'heure ! / À plus tard ! / Salut ! / À la prochaine !*
  See you soon! *À bientôt !*
  see each other (to) *se voir*
seeing-eye dog *chien* (m.) *d'aveugle*
seem (to) *sembler*
  it seems that *il semble que*
sell (to) *vendre*
send (to) *envoyer*
  send a file (to) *envoyer un fichier*
  send an e-mail (to) *envoyer un mail / mèl / e-mail / courriel / courrier électronique*
September *septembre*
series (TV) *feuilleton* (m.) *(télévisé)*
serious *grave, sérieux / sérieuse* (m./f.)
  It's not serious. *Ce n'est pas grave.*
server *serveur / serveuse* (m./f.)
seven *sept*
seventeen *dix-sept*
seventh *septième*

seventy *soixante-dix*
several *plusieurs*
sewing *couture* (f.)
shame *honte* (f.)
  be ashamed (to) *avoir honte*
shampoo *shampooing* (m.)
shape *forme* (f.)
  be in shape (to) *être en forme*
  be in good shape (to) *être en pleine / bonne forme*
sharp *précis / précise* (m./f.)
  at noon sharp *à midi précis*
shave (to) *se raser*
shaving cream *crème* (f.) *à raser*
she *elle*
shelf *étagère* (f.)
ship *bateau* (m.)
shipping department (mail room) *service* (m.) *du courrier*
shirt *chemise* (f.)
shoe *chaussure* (f.)
  shoe store *magasin* (m.) *de chaussures*
  shoe size *pointure* (f.)
shop (small) *boutique* (f.)
shop (to) *faire des / les courses*
short *petit / petite* (m./f.), *court / courte* (m./f.)
shot *piqûre* (f.), *injection* (f.)
should *devoir*
shoulder *épaule* (f.)
show (to) *montrer, présenter, donner*
shower *douche* (f.)
  shower gel *gel* (m.) *douche*
shrimp *crevettes* (f. pl.)
sick *malade*
  make oneself sick (to) *se rendre malade*
  be sick (to) *être malade*
side *côté* (m.)
  at the side of (next to) *à côté de*
  at the side, on the side, to the side *à côté*
  on the other side of *de l'autre côté de*
  side dish *plat* (m.) *d'accompagnement*
  side effect *effet* (m.) *secondaire*
sidewalk *trottoir* (m.)
sign language *langage* (m.) *des signes*
silk *soie* (f.)
silver *argent* (m.)
since *depuis*
  since when? *depuis quand ?*

sincere *sincère*
sing (to) *chanter*
singer *chanteur / chanteuse* (m./f.)
single *célibataire*
sink *lavabo* (m.), *évier* (m.)
sir *monsieur*
sister *sœur* (f.)
sitcom *comédie* (f.) *de situation*
sitting (down) *assis / assise* (m./f.)
situated (to be) *se trouver*
sit-ups *abdominaux* (m. pl.)
six *six*
sixteen *seize*
sixth *sixième*
sixty *soixante*
size (clothing) *taille* (f.)
size (shoe) *pointure* (f.)
skate/skating *patin* (m.)
skateboard *planche* (f.) *à roulettes, skateboard* (m.)
ski (to) *faire du ski, skier*
ski resort *station* (f.) *de sports d'hiver*
ski slope *piste* (f.)
skiing *ski* (m.)
  go skiing (to) *faire du ski*
skin *peau* (f.)
skirt *jupe* (f.)
sky *ciel* (m.)
sleep *sommeil* (m.)
sleeping car/sleeper car *wagon-lit* (m.)
sleepy (to be) *avoir sommeil*
slice *tranche (bread, cheese)* (f.), *part (cake, pie, pizza)* (f.), *rondelle (round - cucumber, banana, sausage, etc.)* (f.)
  slice of cheese *morceau de fromage*
slope (ski) *piste* (f.)
slow *lent / lente* (m./f.)
slowly *lentement*
small *petit / petite* (m./f.)
  small shop *boutique* (f.)
smile *sourire* (m.)
snails *escargots* (m. pl.)
sneaker *basket* (m./f.), *chaussure* (f.) *de basket / tennis*
snow *neige* (f.)
snow (to) *neiger*
  It's snowing. *Il neige.*
snowboarding *surf* (m.) *sur neige*

snowman *bonhomme* (m.) *de neige*
so *alors, donc*
  so that *afin que, pour que*
soak up (to) *éponger*
soap *savon* (m.)
soccer *foot(ball)* (m.)
  soccer player *footballeur / footballeuse* (m./f.)
  soccer stadium *stade* (m.) *de foot*
social *social / sociale* (m./f.)
sock *chaussette* (f.)
sofa *canapé* (m.)
soft *doux / douce* (m./f.)
  soft drink *boisson* (f.) *gazeuse*
softly *doucement*
software *logiciel* (m.)
sojourn *séjour* (m.)
sole (fish) *sole* (f.)
  sole covered in flour and sautéed in butter *sole meunière*
some *du / de la / de l' / des* (m./f./m. or f. before a vowel or silent h/pl.), *en*
someone, somebody *quelqu'un*
  someone else *quelqu'un d'autre*
something *quelque chose*
  something else *autre chose*
sometimes *quelquefois, parfois*
son *fils* (m.)
son-in-law *beau-fils* (m.)
song *chanson* (f.)
soon *bientôt*
  See you soon! *À bientôt !*
sorrow *douleur* (f.)
sorry *désolé / désolée* (m./f.)
  I am sorry. *Je suis désolé / désolée.*
So-so. *Comme ci, comme ça.*
sound system *chaîne* (f.) *hi-fi*
soup *soupe* (f.), *potage* (m.)
  onion soup *soupe à l'oignon*
  consommé (clear soup made from stock) *consommé* (m.)
  vermicelli pasta consommé (noodle soup) *consommé aux vermicelles*
sour *aigre*
south *sud* (m.)
souvenir, memory *souvenir* (m.)
Spain *Espagne* (f.)
Spanish *espagnol / espagnole* (m./f.)
  Spanish language *espagnol* (m.)

speak (to) *parler*
  speak to each other (to) *se parler*
  Speak slower/more slowly, please. *Parlez plus lentement, s'il vous plaît.*
  I speak a little French. *Je parle un peu français.*
specialty *spécialité* (f.)
spectator *spectateur / spectatrice* (m./f.)
spelling *orthographe* (f.)
spend time (to) *passer du temps*
spinach *épinards* (m. pl.)
spoon *cuillère* (f.), *cuiller* (f.)
sport *sport* (m.)
sprain one's ankle (to) *se fouler la cheville*
spring *printemps* (m.)
  in (the) spring *au printemps*
square *carré* (m.)
stadium *stade* (m.)
  soccer stadium *stade de foot*
staff *personnel* (m.)
stairs *escaliers* (m. pl.)
stamp *timbre* (m.)
standing (up) *debout*
star *étoile* (f.)
start (to) *commencer*
station *station* (f.)
  subway/metro station *station* (f.) *de métro*
stationary bike *vélo* (m.) *d'appartement*
  ride a stationary bike (to) *faire du vélo d'appartement*
statue *statue* (f.)
stay *séjour* (m.)
stay (to) *rester*
  stay in shape (to) *rester en forme*
steady job *emploi* (m.) *régulier*
steak *steak* (m.)
  steak and fries *steak frites*
stepdaughter *belle-fille* (f.)
stepfather *beau-père* (m.)
stepmother *belle-mère* (f.)
stepson *beau-fils* (m.)
still *toujours, encore*
stocking (hose) *bas* (m.)
stomach *estomac* (m.)
stop *arrêt* (m.)
  bus stop *arrêt de bus / d'autobus*
stop (to) *cesser*
store *magasin* (m.)

candy store *confiserie* (f.)
pastry and candy store *pâtisserie-confiserie* (f.)
grocery store *épicerie* (f.)
hardware store *quincaillerie* (f.)
storm *orage* (m.)
story *histoire* (f.)
stove *cuisinière* (f.)
straight *droit*
  straight ahead *tout droit*
strange *étrange, bizarre*
  It's strange. *C'est bizarre. / C'est étrange.*
strawberry *fraise* (f.)
  strawberry ice cream *glace* (f.) *à la fraise*
  strawberry pie *tarte* (f.) *aux fraises*
street *rue* (f.)
streetlight *lampadaire* (m.)
strength training *musculation* (f.)
  do strength training (to) *faire de la musculation*
strike *grève* (m.)
  on strike *en grève*
strike (to) *faire (la) grève*
stroke *attaque* (f.) *cérébrale*
strong *fort / forte* (m./f.)
strongly *vivement*
student *étudiant / étudiante* (m./f.), *élève* (m./f.)
  medical student *étudiant / étudiante en médecine*
  high school student *lycéen / lycéenne* (m./f.)
study (to) *étudier*
subject *sujet* (m.), *matière* (f.)
subtitle *sous-titre* (m.)
suburban *de banlieue*
suburbs *banlieue* (f.)
subway *métro* (m.)
  subway station *station* (f.) *de métro*
succeed (to) *réussir*
suddenly *soudain*
  all of a sudden *tout à coup/tout d'un coup*
sugar *sucre* (m.)
suggest (to) *suggérer*
suit (man's) *costume* (m.), *complet* (m., fml.)
  three-piece suit *complet-veston*
  suit (woman's) *tailleur* (m.)
suit someone well (to) *aller à ravir à quelqu'un*
summer *été* (m.)
  in (the) summer *en été*

summer vacation *grandes vacances* (f. pl.)
summer job *emploi* (m.) *saisonnier*
sun *soleil* (m.)
   It's sunny. *Il y a du soleil. / Il fait soleil.*
sunbathe (to) *prendre un bain de soleil*
Sunday *dimanche*
sunglasses *lunettes* (f. pl.) *de soleil*
super *super*
superficial injury *blessure* (f.) *superficielle*
supermarket *supermarché* (m.)
surfing *surf* (m.), *planche à voile* (f.)
surprise (to) *surprendre*
surrender (to) *se rendre*
sweater *pull(-over)* (m.), *tricot* (m.)
sweat *sueur* (f.)
   be sweating (to) *être en sueur, être en nage*
sweet *sucré / sucrée* (m./f.), *doux / douce* (m./f.)
   sweet bun *brioche* (f.)
sweetly *doucement*
swim (to) *nager, faire de la natation*
swimming *natation* (f.)
   go swimming (to) *faire de la natation*
Swiss *suisse*
Switzerland *Suisse* (f.)
synagogue *synagogue* (f.)

T

table *table* (f.)
   table for two *table pour deux*
   table setting *couvert* (m.)
tablecloth *nappe* (f.)
tablet *cachet* (m.), *comprimé* (m.)
tail *queue* (f.)
take (to) *prendre*
   take a bath (to) *prendre un bain*
   take a shower (to) *prendre une douche*
   take a tour (to) *faire un tour*
   take a walk (to) *faire une promenade, se promener*
   take someone or something for a walk (to) *promener*
   take (someone) along (to) *emmener*
   take off (to) *enlever*
   take a picture (to) *prendre une photo*
   Can you take our picture? *Pourriez-vous nous prendre en photo, s'il vous plaît ?*
   take oneself to (a place) (to) *se rendre à (+ location)*

take (a class) (to) *suivre (un cours), assister à (un cours)*
take (a test) (to) *passer (un examen)*
tale *histoire* (f.)
talented *talentueux / talentueuse* (m./f.)
talk (to) *parler*
tall *grand / grande* (m./f.)
tan (color) *beige*
tan (to) *bronzer*
tan (from the sun), tanned *bronzé / bronzée* (m./f.)
tart *tarte* (f.)
taste *goût* (m.)
taxi *taxi* (m.)
   taxi driver *chauffeur* (m.) *de taxi*
tea *thé* (m.)
   herbal tea *tisane* (f.)
   cup of tea *tasse* (f.) *de thé*
   teakettle, teapot *théière* (f.)
teach (to) *enseigner*
teacher *professeur / professeure* (m./f.), *prof* (infml., m./f.), *enseignant / enseignante* (m./f.)
team *équipe* (f.)
   rugby team *équipe de rugby*
teenager *adolescent / adolescente* (m./f.)
telephone *téléphone* (m.), *appareil* (m.)
   telephone extension *poste* (m.)
   cell phone *portable* (m.)
   phone number *numéro* (m.) *de téléphone*
   to answer the phone *répondre au téléphone*
   to make a phone call, to phone *téléphoner*
television *télé(vision)* (f.)
   television program *émission* (f.)
   TV series *feuilleton* (m.) *(télévisé)*
tell (to) *dire*
   tell each other (to) *se dire*
teller *guichetier* (m.)
temperature *température* (f.)
temple *temple* (m.)
ten *dix*
tendon *tendon* (m.)
tennis *tennis* (m.)
   tennis shoe *basket* (m./f.), *chaussure* (f.) *de basket / tennis*
tenth *dixième*
test *examen* (m.)
   fail (a test) (to) *rater (un examen)*
   pass (a test) (to) *réussir à (un examen)*

textbook *livre* (m.) *scolaire*
than *que*
more … than *plus… que*
less … than *moins… que*
as … as *aussi… que*
thank you *merci*
Thank you very much. *Merci bien.*
thanks to … *grâce à…*
that *ce / cet / cette* (m./m. before a vowel or silent h/f.), *ça / c', que, qui*
that one, that one there *celui-là / celle-là* (m./f.)
that way *par là*
That doesn't interest me. *Ça ne m'intéresse pas.*
That interests me. *Ça m'intéresse.*
That makes … /That is … *Ça fait…*
that is *c'est*
That's bad. *C'est mauvais.*
Is that all? *C'est tout ?*
That's all. *C'est tout.*
the *le / l' / la / les* (m./m. before a vowel or silent h/f./pl.)
theater *théâtre* (m.)
movie theater *cinéma* (m.)
their *leur / leurs* (m. or f./pl.)
them *eux / elles* (m./f.), *les* (direct object pronoun)
to them *leur* (indirect object pronoun)
themselves *se / s'* (reflexive pronoun)
then *alors, donc, ensuite, puis*
there *là, là-bas, y*
over there *là-bas*
there is/are *il y a, voilà*
there was/were *il y avait*
there it is/they are *voilà*
therefore *donc*
these *ces*
these ones, these ones here *ceux-ci / celles-ci* (m./f.)
they *ils / elles* (m./f.)
thin *mince*
thing *chose* (f.)
think (to) *penser, réfléchir*
think that (to) *trouver que, penser que*
third *troisième*
third base *troisième base* (f.)
thirst *soif* (f.)
be thirsty (to) *avoir soif*

thirteen *treize*
thirty *trente*
this *ce / cet / cette* (m./m. before a vowel or silent h/f.), *ça / c', ci*
this is *c'est*
this way *par ici*
this one, this one here *celui-ci / celle-ci* (m./f.)
those *ces*
those ones, those ones there *ceux-là / celles-là* (m./f.)
thousand *mille*
threaten (to) *menacer*
three *trois*
thriller *film* (m.) *à suspense, thriller* (m.)
throat *gorge* (f.)
through *à travers*
throw (to) *envoyer, jeter*
throw out/away (to) *jeter*
thunder *tonnerre* (m.)
Thursday *jeudi*
ticket *billet* (m.), *place* (f.)
ticket window *guichet* (m.)
I would like a round-trip ticket. *Je voudrais un billet aller-retour.*
tie *cravate* (f.)
tie (in a game/match) (to) *faire match nul*
time *fois* (f.), *temps* (m.)
at what time? *à quelle heure ?*
What time is it? *Quelle heure est-il ?*
arrival time *heure* (f.) *de l'arrivée*
one time (once) *une fois*
I don't have (the) time. *Je n'ai pas le temps.*
tinker (to) *bricoler*
tire *pneu* (m.)
tissue *mouchoir* (m.)
to *à, pour, en, jusqu'à*
to the *au / à la / à l' / aux* (m./f./m. or f. before a vowel or silent h/pl.)
next to *à côté de*
To your health! *À votre santé !*
to the left/to the right *à gauche / à droite*
today *aujourd'hui*
toe *doigt* (m.) *de pied, orteil* (m.)
toenail *ongle* (m.) *de pied*
together *ensemble*
toilet *toilettes* (f. pl.)
toilet paper *papier* (m.) *hygiénique*
tomato *tomate* (f.)

tomorrow *demain*
tongue *langue* (f.)
tonight *ce soir*
too *aussi (also), trop (much)*
tooth *dent* (f.)
touchdown *essai* (m.)
tour *tour* (m.)
tourist *touriste* (m./f.)
towel *serviette* (f.)
  bath towel *serviette de bain*
tower *tour* (f.)
  Eiffel Tower *Tour Eiffel*
town *ville* (f.)
  town hall *hôtel* (m.) *de ville*
track *voie* (f.), *piste* (f.)
track (and field) *athlétisme* (m.)
traffic *circulation* (f.)
trail *piste* (f.)
train *train* (m.)
  train station *gare* (f.)
  high-speed train *train à grande vitesse (TGV)*
train (to) *s'entraîner*
training *entraînement*
transportation *transport* (m.)
trash can *poubelle* (f.)
travel *voyage* (m.)
travel (to) *voyager*
traveler's check *chèque* (m.) *de voyage*
treadmill *tapis* (m.) *de course / de jogging*
tree *arbre* (m.)
trillion *trillion*
trip *voyage* (m.), *séjour* (m.)
  round-trip *aller-retour*
trout *truite* (f.)
  trout cooked in wine and vinegar *truite au bleu*
truck *camion* (m.)
true *vrai / vraie* (m./f.)
  it is true that *il est vrai que*
truly *vraiment*
try (to) *essayer*
  try on/out (to) *essayer*
T-shirt *T-shirt* (m.)
Tuesday *mardi*
turn *tour* (m.)
turn (to) *tourner*
TV *télé(vision)* (f.)
  TV series *feuilleton* (m.) *(télévisé)*

twelve *douze*
twentieth *vingtième*
twenty *vingt*
twice *deux fois*
two *deux*
  two dozen *deux douzaines*
  two months before *deux mois auparavant, deux mois avant*
  two times *deux fois*
type *genre*

U

ugly *laid / laide* (m./f.)
umbrella *parapluie* (m.)
uncle *oncle* (m.)
under *sous*
  under what name? *sous quel nom ?*
underneath *dessous*
underpants *caleçon* (m.)
undershirt *maillot* (m.) *de corps*
understand (to) *comprendre*
  I don't understand. *Je ne comprends pas.*
  Completely understood. *Bien entendu.*
  understand each other (to) *se comprendre*
underwear *sous-vêtements* (m. pl.)
unemployed *au chômage, sans emploi, sans travail, chômeuse, chômeur*
unemployment *chômage* (m.)
unfortunate *malheureux / malheureuse* (m./f.), *pauvre*
unfortunately *malheureusement*
unfriendly *peu amical / peu amicale* (m./f.)
unhappily *malheureusement*
unhappy *malheureux / malheureuse* (m./f.)
United States *États-Unis* (m. pl.)
university *université* (f.)
unless *à moins que... ne*
until *jusqu'à, jusqu'à ce que, d'ici*
upstairs, up above *en haut*
up until, up to *jusqu'à*
urban *urbain / urbaine* (m./f.)
urgent *urgent / urgente* (m./f.)
  it is urgent that *il est urgent que*
us *nous*
  to us *nous* (indirect object pronoun)
use (to) *employer, utiliser*
  use sign language (to) *utiliser le langage des signes*

usually *normalement, d'habitude, en général*

V

vacation *vacances* (f. pl.)
  summer vacation *grandes vacances* (f. pl.)
  winter vacation *vacances* (f. pl.) *d'hiver*
    400
vaccine *vaccin* (m.)
vain *vain / vaine* (m./f.)
vanilla *vanille* (f.)
  vanilla ice cream *glace* (f.) *à la vanille*
veal *veau* (m.)
vegetable *légume* (m.)
vendor *marchand / marchande* (m./f.)
vermicelli pasta *vermicelle* (m.)
  vermicelli pasta consommé (noodle
    soup) *consommé* (m.) *aux vermicelles*
version *version* (f.)
very *très, bien*
  very good *très bien, très bon / bonne* (m./f.)
  very well *très bien*
veterinarian *vétérinaire* (m.)
video game *jeu* (m.) *vidéo*
Vietnamese *vietnamien / vietnamienne* (m./f.)
village *village* (m.)
violet (purple) *violet / violette* (m./f.)
violin *violon* (m.)
virus *virus* (m.)
visit (a person) (to) *rendre visite à*
visit (a place) (to) *visiter*
vocabulary *vocabulaire* (m.)
volleyball *volley(-ball)* (m.)
voyage *voyage* (m.)

W

waffle *gaufre* (f.)
wait (for) (to) *attendre*
  wait in line (to) *faire la queue*
  can't wait (to look forward to) *avoir hâte*
  (I) can't wait for the end of the
    day! *Vivement la fin de la journée !*
waiter/waitress *serveur / serveuse* (m./f.)
wake (someone) (to) *réveiller*
  wake up (to), wake oneself up (to) *se réveiller*
walk (to) *marcher*
  take a walk (to) *se promener*
  take someone or something for a walk
    (to) *promener*

walk with a cane (to) *marcher avec une canne*
walk with crutches (to) *marcher avec des
  béquilles*
wall *mur* (m.)
want (to) *vouloir, désirer*
  I want … *Je veux…*
  I would like … *Je voudrais…*
wardrobe *armoire* (f.)
warm *chaud / chaude* (m./f.)
  It's warm./It's hot. *Il fait chaud.*
  be warm/hot (to) *avoir chaud*
wash (to) *laver*
  wash up (to), wash oneself (to) *se laver*
washing machine *machine* (f.) *à laver, lave-linge*
  (m.)
washroom *salle* (f.) *de bains*
waste (to) *perdre*
  waste time (to) *perdre du temps*
  waste your time (to) *perdre votre / ton temps*
watch *montre* (f.)
watch (to) *regarder*
  watch each other (to) *se regarder*
water *eau* (f.)
  mineral water *eau minérale*
  pitcher of water *carafe* (f.) *d'eau*
water-ski (to) *faire du ski nautique*
water-skiing *ski* (m.) *nautique*
way *direction* (f.), *chemin* (m.)
  this way *par ici*
  that way *par là*
we *nous, on* (infml.)
weak *faible*
wear (to) *porter*
  wear contact lenses (to) *porter des verres de
    contact, porter des lentilles de contact*
weather *temps* (m.)
  What's the weather today? *Quel temps fait-il
    aujourd'hui ?*
webpage *page* (f.) *web*
website *site* (m.) *web*
wedding ring *alliance* (f.)
Wednesday *mercredi*
week *semaine* (f.)
  in one week *dans une semaine*
  next week *semaine prochaine, dans une
    semaine*
  the week before last *semaine précédente,
    semaine d'avant*

the week after next *semaine d'après, semaine suivante, dans deux semaines*

days of the week *jours* (m. pl.) *de la semaine*

weekend *week-end* (m.)

weigh (to) *peser*

weightlifting *haltérophilie* (f.), *musculation* (f.)

lift weights (to) *faire de la musculation*

Welcome. *Bienvenue.*

You're welcome. *De rien. / Il n'y a pas de quoi. / Je vous en prie.* (fml.)

well *bien*

very well *très bien*

It's going well. *Ça va bien.*

Well done. *Bravo.*

Well ... *Eh bien... / Ben...* (infml.) */ Alors... / Alors là...*

well-dressed *bien habillé / habillée* (m./f.)

west *ouest* (m.)

western *western* (m.)

what *qu'est-ce que, quel / quelle* (m./f.), *quoi, que, qu'est-ce qui*

what happens next *suite* (f.)

what?/of what? *de quel / quelle ?* (m./f.)

at what time? *à quelle heure ?*

What is this/that? *Qu'est-ce que c'est ?*

What is the weather today? *Quel temps fait-il aujourd'hui ?*

What time is it? *Quelle heure est-il ?*

What's your name? *Comment vous appelez-vous ?* (pl./fml.) */ Comment t'appelles-tu ?* (infml.)

What's up?/What's new? *Quoi de neuf ?*

whatever *n'importe quoi*

wheelchair *chaise* (f.) *roulante*

when *quand*

since when? *depuis quand ?*

where *où*

Where is ... ? *Où se trouve... ? / Où est... ?*

Where is the restroom? (lit., Where are the toilets?) *Où sont les toilettes ?*

wherever *n'importe où*

which *que, quel / quelle* (m./f.), *lequel / laquelle / lesquels / lesquelles* (m./f./m. pl./f. pl.)

of which *dont*

while *pendant que*

whipped cream (that is flavored and sweetened) *crème* (f.) *chantilly*

white *blanc / blanche* (m./f.)

white wine *vin* (m.) *blanc*

white wine with black currant liqueur *kir* (m.)

white coat (doctor's coat) *blouse* (f.) *blanche*

who *qui*

Who is it? *Qui est-ce ?*

Who's calling? (on the phone) *C'est de la part de qui ? / Qui est à l'appareil ?*

whoever *n'importe qui*

whom *que*

of whom *dont*

whose *dont*

why *pourquoi*

wide *large*

wife *femme* (f.)

win (to) *gagner*

win a game/match (to) *gagner un match*

wind *vent* (m.)

It's windy. *Il fait du vent. / Il y a du vent.*

window *fenêtre* (f.), *guichet* (ticket) (m.)

wine *vin* (m.)

red/white/rosé/sparkling wine *vin rouge / blanc / rosé / mousseux*

white wine with black currant liqueur *kir* (m.)

type of French sparkling wine *crémant* (m.)

wine list *carte* (f.) *des vins*

winter *hiver* (m.)

in (the) winter *en hiver*

winter vacation *vacances* (f. pl.) *de neige*

wish (to) *désirer, souhaiter, vouloir*

with *avec*

With pleasure. *Avec plaisir.*

without *sans, sans que*

wolf *loup* (m.)

woman *femme* (f.)

wonder (to) *se demander*

wood *bois* (m.)

Bois de Vincennes (Vincennes Wood) *Bois de Vincennes (a large park in Paris)*

Bois de Boulogne (Boulogne Wood) *Bois de Boulogne (a large park in Paris)*

wooden *en bois*

word *mot* (m.)

work *travail* (m.), *boulot* (m.), *emploi* (m.)

work (to) *travailler*

work hard (to) *travailler dur*

worker *employé / employée* (m./f.)

workout *entraînement* (m.)

world *monde* (m.)

worried *inquiet / inquiète* (m./f.)

Don't worry about it. *Ce n'est pas grave.*

worse *pire, plus mauvais / mauvaise* (m./f.)

the worst *le / la pire, le / la plus mauvais / mauvaise*

worth (to be) *valoir*

be worth the trouble (to) *valoir la peine*

wounded *blessé / blessée* (m./f.)

Wow! *Oh là là !*

wrestling *lutte* (f.)

wrist *poignet* (m.)

write (to) *écrire*

writer *écrivain* (m.) (sometimes: *écrivaine*, f.)

wrong *faux / fausse* (m./f.), *mal, tort*

be wrong (to) *avoir tort*

X

x-ray *radio(graphie)* (f.)

Y

year *année* (f.), *an* (m.)

be ... years old (to) *avoir... ans*

final year of high school *classe* (f.) *terminale*

yellow *jaune*

yes *oui, si (negative)*

yesterday *hier*

yield to (to) *se rendre à (+ evidence, an argument, etc.)*

yoga *yoga* (m.)

you *tu* (infml.), *vous* (pl./fml.), *toi* (infml.), *te / t'* (direct object pronoun) (infml.), *vous* (direct object pronoun) (pl./fml.)

to you *te / t'* (infml.), *vous* (pl./fml.) (indirect object pronoun)

you have to/need to/must *il faut*

You're welcome. *De rien. / Je vous en prie.* (fml.)

young *jeune*

youngest child *cadet / cadette* (m./f.)

your (infml.) *ton / ta / tes* (m./f./pl.)

your (pl./fml.) *votre / vos* (m. or f./pl.)

yourself *te / t'* (infml.), *vous* (fml.) (reflexive pronoun)

yourselves *vous* (reflexive pronoun)

youth hostel *auberge* (f.) *de jeunesse*

Z

zero *zéro*

*This low-priced Bantam Book
has been completely reset in a type face
designed for easy reading, and was printed
from new plates. It contains the complete
text of the original hard-cover edition.*
NOT ONE WORD HAS BEEN OMITTED.

THE NEW AEROBICS
*A Bantam Book / published by arrangement with
M. Evans and Company, Inc.*

PRINTING HISTORY
Evans edition published May 1970
Bantam edition / May 1970

printing ...... *June 1970*	15th printing ...... *May 1974*
printing ...... *July 1970*	16th printing ... *January 1975*
printing ... *October 1970*	17th printing ...... *May 1975*
printing .... *March 1971*	18th printing ...... *May 1975*
printing ...... *July 1971*	19th printing . *September 1975*
printing ... *August 1971*	20th printing ... *October 1975*
printing ... *January 1972*	21st printing ... *January 1976*
printing .... *March 1972*	22nd printing ..... *June 1976*
printing ...... *June 1972*	23rd printing ..... *June 1976*
printing ... *October 1972*	24th printing . *December 1976*
printing ... *March 1973*	25th printing ...... *June 1977*
printing . *December 1973*	26th printing . *November 1977*
printing ... *January 1974*	27th printing .. *February 1978*
28th printing ......*August 1978*	
29th printing	

...*and back cover photographs of the author and his wife,
courtesy of Shelly Katz*

*All rights reserved under International and
Pan-American Copyright Conventions.
Copyright © 1970 by Kenneth H. Cooper.
...book may not be reproduced in whole or in part, by
...eograph or any other means, without permission.
...formation address: M. Evans and Company, Inc.,
...16 East 49th Street, New York, N.Y. 10017.*

ISBN 0-553-12360-2

...ed simultaneously in the United States and Canada

*...oks are published by Bantam Books, Inc. Its trade-
...sting of the words "Bantam Books" and the por-
...bantam, is registered in the United States Patent
...in other countries. Marca Registrada. Bantam
...666 Fifth Avenue, New York, New York 10019.*

...D IN THE UNITED STATES OF AMERICA

THE NEW AEROBICS

by Kenneth H. Cooper, M.
Lt. Col., U.S.A.F. Medi

2nd
3rd
4th
5th
6th
7th
8th
9th
10th
11th
12th
13th
14th

Front

This
mir
For

Publis

Bantam B.
mark, con
trayal of
Office and
Books, Inc

PRINT

Author's Preface

WHEN I INTRODUCED aerobics as a new concept of exercise, my chief aim was to counteract the problems of lethargy and inactivity which are so widely prevalent in our American population. Therefore, my first book was mainly a motivational book, but also it was an attempt to encourage people to examine more closely the benefits to be gained from regular exercise. The wide public acceptance of *Aerobics* indicates that these objectives have been at least partially achieved.

The present volume serves a different purpose. As a result of the comments from people in all walks of life and the accumulation of vast amounts of new data, it has been possible to prepare a book which discusses in great detail the specific requirements for safely and effectively entering an age-adjusted exercise program. I tend to classify this book more of an "Aerobics Handbook" or an "Aerobics Guidelines" than a new concept of exercise. For this reason, I hope that the faithful follower of "Aerobics" as well as the unconditioned beginner will find this new version of aerobics both interesting and challenging. Because of the expanded range of exercise options, the adjustment for age, and the comprehensive data tables, I also hope that physical educators and medical personnel concerned with exercise will find this book useful in supervising physical conditioning programs.

Whether this book is used as an individual exercise guide or as a professional reference work, it is my profound hope as a physician that it will serve its readers as a key to health and well-being.

KENNETH H. COOPER, M.D.

San Antonio, Texas

To my wife, *Millie*, who has become a tireless co-worker, an unwavering supporter, and a beautiful example of the benefits of regular exercise—and to my young daughter, *Berkley,* who has learned to live so often and so much without Daddy.

Contents

1: The Impact of Aerobics

I RECEIVED A letter recently from an elderly gentleman who wrote:

> *Dear Dr. Cooper:*
> *I want to take this opportunity to thank you for the Aerobics conditioning program. I have followed the program faithfully for over nine months. During the past six months, I have been averaging at least 30 points per week entirely by walking. I sleep better, feel better, and have gone through the winter without any medical problems for the first time in years—and I am anxiously awaiting my 94th year.*
>
> *Appreciatively,*

This is one example of the thousands of letters I have received from men and women, of all ages, and from all over the world. Many are letters of appreciation. Others ask questions. But nearly all document the beneficial effect aerobics has had on their lives. It has been impossible to respond to all of these letters, so I hope that this book will in some way serve as a means of communicating with dedicated aerobics fans everywhere. Perhaps it will inspire others to began an aerobics program. But my most earnest hope is that the wisdom gained from testing and training tens of thousands of men and women can be imparted to people everywhere who are still seeking healthier, more productive and more effective lives.

Today, the official physical fitness program of the United States Air Force is based on aerobics, with roughly 800,000 members of the Air Force participating. Several foreign military organizations are considering adopting it as their official conditioning program. What's more, aerobics is no longer exclusive to the military. Countless people in every walk of life have found aerobics a workable way to achieve new levels of physical competence and personal well-being. Professional athletic teams have found it to be an excellent way to maintain a high level of fitness during the off season. Many colleges and universities throughout the country have adopted aerobics as a part of their physical education program. All have shown interest in the program because it is the first scientific attempt to validate and quantify the effect of exercise—and to answer the intriguing questions of what kind, how often, and how much.

The age range of the participants in this program has also been remarkable. I was surprised to discover that a large proportion of aerobics fans—women as well as men—are in the 40–60 age bracket. The men in this age group say that they took up aerobics as a type of life insurance. And the women admit just as frankly that they consider aerobics a good way to keep their figures as well as their health.

A middle-aged woman writes:

After raising a family of four children, I could once again concentrate on regaining a youthful figure. I tried dieting but always seemed to lose weight where I didn't want to. When I combined a mild dietary restriction program with aerobics, I lost weight and inches in desirable places—hips, thighs and waist. I dropped three dress sizes and my husband says I look ten years younger! Aerobics has completely changed my life.

I have also learned that these middle-aged men and women respond well to training programs but that their approach must be less vigorous and more prolonged. Consequently, you will notice that there are four age-adjusted conditioning programs in the center of this book. In addition, physical fitness categories have also been age-adjusted. And for the older person, there has been more emphasis placed on achieving 30 points per week as contrasted to meeting the requirement of a physical fitness test. As a result, the program is now more adaptable and easier to accomplish by men and women of all ages.

The widespread interest in exercise has caused physicians and public health authorities to take an appraising look at aerobics. If properly implemented and supervised, some of them see it as a possible countermeasure to the Nation's Number One health problem: heart disease.

Heart disease is a national disaster. Every year, nearly a million Americans die from heart and blood vessel disease—a death rate higher than that of any other country. Millions more are crippled by heart attacks. To make matters even worse, the disease appears to be reaching out to younger people. Men in their 40s and even in their 30s are dropping off at an alarming rate. And, as in everything else, the women are catching up with the men. Death from heart disease in young American women is also the highest of any country in the world. Perhaps this explains why the longevity of American men ranks 17th and that American women rank tenth among the major nations of the world.

A spokesman for the National Heart Institute sums up the situation in a single sentence: "We're faced with a kind of super-epidemic against which every possible resource must be mobilized."

Exercise, without doubt, is one possible resource.

To claim that aerobics is the only solution to the overwhelming problem of heart disease would be foolish and irresponsible. But I can assure each reader that aerobics—if implemented properly and practiced according to the charts and the rules in this book—will lessen his chance of prematurely developing coronary heart disease or related vascular ailments.

Aside from preventing heart trouble, aerobics holds out other promises for public health. The Russians and Germans have already shown that mass programs of exercise are an efficient way to raise the general fitness level of entire populations.

In the United States, where the vast majority of the population can't pass a basic fitness test, we've got a long way to go in public sponsorship of exercise programs. But the impact of aerobics has nudged a few health officials to look more critically at the role of exercise in preventive medicine.

The state of Vermont, for example, is now using aerobics in a statewide preventive medicine program. And the New York Federal Safety Council recently urged Mayor John V. Lindsay of New York City to set up a municipal aerobics fitness program.

I'm often asked just how many people are practicing aerobics. One way to answer this question would be to refer to book sales—nearly one and one-half million copies of the paperback edition of *Aerobics* have been sold. But book sales cannot be considered an accurate indication of program participation. A better indication comes from the Belden Public Opinion Poll, a regional opinion research organization headquartered in Dallas, Texas. A statewide survey of 60 Texas communities in mid-1968 revealed that 26 percent of the citizens in Texas were exercising regularly and that an estimated 186,000 were following the aerobics program. Projected nationally, this figure indicates that several million Americans may have been practicing aerobics in 1968.

Hundreds of private gyms and health clubs have responded to this mass interest by offering aerobic conditioning courses. The YM-YWCA is leading this trend. In most major cities you can now find at least one branch of the YMCA or YWCA with an aerobics group. So if you seek company, encouragement, advice, and expert supervision for your exercise, the Y is a good place to look.

You might also check the National Jogging Association (P.O. Box 19367, Washington, D.C. 20036), to find out if they have any groups in your vicinity. The Association got off to a fine start in 1968 with a highly suitable ceremony at the Jefferson Memorial in Washington, D.C. Former Secretary of the Interior Stewart L. Udall and Lieutenant General Richard L. Bohannon (ret.), once surgeon general of the USAF, led the assembled crowd in a brisk jog around the reflecting pool.

Another rapidly growing group is called Mile-a-thon International. This organization is supported by the Long Beach Community Hospital, Long Beach, California. They sponsor walking and running activities throughout southern California and once yearly hold a large walking/running event. The emphasis is on participation, not competition, and their appropriate motto is "Witness to Fitness." In 1969, the Mile-a-thon attracted nearly a thousand men, women and children.

Even the interest in cycling seems to be increasing. The League of American Wheelmen, the national amateur cycling organization, reports that bicycle sales in 1968 exceeded all previous years.

But one of the most encouraging recent trends is the growing interest of business and industry in the fitness of their employees. This makes good sense from a management viewpoint. Company-sponsored fitness programs tend to reduce absenteeism, accidents and sick pay. What's more, employees in good physical condition are more alert, more productive, and their morale is higher.

Company fitness programs are rarely restricted to top brass. In most firms, any employee can join. As it turns out, most of them are eager to sign up. A California firm scheduling several aerobics sessions per week polled its employees for their reactions. Here's a typical sampling:

"After a workout, the fog clears," says an airframe designer. "I can focus on what I'm doing."

An accountant comments: "I no longer get drowsy in the afternoon—and I've got plenty of energy left when I get home."

"For me it's like insurance," says an assembly-line inspector. "I just can't afford to get sick. Not with hospital costs a hundred dollars a day."

He has a point. *Staying* well is a lot cheaper than *getting* well.

The general manager of a division of one of the country's largest electronics concerns sums up his experience this way: "Our Division was in serious trouble a while ago due to merger and soft market problems. We now seem to be well on our way towards joining the rest of the corporation in achieving some real success. I give no small credit to your 'Aerobics' program for having provided a management and employee team made up of individuals who feel better, look better, and are more physically and mentally alert."

Such reactions strengthen my hope that the increasing use of aerobics in industry-sponsored programs will become a major factor in building fitness and health throughout the country.

And all of this is just a beginning. The stage has been set for developing aerobics on an even broader scale.

In May 1968, I participated in a seminar at the Congress

of International Military Sports in Fontainebleau, France. At this meeting, plans were laid for aerobics programs within the armed forces of Sweden, Austria, Finland, Korea and Brazil. From the military of these countries, aerobics will surely spread to the civilian population, just as it has in the United States. Moreover, nine countries represented at the congress agreed to pool data obtained in connection with aerobics testing. This will create an international information bank from which valuable new knowledge can be derived.

In little more than a year, aerobics has grown from near obscurity to worldwide scope. It is a deep satisfaction for me to have had a leading part in this development. What greater reward can there be for a research physician than to know that his work has put millions of people on a new road to good health.

2: Revisions and Recaps

DOCTORS LEARN FROM their patients, coaches from their teams, and I've learned a great deal from the thousands of people who have told me about their personal experience with aerobics. Also, I have had the opportunity to collect and evaluate data on many civilian and military personnel including a large United States Air Force aerobics study. At the request of the USAF Chief of Staff, an expanded aerobics project was conducted at five Air Force bases during the period of April–October 1968. A total of 15,146 men were studied, representing one of the largest research projects ever attempted in the field of physical conditioning.

The knowledge gained from this massive research effort and from the public participation in aerobics has helped us formulate new guidelines. No basic principles have been altered. In fact, the original concept of aerobics has been greatly strengthened by the new findings. But we have revised many program details and worked out some new ones. Among them:

- Revised progressive point charts
- Adjustments for different age groups
- New fitness testing rules
- New safety tips
- New sports and exercises added to the aerobic reference charts
- Special pointers for women and children
- Medical examination requirements

DEFINING AEROBICS

Aerobics (pronounced: a-er-ó biks) refers to a variety of exercises that stimulate heart and lung activity for a time period sufficiently long to produce beneficial changes in the body. Running, swimming, cycling, and jogging—these are typical aerobic exercises. There are many others.

Aerobics offers you an ample choice of different forms of exercise, including many popular sports. They have one thing in common: by making you work hard, they demand plenty of oxygen. That's the basic idea. That's what makes them aerobic.

The main objective of an aerobic exercise program is to increase the maximum amount of oxygen that the body can process within a given time. This is called your *aerobic capacity*. It is dependent upon an ability to 1) rapidly breathe large amounts of air, 2) forcefully deliver large volumes of blood and 3) effectively deliver oxygen to all parts of the body. In short, it depends upon efficient lungs, a powerful heart, and a good vascular system. Because it reflects the conditions of these vital organs, the aerobic capacity is the best index of overall physical fitness.

TRAINING EFFECT

Collectively, the changes induced by exercise in the various systems and organs of the body are called the *training effect*. Unless the exercise is of sufficient intensity and duration, it will not produce a training effect and cannot be classified as an aerobic exercise. However, this distinction between aerobic and non-aerobic exercises is a laboratory determination, too technical for routine use. Therefore, the point system utilized in the aerobics conditioning program was developed to make this distinction for you. If the program is followed exactly and the required point goals are reached, an adequate training effect is assured. Specifically, aerobic exercise produces a training effect and increases the capacity to utilize oxygen in several ways:

1. It strengthens the muscles of respiration and tends to reduce the resistance to air flow, ultimately facilitating the rapid flow of air in and out of the lungs.
2. It improves the strength and pumping efficiency of the heart, enabling more blood to be pumped with each stroke. This improves the ability to more rapidly transport life-sustaining oxygen from the lungs to the heart and ultimately to all parts of the body.
3. It tones up muscles throughout the body, thereby improving the general circulation, at times lowering blood pressure and reducing the work on the heart.

4. It causes an increase in the total amount of blood circulating through the body and increases the number of red blood cells and the amount of hemoglobin, making the blood a more efficient oxygen carrier.

None of this is speculation. The anatomic and biochemical changes characteristic of the training effect have been documented in the laboratory many times. And throughout this book, reference will be made to many of these studies which have shown the health-building action of the training effect, especially as it concerns the heart.

POINT CHARTS

The training effect is the goal of an aerobic conditioning program. The means for achieving that goal is also provided by the program. That is the purpose of the point charts. Here lies the unique merit of the aerobic system: you can measure your own progress as if you were being monitored in a medical research laboratory. All you need is the point chart and a stopwatch. In effect, aerobics puts the lab in your pocket.

Many people ask, "What is so important about points? Why isn't it sufficient just to add up the total distance you walk or run?"

For an answer, I refer to an experience I had several years ago. Two active runners in their early forties, comparable in weight and height, came to my laboratory for an evaluation on the treadmill. In the interview prior to their evaluation, I discovered that both men were running two miles, five days a week. I immediately assumed that their level of fitness was comparable but was quite surprised at the results of their treadmill test. One of the subjects was clearly in excellent condition and the other barely passed.

Why the difference?

I was perplexed until I asked another question: *"How fast do you run your two miles?"* The first said he averaged between 13:30–14:00 minutes whereas the second took over 20:00 minutes. One was a runner and the other a jogger. It was readily apparent that I needed to consider a factor other than distance—the time.

You achieve a greater training effect if you put more effort into your exercise. Consequently, the point system was developed so that I knew exactly how much effort was being expended.

In hundreds of subsequent studies, we have discovered that it is easy to predict oxygen consumption and fitness based on points but difficult to predict it on miles alone. If you tell me that you are running 20 miles per week, I'm not quite sure what your level of fitness will be, but if you tell me you are averaging 100 points per week, I know that you are in excellent condition!

The aerobic point system was derived from laboratory measurements of the oxygen cost of the exercise, as well as from data obtained in field tests. How these experiments and tests were performed, and how the point charts were calculated, has been explained at length in my earlier book. For the user of these charts all that is necessary is to understand that the aerobic points refer to the energy expended.

The point value assigned to each exercise indicates that amount of oxygen consumed by the body during a particular activity. More points mean more effort expended, that is, more oxygen burned in the body at a faster rate. In short, the point system measures the energy cost of the exercise.

For example, if you run a mile in 11:30 minutes, you can earn 3 points. Run the mile in 8:30 minutes and you earn 4 points.

"Hold it Doc," one of the airmen interrupted when I was explaining this to a test group. "You mean I get more points for exercising less?"

"How so?" I asked, somewhat confused.

"Well, you're giving me 3 points for 11:30 minutes and 4 points for exercising three minutes less, even though the distance is the same."

I finally saw his problem. Throughout the aerobic charts, shorter completion times mean more points. That's what confused him.

"Look at it this way," I explained, "Suppose you're driving your car. To cover a mile faster, you have to step down harder on the gas pedal. Why? Because going faster takes more power from the engine. It's the same when you're running. If you run a mile in a shorter time, your energy output is greater. Your heart and lungs work harder. That's why you get more points for the shorter time span."

Because the point charts let you measure the amount of effort you expend, you can now take exercise in *progressive* doses. And this is vitally important. In fact, it is the key to the aerobic conditioning program. The body must gradually adjust itself to increasing amounts of exercise. Too much too fast can be as damaging as too little too late. That's why the charts for the conditioning program spell out exact exercise rations from week to week. "Why are 30 points per week necessary? Why not 20 or wouldn't 50 be even better?" These are questions that are asked at nearly all of my presentations.

The answer is always the same. From testing and training thousands of men and women, I have been able to show that roughly 80 percent of the people who follow the progressive programs and work up to 30 points per week can reach our minimum standards of fitness.

"And where did you get your standards?"

The standards I have established are based mainly on age-adjusted Swedish standards—and Swedish researchers in exercise physiology have long been recognized as the world's leaders in this field.

AGE CODING

As you may have noticed in the preceding paragraph, I said *age adjusted* standards. And a new feature of this book is not only progressive exercise charts adjusted to age but also new categories of fitness based on age. The breakdown of the four separate age brackets is as follows:

> Under 30
> 30 to 39
> 40 to 49
> 50 and over

Splitting the conditioning programs into four separate training routines permitted me to use a different approach for the older age groups. But the 30 point per week requirement still remains—it just takes a little longer time to reach it.

The original conditioning program was based on data obtained exclusively from my Air Force research group. Their average age was in the middle twenties. After the general public took up aerobics, it became clear that certain modifications were needed. Too many civilians, deskbound, middle aged and maybe a little paunchy, just weren't able to meet exercise norms set up for young airmen.

The physical director of a YMCA branch of mid-Manhattan filed a typical report:

> *In this location we gets lots of businessmen coming in for exercise. Some of the men in our aerobics group are well into middle age, ranging between 47 and 53. At the outset, they didn't seem in any worse shape than the rest. But they soon found that they couldn't keep up with the younger men or with the chart requirements of the aerobics program. They get discouraged, and some would quit. I hated to see them drop out. After all, they needed the exercise most. Should I have modified the chart requirements for them? If so, how?*

Similar letters flowed in by the dozens. In response, I made a special effort to draw older persons into the expanded research program to study their exercise needs. Among them, I even picked several hundred men and women over 50 years of age to evaluate their reactions to the aerobics program. The new age-adjusted charts are the outcome of these studies.

Age is not a major obstacle to fitness. No matter what age bracket you belong to, you can reach a satisfactory level of fitness. But you must work toward the common goal using a different approach and at a different rate.

The new age-coding of the charts, I hope, will open the door to aerobics for even broader segments of the population, particularly those in the over-40 brackets. With aerobics, they can avoid many symptoms of premature aging, regain the vigor and vitality they have long thought lost, and make the "best years of life" just that.

We'll discuss the many new hints and suggestions that have come from our expanding experience with aerobics as we go along. First, let's get started in the new aerobics.

3: The Physical Examination

DIFFERENT PEOPLE HAVE different objectives in their quest for fitness. To an athlete, it's seconds shaved off a mile, or that extra burst of speed in the last minute of the game. To a lawyer, it's alertness after hours of hard bargaining. To a housewife, a dress two sizes smaller, or maybe just the sense of abundant well-being, the positive outlook and regained youthfulness that comes from really being "fit."

No matter what your particular exercise aim may be, the most important thing is to achieve it safely. After all, you want to gain your health, not lose it. That's why a thorough physical examination should be the very first step on your road to fitness.

Emphasizing the importance of such an examination is the following tragic incident. On July 23, 1968, a leading West Coast newspaper exploded a banner headline: TWO MORE JOGGERS DIE! Other newspapers across the country picked up the story. Occurring shortly after a wave of enthusiasm had made jogging something of a nationwide sport, the tragedy suddenly focused national concern on the problem of safety in exercise.

My phone rang almost constantly. Physicians and lay people alike were anxiously asking under what conditions exercise might be dangerous, and prominent doctors were wondering out loud in newspapers and magazines whether perhaps the idea of exercise had been oversold to the public.

In response to this widespread concern, I decided to investigate more closely the case of the two joggers who had suffered fatal heart attacks during the exercise. Both, it turnd out, had severe heart disease, and one of them had been told by a prominent West Coast physician that he should under no circumstances engage in vigorous exercise. Yet, contrary to medical advice, the man started jogging at a strenuous rate, mistakenly believing that this would help him overcome his heart condition more quickly. Instead, jogging at a hard pace strained his weak heart beyond its limits.

The one good thing growing out of this tragedy was the realization on the part of physicians that anyone entering an exercise or physical conditioning program should have a medical checkup before starting. So before you embark on any exercise program, get your doctor's approval.

MEDICAL CHECKUP

Because no standards have yet been set for this pre-exercise checkup, many doctors have asked for recommended procedures. In response to these inquiries, I collaborated with several of my colleagues and with the AMA Committee on Physical Fitness and Exercise to define the kind of examination recommended for this purpose. The full medical details are to be published in a scientific article entitled "Guidelines in the Management of the Exercising Patient." The main objective of this examination is to spot heart, lung, and blood vessel problems that could make exercise potentially dangerous. This is especially important for older persons who are more likely to be affected by such problems.

The following guidelines are proposed for different age groups:

Under 30: You can start exercising if you've had a checkup within the past year and the doctor found nothing wrong with you.

Between 30 and 39: You should have a checkup within three months before you start exercising. The examination should include an electrocardiogram (ECG) taken at rest.

Between 40 and 59: Same as for the 30–39 group with one important addition. Your doctor should also take an ECG to check your heart while you are exercising. Your pulse rate during this test should approach the level it would during aerobic workouts.*

Over 59: The same requirements as for the 40–59 age group except that the examination should be performed immediately before embarking on any exercise program.

* For detailed requirements, physicians may refer to the Appendix for a chart listing the target heart rates to be used in taking an exercise ECG.

The trouble is that not many doctors are equipped to take ECGs during exercise. Ideally, they should have either a stationary bicycle or a treadmill in their office so that they can continuously monitor your ECG while you vigorously exercise. With growing popular interest in exercise, I hope that more doctors will install this kind of equipment. After all, a good stationary bicycle with adjustable brake force costs less than $100. A treadmill is more expensive.

If your doctor doesn't have this kind of equipment, he can still take your ECG while you are under stress by giving you a variant of the so-called Masters two-step test. In this test you rapidly go up and down a single step until your pulse rate reaches the required level. The ECG and pulse should be monitored both during and after such exercise. Occasionally ECG changes produced by the exercise stress do not show up until two to five minutes after the exercise has stopped. That's why the ECG should continue to be monitored during the recovery period.

The purpose of these tests is to spot any heart condition that might cause trouble during exercise. If coronary weakness or some other defect shows up, exercise must be scaled down to levels of physical demand that your heart can meet safely. Your doctor may suggest that you do your exercising in a special medically supervised program until you have made sufficient improvement to continue on your own. In fact, he may recommend that you confine yourself to walking—no running, jogging or other more strenuous forms of exercise.

Don't feel discouraged about this. Done consistently and according to the aerobic charts, walking can gain for you the same benefits as any of the more strenuous exercises. The only difference is that it takes a little longer. Even if you do nothing but walk, you can eventually be as aerobically fit as anyone.

While walking can be recommended to almost anyone, the more vigorous exercises, notably jogging and running, are strictly prohibited for persons suffering from any of the following conditions:

1. Moderate to severe coronary heart disease causing chest pain with minimal activity (angina pectoris).

2. Recent heart attacks. You must wait at least three months after a heart attack before starting on a regular exercise program. Even then your exercise program must be medically supervised.

3. Severe disease of the heart valves, primarily as a result of old rheumatic fever. Some patients of this type should not exercise at all—not even to the extent of fast walking.

4. Certain types of congenital heart disease, particularly those in which the surface of the body turns blue during exercise.

5. Greatly enlarged heart due to high blood pressure or other types of progressive heart disease.

6. Severe irregularities of the heartbeat requiring medication or frequent medical attention.

7. Uncontrolled sugar diabetes constantly fluctuating from too much to not enough blood sugar.

8. High blood pressure not controlled by medication; *i.e.*, blood pressure exceeding 180/110 even with medication.

9. Excessive obesity. If you are more than 35 pounds overweight according to the standard weight charts, you must lose weight on a walking program before you can begin running or jogging.

10. Any infectious disease during its acute stage.

Another group of ailments do not prevent you from exercising altogether but make it necessary to proceed with caution and under medical supervision. In contrast to the above-named conditions, which are absolute *contraindications*, the following are regarded—medically speaking—as *relative* contraindications:

1. Any infectious disease in its convalescent or chronic stage.

2. Sugar diabetes controlled by insulin.

3. A history of recent or active internal bleeding. (Some of these patients should not exercise at all.)

4. Kidney disease, either chronic or acute.

5. Anemia under treatment but not yet corrected (less than 10 grams of hemoglobin).

6. Acute or chronic lung disease resulting in breathing difficulty with even light exercise.

7. Elevated blood pressure which can be lowered only to 150/90 with medication.
8. Blood vessel disease of the legs that produces pain with walking.
9. Arthritis in the back, legs, feet or ankles, requiring frequent medication for relief of pain.
10. Convulsive disease not completely controlled with medication.

Let me stress once more that these relative contraindications do not rule out exercise. To the contrary, in some cases exercise helps reduce their symptoms. But medical judgment and supervision must be applied to each individual case.

AGE RESTRICTIONS

As you grow in years, the efficiency of your heart and lungs gradually decreases. One of the benefits of aerobic exercise is that it slows down this aspect of aging and to some degree helps you retain your youthful fitness. But if you have not been exercising regularly, you should observe certain age restrictions when you consider starting a conditioning program.

Up to 30 years of age: Unless you have some obvious medical problem, you can enter any type of an exercise program—running jogging, swimming, cycling—no restrictions. Just choose one that you enjoy.

Between 30 and 50 years of age: You're still good for almost everything. You have your choice of sports. But if you plan to do some of the more strenuous exercises, be sure to get your doctor's specific approval of your decision.

Between 50 and 59 years: It would be better if you started a walking program. Only after you have conditioned yourself by walking according to the charts should you consider running, jogging, or more demanding competitive sports such as basketball, handball, or squash. Have your doctor check you out again before you start such activities. Othrwise you're better off sticking with less arduous exercises, such as walking, golf, cycling (particularly stationary cycling), and swimming.

Age 60 and over: If you're like most people in this age group, avoid jogging, running and vigorous competitive sports. Walking, swimming and stationary cycling will do you a lot more good.

However, there are exceptions for the over-60 bracket. If you have been keeping in shape by regular exercise for many years so that you have built up and maintained your aerobic capacity, you may safely participate in such vigorous activities as jogging, running, and stationary running. You're also free to engage in more strenuous activities if you do your exercise in a medically supervised group.

If you doubt that regular conditioning exercise can keep you fit way beyond 60, look at 102-year-old Larry Lewis. He's been exercising practically all his life, first as a member of Ringling Brothers and Barnum and Bailey's circus, and since the age of 80, as a regular jogger. Now he is on his feet some eight hours each day as a banquet waiter at San Francisco's St. Francis Hotel.

Larry runs six miles every morning in Golden Gate Park. Then he walks five miles to work, and after his long shift, he usually walks home. On his 102nd birthday he added something extra to this routine. He ran a 100-yard dash in 17.3 seconds—0.5 faster than he was able to do it at the age of 101. It's not official, but I'm pretty sure that this is the world record for the 100-yard dash for men above one hundred years of age!

In this chapter, I have stressed the need for a medical examination prior to entering *any* exercise program, because as a physician it is my duty to warn against possible health risks. But the encouraging fact is that the great majority of people pass their pre-exercise examination with no trouble at all and can enter sensible exercise programs without reservation.

Because of incidents like the death of the California joggers, people sometimes get the idea that all exercise is risky. They think exercise killed those joggers. Exactly the opposite is true. They died because of the severity of their disease whereas proper exercise might have strengthened their hearts and saved their lives—if they had followed reasonable medical advice.

Exercise is the medicine that keeps countless people alive. But like all medicine, it must be taken according to prescription.

4: Fitness Testing and Categories

FITNESS TESTING IS strictly optional. You can put yourself in fine shape without ever taking any test at all. Just follow the conditioning charts. By the time you reach the 30-points-per-week level, just take it for granted that you're in good condition.

Yet, there are many occasions when physical fitness testing is extremely useful. For example, physicians may need to know a patient's level of fitness so that they can determine the amount of physical activity he may safely perform on the job. Coaches may want to test the fitness of individual athletes or even their entire team before starting into seasonal competition. Physical educators may benefit from evaluating their classes as a means of determining their response to a particular training program. Even if you are exercising strictly on your own, you may want to find out just where you stand in comparison with others. Or once you start an exercise program, you may want a method for monitoring your progress.

For all these purposes, we have developed aerobic fitness tests that are both simple and accurate. Basically, the tests measure your aerobic capacity—the maximum amount of oxygen your body can process during exhausting work. This is one of the best, if not the best available indicator of general fitness and physical capability.

MEASURING AEROBIC CAPACITY

The groundwork for developing an aerobic fitness test was done in the laboratory. To measure a man's aerobic capacity, we ask him to walk/run on a motor driven treadmill. Its speed can be varied from a slow walk to a quick dash, and the incline can be raised to simulate an uphill run. The man on the treadmill has no choice but to move at the speed set by the technician. If he doesn't run hard enough, he falls off backwards. That's how we were able to encourage our volunteers to run up to the point of exhaustion—assuring a maximum effort.

During these tests we continuously monitored the electrocardiogram and blood pressure to guard against overexertion. At the first sign of excessive heart strain, we stopped the test. By watching the electrocardiogram, blood pressure and respiration rate, we could also tell whether our test subject was really working to the limit of his capacity.

While the test subjects were running on the treadmill, they breathed into a one-way valve that enabled us to collect the air they exhaled. This air was then analyzed to determine the amount of oxygen their bodies utilized during their exhausting effort. This amount (measured in milliliters per kilogram of total body weight per minute) marks a man's aerobic capacity. It is his fitness index.

Through these lab tests we found, for example, that a man less than 29 years of age and in good physical condition can process upward of 42.5 milliliters of oxygen per kilogram per minute, while a person in very poor shape can process only 25 milliliters or less.

On the basis of these measurements we set up the following five Fitness Categories for men:

FITNESS CATEGORY	OXYGEN CONSUMPTION (Ml/Kg/Min)			
	Under 30	*30–39*	*40–49*	*50+*
I. Very Poor	< 25.0	< 25.0	< 25.0	
II. Poor	25.0–33.7	25.0–30.1	25.0–26.4	< 25.0
III. Fair	33.8–42.5	30.2–39.1	26.5–35.4	25.0–33.7
IV. Good	42.6–51.5	39.2–48.0	35.5–45.0	33.8–43.0
V. Excellent	51.6+	48.1+	45.1+	43.1+

< Means less than.

FIELD TESTING

So much for theory. Obviously, this type of laboratory fitness testing is necessary for research but it isn't very practical. It takes about $10,000 worth of equipment, three technicians and an hour's time to test a single person. For general use, simpler field testing methods had to be developed. Fortunately, we were able to devise field tests requiring only a stop watch and a place to run. Despite their simplicity and ease of administration these field tests are almost as accurate and reliable as laboratory measurements made on the treadmill.

Since your heart rate and blood pressure cannot be monitored continuously during a field test, there is a certain risk if you take such a test without having been properly conditioned by previous exercise. That is why I suggest the following precautions:

1. Don't take a fitness test prior to beginning an exercise program if you are over 30 years of age.

2. Be sure to have a medical examination, as outlined in Chapter 3, before you take a fitness test. If you are over 30, it is still safer to postpone the test until you have completed the six-week "starter program" as described in Chapter Six.

3. If you comply with the above, yet experience extreme fatigue, shortness of breath, light-headedness or nausea during the physical fitness test, stop immediately. Do not try to repeat the test until your fitness level has been gradually improved through regular exercise.

12-MINUTE TEST

The first of these field tests is the 12-minute test. Run and walk as far as you comfortably can in 12 minutes. If you get winded, slow down awhile until you get your breath back. Then run again for a stretch. The idea is to cover the greatest distance you can in those 12 minutes. Our findings show that the distance covered correlates very accurately (coefficient of correlation $= .90$) with treadmill measurements of oxygen consumption and aerobic capacity. In other words, you can measure your aerobic capacity and determine your fitness category simply by a 12-minute run.

The correlation between distance covered in 12 minutes and oxygen consumption works out as follows:

DISTANCE COVERED (Miles)	OXYGEN CONSUMPTION (Ml/Kg/Min)
less than 1.0	less than 25.0
1.0 to 1.24	25.0 to 33.7
1.25 to 1.49	33.8 to 42.5
1.50 to 1.74	42.6 to 51.5
1.75 miles or more	51.6 or more

(Data based on men 17–52 years of age)

If you have no other way to measure how far you have run, you can do it by driving the same stretch of road in your car and reading the distance covered on the odometer. Don't try to measure distance with a pedometer. We've checked out several and none are sufficiently accurate.

The following charts tell you how to rate yourself on the 12-minute test, and in contrast to previously published test charts, these have been adjusted for different age groups. The original 12-minute test chart was designed for male Air Force personnel whose average age was under 30. But since so many people past 30 have expressed interest in the aerobics program, it has become necessary to establish some age-adjusted standards for both men and women. These new factors have been incorporated in the revised charts. As they stand now, these charts are applicable to a broad spectrum of the population, although the chart for women is a preliminary chart only.

12-Minute Test for Men

(Distances in miles covered in 12-minutes)

Fitness Category	Age			
	Under 30	*30–39*	*40–49*	*50+*
I. Very Poor	< 1.0	< .95	< .85	< .80
II. Poor	1.0–1.24	.95–1.14	.85–1.04	.80– .99
III. Fair	1.25–1.49	1.15–1.39	1.05–1.29	1.0 –1.24
IV. Good	1.50–1.74	1.40–1.64	1.30–1.54	1.25–1.49
V. Excellent	1.75+	1.65+	1.55+	1.50+

< Means less than.

12-Minute Test for Women *

(Distance in miles covered in 12 minutes)

Fitness Category	Age			
	Under 30	*30–39*	*40–49*	*50+*
I. Very Poor	< .95	< .85	< .75	< .65
II. Poor	.95–1.14	.85–1.04	.75– .94	.65– .84
III. Fair	1.15–1.34	1.05–1.24	.95–1.14	.85–1.04
IV. Good	1.35–1.64	1.25–1.54	1.15–1.44	1.05–1.34
V. Excellent	1.65+	1.55+	1.45+	1.35+

* Preliminary chart based on limited data.
< Means less than.

1.5 MILE TEST

During the summer of 1968, I was asked to evaluate the physical fitness of more than 15,000 members of the Air Force. For testing such a large group, the 12-minute test described above proved too cumbersome. It was impossible to monitor a thousand men on a single track in a morning, as was required by our tight schedule. Some modification of test procedures had to be made.

To simplify the administration of the test to large groups, we took the information we had accumulated from the 12-minute test and developed new standards based on the time required to run 1.5 miles. The five fitness categories were then related to the age of the subject as well as the time required to run the 1.5 mile distance. If you prefer this type of test to the 12-minute test, rate yourself according to the following charts:

1.5 MILE TEST FOR MEN †

(Running time in minutes for 1.5 mile distance)

FITNESS CATEGORY	AGE			
	Under 30	30–39	40–49	50+
I. Very Poor	16:30+	17:30+	18:30+	19:00+
II. Poor	16:30—14:31	17:30—15:31	18:30—16:31	19:00—17:01
III. Fair	14:30—12:01	15:30—13:01	16:30—14:01	17:00—14:31
IV. Good	12:00—10:16	13:00—11:01	14:00—11:31	14:30—12:01
V. Excellent *	<10:15	<11:00	<11:30	<12:00

† No separate chart is provided for women because available data are still too tentative.

* For military personnel, the Excellent requirements are 15–30 seconds faster.

< Means less than.

With the aid of these field tests we have been able to confirm the effects of aerobic training in thousands of Air Force personnel. Typically, a deconditioned man in the Very Poor category with an aerobic capacity of less than 25 milliliters can increase his capacity by as much as 30 percent in response to aerobic conditioning.

I strongly urge coaches and sports instructors to employ either the 12-minute or the 1.5-mile tests in place of some of the older methods. Many athletic teams will test their athletes by asking them to run one mile or the even shorter distance of 600 yards. Usually the requirement is to run the mile in less than six or seven minutes. If an athlete can do this, he supposedly has sufficient endurance capacity.

The irony is that the one-mile run—let alone the 600-yard run—is much too short to accurately test for endurance or aerobic capacity. Such relatively brief spurts are basically tests of anaerobic capacity; *i.e.* the ability to perform at a high level of energy output for very short periods. It is a poor indicator of the athlete's ability to finish the game without slackening off toward the end. Our observation that a one-mile run does not represent a significant challenge to an athlete's aerobic capacity has recently been confirmed by other researchers. A run of at least 1.5 miles or a duration of at least 12 minutes is necessary to estimate accurately by field-testing methods the maximum oxygen consumption.

An increasing number of athletic teams have been using both the 12-minute and the 1.5-mile tests in conjunction with their off-season and in-season conditioning. The University of Nebraska football team, for example, found that less than half of their men were able to run 1.5 miles in under 12:00 minutes at the beginning of spring training. Yet at the end of spring training, they proudly announced that every man on the team—including the heavy tackles—was able to run 1.5 miles in 12 minutes or less.

Calvert Hall High School, Towson, Maryland, employed intensive aerobic conditioning prior to the football season, then used the 12-minute test weekly during the season to assure that team members were keeping up their fitness. For the first time in the history of the school, the team went through the entire season without time lost due to injuries, indicating that the fitness and added alertness gained from aerobics may be an important factor in avoiding athletic injury. The Green Bay Packers professional football team have publicized the fact that they use aerobics during the off-season. They hope that this off-season conditioning will improve their performance in season by: 1) increasing the stamina and endurance of their players; 2) reducing athletic injuries; and 3) increasing the number of years a player can actively participate as a team member.

FITNESS COMPARISONS

The 12-minute and 1.5-mile tests now, for the first time, provide a practical method for measuring and comparing the fitness of large numbers of people. As these tests become more widely used, we may expect interesting new information about fitness levels at different schools, in different occupations, different states and countries. Such data will be valuable in developing aerobic exercise programs aimed at raising the general level of fitness for men and women of all ages.

One of the first foreign surveys of this kind was made by Arthur Zechner, a captain in the Austrian army. He gave the 12-minute test to 1157 recruits whose average age was 19 years. Here are the results:

1157 AUSTRIAN MALES—INITIAL TESTING
(18–20 Years of Age)

FITNESS CATEGORY	Percent
I. Very Poor	0.6
II. Poor	3.6
III. Fair	20.5
IV. Good	44.5
V. Excellent	30.8

Contrast these findings with our own Air Force personnel in the same age group:

1370 AMERICAN MALES—INITIAL TESTING
(18–20 Years of Age)

FITNESS CATEGORY	Percent
I. Very Poor	3.0
II. Poor	6.7
III. Fair	31.2
IV. Good	52.8
V. Excellent	6.3

The figures speak pretty well for themselves. In Austria, walking and cycling are still common means of transportation, and country hikes are a favorite Sunday activity. We may have better transportation and fancier entertainment, but they don't make us any healthier.

Captain Zechner also used the 12-minute fitness test to compare the performance of smokers and nonsmokers in this group of young men. He found that men smoking as few as *five* cigarettes a day showed an impairment in their running performance, added proof that smoking and fitness don't mix.

FIELD TESTING EXPERIENCE

The field tests described in this chapter have been studied by a number of investigators over the past two years and have been found substantially safe and efficient.

In terms of sheer numbers, my own experience in fitness testing probably exceeds that of any other researcher. In the course of developing the USAF Aerobics Physical Fitness Program, I supervised 12-minute and 1.5-mile tests on more than 30,000 men and women, both in the laboratory and in the field. Only a single serious incident occurred during this whole testing effort. A 51-year-old man suffered a heart attack 30 minutes following a 1.5-mile test.

I can't say with absolute assurance that this heart attack would not have occurred if proper safeguards had been observed. However if, prior to the initial test, this man had been given a medical examination as outlined in Chapter Three, some sign of heart disease might have been evident. He would then have been advised not to participate in any fitness test.

If the precautions set forth in this book are followed, fitness testing carries virtually no risk and is a valuable part of a physical training program. By monitoring the progress of athletic teams or other groups engaged in physical conditioning, it provides an excellent guide for coach and player alike.

However, let me repeat that a person exercising on his own and interested only in improving his personal fitness need not take any fitness test at all. If he just keeps on earning the number of aerobic points set forth in the conditioning charts, he'll achieve a good level of fitness with or without testing.

5: Entering the Aerobics Program

Two WEEKS AGO my phone rang. A long distance call from Nebraska.

"Dr. Cooper?"

"Speaking."

"Well, I have a complaint about aerobics," a rather disgruntled voice said at the other end. "I've been on the program six weeks and now my legs are so sore I can hardly move."

"What program did you start?" I asked.

"Running."

"Did you walk for a couple of weeks before you started running?"

"Oh no. I started running the first day and by the end of the first week I ran a mile in nine minutes."

That's when I had my first inkling of what was wrong with the fellow. To confirm my theory, I asked: "How fast were you going after three weeks?"

"I ran a mile in seven minutes," he said proudly. "And by the time my legs gave out after six weeks, I got it down to six minutes and thirty seconds."

No wonder he was in trouble. He ignored the first rule of aerobics: never get ahead of yourself—or of the charts!

PROGRESS SLOWLY

Most of us are always trying to get there in a hurry—wherever we may be going. In exercise this just doesn't work and merely invites trouble. Don't rush your conditioning program. Work up to your goal gradually.

I discourage people from starting directly on a running program unless they have been exercising regularly. All three of the progressive running programs require at least one week of walking before any running. Working up slowly to more strenuous effort is important not only to accustom the heart to the new demands but also to let tendons and muscles adjust themselves to the new activity.

WARM UP PROPERLY

Any athlete knows that the body doesn't spring suddenly into high gear from a state of rest. It needs a period of gradual warm-up before strenuous effort, in order to minimize muscle and joint problems. This is particularly important for people past 40.

I usually recommend the following five-minute routine: During the first minute do stretching exercises for arms, legs and back. During the second minute do sit-ups (with your knees bent) and push-ups. During the third minute, walk in a circle at a fairly rapid pace. During the fourth minute alternate 15 seconds of walking with 15 seconds of jogging—a sort of half-run. During the fifth minute jog continuously; i.e. run at a very slow speed—approximately at the rate of a 12- 13-minute mile.

Stay flat-footed as much as possible during your warm-up run. That will give the tendons in your feet and ankles a chance to stretch gradually, helping to avoid possible irritation from sudden stress.

After this five-minute routine, start your regular aerobic workout. If you are about to participate in some kind of endurance activity, e.g., a three-mile run, the running part of the warm-up may be incorporated into the first few minutes of the activity itself.

EXERCISE WITHIN YOUR TOLERANCE

One basic rule to be aware of in entering an exercise program is this: Avoid straining and pushing yourself to the extent that you become overly fatigued. Such intense effort at the outset of an exercise program is not only dangerous, it also defeats your basic purpose. Instead of feeling more fit and more vigorous, you'll just feel chronically tired.

COOL DOWN SLOWLY

While a warm-up is a generally accepted practice, few people realize that the body also needs a cooling-down period after exercise. They slump into complete relaxation immediately after exercise. This can cause dizzy spells, fainting and even more serious consequences. Strange as it seems you must get ready for rest.

Five minutes of walking or very slow jogging eases the transition between running and resting.

One dramatic experiment performed back in 1941 documented the importance of cooling down after a workout. One hundred men were asked to run to exhaustion on a treadmill. Then they were told to stand motionless. Seventeen of them promptly fainted. What caused this effect?

Immediately after running, most of the blood was pooled in their legs. Without a gradual cool-down period they couldn't get enough blood back to where it was needed—the heart and the brain. The blood stayed in their legs and they blacked out.

A similar incident occurred to an acquaintance of mine. He was on a vacation trip to Washington, D.C., and being an ardent aerobics fan, he spurned the elevators in the Washington monument and climbed all the way to the top. Then he walked all the way down. Nothing happened.

The next day he climbed the more than 900 steps to the top again—just to keep himself in shape. As he reached the top, it just so happened that the elevator door opened for a ride back down. His willpower sagged momentarily, and he accepted the mute invitation of the open elevator door for the down-trip. As soon as the elevator reached the ground floor, he fainted.

Rushed to the hospital by anxious bystanders, he soon recovered but was kept there for observation for several days. The doctors ran all sorts of tests on him, suspecting heart irregularities and other ailments. But none of the tests showed anything abnormal. Finally, perplexed, he contacted me by phone. After hearing the details of his fainting episode, I immediately suspected what had happened. He very likely collapsed because of an insufficient cool-down period. Standing motionless in the crowded elevator, he suffered the same symptoms as the men whose vigorous treadmill exercise was followed by a sudden standstill. Fortunately, the episode produced no lasting damage and he was able to continue his aerobic program without problems.

Another man was less lucky. He was a well-conditioned,

47-year-old man who had been running regularly for three months. Usually he would trot at a slow pace for 3–5 minutes after his run, allowing his body to relax gradually. But one day because of very cold weather, he sat down in his warm car immediately after the run. He was found slumped over the steering wheel.

What happened is a matter of speculation, since the autopsy did not reveal the cause of his death. However, sudden relaxation, plus the warmth of his car may have combined lethally. The blood had shifted to the legs during the run. At the sudden stop of activity, the muscles no longer helped return the blood to the heart. To make matters worse, the capillary vessels were dilated by the sudden warmth in the car. The heart and brain were suddenly without adequate blood supply, causing heart stoppage. This tragic incident again underlines the importance of two basic precautions:

1. Taper off gradually. Trot or walk for a few minutes after any strenuous exercise, preferably at the same air temperature as that at which the exercise was performed.

2. Avoid going into a hot room or a hot shower immediately after exercise. Wait until you cool down and have stopped sweating before you shower. About the worst thing you can do is to go into a steamroom or sauna immediately after a hard, hot workout.

CALISTHENICS

Because I favor aerobic exercise as the basic requirement for fitness, some readers of my earlier book concluded that I advise against calisthenics. This is definitely not so. It's not an either/or proposition. If you do aerobics, that doesn't rule out calisthenics. Both are good, but each serves a different purpose. Calisthenics builds agility, coordination and muscular strength, particularly in the arms and the upper torso. Aerobics builds basic fitness and endurance. A highly conditioned person needs both.

I do a certain amount of calisthenics in addition to aerobics: sit-ups with the knees bent, toe-touches and push-ups. I recommend doing such calisthenics either before or after aerobic workouts, particularly if the aerobic exercise involves mainly the legs and does not directly engage the muscles of the upper body. The warm-up or cool-down periods are convenient periods for doing such calisthenics.

WHEN TO EXERCISE

You can bolster your willpower by always exercising at the same time of day. Some people like getting their aerobics out of the way first thing in the morning.

Others claim that they can't exercise in the morning because "my body is slow to awaken." I can find no medical evidence in support of this. But for whatever reasons, some people feel sluggish in the morning. They are the so-called "evening types" who don't really come alive until later in the day. Many of them prefer exercise in the late afternoon or evening.

Still others use their lunch hour as an exercise period.

Lunch-hour exercise has a special advantage for weight watchers. Vigorous activity tends to suppress appetite immediately afterward. Therefore, lunch hour athletes may find that they can get by without lunch—"just a bowl of soup or a cold drink." The combined effect of exercise and reduced food intake soon gets rid of those extra pounds and inches.

"Exercise cuts down appetite?" people ask in surprise. "I thought it would make you hungry!"

True, moderate exercise may increase the appetite. But intense exercise for even relatively short periods—such as most aerobic workouts—decreases appetite. Such exercise shunts the blood away from your stomach. As a result, you don't have much of a desire for food. Even after you've recovered from the exercise, your appetite rarely increases above normal. The net result is that you tend to eat less without feeling hungry.

A sergeant at Lackland Air Force Base was about 40 pounds overweight. He had never been able to follow a diet. In addition to eating big meals, he was always snacking between meals. I suggested aerobic workouts just before lunch. The results were excellent. In five weeks, he lost 20 pounds by merely skipping lunch and exercising.

Late afternoon exercise also has certain advantages. Because it dispels tension, after-office exercise is especially helpful to men whose jobs put them under nervous strain. It works as a very effective tranquilizer. People with ulcers and other nervous disturbances often find that after-work exercise greatly reduces their symptoms.

Several people have asked about exercising vigorously after dinner. They like to wait until the day cools. I tell them that it doesn't really matter when you exercise, as long as you wait at least two hours after a meal.

I know people who exercise just before bedtime. Afterwards they feel relaxed and pleasantly tired and drop right off to sleep. That's fine if you can do it. For most people it doesn't work out that way. Exercise gets them physically too agitated to be able to sleep immediately afterward. They need a quiet unwinding period of one to two hours between exercise and sleep.

One thing about exercising late in the day: for some reason it seems to encourage quitting. Bill Bowerman, track coach at the University of Oregon, kept a record on dropouts in a large group of joggers over a period of several years. The quitting rate among morning joggers was less than 30 percent. Among the afternoon and evening joggers it was more than 60 percent.

Why is quitting more prevalent among the afternoon and evening men? I have no medical explanation, but I have a hunch that it is easier to find an excuse for not exercising in the afternoon than it is at 6:00 A.M.

When I discussed early-morning exercise at the International Congress on Military Sports at Fontainebleau, France, some French doctors immediately raised a question: "Exercise before breakfast?" Eating comes first, they insisted.

They have a point. A little sustenance might be preferable, providing it is followed by a sufficient waiting period before the start of exercise. But for most people that is impractical. They haven't got that much time in the morning.

My own experience shows that exercise on an empty stomach does no harm. In our Air Force test group we had thousands of people exercising daily before breakfast without any ill effect. But if you feel that you need to have something in the morning to give you a little quick energy before your workout, I suggest the following: Drink a glass of orange juice; wait 10–15 minutes; then go. To sum up the question of when to exercise, I'd like to make this suggestion: Pick any time that suits your schedule and your needs. The important thing is to make it a regular routine. We are creatures of habit. So let the force of habit help you maintain your exercise pattern.

REGULARITY

If you can't exercise regularly, you're better off not exercising at all. That may sound harsh. But regularity in exercise is an important safety precaution. Now-and-then exercise will not help you build and keep your fitness. It will not increase your aerobic capacity. It will not strengthen your heart so that it can stand a really tough workout.

A case in point was a young Air Force major who liked to play handball whenever he had a chance. Unfortunately, he was able to play only once a week or less. In-between he had no exercise whatsoever.

In the middle of a fast game, he experienced severe chest pain, apparently the result of insufficient blood to the heart. He was taken to the hospital where he spent several weeks although a definite diagnosis was never made.

After his discharge from the hospital, I didn't tell him to quit handball, which he obviously enjoyed, but I advised him to build up his aerobic capacity by doing other exercises between his weekly handball games.

He started cycling and swimming every other day. In response to these closely spaced regular workouts, his aerobic capacity increased to the level where he can now safely and comfortably keep his weekly handball date. While regularity of exercise is important, you should interrupt your exercise program whenever you become ill or excessively fatigued. Avoid vigorous exercise for a 24-hour period after an immunization.

CATCHING UP

But suppose you have to go off on a business trip. Or you come down with a cold. What about these unavoidable interruptions of your exercise routine? How do you catch up?

A lot of people try to pick up where they left off. But that usually proves too strenuous. Your aerobic capacity backslides during a period of inactivity—especially if you're in the upper age brackets.

When you resume exercising after an interruption, you'll have to backtrack on the charts. The question is, how far.

Because different individuals lose aerobic capacity at a different rate during periods of inactivity, you'll have to gauge this for yourself. The main point is, don't push yourself too hard to get back to where you were before.

Wanting to make up for lost time, you might be tempted to overstrain yourself. Fortunately, there are three simple ways to tell if you are exercising too hard during any stage of your conditioning program.

Check 1: Symptoms during exercise

Signs of overexertion during exercise are: tightness or pain in the chest, severe breathlessness, lightheadedness, dizziness, loss of muscle control and nausea. When you experience any of these symptoms, stop exercising immediately.

Check 2: Recovery heart rate

Five minutes after exercise, count your pulse. If it's still over 120, it's a sign that the exercise was too tough for a person in your condition. Ten minutes after exercise, check your pulse again. It should be back below 100. If it isn't let up a little on your exercise program.

The best way to take your pulse is to feel it at your throat. Most people can't feel their own wrist pulse strongly enough for an accurate count. Use a watch with a sweep second hand. Count the pulse for ten seconds, then multiply by six. Or count for 15 seconds and multiply by four.

Check 3: Recovery breathing rate

If you find yourself still short of breath ten minutes after you stop exercising, you can pretty well take it for granted that you're trying too hard. (Normal, resting, respiratory rates range from 12–16 breaths per minute.)

Use these safety checks whenever you think that you might be overexerting.

TEMPERATURE RESTRICTIONS

During extremely hot or extremely cold weather, do not exercise to the point of exhaustion, particularly if you are just starting your conditioning program. The ideal exercise weather is 40° F to 85° F with the humidity less than 60 percent and the wind velocity less than 15 mph. Above or below these limits, reduce the duration and intensity of your exercise.

"But what if the thermometer climbs above 85° F? Should I stop exercising completely?" The answer is a qualified "No!" To some extent you can counteract the effects of heat.

Schedule your exercise in the cooler hours of the morning or evening, at least until you are acclimated.

If you sweat profusely (and this is a characteristic of conditioning), you must increase your salt intake. You can do this either by taking one or two salt tablets with your meals or simply increasing the amount of salt you put on your food. Drink lots of water after working out in a hot and humid environment. That's just as important as getting enough salt. Orange juice and liquid salt solutions are also good fluids to use when sweating excessively.

If there's a sudden heat wave, or if you move to a hotter climate, slow down for at least two weeks to give your body a chance to acclimate itself.

But once the thermometer tops 95 degrees, the best possible advice is to stop all strenuous aerobic exercise. Under conditions of high humidity (above 80 percent), stop when the temperature exceeds 90. Hot and humid weather puts an extra strain on the heart.

Wear light, loose clothing. To avoid chafing, use vaseline or other types of lubricants on the skin areas likely to be affected—particularly the insides of the thighs.

About the worst possible thing you can do is to wear rubberized or other impervious clothing while exercising in hot weather. Rubber suits are advertised as aids to weight reduction. The idea is to work up a sweat in these airtight suits which will enable you to take off weight rapidly. Of course, you gain all those liquid pounds right back as soon as you quench your thirst.

I know of one case involving a heavily overweight businessman in his forties who ran himself nearly to exhaustion in a rubber suit on a hot day, hoping to sweat off a chunk of his midriff. At the end of his run, he collapsed. On his arrival at the hospital he had a temperature above 108° F and only by immediate and competent medical attention was it possible to save his life. Such damaging effects may be due to heat alone but are frequently the result of heat and humidity. Lately, attempts have been made to express both these factors by a single measure, such as the T.H.I. (Temperature-Humidity Index) used by the weather bureau or the H.S.I. (Heat-Stress Index). There is a section in the appendix showing how to determine the severity of the heat stress (WBGT) and a chart detailing exercise limitations advisable when the WBGT reaches certain points.

Cold weather is less dangerous, though by no means harmless. Curiously, people seem more concerned about cold weather than about hot.

Joggers, particularly, can't stand the idea of sitting out the winter. "A day without jogging," one of them writes, "is incomplete to me. I just don't feel right without it. Will jogging in the cold air frostbite my lungs?" he asks.

If anything "frostbites," it will be his ears or his nose, not his lungs. By the time the air gets down into the chest, it's adequately warmed, even if you breathe mainly through your mouth when you exercise.

If the temperature drops below zero, the normal air-warming mechanism of your body may no longer be sufficient, especially if you're heading into an icy wind. Under those conditions too much cold air may be rushing down your windpipe to be adequately warmed. It won't frostbite your lungs, but it may cause constriction of the coronary arteries. (The exact action of the cold air on the circulatory system is not yet fully understood. Research in this area is still under way at the National Heart Institute.)

That's probably what happens to people who suffer heart attacks while shoveling snow in icy air. Of course, most of them are in poor condition to begin with. They exhaust themselves by shoveling, and the added strain imposed by the cold air is more than they can tolerate.

Some of our Air Force personnel in Alaska ran throughout the winter without difficulty, showing that cold weather is no deterrent to exercise if one is physically fit, and if sensible safeguards are taken. One of these is cooling down very gradually after you've worked up a sweat. Don't allow yourself to get chilled. Another is putting a scarf over your mouth to help warm up the air. Of course, the fabric has to be loose-knit for fairly free air passage. A dental or surgical mask also works well for this purpose. And always let someone know when and where you will be exercising.

Summing up cold weather precautions, I'm not saying that you should quit outdoor exercise when the weather gets below freezing, but I am saying that you should observe the above-mentioned precautions. By all means, stop at the first sign of chest pain. That's a basic rule under any condition; even more important when exercising in cold weather.

ALTITUDE

Another environmental factor you should take into consideration when entering an aerobics program is altitude. The 1968 Olympics in Mexico City (elevation 7300 feet above sea level) focused attention on the fact that sports and other forms of physical activity are affected by high altitude. I have received many letters from people all over the world asking if some special compensation should be made in the aerobics program when exercising at altitude.

Since the pressure of oxygen is lower at high altitude, it is obvious that performances will be impaired and some compensation must be made. The first compensation is in physical fitness testing. If a person takes a 12-minute or 1.5-mile fitness categorization test the following altitude adjustments for distance or time should be made:

12-MINUTE FITNESS CATEGORIZATION TEST

Altitude in Feet at Which Acclimatized	Distances to be subtracted from the 12-Minute Age Adjusted requirements †
* 5,000	.05 miles
6,000	.06 miles
7,000	.08 miles
8,000	.10 miles
9,000	.125 miles
10,000	.150 miles
11,000	.175 miles
12,000	.20 miles

* Up to 5,000 feet, use the 12-Minute Test charts without altitude correction.

† 12-Minute Test for Men (page 30) and 12-Minute Test for Women (page 30).

1.5 Mile Fitness Categorization Test

Altitude in Feet at Which Acclimatized	Times to be added to the age requirements for running 1.5 miles †
* 5,000	30 seconds
6,000	40 seconds
7,000	50 seconds
8,000	1 minute
9,000	1 min 15 sec
10,000	1 min 30 sec
11,000	1 min 45 sec
12,000	2 minutes

* Up to 5,000 feet, use the 1.5-Mile Test chart without altitude correction (page 31).

† 1.5-Mile Test for Men (page 31).

The second compensation is an adjustment in the point charts when exercising at altitude. It would be impractical to adjust all the charts so that the effect of altitude is considered but, as an example, I have revised the points for running one mile at 5000, 8000 and 12,000 feet.

Point Value for Walking and Running
One Mile at Various Altitudes

1.0 Mile	Standard	5,000 Feet	Points
	19:59–14:30 Min	20:29–15:00	1
	14:29–12:00 Min	14:59–12.30	2
	11:59–10:00 Min	12:29–10:30	3
	9:59– 8:00 Min	10:29– 8:30	4
	7:59– 6:30 Min	8:29– 7:00 Min	5
	Under 6:30 Min	Under 7:00 Min	6

	8,000 Feet	12,000 Feet	Points
	20:59–15:30 Min	21:29–16:30	1
	15:29–13:00 Min	16:29–14:00	2
	12:59–11:00 Min	13:59–12:00	3
	10:59– 9:00 Min	11:59–10:00	4
	8:59– 7:30 Min	9:59– 8:30	5
	Under 7:30 Min	Under 8:30	6

With these compensations, the aerobics program can be used very effectively as a means of both physical fitness testing and training at altitude.

In this chapter, I have tried to give you some general advice on how to enter the aerobics program safely and effectively. But don't forget to use "common sense" in your program.

In the next chapter, we'll discuss in detail the proper way to start in the aerobics program.

6: The Age-Adjusted Exercise Charts

BEFORE STARTING INTO the aerobics program, you should classify yourself into one of two categories: either you are already in good physical condition and want to remain that way, or you are in poor condition and want to do something about it. In the first case, you are classified as a "Conditioned Beginner" and, in the second case, as an "Unconditioned Beginner." The rules for entering and proceeding through the aerobics program are different for conditioned and unconditioned people, so be certain to read the following instructions very carefully.

CONDITIONED BEGINNERS

If you have been exercising regularly, that is at least three times a week for a minimum of six weeks, and have been given the necessary medical clearance for your age (Chapter Three), you may take the 12-minute test to determine your current level of fitness.

12-MINUTE TEST
(Distances in miles covered in 12 minutes)

FITNESS CATEGORY	AGE (YEARS)			
	Under 30	30–39	40–49	50+
I. Very Poor	<1.0	<.95	<.85	<.80
	<.95	<.85	<.75	<.65
II. Poor	1.0–1.24	.95–1.14	.85–1.04	.80– .99
	.95–1.14	.85–1.04	.75– .94	.65– .84
III. Fair	1.25–1.49	1.15–1.39	1.05–1.29	1.0–1.24
	1.15–1.34	1.05–1.24	.95–1.14	.85–1.04
IV. Good	1.50–1.74	1.40–1.64	1.30–1.54	1.25–1.49
	1.35–1.64	1.25–1.54	1.15–1.44	1.05–1.34
V. Excellent	1.75+	1.65+	1.55+	1.50+
	1.65+	1.55+	1.45+	1.35+

(The second requirement in each case is for women.)
< Means less than.

If you pass this test, reaching either category IV or V, proceed directly to page 107 and follow one of the suggested 30-point per week programs, or make up a 30-point per week program of your own from the reference charts beginning on page 111. If you failed the test, reaching only categories I, II or III, go to the instructions for "unconditioned beginners" following below.

UNCONDITIONED BEGINNERS

If you have not been exercising regularly, DO NOT take any fitness test at the start of your exercise program. Instead, begin one of the progressive, age-adjusted starter programs outlined in this chapter.

Particularly if you are over 30 and for some reason have not been able to get the kind of medical examination suggested in Chapter Three, it is absolutely essential for your safety that you begin with one of the age-adjusted *starter* programs, observing its rules strictly.

After following the starter program for *six weeks,* you have two choices:

1 You may continue the Category I program for a full 16 weeks without ever taking any fitness test at all.

2. You may want to speed up your conditioning and reach your goal in less than 16 weeks. In that case, take the 12-minute fitness test after six weeks of initial training to place yourself into one of the five fitness categories. Then proceed according to the charts for your fitness category and your age.

The charts are self-explanatory. All you need to work with them successfully is a stopwatch or a shock-resistant wristwatch with a sweep second hand. However, a few additional hints about reading the charts and setting up your exercise routine may prove helpful.

TIME GOALS

You should reach the time goals listed for each week of the conditioning program at the *end* of that particular week. Don't try to make a time goal at the beginning of the week. If you do, you may run into a snag.

People have become discouraged right at the start because they misunderstand this. For example, a man of 52, apparently in very poor condition, wrote to me: "I'm trying to follow the stationary running program. But I can't even make it for the first day. I get winded long before those 2½ minutes." Apparently he believed that it was necessary to reach the first week's goal on the first day and as a result he exceeded his endurance capacity.

He should have started his stationary running program by working out as little as 30 seconds on the first day. The next day he could have tried 60 seconds, then to 1½ minutes and so on. By the end of the first week, 2½ minutes would have been a more realistic time goal. Gradual increments are the key to the whole conditioning program. I cannot emphasize this strongly enough.

STICKING WITH IT

Let's face the facts honestly: the first six weeks are the hardest.

It takes quite a bit of push to go through the initial phase of the conditioning program. Much depends on your frame of mind. Make a firm resolution to stick with the program for eight weeks—and no weaseling out of it. Once you're past that period, I can promise you that you'll begin to enjoy your workout. After eight to ten weeks, you sense the change. You'll find yourself looking forward to your exercise, longing for it as an accustomed pleasure.

GROUP EXERCISE

If your morale needs boosting along the way, by far the sturdiest prop for sagging spirits is group exercise. It stirs your sense of competition, providing a spur as well as the reassurance of shared experience. So if you can, join an aerobics group—at least until you're over that first hurdle.

In my own neighborhood on the outskirts of San Antonio, Texas, a community aerobics group sprang up almost spontaneously. About a dozen residents started getting together every evening at a local high school track. The wives and children would come along and it soon became a family affair. Now, we have some friendly competition from time-to-time including husband-and-wife relay races. Actually any couple can join—married or not. The rules are simple. The woman starts off, running, walking, or jogging a mile as fast as she can. Then she passes the baton to her partner, who continues for another two miles. Their combined run is timed and prizes are awarded in four age-adjusted categories, based on the average age of the couple. (Women who take a few years off their age just have to run a little harder.)

To encourage beginners who are not yet in good enough shape to compete in such events, we are now planning some games and contests not based on competition with others. For example, we ask each contestant to predict the time it will take him to walk, jog, or run a certain distance. The one coming closest to his own prediction is the winner—no matter how long it takes him.

Group activities have helped many beginners get through those hard weeks at the outset by stimulating their interest and giving them moral support.

CHANGING PROGRAMS

Once you have started a conditioning program, don't switch to a different exercise until you have completed it. Your muscles become adjusted to one type of exercise and you may not be able to keep up your rate of conditioning when you go to another form of exercise. But once you have reached the 30-point-per-week level, you are free to pick any combination of activities that will add variety and pleasure to your exercise program.

PERSONAL VARIATIONS

While the eager beavers tell me the charts are too slow, others tell me they're too fast. They find it difficult to keep up with the time goals spelled out for each week.

Such cases are exceptions, but you may be one of them. It's nothing to worry about. If you find yourself trailing behind the specified rate of progress, drop back to an easier chart or just repeat the exercise program for the last week you were able to complete without trouble.

By this repetition you will build the added aerobic capacity you need to take the next step forward on the conditioning charts. If one repetition won't do it, repeat again. Eventually you'll reach the full 30-point-per-week level.

Think of it this way: it took you five, ten or maybe twenty years to get out of shape. So don't be surprised if it takes you a few extra weeks to get back into shape. I know a middle-aged businessman here in San Antonio who took 31 weeks to complete the 16-week conditioning program. More power to him! I am proud of him for sticking with it despite obvious difficulties. Now he's reaching 30 points a week and enjoying to the ultimate his newly acquired fitness.

There's no minimum rate of progress. The only really important thing is to keep earning points every week. As long as you accumulate those points, you are building aerobic capacity. You are progressing toward the goal of good cardiovascular-pulmonary fitness.

THE AEROBICS CHART PACK

1. Follow the instructions at the beginning of Chapter Six before starting into one of the following age-adjusted progressive exercise programs.

2. Then, select one of the exercise programs compatible with your age.

IF YOU ARE:	YOUR PROGRAMS ARE FOUND ON PAGES:
under 30 years of age	53–64
30–39 years of age	65–78
40–49 years of age	79–92
Ages 50 and older	93–106

3. When you have completed one of the age-adjusted progressive exercise programs, continue averaging at least 30 points per week, following the program of your choice.

THE 12-MINUTE TEST OF FITNESS

Do not take this test until you have complied with the instructions at the beginning of Chapter Six.

12-MINUTE TEST
(DISTANCES IN MILES)

FITNESS CATEGORY		UNDER 30	30-39	40-49	50+
I	Very Poor	$<$1.0	$<$.95	$<$.85	$<$.80
II	Poor	1.0 -1.24	.95-1.14	.85-1.04	.80- .99
III	Fair	1.25-1.49	1.15-1.39	1.05-1.29	1.0 -1.24
IV	Good	1.50-1.74	1.40-1.64	1.30-1.54	1.25-1.49
V	Excellent	1.75+	1.65+	1.55+	1.50+

$<$ means less than

WALKING EXERCISE PROGRAM
(under 30 years of age)

STARTER

WEEK	DISTANCE (miles)	TIME (min)	FREQ/WK	POINTS/WK
1	1.0	15:00	5	5
2	1.0	14:00	5	10
3	1.0	13:45	5	10
4	1.5	21:30	5	15
5	1.5	21:00	5	15
6	1.5	20:30	5	15

After completing the above starter program, continue with the Category 1 conditioning program below or, if you wish to speed up your program, take the 12-minute test of fitness. If you take the test, find your category from the table at the beginning of the chart pack (page 52). If your category is I, II, or III, continue with the appropriate category below. If your category is IV or V, follow the instructions in the note at the bottom of page 54.

CONDITIONING

FITNESS CATEGORY I   (Less than 1.0 mile on 12-minute test)

WEEK	DISTANCE (miles)	TIME (min)	FREQ/WK	POINTS/WK
7	2.0	28:00	5	20
8	2.0	27:45	5	20
9	2.0	27:30	5	20
10	2.0	27:30	3	22
	and			
	2.5	33:45	2	
11	2.0	27:30	3	22
	and			
	2.5	33:30	2	
12	2.5	33:15	4	26
	and			
	3.0	41:30	1	
13	2.5	33:15	3	27
	and			
	3.0	41:15	2	
14	2.5	33:00	3	27
	and			
	3.0	40:00	2	
15	3.0	41:00	5	30
16	4.0	55:00	3	33

WALKING EXERCISE PROGRAM
(under 30 years of age)

CONDITIONING

FITNESS CATEGORY II   (1.0–1.24 miles on 12-minute test)

WEEK	DISTANCE (miles)	TIME (min)	FREQ/WK	POINTS/WK
7	2.0	27:30	5	20
8	2.0	27:30	3	22
	and			
	2.5	33:45	2	
9	2.0	27:30	3	22
	and			
	2.5	33:30	2	
10	2.5	33:15	3	27
	and			
	3.0	41:15	2	
11	2.5	33:00	3	27
	and			
	3.0	40:00	2	
12	3.0	41:00	5	30
13	4.0	55:00	3	33

FITNESS CATEGORY III   (1.25–1.49 miles on 12-minute test)

WEEK	DISTANCE (miles)	TIME (min)	FREQ/WK	POINTS/WK
7	2.5	33:15	4	26
	and			
	3.0	41:30	1	
8	2.5	33:00	3	27
	and			
	3.0	40:00	2	
9	3.0	41:00	5	30
10	4.0	55:00	3	33

After completing the progressive walking program, go to pages 107-8 and select one of the 30-point-per-week programs or develop one of your own from the point value charts beginning on page 111.

RUNNING EXERCISE PROGRAM
(under 30 years of age)

STARTER *

WEEK	DISTANCE (miles)	TIME (min)	FREQ/WK	POINTS/WK
1	1.0	13:30	5	10
2	1.0	13:00	5	10
3	1.0	12:45	5	10
4	1.0	11:45	5	15
5	1.0	11:00	5	15
6	1.0	10:30	5	15

After completing the above starter program, continue with the Category I conditioning program below or, if you wish to speed up your program, take the 12-minute test of fitness. If you take the test, find your category from the table at the beginning of the chart pack (page 52). If your category is I, II, or III, continue with the appropriate category below. If your category is IV or V, follow the instructions in the note at the bottom of page 56.

* Start the program by walking, then walk and run, or run, as necessary to meet the changing time goals.

CONDITIONING

FITNESS CATEGORY I   (Less than 1.0 mile on 12-minute test)

WEEK	DISTANCE (miles)	TIME (min)	FREQ/WK	POINTS/WK
7	1.5	18:30	5	15
8	1.5	17:30	5	15
9	1.5	16:30	4	18
10	1.0	9:30	3	21
	and			
	1.5	15:30	2	
11	1.0	8:45	3	24
	and			
	1.5	14:45	2	
12	1.0	8:30	3	24
	and			
	1.5	14:00	2	
13	1.0	8:15	3	24
	and			
	1.5	13:30	2	
14	1.0	7:55	3	27
	and			
	1.5	13:00	2	
15	1.0	7:45	2	31
	and			
	1.5	12:30	2	
	and			
	2.0	18:00	1	
16	1.5	11:55	2	32
	and			
	2.0	17:00	2	

RUNNING EXERCISE PROGRAM
(under 30 years of age)

CONDITIONING

FITNESS CATEGORY II   (1.0–1.24 miles on 12-minute test)

WEEK	DISTANCE (miles)	TIME (min)	FREQ/WK	POINTS/WK
7	1.5	17:30	5	15
8	1.5	16:30	4	18
9	1.0	9:30	3	21
	and			
	1.5	15:30	2	
10	1.0	8:45	3	24
	and			
	1.5	14:15	2	
11	1.0	8:15	2	26
	and			
	1.5	13:00	3	
12	1.0	7:45	2	31
	and			
	1.5	12:30	2	
	and			
	2.0	18:00	1	
13	1.5	11:55	2	32
	and			
	2.0	17:00	2	

FITNESS CATEGORY III   (1.25–1.49 miles on 12-minute test)

WEEK	DISTANCE (miles)	TIME (min)	FREQ/WK	POINTS/WK
7	1.5	16:30	5	22
8	1.0	9:00	3	24
	and			
	1.5	14:45	2	
9	1.0	7:55	1	32
	and			
	2.0	18:00	3	
10	1.5	11:55	2	32
	and			
	2.0	17:00	2	

After completing the Category I, II, or III progressive running program, go to pages 107-8 and select one of the 40-point-per-week programs or develop one of your own from the point value charts beginning on page 111.

CYCLING EXERCISE PROGRAM
(under 30 years of age)

STARTER

WEEK	DISTANCE (miles)	TIME (min)	FREQ/WK	POINTS/WK
1	2.0	10:00	5	5
2	2.0	9:00	5	5
3	2.0	7:45	5	10
4	3.0	11:50	5	15
5	3.0	11:00	5	15
6	3.0	10:30	5	15

After completing the above starter program, continue with the Category I conditioning program below or, if you wish to speed up your program, take the 12-minute test of fitness. If you take the test, find your category from the table at the beginning of the chart pack (page 52). If your category is I, II, or III, continue with the appropriate category below. If your category is IV or V, follow the instructions in the note at the bottom of page 58.

CONDITIONING

FITNESS CATEGORY I (Less than 1.0 mile on 12-minute test)

WEEK	DISTANCE (miles)	TIME (min)	FREQ/WK	POINTS/WK
7	4.0	15:45	5	20
8	4.0	15:30	5	20
9	4.0	14:30	5	20
10	4.0 and	14:00	4	21
	5.0	18:30	1	
11	4.0 and	14:00	3	22
	5.0	18:00	2	
12	4.0 and	13:45	3	24
	6.0	23:30	2	
13	4.0 and	13:30	3	24
	6.0	23:00	2	
14	5.0 and	17:00	3	27
	6.0	22:00	2	
15	6.0	21:00	5	30
16	8.0	28:30	3	31½

CYCLING EXERCISE PROGRAM
(under 30 years of age)

CONDITIONING

FITNESS CATEGORY II   (1.0–1.24 miles on 12-minute test)

WEEK	DISTANCE (miles)	TIME (min)	FREQ/WK	POINTS/WK
7	4.0	14:30	5	20
8	4.0	14:00	4	21
	and			
	5.0	18:30	1	
9	4.0	14:00	3	22
	and			
	5.0	18:00	2	
10	4.0	13:30	3	24
	and			
	6.0	23:00	2	
11	5.0	17:00	3	27
	and			
	6.0	22:00	2	
12	6.0	21:00	5	30
13	8.0	28:30	3	31½

FITNESS CATEGORY III   (1.25–1.49 miles on 12-minute test)

WEEK	DISTANCE (miles)	TIME (min)	FREQ/WK	POINTS/WK
7	4.0	13:45	3	24
	and			
	6.0	23:30	2	
8	5.0	17:00	3	27
	and			
	6.0	22:00	2	
9	6.0	21:00	5	30
10	8.0	28:30	3	31½

After completing the progressive cycling program, go to pages 107-8 and select one of the 30-point-per-week programs or develop one of your own from the point value charts beginning on page 111.

SWIMMING EXERCISE PROGRAM
(under 30 years of age)

Overhand Crawl *

STARTER

WEEK	DISTANCE (yards)	TIME (min)	FREQ/WK	POINTS/WK
1	100	2:30	5	6
2	150	3:00	5	7½
3	200	4:00	5	7½
4	250	5:00	5	10
5	250	5:30	5	10
6	300	6:00	5	12½

After completing the above starter program, continue with the Category I conditioning program below or, if you wish to speed up your program, take the 12-minute test of fitness. If you take the test, find your category from the table at the beginning of the chart pack (page 52). If your category is I, II, or III, continue with the appropriate category below. If your category is IV or V, follow the instructions in the note at the bottom of page 60.

* Breaststroke is less demanding an so is backstroke. Butterfly is considerably more demanding.

CONDITIONING

FITNESS CATEGORY I   (Less than 1.0 mile on 12-minute test)

WEEK	DISTANCE (yards)	TIME (min)	FREQ/WK	POINTS/WK
7	300	6:00	5	12½
8	400	8:30	5	17½
9	400	8:30	5	17½
10	400	8:00	2	19
	and			
	500	10:30	3	
11	400	8:00	2	22
	and			
	600	12:30	3	
12	500	10:30	3	24
	and			
	700	14:30	2	
13	600	12:00	4	27½
	and			
	800	16:30	1	
14	600	11:30	3	29½
	and			
	800	16:00	2	
15	800	15:30	4	30
16	1000	19:30	3	31½

SWIMMING EXERCISE PROGRAM
(under 30 years of age)

Overhand Crawl *

CONDITIONING

FITNESS CATEGORY II   (1.0–1.24 miles on 12-minute test)

WEEK	DISTANCE (yards)	TIME (min)	FREQ/WK	POINTS/WK
7	400	8:30	5	17½
8	400	8:00	2	19
	and			
	500	10:30	3	
9	400	8:00	2	22
	and			
	600	12:30	3	
10	600	12:30	4	27¼
	and			
	800	16:30	1	
11	600	12:30	3	29½
	and			
	800	16:00	2	
12	800	15:30	4	30
13	1000	19:30	3	31½

FITNESS CATEGORY III   (1.25–1.49 miles on 12-minute test)

WEEK	DISTANCE (yards)	TIME (min)	FREQ/WK	POINTS/WK
7	500	10:30	3	24
	and			
	700	14:30	2	
8	600	12:30	3	29½
	and			
	800	16:00	2	
9	800	15:30	4	30
10	1000	19:30	3	31½

* Breaststroke is less demanding and so is backstroke. Butterfly is considerably more demanding.

After completing the progressive swimming program, go to pages 107–8 and select one of the 30-point-per-week programs or develop one of your own from the point value charts beginning on page 111.

STATIONARY RUNNING EXERCISE PROGRAM
(under 30 years of age)

STARTER

WEEK	DURATION (min)	STEPS/MIN °	FREQ/WK	POINTS/WK
1	2:30	70–80	5	4
2	5:00	70–80	5	7½
3	5:00	70–80	5	7½
4	7:30	70–80	5	11¼
5	7:30	70–80	5	11¼
6	10:00	70–80	5	15

After completing the above starter program, continue with the Category I conditioning program below or, if you wish to speed up your program, take the 12-minute test of fitness. If you take the test, find your category from the table at the beginning of the chart pack (page 52). If your category is I, II, or III, continue with the appropriate category below. If your category is IV or V, follow the instructions in the note at the bottom of page 62.

° Count only when the left foot hits the floor. Feet must be brought at least eight inches from the floor.

CONDITIONING

FITNESS CATEGORY I   (Less than 1.0 mile on 12-minute test)

WEEK	DURATION (min)	STEPS/MIN °	FREQ/WK	POINTS/WK
7	10:00	70–80	5	15
8	12:30	70–80	5	18¾
9	12:30	70–80	5	18¾
10	15:00	70–80	5	22½
11	15:00	70–80	5	22½
12	10:00 and	80–90	1	24¼
	17:30	70–80	3	
13	12:30 and	80–90	3	27
	15:00	80–90	2	
14	12:30 and	80–90	2	28
	15:00	80–90	3	
15	15:00	80–90	5	30
16	15:00	90–100	4	30

° Count only when the left foot hits the floor. Feet must be brought at least eight inches from the floor.

STATIONARY RUNNING EXERCISE PROGRAM
(under 30 years of age)

CONDITIONING

FITNESS CATEGORY II   (1.0–1.24 miles on 12-minute test)

WEEK	DURATION (min)	STEPS/MIN *	FREQ/WK	POINTS/WK
7	12:30	70–80	5	18¾
8	15:00	70–80	5	22½
9	15:00	70–80	5	22½
10	12:30	80–90	3	27
	and			
	15:00	80–90	2	
11	12:30	80–90	2	28
	and			
	15:00	80–90	3	
12	15:00	80–90	5	30
13	15:00	90–100	4	30

* Count only when the left foot hits the floor. Feet must be brought at least eight inches from the floor.

FITNESS CATEGORY III   (1.25–1.49 miles on 12-minute test)

WEEK	DURATION (min)	STEPS/MIN *	FREQ/WK	POINTS/WK
7	10:00	80–90	1	24¼
	and			
	17:30	70–80	3	
8	12:30	80–90	2	28
	and			
	15:00	80–90	3	
9	15:00	80–90	5	30
10	15:00	90–100	4	30

* Count only when the left foot hits the floor. Feet must be brought at least eight inches from the floor.

After completing the progressive program, go to pages 107-8 and select one of the 30-point-per-week programs or develop one of your own from the point value charts beginning on page 111.

HANDBALL/BASKETBALL/SQUASH EXERCISE PROGRAM
(under 30 years of age)

STARTER

WEEK	TIME (min)°	FREQ/WK	POINTS/WK
1	10	5	7½
2	15	5	11¼
3	15	5	11¼
4	20	5	15
5	20	5	15
6	20	5	15

After completing the above starter program, continue with the Category I conditioning program below or, if you wish to speed up your program, take the 12-minute test of fitness. If you take the test, find your category from the table at the beginning of the chart pack (page 52). If your category is I, II, or III, continue with the appropriate category below. If your category is IV or V, follow the instructions in the note at the bottom of page 64.

° Continuous exercise. Do not count breaks, time-outs, etc.

CONDITIONING

FITNESS CATEGORY I   (Less than 1.0 mile on 12-minute test)

WEEK	TIME (min)°	FREQ/WK	POINTS/WK
7	30	5	22½
8	30	5	22½
9	30	5	22½
10	35	5	26¼
11	35	5	26¼
12	35 and	3	27¼
	40	2	
13	35 and	3	27¼
	40	2	
14	30 and	2	29¼
	45	3	
15	40	5	30
16	50	4	30

° Continuous exercise. Do not count breaks, time-outs, etc.

HANDBALL/BASKETBALL/SQUASH EXERCISE PROGRAM
(under 30 years of age)

CONDITIONING

FITNESS CATEGORY II   (1.0–1.24 miles on the 12-minute test)

WEEK	TIME (min)*	FREQ/WK	POINTS/WK
7	30	5	22½
8	35	5	26¼
9	35	5	26¼
10	35 and 40	3 2	27¼
11	30 and 45	2 3	29¼
12	40	5	30
13	50	4	30

* Continuous exercise. Do not count breaks, time-outs, etc.

FITNESS CATEGORY III   (1.25–1.49 miles on the 12-minute test)

WEEK	TIME (min)*	FREQ/WK	POINTS/WK
7	35 and 40	3 2	27¼
8	30 and 45	2 3	29¼
9	40	5	30
10	50	4	30

* Continuous exercise. Do not count breaks, time-outs, etc.

After completing the progressive program, go to pages 107-8 and select one of the 30-point-per-week programs or develop one of your own from the point value charts beginning on page 111.

WALKING EXERCISE PROGRAM
(30–39 years of age)

STARTER

WEEK	DISTANCE (miles)	TIME (min)	FREQ/WK	POINTS/WK
1	1.0	17:30	5	5
2	1.0	15:30	5	5
3	1.0	14:15	5	10
4	1.0	14:00	5	10
5	1.5	21:40	5	15
6	1.5	21:15	5	15

After completing the above starter program, continue with the Category I conditioning program below, or if you wish to speed up your program, take the 12-minute test of fitness. If you take the test, find your category from the table at the beginning of the chart pack (page 52). If your category is I, II, or III, continue with the appropriate category below. If your category is IV or V, follow the instructions in the note at the bottom of page 66.

CONDITIONING

FITNESS CATEGORY I (Less than 0.95 mile on 12-minute test)

WEEK	DISTANCE (miles)	TIME (min)	FREQ/WK	POINTS/WK
7	1.5	21:00	5	15
8	2.0	28:45	5	20
9	2.0	28:30	5	20
10	2.0	28:00	5	20
11	2.0	28:00	3	22
	and			
	2.5	35:30	2	
12	2.5	35:00	3	27
	and			
	3.0	43:15	2	
13	2.5	34:45	3	27
	and			
	3.0	43:00	2	
14	2.5	34:30	3	27
	and			
	3.0	42:30	2	
15	3.0	42:30	5	30
16	4.0	56:30	3	33

WALKING EXERCISE PROGRAM
(30–39 years of age)

CONDITIONING

FITNESS CATEGORY II   (0.95–1.14 miles on 12-minute test)

WEEK	DISTANCE (miles)	TIME (min)	FREQ/WK	POINTS/WK
7	2.0	28:30	5	20
8	2.0	28:00	5	20
9	2.0	28:00	3	22
	and			
	2.5	35:30	2	
10	2.5	34:45	3	27
	and			
	3.0	43:00	2	
11	2.5	34:30	3	27
	and			
	3.0	42:30	2	
12	3.0	42:30	5	30
13	4.0	56:30	3	33

FITNESS CATEGORY III   (1.15–1.39 miles on 12-minute test)

WEEK	DISTANCE (miles)	TIME (min)	FREQ/WK	POINTS/WK
7	2.5	35:00	3	27
	and			
	3.0	43:15	2	
8	2.5	34:30	3	27
	and			
	3.0	42:30	2	
9	3.0	42:30	5	30
10	4.0	56:30	3	33

After completing the Category I, II, or III progressive running program, go to pages 107–8 and select one of the 30-point-per-week programs or develop one of your own from the point value charts beginning on page 111.

RUNNING EXERCISE PROGRAM
(30–39 years of age)

STARTER *

WEEK	DISTANCE (miles)	TIME (min)	FREQ/WK	POINTS/WK
1	1.0	17:30	5	5
2	1.0	15:30	5	5
3	1.0	14:15	5	10
4	1.0	13:30	5	10
5	1.0	11:45	5	15
6	1.0	11:15	5	15

After completing the above starter program, continue with the Category I conditioning program below or, if you wish to speed up your program, take the 12-minute test of fitness. If you take the test, find your category from the table at the beginning of the chart pack (page 52). If your category is I, II, or III, continue with the appropriate category below. If your category is IV or V, follow the instructions in the note at the bottom of page 70.

* Start the program by walking. Then walk and run, or run, as necessary to meet the changing time goals.

RUNNING EXERCISE PROGRAM
(30–39 years of age)

CONDITIONING -

FITNESS CATEGORY I (Less than 0.95 mile on 12-minute test)

WEEK	DISTANCE (miles)	TIME (min)	FREQ/WK	POINTS/WK
7	1.5	19:30	5	15
8	1.5	18:30	5	15
9	1.5	17:30	4	18
10	1.0	10:00	2	19½
	and			
	1.5	16:30	3	
11	1.0	9:30	3	21
	and			
	1.5	15:30	2	
12	1.0	9:00	3	24
	and			
	1.5	14:30	2	
13	1.0	8:30	3	24
	and			
	1.5	14:00	2	
14	1.0	8:15	3	30
	and			
	2.0	19:30	2	
15	1.0	8:00	2	31½
	and			
	1.5	12:55	2	
	and			
	2.5	22:30	1	
16	1.0	8:00	1	34
	and			
	1.5	12:25	2	
	and			
	2.0	18:30	2	

RUNNING EXERCISE PROGRAM
(30–39 years of age)

CONDITIONING

Fitness Category II   (0.95–1.14 miles on 12-minute test)

WEEK	DISTANCE (miles)	TIME (min)	FREQ/WK	POINTS/WK
7	1.5	18:30	5	15
8	1.5	17:00	4	18
9	1.0 and	10:00	3	21
	1.5	15:45	2	
10	1.0 and	9:15	3	24
	1.5	14:30	2	
11	1.0 and	8:45	2	26
	1.5	13:00	3	
12	1.0 and	8:15	3	30
	2.0	19:30	2	
13	1.0 and	8:00	1	34
	1.5 and	12:25	2	
	2.0	18:30	2	

RUNNING EXERCISE PROGRAM
(30–39 years of age)

CONDITIONING

FITNESS CATEGORY III   (1.15–1.39 miles on 12-minute test)

WEEK	DISTANCE (miles)	TIME (min)	FREQ/WK	POINTS/WK
7	1.5	17:30	4	18
8	1.0 and	10:00	1	21
	1.5	15:15	4	
9	1.5 and	13:15	3	27
	2.0	19:30	1	
10	1.0 and	8:00	1	34
	1.5 and	12:25	2	
	2.0	18:30	2	

After completing the Category I, II, or III progressive running program, go to pages 107–8 and select one of the 30-point-per-week programs or develop one of your own from the point value charts beginning on page 111.

CYCLING EXERCISE PROGRAM
(30–39 years of age)

STARTER

WEEK	DISTANCE (miles)	TIME (min)	FREQ/WK	POINTS/WK
1	2	10:30	5	5
2	2	9:30	5	5
3	2	8:30	5	5
4	2	7:45	5	10
5	2	7:30	5	10
6	3	11:50	5	15

After completing the above starter program, continue with the Category I conditioning program below or, if you wish to speed up your program, take the 12-minute test of fitness. If you take the test, find your category from the table at the beginning of the chart pack (page 52). If your category is I, II, or III, continue with the appropriate category below. If your category is IV or V, follow the instructions in the note at the bottom of page 72.

CONDITIONING

FITNESS CATEGORY I   (Less than 0.95 mile on 12-minute test)

WEEK	DISTANCE (miles)	TIME (min)	FREQ/WK	POINTS/WK
7	3.0	11:30	5	15
8	4.0	15:45	5	20
9	4.0 and	15:30	4	21
	5.0	19:45	1	
10	4.0 and	15:00	3	22
	5.0	19:00	2	
11	3.0 and	11:00	2	24
	6.0	23:45	3	
12	3.0 and	10:30	2	24
	6.0	23:30	3	
13	3.0 and	10:30	2	24
	6.0	23:00	3	
14	5.0 and	18:30	3	27
	6.0	22:30	2	
15	6.0	22:00	5	30
16	8.0	29:30	3	31½

CYCLING EXERCISE PROGRAM
(30–39 years of age)

CONDITIONING

FITNESS CATEGORY II   (0.95–1.14 miles on 12-minute test)

WEEK	DISTANCE (miles)	TIME (min)	FREQ/WK	POINTS/WK
7	4.0	15:30	4	21
	and			
	5.0	19:45	1	
8	4.0	15:00	3	22
	and			
	5.0	19:00	2	
9	3.0	11:00	2	24
	and			
	6.0	23:45	3	
10	3.0	10:30	2	24
	and			
	6.0	23:00	3	
11	5.0	18:30	3	27
	and			
	6.0	22:30	2	
12	6.0	22:00	5	30
13	8.0	29:30	3	31½

FITNESS CATEGORY III   (1.15–1.39 miles on 12-minute test)

WEEK	DISTANCE (miles)	TIME (min)	FREQ/WK	POINTS/WK
7	3.0	10:30	2	24
	and			
	6.0	23:30	3	
8	5.0	18:30	3	27
	and			
	6.0	22:30	2	
9	6.0	22:00	5	30
10	8.0	29:30	3	31½

After completing the Category I, II, or III progressive cycling program, go to pages 107–8 and select one of the 30-point-per-week programs or develop one of your own from the point value charts beginning on page 111.

SWIMMING EXERCISE PROGRAM
(30–39 years of age)

Overhand Crawl *

STARTER

WEEK	DISTANCE (yards)	TIME (min)	FREQ/WK	POINTS/WK
1	100	2:30	5	4
2	150	3:00	5	5
3	175	3:45	5	6
4	200	4:00	5	7½
5	250	5:15	5	10
6	250	5:00	5	10

After completing the above starter program, continue with the Category I conditioning program below or, if you wish to speed up your program, take the 12-minute test of fitness. If you take the test, find your category from the table at the beginning of the chart pack (page 52). If your Category is I, II, or III, continue with the appropriate category below. If your category is IV or V, follow the instructions in the note at the bottom of page 74.

* Breaststroke is less demanding and so is backstroke. Butterfly is considerably more demanding.

CONDITIONING

FITNESS CATEGORY I   (Less than 0.95 mile on 12-minute test)

WEEK	DISTANCE (yards)	TIME (min)	FREQ/WK	POINTS/WK
7	300	6.15	5	12½
8	300	6:00	5	12½
9	400	8:30	5	17½
10	400	8:00	5	17½
11	400 and	8:00	2	19
	500	10:30	3	
12	400 and	8:30	2	22
	600	12:30	3	
13	500 and	10:30	3	24
	700	15:00	2	
14	600 and	12:00	4	27¼
	800	16:30	1	
15	800	16:00	4	30
16	1000	20:30	3	31½

SWIMMING EXERCISE PROGRAM
(30–39 years of age)

Overhand Crawl *

FITNESS CATEGORY II   (0.95–1.14 miles on 12-minute test)

WEEK	DISTANCE (yards)	TIME (min)	FREQ/WK	POINTS/WK
7	400	8:30	5	17½
8	400	8:00	5	17½
9	400	8:00	2	19
	and			
	500	10:30	3	
10	500	10:30	3	24
	and			
	700	15:00	2	
11	600	12:00	4	27¼
	and			
	800	16:30	1	
12	800	16:00	4	30
13	1000	20:30	3	31½

FITNESS CATEGORY III   (1.15–1.39 miles on 12-minute test)

WEEK	DISTANCE (yards)	TIME (min)	FREQ/WK	POINTS/WK
7	400	8:30	2	22
	and			
	600	12:30	3	
8	600	12:00	4	27¼
	and			
	800	16:30	1	
9	800	16:00	4	30
10	1000	20:30	3	31½

* Breaststroke is less demanding and so is backstoke. Butterfly is considerably more demanding.

After completing the Category I, II, or III progressive swimming program, go to pages 107–8 and select one of the 30-point-per-week programs or develop one of your own from the point value charts beginning on page 111.

STATIONARY RUNNING EXERCISE PROGRAM
(30–39 years of age)

STARTER

WEEK	DURATION (min)	STEPS/MIN *	FREQ/WK	POINTS/WK
1	2:30	70–80	5	4
2	2:30	70–80	5	4
3	5:00	70–80	5	7½
4	5:00	70–80	5	7½
5	7:30	70–80	5	11¼
6	7:30	70–80	5	11¼

After completing the above starter program, continue with the Category I conditioning program below or, if you wish to speed up your program, take the 12-minute test of fitness. If you take the test, find your category from the table at the beginning of the chart pack (page 52). If your category is I, II, or III, continue with the appropriate category below. If your category is IV or V, follow the instructions in the note at the bottom of page 76.

* Count only when the left foot hits the floor. Feet must be brought at least eight inches from the floor.

CONDITIONING

Fitness Category I   (Less than 0.95 mile on 12-minute test)

WEEK	DURATION (min)	STEPS/MIN *	FREQ/WK	POINTS/WK
7	10:00	70–80	5	15
8	10:00	70–80	5	15
9	12:30	70–80	5	18¾
10	12:30	70–80	5	18¾
11	15:00	70–80	5	22½
12	10:00 and	80–90	1	24¼
	17:30	70–80	3	
13	10:00 and	80–90	1	24¼
	17:30	70–80	3	
14	12:30 and	80–90	2	28
	15:00	80–90	3	
15	15:00	80–90	5	30
16	15:00	90–100	4	30

* Count only when the left foot hits the floor. Feet must be brought at least eight inches from the floor.

STATIONARY RUNNING EXERCISE PROGRAM
(30–39 years of age)

CONDITIONING

FITNESS CATEGORY II   (0.95–1.4 miles on 12-minute test)

WEEK	DURATION (min)	STEPS/MIN *	FREQ/WK	POINTS/WK
7	12:30	70–80	5	18¾
8	12:30	70–80	5	18¾
9	15:00	70–80	5	22½
10	10:00 and	80–90	1	24¼
	17:30	70–80	3	
11	12:30 and	80–90	2	28
	15:00	80–90	3	
12	15:00	80–90	5	30
13	15:00	90–100	4	30

* Count only when the left foot hits the floor. Feet must be brought at least eight inches from the floor.

FITNESS CATEGORY III   (1.15–1.39 miles on 12-minute test)

WEEK	DURATION (min)	STEPS/MIN *	FREQ/WK	POINTS/WK
7	10:00 and	80–90	1	24¼
	17:30	70–80	3	
8	12:30 and	80–90	2	28
	15:00	80–90	3	
9	15:00	80–90	5	30
10	15:00	90–100	4	30

* Count only when the left foot hits the floor. Feet must be brought at least eight inches from the floor.

After completing the Category I, II, or III progressive stationary running program, go to pages 107–8 and select one of the 30-point-per-week programs or develop one of your own from the point value charts beginning on page 111.

HANDBALL/BASKETBALL/SQUASH EXERCISE PROGRAM
(30–39 years of age)

STARTER

WEEK	TIME (min)*	FREQ/WK	POINTS/WK
1	10	5	7½
2	10	5	7½
3	15	5	11¼
4	15	5	11¼
5	20	5	15
6	20	5	15

After completing the above starter program, continue with the Category I conditioning program below or, if you wish to speed up your program, take the 12-minute test of fitness. If you take the test, find your category from the table at the beginning of the chart pack (page 52). If your category is I, II, or III, continue with the appropriate category below. If your category is IV or V, follow the instructions in the note at the bottom of page 78.

* Continuous exercise. Do not count breaks, time-outs, etc.

CONDITIONING

FITNESS CATEGORY I   (Less than 0.95 mile on 12-minute test)

WEEK	TIME (min)*	FREQ/WK	POINTS/WK
7	20	5	15
8	25	5	18¾
9	20	1	21
	and		
	30	4	
10	20	1	21
	and		
	30	4	
11	25	1	24¾
	and		
	35	4	
12	25	1	24¾
	and		
	35	4	
13	35	3	27¾
	and		
	40	2	
14	35	3	27¾
	and		
	40	2	
15	40	5	30
16	50	4	30

* Continuous exercise. Do not count breaks, time-outs, etc.

HANDBALL/BASKETBALL/SQUASH EXERCISE PROGRAM
(30–39 years of age)

CONDITIONING

FITNESS CATEGORY II   (0.95–1.14 miles on 12-minute test)

WEEK	TIME (min) *	FREQ/WK	POINTS/WK
7	20	1	21
	and		
	30	4	
8	20	1	21
	and		
	30	4	
9	25	1	24¾
	and		
	35	4	
10	35	3	27¾
	and		
	40	2	
11	35	3	27¾
	and		
	40	2	
12	40	5	30
13	50	4	30

* Continuous exercise. Do not count breaks, time-outs, etc.

FITNESS CATEGORY III   (1.15–1.39 miles on 12-minute test)

WEEK	TIME (min) *	FREQ/WK	POINTS/WK
7	25	1	24¾
	and		
	35	4	
8	35	3	27¾
	and		
	40	2	
9	40	5	30
10	50	4	30

* Continuous exercise. Do not count breaks, time-outs, etc.

After completing the Category I, II, or III progressive program, go to pages 107–8 and select one of the 30-point-per-week programs or develop one of your own from the point value charts beginning on page 111.

WALKING EXERCISE PROGRAM
(40–49 years of age)

STARTER

WEEK	DISTANCE (miles)	TIME (min)	FREQ/WK	POINTS/WK
1	1.0	18:00	5	5
2	1.0	16:00	5	5
3	1.5	24:00	5	7½
4	1.5	22:30	5	7½
5	2.0	31:00	5	10
6	2.0	30:00	5	10

After completing the above starter program, continue with the Category I conditioning program below or, if you wish to speed up your program, take the 12-minute test of fitness. If you take the test, find your category from the table at the beginning of the chart pack (page 52). If your category is I, II, or III, continue with the appropriate category below. If your category is IV or V, follow the instructions in the note at the bottom of page 80.

CONDITIONING

FITNESS CATEGORY I   (Less than 0.85 mile on 12-minute test)

WEEK	DISTANCE (miles)	TIME (min)	FREQ/WK	POINTS/WK
7	2.5	37:45	5	12½
8	2.5	36:30	5	12½
9	2.0 and	29:30	3	16
	2.5	36:00	2	
10	1.5 and	21:30	3	19
	2.5	35:30	2	
11	2.0 and	28:00	3	22
	2.5	36:00	2	
12	2.5 and	35:30	4	23
	3.0	43:45	1	
13	2.0 and	28:00	2	26
	3.0	43:00	3	
14	2.5 and	34:45	3	27
	3.0	42:45	2	
15	3.0	42:45	5	30
16	4.0	56:45	3	33

WALKING EXERCISE PROGRAM
(40–49 years of age)

CONDITIONING

FITNESS CATEGORY II   (0.85–1.04 miles on 12-minute test)

WEEK	DISTANCE (miles)	TIME (min)	FREQ/WK	POINTS/WK
7	2.0	29:30	3	16
	and			
	2.5	36:00	2	
8	1.5	21:30	3	19
	and			
	2.5	35:30	2	
9	2.0	28:00	3	22
	and			
	2.5	36:00	2	
10	2.0	28:00	2	26
	and			
	3.0	43:00	3	
11	2.5	34:45	3	27
	and			
	3.0	42:45	2	
12	3.0	42:45	5	30
13	4.0	56:45	3	33

FITNESS CATEGORY III   (1.05–1.29 miles on 12-minute test)

WEEK	DISTANCE (miles)	TIME (min)	FREQ/WK	POINTS/WK
7	2.5	35:30	4	23
	and			
	3.0	43:45	1	
8	2.5	34:45	3	27
	and			
	3.0	42:45	2	
9	3.0	42:45	5	30
10	4.0	56:45	3	33

After completing the Category I, II, or III progressive walking program, go to pages 107–8 and select one of the 30-point-per-week programs or develop one of your own from the point value charts beginning on page 111.

RUNNING EXERCISE PROGRAM
(40–49 years of age)

STARTER *

WEEK	DISTANCE (miles)	TIME (min)	FREQ/WK	POINTS/WK
1	1.0	18:00	5	5
2	1.0	16:00	5	5
3	1.0	15:00	5	5
4	1.0	14:15	5	10
5	1.0	13:45	5	10
6	1.0	12:45	5	10

After completing the above starter program, continue with the Category I conditioning program below or, if you wish to speed up your program, take the 12-minute test of fitness. If you take the test, find your category from the table at the beginning of the chart pack (page 52). If your category is I, II, or III, continue with the appropriate category below. If your category is IV or V, follow the instructions in the note at the bottom of page 84.

* Start the program by walking, then walk and run, or run as necessary to meet the changing time goals.

RUNNING EXERCISE PROGRAM
(40–49 years of age)

CONDITIONING

FITNESS CATEGORY I   (Less than 0.85 mile on 12-minute test)

WEEK	DISTANCE (miles)	TIME (min)	FREQ/WK	POINTS/WK
7	1.5	20:30	5	15
8	1.5	19:30	5	15
9	1.5	18:30	5	15
10	1.0	10:45	2	19½
	and			
	1.5	17:30	3	
11	1.0	10:15	2	19½
	and			
	1.5	16:30	3	
12	1.0	9:45	3	21
	and			
	1.5	15:30	2	
13	1.0	9:15	3	24
	and			
	1.5	14:55	2	
14	1.0	8:55	3	26
	and			
	2.0	20:30	2	
15	1.0	8:45	2	27
	and			
	1.5	14:00	2	
	and			
	2.0	20:00	1	
16	1.0	8:30	1	34
	and			
	1.5	13:25	2	
	and			
	2.0	19:30	2	

RUNNING EXERCISE PROGRAM
(40–49 years of age)

CONDITIONING

FITNESS CATEGORY II   (0.85–1.04 miles on 12-minute test)

WEEK	DISTANCE (miles)	TIME (min)	FREQ/WK	POINTS/WK
7	1.5	19:30	5	15
8	1.5	18:00	5	15
9	1.0	10:45	3	18
	and			
	1.5	17:00	2	
10	1.0	10:00	1	21
	and			
	1.5	15:45	4	
11	1.0	9:30	2	26
	and			
	1.5	14:30	3	
12	1.0	9:00	1	32
	and			
	2.0	20:30	4	
13	1.0	8:30	1	34
	and			
	1.5	13:25	2	
	and			
	2.0	19:30	2	

RUNNING EXERCISE PROGRAM
(40–49 years of age)

CONDITIONING

Fitness Category III   (1.05–1.29 miles on 12-minute test)

WEEK	DISTANCE (miles)	TIME (min)	FREQ/WK	POINTS/WK
7	1.5	18:30	5	15
8	1.0	10:45	3	18
	and			
	1.5	16:30	2	
9	1.5	14:15	2	26
	and			
	2.0	20:30	2	
10	1.0	8:30	1	34
	and			
	1.5	13:25	2	
	and			
	2.0	19:30	2	

After completing the Category I, II, or III progressive running program, go
to pages 107–8 and select one of the 30-point-per-week program or develop
one of your own from the point value charts beginning on page 111.

CYCLING EXERCISE PROGRAM
(40–49 years of age)

STARTER

WEEK	DISTANCE (miles)	TIME (min)	FREQ/WK	POINTS/WK
1	2.0	11:00	5	5
2	2.0	10:00	5	5
3	3.0	15:00	5	7½
4	3.0	14:00	5	7½
5	4.0	19:00	5	10
6	4.0	17:30	5	10

After completing the above starter program, continue with the Category I conditioning program below or, if you wish to speed up your program, take the 12-minute test of fitness. If you take the test, find your category from the table at the beginning of the chart pack (page 52). If your category is I, II, or III, continue with the appropriate category below. If your category is IV or V, follow the instructions in the note at the bottom of page 86.

CONDITIONING

FITNESS CATEGORY I   (Less than 0.85 mile on 12-minute test)

WEEK	DISTANCE (miles)	TIME (min)	FREQ/WK	POINTS/WK
7	4.0	16:30	5	10
8	5.0	21:30	5	12½
9	3.0 and	13:00	2	15
	4.0	15:45	3	
10	3.0 and	11:45	1	18
	4.0	15:30	4	
11	4.0 and	15:00	3	22
	5.0	19:45	2	
12	3.0 and	11:30	2	24
	6.0	23:45	3	
13	3.0 and	11:00	2	24
	6.0	23:30	3	
14	5.0 and	19:00	3	27
	6.0	23:15	2	
15	6.0	23:00	5	30
16	8.0	31:30	3	31½

CYCLING EXERCISE PROGRAM
(40–49 years of age)

CONDITIONING

FITNESS CATEGORY II   (0.85–1.04 miles on 12-minute test)

WEEK	DISTANCE (miles)	TIME (min)	FREQ/WK	POINTS/WK
7	3.0 and	13:00	2	15
	4.0	15:45	3	
8	3.0 and	11:45	1	18
	4.0	15:30	4	
9	4.0 and	15:00	3	22
	5.0	19:45	2	
10	3.0 and	11:00	2	24
	6.0	23:30	3	
11	5.0 and	19:00	3	27
	6.0	23:15	2	
12	6.0	23:00	5	30
13	8.0	31:30	3	31½

FITNESS CATEGORY III   (1.05–1.29 miles on 12-minute test)

WEEK	DISTANCE (miles)	TIME (min)	FREQ/WK	POINTS/WK
7	3.0 and	11:30	2	24
	6.0	23:45	3	
8	5.0 and	19:00	3	27
	6.0	23:15	2	
9	6.0	23:00	5	30
10	8.0	31:30	3	31½

After completing the Category I, II, or III progressive cycling program, go to pages 107–8 and select one of the 30-point-per-week programs or develop one of your own from the point value charts beginning on page 111.

SWIMMING EXERCISE PROGRAM
(40–49 years of age)

Overhand Crawl *

STARTER

WEEK	DISTANCE (yards)	TIME (min)	FREQ/WK	POINTS/WK
1	100	2:30	5	4
2	150	3:15	5	5
3	175	4:00	5	6
4	200	4:30	5	7½
5	200	4:15	5	7½
6	250	5:30	5	10

After completing the above starter program, continue with the Category I conditioning program below or, if you wish to speed up your program, take the 12-minute test of fitness. If you take the test, find your category from the table at the beginning of the chart pack (page 52). If your category is I, II, or III, continue with the appropriate category below. If your category is IV or V, follow the instructions in the note at the bottom of page 88.

* Breaststroke is less demanding and so is backstroke. Butterfly is considerably more demanding.

CONDITIONING

FITNESS CATEGORY I   (Less than 0.85 mile on 12-minute test)

WEEK	DISTANCE (yards)	TIME (min)	FREQ/WK	POINTS/WK
7	250	5:15	5	10
8	300	6:45	5	12½
9	300	6:15	5	12½
10	400	9:00	5	17½
11	400	8:30	5	17½
12	400 and	8:30	2	19
	500	10:45	3	
13	400 and	9:00	2	22
	600	13:00	3	
14	500 and	11:00	3	24
	700	15:30	2	
15	700	15:00	5	30
16	800	16:30	4	30

SWIMMING EXERCISE PROGRAM
(40–49 years of age)

Overhand Crawl *

CONDITIONING

FITNESS CATEGORY II   (0.85–1.04 miles on 12-minute test)

WEEK	DISTANCE (yards)	TIME (min)	FREQ/WK	POINTS/WK
7	300	6:15	5	12½
8	400	9:00	5	17½
9	400	8:30	5	17½
10	400	9:00	2	22
	and			
	600	13:00	3	
11	500	11:00	3	24
	and			
	700	15:30	2	
12	700	15:00	5	30
13	800	16:30	4	30

FITNESS CATEGORY III   (1.05–1.29 miles on 12-minute test)

WEEK	DISTANCE (yards)	TIME (min)	FREQ/WK	POINTS/WK
7	400	8:30	2	19
	and			
	500	10:45	3	
8	500	11:00	3	24
	and			
	700	15:30	2	
9	700	15:00	5	30
10	800	16:30	4	30

* Breaststroke is less demanding and so is backstroke. Butterfly is considerably more demanding.

After completing the Category I, II, or III progressive swimming program, go to pages 107–8 and select one of the 30-point-per-week programs or develop one of your own from the point value charts beginning on page 111.

STATIONARY RUNNING EXERCISE PROGRAM
(40–49 years of age)

STARTER

WEEK	DURATION (min)	STEPS/MIN *	FREQ/WK	POINTS/WK
1	2:30	70–80	5	4
2	2:30	70–80	5	4
3	5:00	70–80	5	7½
4	5:00	70–80	5	7½
5	5:00	70–80	5	7½
6	7:30	70–80	5	11¼

After completing the above starter program, continue with the Category I conditioning program below or, if you wish to speed up your program, take the 12-minute test of fitness. If you take the test, find your category from the table at the beginning of the chart pack. (page 52). If your category is I, II, or III, continue with the appropriate category below. If your category is IV or V, follow the instructions in the note at the bottom of page 90.

* Count only when the left foot strikes the floor. Feet must be brought at least eight inches from the floor.

CONDITIONING

FITNESS CATEGORY I   (Less than 0.85 mile on 12-minute test)

WEEK	DURATION (min)	STEPS/MIN *	FREQ/WK	POINTS/WK
7	7:30	70–80	5	11¼
8	10:00	70–80	5	15
9	10:00	70–80	5	15
10	12:30	70–80	5	18¾
11	12:30	70–80	5	18¾
12	15:00	70–80	5	22½
13	10:00 and	80–90	1	24¼
	17:30	70–80	3	
14	12:30 and	80–90	2	28
	15:00	80–90	3	
15	17:30	70–80	4	27
16	20:00	80–90	3	30

* Count only when the left foot strikes the floor. Feet must be brought at least eight inches from the floor.

STATIONARY RUNNING EXERCISE PROGRAM
(40–49 years of age)

CONDITIONING

FITNESS CATEGORY II   (0.85–1.04 miles on 12-minute test)

WEEK	DURATION (min)	STEPS/MIN *	FREQ/WK	POINTS/WK
7	10:00	70–80	5	15
8	12:30	70–80	5	18¾
9	12:30	70–80	5	18¾
10	10:00	80–90	1	24¼
	and			
	17:30	70–80	3	
11	12:30	80–90	2	28
	and			
	15:00	80–90	3	
12	17:30	70–80	4	27
13	20:00	80–90	3	30

* Count only when the left foot strikes the floor. Feet must be brought at least eight inches from the floor.

FITNESS CATEGORY III   (1.05–1.29 miles on 12-minute test)

WEEK	DURATION (min)	STEPS/MIN *	FREQ/WK	POINTS/WK
7	15:00	70–80	5	22½
8	12:30	80–90	2	28
	and			
	15:00	80–90	3	
9	17:30	70–80	4	27
10	20:00	80–90	3	30

* Count only when the left foot strikes the floor. Feet must be brought at least eight inches from the floor.

After completing the Category I, II, or III progressive stationary running program, go to pages 107–8 and select one of the 30-point-per-week programs or develop one of your own from the point value charts beginning on page 111.

HANDBALL/BASKETBALL/SQUASH EXERCISE PROGRAM
(40–49 years af age)

STARTER

WEEK	TIME (min) *	FREQ/WK	POINTS/WK
1	10	5	7½
2	10	5	7½
3	10	5	7½
4	15	5	11¼
5	15	5	11¼
6	15	5	11¼

After completing the above starter program, continue with the Category I conditioning program below or if, you wish to speed up your program, take the 12-minute test of fitness. If you take the test, find your category from the table at the beginning of the chart pack (page 52). If your category is I, II, or III, continue with the appropriate category below. If your category is IV or V, follow the instructions in the note at the bottom of page 92.

* Continuous exercise. Do not count breaks, time-outs, etc.

CONDITIONING

FITNESS CATEGORY I   (Less than 0.85 mile on 12-minute test)

WEEK	TIME (min) *	FREQ/WK	POINTS/WK
7	20	5	15
8	20	5	15
9	20	5	15
10	25	5	18¾
11	25	5	18¾
12	20 and 30	1 4	21
13	20 and 30	1 4	21
14	25 and 35	1 4	24¾
15	35 and 40	3 2	27¾
16	40	5	30

* Continuous exercise. Do not count breaks, time-outs, etc.

HANDBALL/BASKETBALL/SQUASH EXERCISE PROGRAM

(40–49 years af age)

CONDITIONING

FITNESS CATEGORY II (0.85–1.04 miles on 12-minute test)

WEEK	TIME (min)*	FREQ/WK	POINTS/WK
7	20	5	15
8	25	5	18¾
9	25	5	18¾
10	20	1	21
	and		
	30	4	
11	25	1	24¾
	and		
	35	4	
12	35	3	27¾
	and		
	40	2	
13	40	5	30

* Continuous exercise. Do not count breaks, time-outs, etc.

FITNESS CATEGORY III (1.05–1.29 miles on 12-minute test)

WEEK	TIME (min)*	FREQ/WK	POINTS/WK
7	20	1	21
	and		
	30	4	
8	25	1	24¾
	and		
	35	4	
9	35	3	27¾
	and		
	40	2	
10	40	5	30

* Continuous exercise. Do not count breaks, time-outs, etc.

After completing the Category I, II, or III progressive program, go to pages 107–8 and select one of the 30-point-per-week programs or develop one of your own from the point value charts beginning on page 111.

WALKING EXERCISE PROGRAM
(age 50 and over)

STARTER

WEEK	DISTANCE (miles)	TIME (min)	FREQ/WK	POINTS/WK
1	1.0	18:30	5	5
2	1.0	16:30	5	5
3	1.0	15:00	5	5
4	1.5	24:30	5	7½
5	1.5	23:00	5	7½
6	1.5	22:30	5	7½

After completing the above starter program, continue with the Category I conditioning program below or, if you wish to speed up your program, take the 12-minute test of fitness. If you take the test, find your category from the table at the beginning of the chart pack (page 52). If your category is I, II, or III, continue with the appropriate category below. If your category is IV or V, follow the instructions in the note at the bottom of page 94.

CONDITIONING

FITNESS CATEGORY I   (Less than 0.80 mile on 12-minute test)

WEEK	DISTANCE (miles)	TIME (min)	FREQ/WK	POINTS/WK
7	2.0	32:00	5	10
8	2.0	31:00	5	10
9	2.5	38:30	5	12½
10	2.0 and	28:45	2	15½
	2.5	27:30	3	
11	2.0 and	28:30	3	17
	2.5	37:00	2	
12	2.5 and	36:00	3	21
	3.0	44:30	2	
13	2.0 and	28:00	2	26
	3.0	43:15	3	
14	2.5 and	35:00	3	27
	3.0	43:00	2	
15	3.0	43:00	5	30
16	4.0	57:00	3	33

WALKING EXERCISE PROGRAM
(age 50 and over)

CONDITIONING

FITNESS CATEGORY II   (0.80–0.99 mile on 12-minute test)

WEEK	DISTANCE (miles)	TIME (min)	FREQ/WK	POINTS/WK
7	2.5	38:30	5	12½
8	2.0 and	28:45	2	15½
	2.5	37:30	3	
9	2.0 and	28:30	3	17
	2.5	37:00	2	
10	2.0 and	28:00	2	26
	3.0	43:15	3	
11	2.5 and	35:00	3	27
	3.0	43:00	2	
12	3.0	43:00	5	30
13	4.0	57:00	3	33

FITNESS CATEGORY III   (1.0–1.24 miles on 12-minute test)

WEEK	DISTANCE (miles)	TIME (min)	FREQ/WK	POINTS/WK
7	2.5 and	36:00	3	21
	3.0	44:30	2	
8	2.5 and	35:00	3	27
	3.0	43:00	2	
9	3.0	43:00	5	30
10	4.0	57:00	3	33

After completing the progressive walking program, go to pages 107–8 and select one of the 30-point-per-week programs or develop one of your own from the point value charts beginning on page 111.

RUNNING EXERCISE PROGRAM
(age 50 and over)

STARTER *

WEEK	DISTANCE (miles)	TIME (min)	FREQ/WK	POINTS/WK
1	1.0	18:30	5	5
2	1.0	17:00	5	5
3	1.0	16:00	5	5
4	1.0	15:00	5	5
5	1.0	14:15	5	10
6	1.0	13:45	5	10

After completing the above starter program, continue with the Category I conditioning program below or, if you wish to speed up your program, take the 12-minute test of fitness. If you take the test, find your category from the table at the beginning of the chart pack (page 52). If your category is I, II, or III, continue with the appropriate category below. If your category is IV or V, follow the instructions in the note at the bottom of page 98.

* Start the program by walking, then walk and run, or run, as necessary to meet the changing time goals.

RUNNING EXERCISE PROGRAM
(age 50 and over)

CONDITIONING

FITNESS CATEGORY I   (Less than 0.80 mile on 12-minute test)

WEEK	DISTANCE (miles)	TIME (min)	FREQ/WK	POINTS/WK
7	1.5	22:00	5	15
8	1.5	20:30	5	15
9	1.5	19:30	5	15
10	1.0	11:30	1	15
	and			
	1.5	18:30	4	
11	1.0	10:45	1	21
	and			
	1.5	17:30	4	
12	1.0	10:15	1	21
	and			
	1.5	16:30	4	
13	1.5	16:00	3	27½
	and			
	2.0	22:00	2	
14	1.0	9:45	2	29
	and			
	2.0	21:15	3	
15	1.5	15:05	2	30
	and			
	2.0	20:30	3	
16	1.0	9:30	1	34
	and			
	1.5	14:25	2	
	and			
	2.0	19:55	2	

RUNNING EXERCISE PROGRAM
(age 50 and over)

CONDITIONING

FITNESS CATEGORY II   (0.80–0.99 mile on 12-minute test)

WEEK	DISTANCE (miles)	TIME (min)	FREQ/WK	POINTS/WK
7	1.5	20:30	5	15
8	1.5	19:00	5	15
9	1.0 and	11:30	2	16½
	1.5	17:45	3	
10	1.0 and	10:45	1	21
	1.5	16:45	4	
11	1.0 and	10:15	2	24
	1.5	22:00	3	
12	1.0 and	9:45	2	26
	2.0	21:00	3	
13	1.0 and	9:30	1	32
	1.5 and	14:25	2	
	2.0	19:55	2	

RUNNING EXERCISE PROGRAM
(age 50 and over)

CONDITIONING

FITNESS CATEGORY III   (1.0–1.24 miles on 12-minute test)

WEEK	DISTANCE (miles)	TIME (min)	FREQ/WK	POINTS/WK
7	1.5	19:00	5	15
8	1.0	11:30	3	18
	and			
	1.5	17:30	2	
9	1.5	15:15	3	25
	and			
	2.0	22:00	2	
10	1.0	9:30	1	32
	and			
	1.5	14:25	2	
	and			
	2.0	19:55	2	

After completing the progressive running program, go to pages 107–8 and select one of the 30-point-per-week programs or develop one of your own from the point value charts beginning on page 111.

CYCLING EXERCISE PROGRAM
(age 50 and over)

STARTER

WEEK	DISTANCE (miles)	TIME (min)	FREQ/WK	POINTS/WK
1	2.0	11:30	5	5
2	2.0	10:30	5	5
3	2.0	10:00	5	5
4	3.0	16:00	5	7½
5	3.0	15:30	5	7½
6	3.0	15:00	5	7½

After completing the above starter program, continue with the Category I conditioning program below or, if you wish to speed up your program, take the 12-minute test of fitness. If you take the test, find your category from the table at the beginning of the chart pack (page 52). If your category is I, II, or III, continue with the appropriate category below. If your category is IV or V, follow the instructions in the note at the bottom of page 100.

CONDITIONING

FITNESS CATEGORY I   (Less than 0.80 mile on 12-minute test)

WEEK	DISTANCE (miles)	TIME (min)	FREQ/WK	POINTS/WK
7	4.0	21:00	5	10
8	4.0	20:00	5	10
9	5.0	26:30	5	12½
10	5.0 and	25:00	1	14½
	6.0	32:00	4	
11	5.0 and	25:00	3	18½
	7.0	39:30	2	
12	7.0	38:00	4	22
13	5.0 and	24:00	2	24½
	8.0	42:00	3	
14	8.0 and	40:00	3	28
	10.0	57:30	1	
15	10.0	55:00	4	34
16	12.0	65:00	3	31½

CYCLING EXERCISE PROGRAM
(age 50 and over)

CONDITIONING

Fitness Category II   (0.80–0.99 mile on 12-minute test)

WEEK	DISTANCE (miles)	TIME (min)	FREQ/WK	POINTS/WK
7	5.0	26:30	5	12½
8	5.0 and	25:00	1	14½
	6.0	32:00	4	
9	5.0 and	25:00	3	18½
	7.0	39:30	2	
10	5.0 and	24:00	2	24½
	8.0	42:00	3	
11	8.0 and	40:00	3	28
	10.0	57:30	1	
12	10.0	55:00	4	34
13	12.0	65:00	3	31½

Fitness Category III   (1.0–1.24 miles on 12-minute test)

WEEK	DISTANCE (miles)	TIME (min)	FREQ/WK	POINTS/WK
7	7.0	38:00	4	22
8	8.0 and	40:00	3	28
	10.0	57:30	1	
9	10.0	55:00	4	34
10	12.0	65:00	3	31½

After completing the progressive cycling program, go to pages 107–8 and select one of the 30-point-per-week programs or develop one of your own from the point value charts beginning on page 111.

SWIMMING EXERCISE PROGRAM
(age 50 and over)

Overhand Crawl *

STARTER

WEEK	DISTANCE (yards)	TIME (min)	FREQ/WK	POINTS/WK
1	100	2:30	5	4
2	150	3:45	5	5
3	175	4:15	5	6
4	200	4:45	5	7½
5	200	4:30	5	7½
6	200	4:15	5	7½

After completing the above starter program, continue with the Category I
conditioning program below or, if you wish to speed up your program, take
the 12-minute test of fitness. If you take the test, find your category from the
table at the beginning of the chart pack (page 52). If your category is
I, II, or III, continue with the appropriate category below. If your category
is IV or V, follow the instructions in the note at the bottom of page 102.

* Breaststroke is less demanding and so is backstroke. Butterfly is considerably more demanding.

CONDITIONING

FITNESS CATEGORY I   (Less than 0.80 mile on 12-minute test)

WEEK	DISTANCE (yards)	TIME (min)	FREQ/WK	POINTS/WK
7	200	5:45	5	10
8	250	5:30	5	10
9	300	7:15	5	12½
10	300	6:45	5	12½
11	400	9:45	5	17½
12	400 and	9:30	2	19
	500	12:00	3	
13	400 and	9:15	2	22
	600	13:45	3	
14	500 and	11:30	2	26
	700	16:30	3	
15	700	16:00	5	30
16	800	18:00	4	30

SWIMMING EXERCISE PROGRAM
(age 50 and over)

Overhand Crawl *

CONDITIONING

FITNESS CATEGORY II   (0.80–0.99 mile on 12-minute test)

WEEK	DISTANCE (yards)	TIME (min)	FREQ/WK	POINTS/WK
7	300	7:15	5	12½
8	300	6:45	5	12½
9	400	9:45	5	17½
10	400	9:15	2	22
	and			
	600	13:45	3	
11	500	11:30	2	26
	and			
	700	16:30	3	
12	700	16:00	5	30
13	800	18:00	4	30

FITNESS CATEGORY III   (1.0–1.24 miles on 12-minute test)

WEEK	DISTANCE (yards)	TIME (min)	FREQ/WK	POINTS/WK
7	400	9:30	2	19
	and			
	500	12:30	3	
8	500	11:30	2	26
	and			
	700	16:30	3	
9	700	16:00	5	30
10	800	18:00	4	30

* Breaststroke is less demanding and so is backstroke. Butterfly is considerably more demanding.

After completing the progressive swimming program, go to pages 107–8 and select one of the 30-point-per-week programs or develop one of your own from the point value charts beginning on page 111.

STATIONARY RUNNING EXERCISE PROGRAM
(age 50 and over)

STARTER

WEEK	DURATION (min)	STEPS/MIN *	FREQ/WK	POINTS/WK
1	1:30	70–80	5	—
2	2:30	70–80	5	4
3	2:30	70–80	5	4
4	5:00	70–80	5	7½
5	5:00	70–80	5	7½
6	5:00	70–80	5	7½

After completing the above starter program, continue with the Category I conditioning program below or, if you wish to speed up your program, take the 12-minute test of fitness. If you take the test, find your category from the table at the beginning of the chart pack (page 52). If your category is I, II, or III, continue with the appropriate category below. If your category is IV or V, follow the instructions in the note at the bottom of page 104.

* Count only when the left foot hits the floor. Feet must be brought at least eight inches from the floor.

CONDITIONING

FITNESS CATEGORY I   (Less than 0.80 mile on 12-minute test)

WEEK	DURATION (min)	STEPS/MIN *	FREQ/WK	POINTS/WK
7	7:30	70–80	5	11¼
8	7:30	70–80	5	11¼
9	10:00	70–80	5	15
10	10:00	70–80	5	15
11	10:00	70–80	5	15
12	12:30	70–80	5	18¾
13	10:00 (1x in A.M.) and	70–80	2	23¼
	10:00 (1x in P.M.) and	70–80		
	12:30	70–80	3	
14	10:00 (1x in A.M.) and	70–80	2	25½
	10:00 (1x in P.M.) and	70–80		
	15:00	70–80	3	
15	12:30 (1x in A.M.) and	70–80	2	28½
	12:30 (1x in P.M.) and			
	15:00	70–80	3	
16	20:00	70–80	4	32

* Count only when the left foot hits the floor. Feet must be brought at least eight inches from the floor.

STATIONARY RUNNING EXERCISE PROGRAM
(age 50 and over)
CONDITIONING

FITNESS CATEGORY II   (0.80–0.99 mile on 12-minute test)

WEEK	DURATION (min)	STEPS/MIN *	FREQ/WK	POINTS/WK
7	10:00	70–80	5	15
8	10:00	70–80	5	15
9	10:00	70–80	5	15
10	10:00 (1x in A.M.) and	70–80	2	23¼
	10:00 (1x in P.M.) and	70–80		
	12:30	70–80	3	
11	10:00 (1x in A.M.) and	70–80	2	25½
	10:00 (1x in P.M.) and	70–80		
	15:00	70–80	3	
12	12:30 (1x in A.M.) and	70–80	2	28½
	12:30 (1x in P.M.) and	70–80		
	15:00	70–80	3	
13	20:00	70–80	4	32

* Count only when the left foot hits the floor. Feet must be brought at least eight inches from the floor.

FITNESS CATEGORY III   (1.0–1.24 miles on 12-minute test)

WEEK	DURATION (min)	STEPS/MIN *	FREQ/WK	POINTS/WK
7	12:30	70–80	5	18¾
8	10:00 (1x in A.M.) and	70–80	2	25½
	10:00 (1x in P.M.) and	70–80		
	15:00	70–80	3	
9	12:30 (1x in A.M.) and	70–80	2	28½
	12:30 (1x in P.M.) and	70–80		
	15:00	70–80	3	
10	20:00	70–80	4	32

* Count only when the left foot hits the floor. Feet must be brought at least eight inches from the floor.

After completing the progressive stationary running program, go to pages 107–8 and select one of the 30-point-per-week programs or develop one of your own from the point value charts beginning on page 111.

HANDBALL/BASKETBALL/SQUASH EXERCISE PROGRAM
(age 50 and over)

STARTER

WEEK	TIME (min) *	FREQ/WK	POINTS/WK
1	7:30	5	5
2	7:30	5	5
3	10:00	5	7½
4	10:00	5	7½
5	12:30	5	10
6	12:30	5	10

After completing the above starter program, continue with the Category I
conditioning program below or, if you wish to speed up your program, take
the 12-minute test of fitness. If you take the test, find your category from the
table at the beginning of the chart pack (page 52). If your category is
I, II, or III, continue with the appropriate category below. If your category
is IV or V, follow the instructions in the note at the bottom of page 106.

* Continuous exercise. Do not count breaks, time-outs, etc.

CONDITIONING

FITNESS CATEGORY I   (Less than 0.80 mile on 12-minute test)

WEEK	TIME (min) *	FREQ/WK	POINTS/WK
7	15:00	5	11¼
8	15:00	5	11¼
9	20:00	5	15
10	20:00	5	15
11	25:00	5	18¾
12	25:00	5	18¾
13	20:00 and 30:00	1 4	21
14	20:00 and 30:00	1 4	24
15	35:00 and 40:00	3 2	27¾
16	40:00	5	30

* Continuous exercise. Do not count breaks, time-outs, etc.

HANDBALL/BASKETBALL/SQUASH EXERCISE PROGRAM
(age 50 and over)

CONDITIONING

FITNESS CATEGORY II   (0.80–0.99 mile on 12-minute test)

WEEK	TIME (min)*	FREQ/WK	POINTS/WK
7	20:00	5	15
8	20:00	5	15
9	25:00	5	18¾
10	20:00	1	21
	and		
	30:00	4	
11	20:00	1	
	and		
	30:00	4	24
12	35:00	3	27¾
	and		
	40:00	2	
13	40:00	5	30

* Continuous exercise. Do not count breaks, time-outs, etc.

FITNESS CATEGORY III   (1.0–1.24 miles on 12-minute test)

WEEK	TIME (min)*	FREQ/WK	POINTS/WK
7	25:00	5	18¾
8	20:00	1	24
	and		
	30:00	4	
9	35:00	3	27¾
	and		
	40:00	2	
10	40:00	5	30

* Continuous exercise. Do not count breaks, time-outs, etc.

After completing the progressive handball/basketball/squash program, go to pages 107–8 and select one of the 30-point-per-week programs or develop one of your own from the point value charts beginning on page 111.

PROGRAMS FOR CATEGORIES IV AND V
(all ages)

FITNESS LEVEL IS SATISFACTORY AT THE OUTSET. THE ONLY REQUIREMENT IS TO MAINTAIN FITNESS USING ONE OF THE FOLLOWING EXERCISE PROGRAMS.

	DISTANCE (miles)	TIME (min) REQUIREMENT	FREQ/WK	POINTS/WK
WALKING	2.0	24:00–29:00	8	32
	or			
	3.0	36:00–43:30	5	30
	or			
	4.0	58:00–79:59	5	35
	or			
	4.0	48:00–58:00	3	33
RUNNING	1.0	6:30– 7:59	6	30
	or			
	1.5	12:00–14:59	5	30
	or			
	1.5	9:45–11:59	4	30
	or			
	2.0	16:00–19:59	4	36
	or			
	2.0	13:00–15:59	3	33
CYCLING	5.0	15:00–19:59	6	30
	or			
	6.0	18:00–23:59	5	30
	or			
	7.0	21:00–27:59	4	36
	or			
	8.0	24:00–31:59	3	31
	YARDS			
SWIMMING	500	8:20–12:59	8	32
	or			
	600	10:00–14:59	6	30
	or			
	800	13:20–19:59	4	30
	or			
	1000	16:40–24:59	3	31½

PROGRAMS FOR CATEGORIES IV AND V
(all ages)

	DURATION (min)	STEPS/MIN *	FREQ/WK	POINTS/WK
STATIONARY RUNNING	10:00 in A.M. and	70–80	5	30
	10:00 in P.M. or	70–80		
	15:00 or	70–80	7	30
	15:00 or	80–90	5	30
	20:00	70–80	4	32

* Count only when the left foot hits the floor. Feet must be brought at least eight inches from the floor.

HANDBALL BASKETBALL SQUASH	40:00 or	—	5	30
	50:00 or	—	4	30
	70:00	—	3	30

SUGGESTED PROGRESSIVE WALKING PROGRAM FOR CARDIAC PATIENTS—A

(Minimal Disease—Uncomplicated)

WEEKS	DISTANCE (miles)	TIME GOAL (min)	FREQ/WK	POINTS/WK
1–2	1.0	20:00	5	—
3–4	1.0	17:30	5	5
5–6	1.0	15:00	5	5
7–8	1.5	23:00	5	7½
9–10	1.5	22:30	5	7½
11–12	2.0	31.00	5	10
13–14	2.0	30:00	5	10
15–16	1.5	21:30	5	15
17–18	1.5	21:00	5	15
19–20	2.0	28:45	3	22
	and			
	2.5	36:00	2	
21–22	2.0	28:30	3	22
	and			
	2.5	35:45	2	
23–24	2.5	35:30	4	26
	and			
	3.0	43:15	1	
25–26	2.5	35:15	3	27
	and			
	3.0	43:15	2	
27–28	2.5	35:00	3	27
	and			
	3.0	42:30	2	
29–30	3.0	42:00	5	30
31–32	4.0	55:00	3	33

MINIMAL REQUIREMENTS TO MAINTAIN FITNESS AFTER COMPLETION OF CONDITIONING PROGRAM—A

DISTANCE (miles)	TIME GOAL (min)	FREQ/WK	POINTS/WK
1.5 (twice a day)	18:00–21:44	5	30
or 2.0	24:00–28:59	8	32
or 3.0	36:00–43:29	5	30
or 4.0	48:00–57:59	3	33
or 5.0	72:30–99:59	4	36

SUGGESTED PROGRESSIVE WALKING PROGRAM FOR CARDIAC PATIENTS—B

(Moderate Disease)

WEEKS	DISTANCE (miles)	TIME GOAL (min)	FREQ/WK	POINTS/WK
1–2	1.0	24:00	5	—
3–4	1.0	20:00	5	—
5–6	1.0	18:00	5	5
7–8	1.0	16:00	5	5
9–10	1.5	25:00	5	7½
11–12	1.5	24:00	5	7½
13–14	2.0	33:00	5	10
15–16	2.0	32:00	5	10
17–18	1.5	23:00	2	10½
	and			
	2.5	40:00	3	
19–20	1.5	22:30	2	12
	and			
	3.0	47:00	3	
21–22	2.5	38:00	2	15½
	and			
	3.5	54:00	3	
23–24	2.5	36:00	3	21
	and			
	3.0	44:00	2	
25–26	3.0	43:15	3	26
	and			
	4.0	61:00	2	
27–28	3.0	43:15	3	26
	and			
	4.0	60:00	2	
29–30	3.0	43:00	5	30
31–32	4.0	57:45	3	33

MINIMUM REQUIREMENTS TO MAINTAIN FITNESS AFTER COMPLETION OF CONDITIONING PROGRAM—B

DISTANCE (miles)	TIME GOAL (min)	FREQ/WK	POINTS/WK
1.5 (twice a day)	18:00–21:44	5	30
or 2.0	24:00–28:59	8	32
or 3.0	36:00–43:29	5	30
or 4.0	48:00–57:59	3	33
or 4.0	58:00–79:59	4	28
or 5.0	72:30–99:59	3	27

POINT VALUE CHARTS

For a more complete breakdown of these point values, see Appendix.

WALKING

1 Mile	POINTS	3.5 Miles	POINTS
19:59—14:30 min	1	70:00 min or longer	1½*
14:29—12:00 min	2	69:59—50:45 min	3½
		50:44—42:00 min	7

1.5 Miles	POINTS	4 Miles	POINTS
29:59—21:45 min	1½	80:00 min or longer	4*
21:44—18:00 min	3	79:59—58:00 min	7
		57:59—48:00 min	11

2 Miles	POINTS	4.5 Miles	POINTS
40:00 min or longer	1*	90 min or longer	4½*
39:59—29:00 min	2	89:59—65:15 min	8
28:59—24:00 min	4	65:14—54:00 min	12½

2.5 Miles	POINTS	5 Miles	POINTS
50:00 min or longer	1*	100:00 min or longer	5*
49:59—36:15 min	2½	99:59—72:30 min	9
36:14—30:00 min	5	72:29—60:00 min	14

3 Miles	POINTS
60:00 min or longer	1½*
59:59—43:30 min	3
43:29—36:00 min	6

RUNNING

1 Mile	POINTS	2 Miles	POINTS
14:29—12:00 min	2	28:59—24:00 min	4
11:59—10:00 min	3	23:59—20:00 min	7
9:59— 8:00 min	4	19:59—16:00 min	9
7:59— 6:30 min	5	15:59—13:00 min	11
under 6:30 min	6	under 13:00 min	13

1.5 Miles	POINTS	2.5 Miles	POINTS
21:44—18:00 min	3	36:14—30:00 min	5
17:59—15:00 min	4½	29:59—25:00 min	9
14:59—12:00 min	6	24:59—20:00 min	11½
11:59— 9:45 min	7½	19:59—16:15 min	14
under 9:45 min	9	under 16:15 min	16½

* Exercise of sufficient duration to be of cardiovascular benefit. At this speed, ordinarily no training effect would occur. However, the duration is of such extent that a training effect does begin to occur.

POINT VALUE CHARTS

For a more complete breakdown of these point values, see Appendix.

RUNNING (CONTINUED)

3 Miles	POINTS	4 Miles	POINTS
43:29—36:00 min	6	57:59—48:00 min	11
35:59—30:00 min	11	47.59—40:00 min	15
29:59—24:00 min	14	39:59—32:00 min	19
23:59—19:30 min	17	31:59—26:00 min	23
under 19:30 min	20	under 26:00 min	27

3.5 Miles	POINTS	5 Miles	POINTS
50:44—42:00 min	7	72:29—60:00 min	10
41:59—35:00 min	13	59:59—50:00 min	15
34:59—28:00 min	16½	49:59—40:00 min	20
27:59—22:45 min	20	39:59—32:30 min	25
under 22:45 min	23½	under 32:30 min	30

CYCLING

2 Miles	POINTS	6 Miles	POINTS
12 min or longer	0	36 min or longer	1*
11:59— 8:00 min	1	35:59—24:00 min	3
7:59— 6:00 min	2	23:59—18:00 min	6
under 6:00 min	3	under 18:00 min	9

3 Miles	POINTS	8 Miles	POINTS
18 min or longer	0	48 min or longer	3½*
17:59—12:00 min	1½	47:59—32:00 min	6½
11:59— 9:00 min	3	31:59—24:00 min	10½
under 9:00 min	4½	under 24:00 min	14½

4 Miles	POINTS	10 Miles	POINTS
24 min or longer	0	60 min or longer	5½*
23:59—16:00 min	2	59:59—40:00 min	8½
15:59—12:00 min	4	39:59—30:00 min	13½
under 12:00 min	6	under 30:00 min	18½

5 Miles	POINTS
30 min or longer	1*
29:59—20:00 min	2½
19:59—15:00 min	5
under 15:00 min	7½

* Exercise of sufficient duration to be of cardiovascular benefit. At this speed, ordinarily no training effect would occur. However, the duration is of such extent that a training effect does begin to occur.

POINT VALUE CHARTS

For a more complete breakdown of these point values, see Appendix.

SWIMMING

200 Yards	POINTS	600 Yards	POINTS
6:40 min or longer	0	20:00 min or longer	1½*
6:39— 5:00 min	1	19:59—15:00 min	4
4:59— 3:20 min	1½	14:59—10:00 min	5
under 3:20 min	2½	under 10:00 min	7½

300 Yards	POINTS	700 Yards	POINTS
10:00 min or longer	1*	23:20 min or longer	1½*
9:59— 7:30 min	1½	23:19—17:30 min	4½
7:29— 5:00 min	2½	17:29—11:40 min	6
under 5:00 min	3½	under 11:40 min	8½

400 Yards	POINTS	800 Yards	POINTS
13:20 min or longer	1*	26:40 min or longer	2¼*
13:19—10:00 min	2½	26:39—20:00 min	5¾
9:59— 6:40 min	3½	19:59—13:20 min	7¼
under 6:40 min	5	under 13:20 min	10¾

500 Yards	POINTS	1000 Yards	POINTS
16:40 min or longer	1*	33:20 min or longer	4*
16:39—12:30 min	3	33:19—25:00 min	8¼
12:29— 8:20 min	4	24:59—16:40 min	10½
under 8:20 min	6	under 16:40 min	14½

* Exercise of sufficient duration to be of cardiovascular benefit. At this speed, ordinarily no training effect would occur. However, the duration is of such extent that a training effect does begin to occur.

POINT VALUE CHARTS

For a more complete breakdown of these point values, see Appendix.

HANDBALL/BASKETBALL/SQUASH *

DURATION	POINTS	DURATION	POINTS
10	1½	55	8¼
15	2¼	60	9
20	3	65	9¾
25	3¾	70	10½
30	4½	75	11¼
35	5¼	80	12
40	6	85	12¾
45	6¾	90	13½
50	7½		

* Continuous exercise. Do not include breaks, time-outs, etc.

STATIONARY RUNNING

TIME	*60-70 STEPS/MIN	POINTS	*70-80 STEPS/MIN	POINTS	*80-90 STEPS/MIN	POINTS
2:30			175-200	¾	200-225	1
5:00	300-350	1¼	350-400	1½	400-450	2
7:30			525-600	2¼	600-675	3
10:00	600-700	2½	700-800	3	800-900	4
12:30			785-1000	3¾	1000-1125	5
15:00	900-1050	3¾	1050-1200	4½	1200-1350	6
17:30			1225-1400	6¾	1400-1575	8½
20:00	1200-1400	7	1400-1600	8	1600-1800	10

* Count only when the left foot hits the floor. Feet must be brought at least eight inches from the floor.

7: Tips and Safeguards

THAT PROVERBIAL OUNCE of prevention also applies to aerobics. This chapter is basically a discussion of possible problems occurring with an exercise program, along with tips on how to avoid them—and hints on how to treat them if they occur.

FOOT TROUBLE

Since foot and ankle troubles are the most frequently encountered exercise problems, they deserve special attention.

The human foot is a marvel of engineering, but it is not well adapted for pounding hard pavements or hard floors. Because of this, some runners develop back pains, leg muscle pains, and swollen ankles. Others develop Achilles tendonitis—soreness and inflammation of the big tendon connecting the heel with the calf. Tendonitis even strikes well-trained athletes, usually without warning, and it may take several weeks to clear up.

To prevent some of these problems, it helps to have a proper warm-up, as discussed in Chapter Five. Occasionally tendonitis occurs when a runner resumes regular workouts after a long layoff. In such cases, it is just as important to stress progressive reentry into the exercise program as it is a proper warm-up.

Stationary running is harder on the feet and ankles than normal running, particularly when it is done in bare feet. Without the support provided by the heel of the shoe, you become a prime candidate for tendonitis and other ankle problems. So keep your shoes on for indoor running.

The so-called "jogger's heel" also occurs occasionally in adult runners. The symptom is a very sore heel caused by landing hard on the heel while running on a concrete or solid surface. To avoid this problem: 1) run flatfooted, touching down with more of the entire sole; 2) avoid running on hard surfaces; and 3) use a cushion-soled shoe.

A more troublesome, but fortunately rare complication is the stress or march fracture of the foot. This happens mostly to older people, whose bones are more brittle. But it may occur at any age.

The sign of a stress or march fracture is a sharp and persistent pain in the foot. It is not a serious matter and with immobilization it usually heals within weeks. Nonetheless, it should be x-rayed, properly treated, and complete healing should be confirmed by your doctor before you resume exercise.

Anytime you develop a problem with your feet and ankles, the best immediate treatment is to reduce the speed and duration of your exercise. If this doesn't work, stop exercising completely and rest the affected part. (Many people follow this rule: If exercise aggravates the pain, stop; if the pain disappears with exercise, continue.)

If your problems persist, it may be necessary to change to another exercise program. For example, a middle-aged man from Houston writes:

> Even though I responded well to the running program and was able to meet all the time requirements, my arthritic ankles couldn't stand the strain. My physician said I had to stop running. With his consent I started cycling and can now cycle five miles in less than 20:00 minutes—and the pain in my ankles completely disappeared.

The proper running style is also of great help in avoiding foot and leg problems. In general, people run too much on either their heels or their toes. I encourage people to run mostly flatfooted.

After the flatfooted touchdown, roll the weight forward on the foot, from heel to toe. Don't run with rigid knees and allow the slightly flexed knee to absorb some of the impact when the foot strikes the ground. Avoid bouncing when running. You can determine how much you are bouncing by watching a stationary object. Let the arms swing comfortably at your side, parallel to your body movement.

Another important point, as I've mentioned before, is the running surface. For stationary running I would recommend a soft rug, preferably with a spongy underlayer. For outdoor running, unfortunately, you have to use whatever is available. A dirt road is good; a quarter mile track is better (particularly if it is covered with the new, resilient, Olympic-type plastic surface) but the best surface is a smooth, well-kept grass field. Since the ideal surface is rarely available, the necessity for good, cushioned-sole shoes is reemphasized.

Picking the right kind of running shoes is probably the biggest factor in avoiding ankle, foot and leg problems. Light, crosscountry shoes are good for running on hard surfaces, but I prefer special long-distance, ripple-sole shoes. The best of these have cushioned innersoles made of some spongy material that gives springy resilience to your step. Avoid standard basketball or tennis shoes, which have an unusually hard sole.

As for socks, it's entirely up to you whether you prefer cotton or nylon. One drawback of nylon socks is that they do not absorb perspiration. Cotton absorbs perspiration, but does not insulate as well against friction.

If your shoes fit well, you may not even need socks. In long-distance running, socks mean extra weight, and some athletes—particularly marathon runners—prefer to run without them. There are insoles that can be inserted in your shoes to reduce friction and blisters.

In case blisters do occur, treat them immediately after running. Keep your feet clean and dry, and the toenails closely clipped.

With these guidelines, you stand an excellent chance of minimizing foot and ankle problems.

KNEE AND LEG PROBLEMS

The most common leg problem with runners is "shin splints." The symptoms are pain and tightness in the muscles in the front of the leg below the knee. Shin splints usually result from running on hard surfaces with hard shoes and are successfully treated by the reverse, that is soft surfaces and cushioned-sole shoes.

Knee problems commonly occur in conditioning programs, particularly among people with old knee injuries. However, even with severe knee and joint problems, some people have been able to run effectively. Let me give you an example.

Sergeant Elmer Jones, a 51-year-old retired member of the USAF has been running with us for over 1½ years. Several years ago, he had an operation on his left knee to correct some chronic changes occurring in the joint. The left kneecap and some cartilage had to be removed. However, progressive exercise strengthened and stabilized his knee and just a few weeks ago he ran 1½ miles in 10:28 minutes—placing him in the Excellent fitness category.

Running distances exceeding one mile on small, unbanked tracks, requiring 25 or more laps to the mile, often causes pain in ankles and knees. For this reason it is preferable to do your outdoor running on larger tracks or on indoor tracks with banked curves. If no such track is available, you can minimize the problems of the smaller track by running 25 laps in one direction and then reversing your direction if you desire to run further. Remember also that a good pair of shoes is just as important for the protection of the knees as it is for the protection of the ankles when you must exercise on a hard surface.

Muscle cramps or spasms in the legs are not uncommon during the early stages of a conditioning program. A muscle only partially conditioned is especially likely to develop cramps. However, this is a transient problem, usually disappearing as a good state of fitness is reached.

BACK TROUBLE

A few individuals who limited their exercise program exclusively to jogging on hard surfaces have written complaining of pain in the lower region of the back. This is not a serious matter, but such discomfort can usually be avoided by supplementing jogging with some calisthenic exercise, notably 15–20 repetitions of both sit-ups with the knees bent and push-ups. These exercises strengthen the back and help to relieve back pain. Cyclists also complain of back aches, and I recommend that they try the same calisthenic routines.

SWIMMERS' PROBLEMS

Swimmers sometimes suffer from a chronic infection of the ear canal. This used to be a common complaint before the chlorination of swimming pools became general practice. If it does occur, see your doctor and have the infection treated. If you find that you are frequently troubled with such infections, swab out your ears after each swim with cotton (or a cotton swab) dipped in alcohol.

Some swimmers develop chronic sinus trouble. An effective precaution is the use of a nose clip while swimming. Competition swimmers report that this increases breathing resistance and tends to lower their performance. But the difference is so slight that I recommend using the nose clip for non-competitive swimming, particularly if the swimming is done as part of an aerobic conditioning program.

EXCESS FATIGUE

A man from Ohio wrote: "Your aerobics program is really great! I run a mile five days a week and now I can go home, go to bed at 6:30, and sleep the rest of the night."

He obviously had missed the point.

Being pleasantly tired for a short period after exercise is one thing. You'd normally expect that. But feeling worn out all the time is something else. Chronic fatigue is a sign that you are exercising at a pace for which you are not yet ready. It is a sign that you need some rest.

I advised my Ohio correspondent to ease up on his exercise until he could get by with seven or eight hours of sleep. "Drop back a couple of weeks in the chart or stay at a level you can tolerate without feeling tired all the time," I wrote him. "Aerobics shouldn't make you constantly sleepy; it should help keep you awake."

Aerobics can be a highly effective cure for ordinary types of insomnia. But the idea is to make you sleep better—not longer. Because exercise reduces your tensions, it helps you to sleep more easily and more deeply. It increases the efficiency of your sleep, so you feel more rested on less sleep. Combined with the general invigoration of your whole system, this should give you extra alertness during your waking hours.

If you do feel overly tired during the later weeks of your conditioning program, you can probably lick the problem by changing your schedule. For example, schedule one resting day after two days of exercise. Of course, to maintain a high level of fitness you should exercise at least four times per week. But that doesn't mean four consecutive days.

There's another way to lick fatigue problems and still earn enough points.

The speed of exercise (the intensity of your workout) may contribute more to fatigue than the duration. So if you have a persistent fatigue problem, I suggest that you exercise at a slower rate for a longer time. You still earn your points but with less strain.

For example, I like to run three miles during the lunch hour several days a week. My time is usually 20:00–21:00 minutes. This is worth 15 points. However, if it is really hot, as at times it can be in south Texas, I tend to get overly fatigued and may be tired the remainder of the day. By running the same distance but slowing the time to 23:30–23:59 minutes, I don't become fatigued at all. In fact, I sometimes feel guilty and feel as though I didn't work out hard enough. But I still get 15 points and I'm wide awake the rest of the day.

Another personal example: At times I have to miss my noon workout due to a multitude of commitments, and I may end up mentally exhausted before 5:00 P.M. Yet, I have several hours of work to accomplish that evening. If I run 1½–2 miles prior to dinner, shower and clean up, it completely revitalizes me. It may be purely psychosomatic but try it, it works!

One of my correspondents summed up all the problems, difficulties and benefits of aerobics this way: "After eight weeks on the conditioning program, I feel younger, stronger, and more alive. And my problems—the ones that looked so big before—well, they haven't gone away. But somehow they look smaller."

Of course, these are subjective reactions. But they also reflect real changes: the strengthening of the heart and lungs, improved circulation, and the ability to distribute more oxygen throughout the body—all the changes that really count.

8: Aerobic Therapy

To MAINTAIN A satisfactory level of fitness and show improvement in various medical conditions, you should average a minimum of 30 points per week.

"And what's so wonderful about 30 points? Why do you set this figure as a goal?"

Let me try to answer this often-asked question. Thirty points per week is enough of a demand on the body to make it respond. With 30 points your body will show definite signs of conditioning—you will fatigue less easily, your heart and lungs will work more efficiently, your capacity for transporting oxygen will increase, and you will probably look and feel better.

Many people who faithfully earn their 30 points each week think of it as a type of health insurance. In a way it is. It will enable you to live a healthier and more productive life, but it is not the fountain of youth. It will help you to lose weight, but you won't lose it rapidly unless you diet along with your exercise program. It will decrease the severity and frequency of many of your medical problems although it may not eliminate them altogether. And as I have already mentioned, it is no guarantee against heart disease, but it is of value in the prevention and rehabilitation of this disease. In that sense, maintaining your 30-point-per-week exercise routine is buying you a lot of health insurance.

Now let us consider the use of aerobic conditioning in treating selected medical problems.

HEART AND BLOOD VESSEL DISEASE

At least one million Americans die each year from heart and blood vessel disorders—600,000, which adds up to one death every 50 seconds, from coronary disease alone. Coronary heart disease has a number of causes: heredity, stress, diet, smoking and inactivity. Some of these causes cannot be changed but patterns of inactivity definitely can be changed. Fortunately, more and more people are starting exercise programs as a means of practicing both preventive and rehabilitative medicine.

In the practice of rehabilitative medicine, physicians are beginning to encourage progressive exercise for selected patients with heart disease.

For example, Master Sergeant J. D. Mott, USAF, suffered a severe heart attack at the age of 41. At that time he was overweight, anxious, smoking heavily and inactive. He survived his heart attack, and four months later decided to join the aerobics program we were conducting for cardiac patients. At that point, his only symptom was occasional chest pain.

Sergeant Mott was placed into the walking program for cardiac patients, moderate disease. In addition, he was placed on a low-cholesterol diet and was encouraged to give up smoking.

His exercise program consisted exclusively of walking, progressing from one to four miles daily. After 12 months, all of his symptoms had disappeared, and the electrocardiogram was normal except for evidence of the old heart attack. At that time, Sergeant Mott was able to switch from the cardiac rehabilitation program to the regular aerobic conditioning program, and he started running. "Never felt better," he said, as he worked happily toward his 30–50-point-per-week goal.

After two years of such conditioning, an x-ray study of his heart showed that he had developed unusually good "collateral" circulation in his coronary system. His working capacity also had increased, and the progress of his potentially crippling and even fatal disease had apparently been slowed.

Another remarkable recovery was made by my neighbor, Mr. Bill Linder. About two years ago, Bill and I were taking an afternoon walk. Whenever we came to a hill, I noticed that Bill would grab his left elbow and complain of pain.

"Oh, it's just that old arthritis," he explained.

But I noticed that the "arthritis" bothered him only on the uphill parts of the walk. That seemed odd indeed. I began to suspect that, since the pain occurred only under stress, it might be "referred" pain from a heart condition. This type of pain, can occur almost anywhere in the upper part of the body.

I suggested to Bill that he have an exercise electrocardiogram.

He just laughed. For years he thought that his pain was arthritis. His electrocardiogram had always been normal.

"Did anyone ever check your electrocardiogram while you were exercising?" I asked.

No, Bill admitted. His doctor had only tested him in a resting condition. I promptly made arrangements for him to have an exercise electrocardiogram—the so-called Masters two-step Test. Under stress, the ECG showed clear signs of moderate to severe heart disease.

Unfortunately, such tests are not normally given with routine checkups. Perhaps we need a revamping of standard procedures or the establishment of special cardiac diagnostic centers to look for "hidden" heart disease. If I had not, by sheer chance, noticed Bill's elbow-grabbing on the uphill stretch, his condition might have remain undetected and untreated. One day he simply might have collapsed with a serious and perhaps fatal attack. Of course, everyone would have said that there had been no previous warning.

Under the supervision of his doctor, Bill started a mild, progressive walking program. After ten months, the progress of his disease had been altered and symptomatically he had improved. His ECG had reverted to normal—even with exercise. Apparently, aerobic exercise had sufficiently improved the blood supply to his heart to change the natural course of his disease.

It goes without saying that the early rehabilitative exercise programs for cardiac patients must remain quite mild. If the patient drives too hard, he may push himself to a point his damaged heart is unable to tolerate. For this reason, it is advisable to recommend to heart patients that they exercise at a level which does not cause their heart rate to exceed the age-adjusted rates listed below. This is particularly important during the early stages of a cardiac rehabilitation program.

MAXIMAL HEART RATES IN CARDIAC REHABILITATION PROGRAMS

Age (Years)	Heart Rate (Beats Per Minute)
Under 30	150
30–34	145
35–39	140
40–44	135
45–49	135
50–54	130
55–59	125
60–64	120
65+	120

A crude way to estimate the maximal heart rate during exercise is to take the pulse during the first ten seconds after exercise and multiply that number by six. However, more sophisticated monitoring methods are available today. One is an electronic device worn by the patient during exercise which sounds a warning through an earphone when his heart rate exceeds a preset limit. Soon to be available is a stationary bicycle with a built-in monitor. As the patient grabs the handlebar, he closes a circuit and can read his heart rate continuously on a meter.

Another important contributory factor to the development of coronary heart disease is a high blood-cholesterol level. The usual way to combat this condition is through diets low in cholesterol and animal fats.

However, several studies have recently shown that exercise, too, may play a role. This lowering effect may be seen in subjects involved in endurance activities even though their diets remain unchanged. To the contrary, exercise programs that tend to build large muscle mass may cause an increase in blood cholesterol levels.

Many patients with high blood pressure have responded well to aerobic therapy. Among my patients at Wilford Hall, I'd like to single out 45-year-old Lieutenant Colonel Gregory Skafidas. Two years ago he joined our program and at that time he had a blood pressure of 180/118. Over the next year, he lost 30 pounds on the aerobics program and his blood pressure dropped to 132/80. He then entered our city-wide ten-mile marathon, finishing in 72 minutes.

Now, two years later, Colonel Skafidas is averaging over 100 points per week and is a living example of the benefits of aerobic therapy.

A mechanism similar to that which restores coronary circulation in damaged hearts also operates in blood vessels in the body. The legs, for example, are frequently affected by blood vessel obstructions, and such conditions can in some instances be helped by exercise.

It should be noted, however, that not all cases of blood vessel disease respond to aerobics. For example, some sufferers from varicose veins claim that exercise aggravated their condition. Others have clearly benefited. Caution and close supervision are therefore advised in using exercise therapy in patients with blood vessel disease.

A moderately successful case of aerobic therapy for advanced vascular disease involved one of our 38-year-old patients with intermittent claudication, a blood vessel ailment causing pain in the legs with even minimal exertion. When he was first studied in our laboratory, he was unable to walk more than a few yards without severe leg pain. In fact, he had difficulty supporting his own weight for more than three minutes without intolerable pain.

He was placed into a very slow walking program and gradually, over a period of many months, his persistence paid off. The effort of walking forced an improvement in the blood supply to his legs. Slowly this new collateral circulation was able to take over, at least partly, the function of the damaged vessels. At the end of his therapy, he was able to walk a distance of one mile without incapacitating pain.

For blood vessel disease, too, I should like to stress the preventive role of aerobics. Prime candidates for blood vessel problems are people who spend a lot of time on their feet without vigorous movement, thereby placing a stress on the blood vessels in their legs. Salesmen standing long hours behind the counter, dentists bending over their patients all day, traffic cops restricted to an intersection—these are the kind of occupations with built-in risk of blood vessel disease.

LUNG DISEASE

Because aerobic exercise improves the efficiency of breathing, it is of value in treating some patients with pulmonary emphysema.

This ailment, frequently related to smoking, is now reaching epidemic proportions in the United States. Since it progressively deprives the patient of lung capacity it is important for him to adequately utilize whatever lung capacity he has remaining. Aerobics helps to accomplish this by increasing the ability to move air in and out of the lungs, by improving oxygen distribution throughout the body, and by providing for more efficient oxygen extraction in the tissues.

At Wilford Hall Hospital we have seen several emphysema patients who had been almost completely incapacitated by their disease restored to a level of competence which enabled them to lead productive lives. One of these patients is now able to walk a mile in 16 minutes.

MISCELLANEOUS MEDICAL PROBLEMS

The broad applicability of exercise therapy, and of aerobics in particular, rests on the fact that such exercise affects the total organism by improving the circulation and oxygen supply to both diseased and normal tissues, by increasing muscle tone and strength, and by decreasing body fat deposits.

In diabetes, for example, the reduction of fat through exercise apparently is a change which improves the body's ability to handle sugar. As a result, some diabetic patients (particularly those with adult onset diabetes) have been able to reduce their insulin requirement after starting a regular exercise program.

I have repeatedly pointed to the fact that exercise is a natural relaxant. This alone is highly beneficial in many clinical conditions. Ulcer patients, for example, probably owe their improvement to the fact they become less tense and nervous. Likewise, chronic insomniacs find that exercise relieves their anxieties and induces healthy fatigue.

The reduction of anxiety through exercise also is helpful in treating some patients with emotional problems.

We know from psychological testing that a patient's self-image improves as the result of systematic exercise. This in itself may be a great help in treating certain emotional problems.

Several psychiatrists have reported good results using

exercise as an adjunct to therapy in patients with certain psychiatric problems, particularly states of mild depression. One of my psychiatric correspondents expressed the thought that a "physically fit patient responds more readily to psychotherapy."

Exercise has recently been employed in the treatment of chronic alcoholics in clinics in Sweden. The initial observations are encouraging, but it is too early to draw conclusions.

A few readers of *Aerobics* claimed that exercise helped, and in some cases, relieved them of their problem with migraine headaches. I can't scientifically document such a statement and therefore report it only as an observation.

The embarrassing problem of incontinence (passing urine when coughing or sneezing) frequently occurs in women after several pregnancies. Some women have written claiming that this condition either disappeared or improved in response to exercise. Apparently the improvement in muscle tone through walking and running enabled these women to regain better control over their bladders.

Many older people have informed me that the arthritis in their legs and back improved with aerobic training. To the contrary, others claim that their arthritis was aggravated by exercise. So the evidence for the beneficial effect of aerobics is still inconclusive.

The whole field of exercise therapy is now in a state of transition from faddism to scientific legitimacy. Hardly a month passes without the publication of a significant new report on the numerous medical applications of exercise. As research expands, I hope that it will be possible to formulate specific aerobic routines for a variety of therapeutic uses.

9: Mostly About Women

I TEND TO disagree with the fellow who first remarked that "beauty is only skin-deep." Quite to the contrary, I believe that beauty in a woman is a reflection of her total well-being, of her basic health and vitality.

It depends, of course, on what you mean by beauty. At one time in our history, it was considered very elegant for a woman to look as though she were in imminent danger of physical collapse. Later on beauty grew more robust. A good-looking woman was supposed to be "pleasantly plump," (her plumpness size) being regarded as a sign of prosperity and good social standing.

Today's ideas are different. The emancipation of women in the twentieth century has given rise to a new ideal of feminine beauty. Today we admire women whose appearance shows that they are competent and capable—women with lean but strong bodies moving with the natural grace of a healthy creature.

This kind of beauty is definitely not just skin-deep. It involves posture, gait, and personality—it is the assurance and the glow that springs from fitness, alertness, and high spirits.

Feminine appeal, of course, is something every man judges for himself. But many, I think, will agree with me that a trim shape and graceful movement add as much to a girl's attractiveness as a pretty face. What really counts is charm—that subtle mixture compounded of both physical and mental attributes that is reflected in stance, motion, manner and voice.

All this may seem a long way from aerobics, but really it isn't. Because exercise changes a person both physically and mentally, it directly affects those factors of physique and personality that are the secret of feminine charm.

I am not peddling miracles. Obviously, exercise alone cannot completely transform you and your personality but, quite aside from physical improvements, exercise may help you to gain self-confidence and give you a feeling of calm complaisance. Granted, exercise cannot—and should not—make you a basically different person. But it can—and should—help you make the most of what you have and what you are.

The kind of personal attractiveness that comes from fitness and health is by no means confined to young women only. When you see a woman of 50 looking like 30, or a woman of 60 looking—and acting—like 40, chances are that she is one of the growing number of middle-aged women who prolong their youthfulness by preventive health care including regular exercise. Their outward signs of age-defying youthfulness—the straight back, taut, smooth skin on face, neck, arms and legs, and supple muscle contours—are evidence that these women don't spend all their spare time sitting before a TV set, moping over their lost youth.

I recall with pleasure the exhilarating sight of a woman, well past 40, giving her daughter a hard time on the tennis court. Both were good players, but the older woman was faster on her feet. Repeatedly rushing the net, she gained an advantage from her agility that enabled her to beat her daughter, who was less than half her age.

Later when she joined us on the club terrace, looking every bit as handsome and vigorous as her own daughter, I complimented her on her game. "Oh," she laughed, "nowadays parents have to keep up with their children."

That is an important point, in more than one way. I am convinced that if parents and their children found active companionship in sports, there would be less of a "generation gap." Shared physical activity is a common ground on which to build mutual understanding.

Recent medical research has given us new insights into the process of aging, and there is evidence indicating that premature aging is accelerated by inactivity. True, other factors are involved, especially heredity and diet. But physical stagnation due to lack of exercise seems to be a major factor in premature aging.

Aerobics therefore has a special significance for the older woman. By prolonging her good looks and vitality, aerobics can help a middle-aged woman attain what may well be her happiest years.

WEIGHT AND FIGURE

Even more than men, women have fallen victims to our sedentary era. At one time, women got a fair amount of exercise just by working in the garden and walking to the grocery store. Few women today tend a kitchen garden; the vegetables are frozen, and you order them by phone.

This avoidance of physical effort extends to every phase of life. Since two-car families are now the suburban rule, the only walking many women do is in parking lots. And city women tell me that, times being what they are, they find it safer not to go out after working hours. Increasingly, women have been deprived of walking and other natural forms of exercise. No wonder so many of them gain weight and lose their figures.

Modern women, therefore, have a particular need of a systematic exercise program, and aerobics has helped countless women take off extra pounds and inches.

Of all the women who have told me of their experience with aerobics, Bertha Whitson is my favorite. She lived in our neighborhood and everyone noticed her, but not in the way a woman likes to be noticed.

Bert was 5′ 2″ and had a sweet and pretty face. Few people ever looked at it. They were too busy staring at—or away from—her excessively overweight frame.

Bert read about aerobics in the *Reader's Digest*. Realizing the need for a change, she asked her physician about starting into an exercise program.

After making sure that her obesity was not due to a medical problem, he said: "What you need is a combination of both diet and exercise. The diet gets rid of excess weight. And the exercise keeps you from gaining it right back after you stop dieting."

Bert was willing to try anything. She went on a moderate diet and began exercising with a kind of brave determination I have rarely seen in anyone.

At first she could hardly move. Running was out of the question. Her thighs were so thick that it was difficult for her to move her legs back and forth in a straight line.

Yet despite these handicaps, and the enormous effort they entailed, Bert started walking every day. Gradually she increased the distance she walked. By the end of six months, she was walking ten miles a day—five miles during the morning, and another five miles in the evening.

Her daily route led her past the football field of the local high school, where her regular appearance was eagerly awaited by some ungentlemanly young athletes who hooted at her laborious progress. But after a few weeks, the boys' attitude changed. Something in Bert's undaunted persistence won their respect. "I felt like a turtle in a turtle race," recalls Bert, "what with all the bystanders cheering and egging me on."

Bystanders weren't the only ones cheering for Bert. Her husband was delighted by both the physical and emotional changes in her. Within one year of daily walking and moderate dieting she lost 50 pounds. Instead of size 18, she now wears size ten. Once again, her husband saw the small, graceful girl he had married.

Not only did she regain her looks; her former sprightliness and good humor returned also. This change of mood partly reflected her pride in her own accomplishment, and the pleasure any woman feels in being physically attractive. But her high spirits also stemmed from the fact that regular exercise gave her more energy.

"I never really lived through the day, when I was so heavy," Bert admits. "I just dragged myself through it. By the time my husband came home at night, I was exhausted and disgusted. Now I have the energy to feel alive in the evening. And I'm better company for my husband."

I never think of Bert as just a case history. I'm frankly touched by this woman's determination. If there were more like her there would be a lot more happy women and happy families in this country.

My own wife, Millie, also relies on aerobics to keep in condition and to keep her shape. Looking at her now—a trim 5'5", 120 pounds—nobody would believe she ever had a weight problem. But she likes Southern style cooking, and has a yen for second helpings. Not surprisingly, she tended to be a little heavier than she wanted to be—by about fifteen pounds or so.

Being a tidy person with a natural concern about her appearance, Millie used to go on crash diets, eating only dry salads and hardboiled eggs, with nothing for breakfast except a cup of black coffee. By such a drastic means, she'd drop in weight fairly rapidly.

Then she'd get ravenously hungry, quit her diet and gain it all back. Exercise, I knew, could help her with her problem. I asked her to start jogging with me, but with my longer stride and better physical condition, I usually got far ahead of her. I had to give myself a handicap. We finally hit on the idea of taking our young daughter along with us. Pushing her in the stroller slowed me down enough so Millie could keep up and it gave me an excellent work out!

Five times a week we jogged, alternately walking and running, up to 1.5 miles. At first, Millie would run only on the downhill stretches, walking the remainder of the way. But gradually, as she got into condition, the walking segments got shorter and shorter. Now she runs the entire distance, and covers the 1.5 miles in just over 12 minutes. This earns her 6 points per run or 30 points per five-day week.

She's eating normally now—with second helpings. But thanks to the exercise, she doesn't put on weight. She's particularly pleased that exercise accomplished what diet alone never could: taking inches off her hips and thighs.

It also reduced her resting heart rate. One night, before Millie started exercising, we counted each other's heart beat just before going to sleep. Mine was 45 beats per minute. Hers was 85.

"I don't want to wear out so much faster than you do!" she said.

Actually, there is no medical evidence that a person has a fixed number of heartbeats per lifetime and that a faster pulse uses up his quota that much sooner. Yet there is no doubt that a slower resting heart rate is less work for the heart.

At any rate, after Millie began exercising regularly, her resting heart rate dropped to less than 60. Her attitude toward exercise is different from mine. I enjoy it. She doesn't. But she keeps at it just the same.

"I still don't really like running," she confessed to me not long ago. "I just look at it as something I do for my health. Like brushing my teeth."

"You mean you don't get any pleasure from it at all?" I asked.

"Oh, sure," she replied. "Every step of the way I think

how I'm going to fit into that size eight dress and how good that cherry pie is going to taste."

Some women go on crash diets to lose weight, but from a medical viewpoint this is certainly not advisable. With a crash diet, which is basically a form of fasting, you may lose as much muscle as fat. True, it takes off pounds and inches, but it certainly doesn't contribute to your fitness. To the contrary, on such a strict diet you'll soon notice the onset of weakness and fatigue.

Yet a moderate diet combined with exercise lets you lose fat and weight while at the same time it strengthens your muscles. And by increasing your aerobic capacity you gain new energy reserves as you reduce. Instead of feeling weak and nervous as a result of your diet, the addition of exercise makes you feel fit and vigorous.

Women are usually surprised when I tell them that exercise also can change their shape even without changing their weight. It lets them take off inches without taking off pounds.

"How can you get smaller without getting lighter?" they ask. The answer is that exercise changes the fat–muscle ratio. Since muscle tissue is a lot more dense than fat, the same weight takes up less space.

While most women use aerobics to take off inches, I know of at least one who put on some inches just where she wanted them.

"I didn't like the looks of my bird legs," writes Mrs. Martha Frank from Lake Village, Arkansas. "I wanted a pair of legs I wouldn't have to hide in slacks.

"So, I started on a running program—on a seldom used blacktop road near the house and barn. I'm 43 years old, and now my family calls me 'Supersport.' I had a little trouble at first with sore arches, but now I'm doing 1.5 miles in 14 minutes and 30 seconds and hope to work my way up into the top fitness category.

"I knew I needed the exercise. I spend most of my time sitting in the truck, driving to cattle auctions—and on weekends sitting at the desk doing the paper work. It made a great difference in the way I feel. And, oh yes, those legs really shaped up. . . ."

Most women frankly admit that they exercise mainly for the sake of their looks. "It makes you feel just fantastic," writes one of my correspondents, "to receive flattering remarks about your youthful looking figure."

Vanity? Not really. The way a woman looks has a great deal to do with the way she feels—and how others feel about her. It's not just a matter of catching or keeping a husband. The attitude of other women toward her, her effectiveness in the community, her chances in a career, even the respect of her children depend to some degree on her appearance. Perhaps it is unfortunate that a woman's total personality is so strongly linked to her appearance. Yet, undeniably, it's part of our culture. Every woman senses it. So to be concerned about her figure is not just vanity but solid good sense.

The way it works out, women earn a double payoff from aerobics: they go on the program to improve their looks, and they get fitness and health as fringe benefits.

PREGNANCY AND AFTER

The greatest physical challenge the average woman faces during her life is childbearing. Far too many women are unprepared for the muscular strain of pregnancy and childbirth. By toning up the abdominal and back muscles, aerobics enables women to carry and deliver their infants more easily and swiftly regain their figures afterward. Besides, the overall improvement of health may have a favorable effect on the child's prenatal development. And it may reduce the danger of circulatory and cardiac complications for the mother.

The muscular conditioning obtained through aerobics also helps avoid some of the painful aftereffects of pregnancy and childbirth.

"Oh, my aching back!" is one of the most common complaints a doctor hears from women after pregnancy and childbirth. Even very young mothers often suffer severe and chronic back pains.

In an article published in the *Journal of the American Medical Association*, it was reported that a lack of exercise in women 18–23 years of age was a frequent cause of backache following pregnancy.

Ideally, a woman should be in good condition before the onset of pregnancy. But she can start into an exercise program during pregnancy, if she consults her obstetrician. She may have a condition that would make exercise inadvisable. Normally it is possible for women to continue their regular aerobic exercise program up to the sixth month of pregnancy. After that, exercise should be less strenuous. A simple walking program may be the most suitable during the last three months.

Of course, there are exceptions to every rule. One of my correspondents in Ann Arbor, Michigan, kept right on jogging throughout her pregnancy. "Even during the ninth month," she writes, "I kept up my daily routine. A 12-minute morning jog, and another 12 minutes jogging late in the evening. All with my obstetrician's approval, of course.

"As a result I felt absolutely marvelous all through my pregnancy and had no difficulty keeping my weight down. My doctor wanted me to do this because he was considering the possibility of a Caesarean section.

"The Caesarean section was not necessary and due to the jogging, I still have my waistline and a flat tummy—not the deflated beach ball I thought I'd end up with."

And then she ended her letter with an amusing comment. "But you know what, Dr. Cooper?—my baby seems to have an unusual fondness for being bounced on the knee!"

Even if your obstetrician decides that exercise is not advisable for you during pregnancy, he will probably permit you to resume exercise after the birth of your child. Any of the aerobic conditioning programs will tone up slack muscles, and help give you your old shape back.

MEN AND WOMEN—THE DIFFERENCE

Whatever may be said of women's hearts in other respects, medically speaking they have less of a problem with coronary disease than men—at least before the age of 40. Coronary heart disease is rare in women of childbearing age. After menopause, though, women begin to lose this advantage. Consequently, a woman's exercise program should be geared to this natural timetable.

This brings us to the difference in exercise requirements for women as compared with men. Since younger women are somewhat immune to heart and blood vessel disease, they do not share a man's need for aerobics as a basic life preserver. Consequently, they don't need to build up as many points as men. Probably, 20–24 points per week is enough. But after menopause, when women begin to lose their natural resistance to cardiovascular disease, they should definitely work up to at least 24 points per week to gain the full preventive effect.

The distance requirements for the 12-minute test for women (page 30) are based on accumulating 24 points per week. With this level of activity, the age adjusted requirements should be achieved easily.

CALISTHENICS FOR WOMEN

Calisthenics develop certain qualities of special interest to women, particularly graceful coordination of movement. For younger women I frequently suggest the addition of calisthenics to their aerobic routine. With calisthenics enhancing the grace of movement and aerobics providing basic fitness and reserve energy, it's a winning combination.

Of the many kinds of calisthenics, I particularly recommend five basic exercises that have been developed for women members of the United States Marine Corps:

1. *Trunk circling:* Stand with your legs apart and twist the upper part of your body alternately to the left and the right, rotating mainly from the waist.

2. *Toe touching:* with your legs fairly close together, bend from the waist to touch your toes with outstretched arms. If you cannot reach all the way down with your knees straight, bend your knees slightly.

3. *Side leg-raise:* Lie on the floor on your side and raise the leg from the hip, then lower it again. Repeat about ten times, then turn to the other side and raise and lower the other leg ten times.

4. *Sit-ups:* Lie on the floor, on your back, with your knees bent. Raise the trunk to a sitting position without the help of arms, then lie down again *slowly.* Start with about ten repetitions. (Sit-ups are traditionally attempted with legs stretched out flat against the floor. I advise against this because the stress on the knees and back may cause pain and even injury. It is far safer to bend the knees slightly during sit-up exercises.)

5. *Side bends:* Stand with your feet apart and extend your arms above your head with fingertips touching. Bend slowly sideways from the waist as far as possible. Keep your arms straight and don't bend your elbows. Remain bent sideways for several seconds. Then straighten up and make a similar bend to the other side, again remaining in a bent position for a few seconds.

Working up to 20 repetitions of each of these five forms of calisthenic, in combination with aerobic exercise, will give younger women an optimum exercise blend.

I have been asked why I specifically recommend calisthenics for women but not for men. Some people draw the inference that I am against calisthenics for men. This is definitely not so. A man may gain from calisthenics the same benefits as a woman. Also, he tends to build certain muscles that otherwise might not be fully developed. But what men need most—heart protection and overall fitness—calisthenics alone can't provide.

Put it this way: Calisthenics are fine as long as they are done *in addition to* rather than *in place of* one of the primary aerobics exercises.

SPECIAL PROBLEMS

Women often ask whether they should exercise during their menstrual period. It depends on the individual case. Women suffering from cramps find exercise extremely uncomfortable. Common sense alone tells them to skip exercise during those days. But, in principle, there is no reason why a woman should stop exercising during her menstrual period, except when it proves painful.

Women frequently develop painful or swollen muscles and joints in response to jogging or stationary running. One possible reason is that in their younger years they do not engage in sports as regularly as men. As a result, their muscles may not be adequately prepared for vigorous aerobic conditioning.

But this problem does not usually persist. After a few days of light exercise or complete rest, the pain tends to disappear. In those rare cases where muscle pains persist with exercise, the best thing to do is simply prolong the conditioning program. Progress very slowly. If necessary, repeat each week so that the muscles get a better chance to adapt themselves to the increasing work load. Another possibility is to alternate different kinds of exercise. Suppose your ankles get sore after stationary running. Switch to cycling for a while to give your ankles a different kind of workout. This enables you to continue your progressive aerobic program without aggravating a joint problem.

Some of the special problems encountered by women aren't physical at all. They're purely a matter of attitude. One of the WAF's in the Air Force aerobics test project seemed obviously reluctant during the daily workouts I supervised. When I asked her about this she responded with a pleasant smile: "It's not ladylike to run!"

"Well, is it ladylike for a woman to participate in any type of exercise?" I asked her.

The point I was trying to get through her pretty head is that outmoded notions of femininity just no longer apply. In an age when young women may join military organizations, win Olympic medals, and compete with men on terms of equality in almost any field, we had better get rid of our notions about what's ladylike and what isn't. I can't imagine why healthful exercise should be considered improper or unsuitable.

In the course of administering aerobics programs, I've seen women as eager and determined as any man in pursuit of physical fitness. Yet I have also observed that some women have a talent for self-pity. They slow down as soon as the exercise gets the least bit strenuous. This ruins any accurate comparison between field and laboratory testing. Specifically, the field test/treadmill correlation for women was only 0.57 as compared with 0.9 for men. Again, it appears to be a matter of motivation and attitude.

I know of at least one woman who certainly has no motivation problems and who has done more than anyone to dispel the myth that women can't do as well as men when it comes to athletics. In the sports world, she is known as Super Sue. Her real name is Susan Bailey, 25 years old, and mother of two children. Her hobby is long-distance running.

Sue has run as far as 38 miles nonstop. In 1968, she entered the national YMCA 3000-mile marathon as the only girl in the 24-man 1-woman team from her home town of Canton, Ohio. The Canton team dropped their national record from 6.5 days to a phenomenal 4.5 days, and Sue contributed 208 miles to the 3000 mile total—the third highest contribution made by any individual team member.

You would think that a woman of this kind would look tough and musclebound. But when I show pictures of Sue at my lectures, there is always an appreciative "Ah!" from the audience. No wonder—for Sue is as pretty and graceful a girl as you will ever see—living proof that sports and true feminine charm go well together.

Since most exercise research has been conducted on men, we still do not have quite enough information on the special needs and problems of exercising women. I would be grateful for any data my readers can contribute on the subject of fitness testing and exercise programs for women.

OVER 40

That life begins at 40 is hardly true. But it certainly doesn't stop there either. I wish more women could convince themselves that the age of 40, or 50, or 60, is not some magic dividing line beyond which nothing good ever happens.

Modern medicine can successfully deal with many of the physical symptoms of aging, minimizing their discomfort. Just within the past few years great strides have been made in this area, and exercise is of considerable importance to a woman who wants to keep young regardless of age.

Quite aside from the physical benefits of exercise, postmenopausal women get a special psychological lift from a regular exercise program. Too often women in that age group suffer a kind of melancholy or mental slump. They go into a depression, becoming cranky and difficult to live with.

I have seen such women improve remarkably through regular exercise. Just why aerobics has the effect of a psychological tonic, I cannot say with scientific precision. But the final effect is obvious. Physical well-being due to regular exercise, plus awareness of improved appearance, evidently gives a needed lift to a woman's mental attitude.

I encountered a striking example of this when we asked the wives of some retired military personnel to join in an aerobics program at our laboratory. About two months after the start of this project I received a visit from a retired officer. He came right to the point and said simply: "I want to thank you for really helping our marriage."

His wife, he told me, had become quite erratic at the age of 48, suffering unpredictable emotional ups and downs. "One day she'd feel all keyed up—all smiles and chatter. The next day she'd sulk and hardly say a word. Sometimes she'd have sudden bitter outbursts, complaining how our lives had been wasted, and how I had robbed her of every chance of happiness. She had illusions of poverty, even though we live quite comfortably. Then she'd go out on a spending spree. She even started interfering in the married lives of our two children. The whole thing was irrational. I didn't know how to deal with it, but I knew it couldn't go on that way."

Then came the turning point. A friend told her about our aerobics club for women. Prompted by her feelings of loneliness, the woman probably would have joined any group that asked her. Luckily, this happened to be just what she needed. Under the stimulus of regular exercise, a set goal, new companions and, above all, improved physical health, she regained her emotional balance. "I think it occurred without her realizing what was happening," her husband said. "She simply went back to normal."

I am not saying that aerobics can be relied on as a cure for emotional disturbances. Obviously, most situations of this type need psychiatric treatment. I am merely reporting an observation: Some women suffering post-menopausal depression have been greatly helped by participation in a regular exercise program.

In one respect, older women should practice special caution during exercise. After menopause, they frequently suffer a condition known as osteoporosis. This causes loss of calcium from the bones, making them brittle. Consequently, older women are more likely to suffer bone fractures. I therefore caution older women about stationary running or rope skipping since these exercises put high stress on the bones of the foot and lower leg.

INDOOR EXERCISE

Women often are housebound. They have to watch the kids, clean the house, cook, do the washing and wait for the delivery man. Their chances to go outdoors for exercise are often limited, and quite aside from the restriction of climate, many women hesitate to go out running in the street.

"People think I'm crazy. They gawk at me," complains a Baltimore housewife who tried jogging around her neighborhood. In contrast to European cities, our own metropolitan areas suffer a drastic shortage of safe, usable parkland and walking paths. As a result, many people—especially women —depend on indoor exercise to earn aerobic points.

Women also like indoor exercise because they can do it without really having to concentrate on it. "I do my stationary running right in front of the TV set," writes an Idaho girl. "That way I get my points, I'm entertained, and the time passes rapidly."

Among the most efficient indoor exercises are stationary running, skipping rope, climbing stairs, stationary cycling and running on a treadmill. A few brief comments on these exercises now, and then I will discuss them in more detail in Chapter Ten.

STATIONARY RUNNING

To avoid foot and ankle trouble, wear cushioned-soled shoes and run on a soft surface, preferably on a thick rug. Pick your knees up in front lifting your feet at least 8 inches off the floor and run at the rate of 80–90 steps per minute. If that seems too fast for you, try 70–80 steps.

To check your speed, count every time your left foot hits the floor. Do this for 15 seconds, then multiply by 4. This gives you your step-per-minute figure.

Some women like to do their stationary running in time to music. It helps keep the rhythm steady and reduces boredom. The trick is finding a record with the proper beat and one that maintains a steady rhythm for a long enough period. There are some jogging records on the market that can be used very effectively in a stationary running program.

ROPE SKIPPING

In some ways, rope skipping is an ideal indoor exercise. It not only gives you the same aerobic benefits as stationary running, but it also provides additional exercise for the muscles of arms, shoulders, and upper torso. This may help to improve a woman's appearance, by toning up the muscles in the arms, shoulders and chest, giving added support to the bust.

What's more, rope skipping is not as likely to cause ankle and leg pain and swelling as stationary running because it lessens the impact of the feet against the floor.

You can skip rope in four different ways: 1) jumping with both feet together; 2) alternating left and right foot; 3) jumping up and down on one leg only; 4) stepping over the rope, one foot at a time.

My recommendation is to use modes one and two. Of course, rope skipping can be done at widely different speeds, from a very slow rate to the fast routine used by professional boxers as part of their conditioning. I recommend about 70–80 steps per minute—the same rate as in stationary running.

Under these conditions, rope skipping has the same point value as stationary running.

STAIR CLIMBING

"Who do you suppose earns more aerobic points: a woman who keeps running up and down the first three steps of her staircase for five minutes or a woman who runs up and down several flights of stairs for the same length of time?"

I threw that question at one of my lab assistants as a teaser. His answer was absolutely correct: the woman running only three steps at a time earns more points. The woman running up and down several flights of stairs loses some of the aerobic benefit because the down trip allows her body time to recover. The three-step course provides more continuity of effort—an essential factor in earning aerobic points.

The point value of stair climbing as well as the use of stationary bicycles, self-propelled and motorized treadmills will be discussed in detail in Chapter Ten.

While it is usually women who are chiefly interested in indoor exercise, there's no reason why men can't join them.

Certainly one of the most important things a woman can do for her husband is to motivate him to join her in regular exercise. Just recently, I received a letter from a Wisconsin housewife describing such a joint venture.

"I love my husband," she writes, "and I want to keep him with me as long as possible—that's why I persuaded him to exercise with me. During the winter we can't run outdoors. So we laid out a track in our basement: Sure, it's short. It takes 80 laps to the mile. But when my husband and I do it together, it's fun."

In their domestic lives, women often become the victims of routine. Many of them lack the challenges that men face in their work. For a woman whose home is her career, the years can become a long, losing battle against boredom. Aerobics has proved to be a turning point in the lives of many such women. Getting on the program marks for them the point of a new departure. They shed boredom and become alert and responsive again. The vitality women gain from upgrading their fitness sometimes opens the door to many other interests, giving their whole existence new dimensions of meaning.

A POSTSCRIPT ON CHILDREN

Every mother teaches her children how to wash, brush their teeth, and perform other habits of personal care and hygiene. Training children to exercise is just as vital to their future health.

In this respect, we, as a nation, don't do a very good job in bringing up our children. Physical fitness is widely neglected by the younger generation, as proved by the rejection rate from the armed forces. As much as 40 percent of all eligible draftees don't measure up to the minimum fitness standards for military service. In terms of national health, this is clearly an emergency situation. Early parental teaching of the value of exercise would be a most effective countermeasure.

Little is yet known about the specific exercise needs of children in the six to 16 age group, and I am trying to obtain additional information in this field. I shall be grateful to any parent, grade school teacher, or junior high school athletics instructor, who can provide me with pertinent observations regarding 12-minute or other field test data, particularly before and after a conditioning program.

Yet some basic facts have been uncovered. Dr. Ernst Jokl, director of the Exercise Research Laboratories of the University of Kentucky, tested 4000 children aged six to 18, by checking their performance in a 600-yard run. He found that girls reach maximum fitness during puberty, but soon lose it again unless their fitness level is maintained by exercise. This may account for the fact that girl swimmers of Olympic caliber are usually in their early teens.

Boys achieve a high-level endurance capacity between the ages of 18 and 21. Not surprisingly, our fastest milers are young men in this age bracket. Marathon champions are usually a little older—24–28 years of age.

Even very young children are sometimes capable of surprising feats of endurance. For example, at the Dipsia Marathon, a 6.8-mile race held annually in California, a five-year-old girl entered the race and finished a very respectable 441st among 900 entries. Among the adult contestants outrun by the little girl were both her parents.

However, I do not advise any kind of endurance exercise for children before the age of six. If such small children enjoy the simpler forms of calisthenics, they might practice them for a few minutes each day. This will give them agility and coordination. Especially if they are encouraged to do these simple exercises while their mother does her aerobics, children form a positive attitude toward physical training. They learn early in life that fitness can be fun.

From the age of six onward, children may participate in low-level aerobic exercise, though the quantitative norms for small children yet remain to be worked out. Running, cycling and swimming are excellent for children, but parents should see to it that children do not exhaust themselves in such activities. Often their abundant energy tempts children beyond their endurance. A parent's common sense should be a safeguard against overexertion.

EXERCISE AT SCHOOL

For children of school age, regular exercise should be part of their school curriculum. In October 1968, the American Academy of Pediatrics issued a set of guidelines for athletics for elementary school children. It is an excellent paper which I strongly recommend to school principals and physical education teachers. In particular, I agree with the academy's objection to competitive team sports for young children. Too much emotional stress is associated with such competition. In particular, the Academy cautions against "undesirable corollaries to organized competitive athletics, such as excessive publicity, pep squads, commercial promoting, victory celebrations, paid admissions, inappropriate spectator behavior, high-pressure public contests and exploitation of children in any form."

The child should learn to enjoy sports and exercise for their own sake—not for commercial or competitive reasons.

The importance of regular exercise in school has been shown by the fact that California school children have enjoyed a much higher fitness level than children from most other states. This was probably attributable to the fact that they had a state law requiring a scheduled daily exercise for students in all grades. Unfortunately, in 1968, the law was modified to allow more flexibility in scheduling of exercise periods, eliminating the mandatory daily requirement.

A high school science teacher of my acquaintance once told me that, in his experience, youngsters active in athletics tend to do better in their classwork. I knew that he himself was an avid sports fan, and so I dismissed his observation as a reflection of his own attitudes and prejudices. To imply that school athletics were directly beneficial to academic work seemed a little far-fetched.

Yet several studies with high school and college students have shown that those students who are more physically fit consistently make better grades. It isn't realistic to believe that physically fit students are more intelligent. But that they are probably more alert and receptive may be the reason that they make better grades.

In view of this apparent link between physical and mental achievement, it is all the more regrettable that our school systems offer so little in the way of physical conditioning.

"Many children in the United States," says Dr. Stanley L. Harrison of the American Academy of Pediatrics, "although healthy and well-nourished, are still in relatively poor physical condition simply because they live in a civilization on wheels. They ride to school in the bus or the family car.

And physical education in school too often consists of just a softball game, which provides a minimum of strenuous exertion."

This is an area where parents, and mothers in particular, can make their influence felt. Through organizations like the PTA, they can insist on properly managed exercise programs in the schools, especially at the grade school and junior high school level. A young mother in Houston wrote to tell me she was running for the school board and one of her campaign promises was to replace baseball in grade school with aerobics exercise. More power to her!

No school program, however well conceived, can in itself offset the damaging influence on a child of our physically passive way of life. It's clearly up to the family, and the mother in particular, to bring up the children with a keen awareness of the physical requirements of a healthful life. She can do a great service to her children by implanting the idea that exercise is not just "something you have to do" but a lifelong source of pleasure.

10: Indoor Exercising

WITH THE WIDESPREAD lack of public recreation facilities in our cities, our inadequate parks, crowded sidewalks, and the absence of walking paths or country lanes suitable for extended walking or running, I often hear the complaint, "I just don't have any place to exercise." Usually this is followed by the question, "What can I do in my own home?"

I have received hundreds of letters with questions related to home exercise: How many points can I earn by stationary cycling? Must I subtract point value for walking on a self-propelled treadmill? Does it make any difference if the treadmill is set at an incline? And—the most commonly asked question on indoor exercise—How many points for walking up a flight of stairs?

The purpose of this chapter is to deal with questions of this kind and to help you plan an aerobics conditioning program you can complete without ever leaving your home.

STATIONARY RUNNING (MODIFIED)

One of the basic indoor aerobics exercises is stationary running. It has, however, several drawbacks. It is hard on the ankles, and most people find it boring. Consequently, they are looking for variations in this tedious routine.

You might, to add variety to your exercise program, use a single step—preferably a cushioned step to prevent slipping. Start with both feet on the floor and step up, bringing boht feet onto the step (one after the other—do not jump), then return your feet to the floor, one at a time. Do this rapidly, at the rate of 30–40 full cycles per minute. The aerobic point value for this type of exercise is as follows:

POINT VALUE FOR EXERCISE USING A SINGLE STEP
(Approximately 7 inches in height)

Stepping Rate (per Min)	Time (Min)	Points
30	6:30	1½
	9:45	2¼
	13:00	3
35	6:00	2
	9:00	3
	12:00	4
40	5:00	2½
	7:30	3¾
	10:00	5

Another variant of stationary running is to use three steps and run up and down the steps, turning around at the top so that you always face forward. Do this at the rate of about 20 complete trips per minute. The point value for this exercise is roughly equivalent to the point value for stationary running at a rate of 70–80 steps per minute. At a rate of 25–30 complete trips per minute, it is equivalent to stationary running at 80–90 steps per minute.

STAIR CLIMBING (AEROBICALLY)

"On my way to work, I walk up several flights of stairs every morning. It takes me about two minutes. How many points do I get?"

My questioner was quite disappointed when I told him that he gets no points at all. Even walking eight to ten flights or more doesn't really help to condition the cardiovascular system because the time interval is too short. True, it may leave you breathless—because you have built up a big oxygen debt during your climb. But the climb just didn't last long enough for the training effect to set in.

Yet there is a way to make good use of a single flight of stairs for aerobic conditioning. Making complete trips up and down that flight can be an excellent way to earn aerobic points. You can even carry some weight with you to increase the point value of this exercise.

For people who find this a convenient exercise method, I have developed the following point-value charts for stair-climbing with and without a load.

POINT VALUE FOR STAIR CLIMBING USING A SINGLE FLIGHT OF STAIRS

(10 Steps; 6–7 inches in height; 25–30° incline)

Round trips (Average Number per Min)	Duration (Min)	Points Without Load	Points (With 10 lb. Load)
6	6:30	1½	2
	9:45	2¼	3
	13:00	3	4
7	6:00	2	2½
	9:00	3	3¾
	12:00	4	5
8	5:30	2½	3
	8:15	3¾	4½
	11:00	5	6
9	4:30	2¾	3¼
	6:45	4¼	4½
	9:00	5¾	6¾
10	4:00	3¼	3¾
	6:00	4¾	5½
	8:00	6½	7½

STATIONARY BICYCLES

These increasingly popular home exercise devices come in various price ranges with different design features.

1. Low cost models ($25–35): No brake resistance device, no speed or mileage indicator. Usually of limited value in aerobic conditioning programs since it is impossible to measure performance accurately enough to follow the progressive exercise charts.

2. Medium-cost models ($75–120): Equipped with speed and mileage indicators and brake resistance devices—everything you need to follow the aerobic charts accurately.

3 Moderately expensive models (about $350): In this category I should like to single out a Swedish exercise bicycle with speed and mileage indicators and a *calibrated* brake resistance device—excellent for either testing or conditioning programs.

4. Expensive models (about $650): These models are motor-driven. You don't supply the energy by pedaling. Hence they are of little value for aerobic conditioning unless you compensate for the work contributed by the motor. You can buy an auxiliary meter that shows how much energy you are expending.

5. Very expensive models (about $900): A stationary bicycle with built-in heart rate monitor and "electronic coach." This provides hills and valleys along the simulated ride by means of pre-programmed variations of brake resistance. You can watch your heart rate on a monitor, making sure that it does not go too high. This is an excellent bike for rehabilitation programs, gyms, YMCAs, and health clubs, though it may be too expensive for the average home user.

Whatever stationary bicycle you may buy, follow these rules as you use it in your aerobic conditioning program:

1. Cycle at an indicated speed of 15–20 miles per hour. Some bikes have a tachometer instead of a speedometer. In that case, keep a cycling rate of 60–80 rpm.

2. Watch your mileage indicator and cycle the distance specified in the charts for one of the progressive cycling programs (see Chapter Six). Generally, I recommend starting with the Category I program.

3. Add enough brake resistance so that immediately after the conclusion of the exercise your heart rate is slightly in excess of the age-adjusted rates given below:

Age (Years)	Heart Rate (beats per minute)
Under 30	160
30–34	155
35–39	150
40–44	145
45–49	145
50–54	140
55–59	140
60–64	135
65+	130

(To check your heart rate, count the beats for the first ten seconds after exercise and then multiply by six).

If you follow these simple rules, you can get on your bicycle and ride your way to physical fitness without ever leaving home.

TREADMILLS

Judging by my correspondence, there is even greater interest in treadmills than in stationary bicycles. As to your choice of a treadmill, again you have a variety of models in different price ranges:

1. Inexpensive ($99–285): These treadmills are muscle-powered and can be used effectively if you can learn to walk or run on them without holding on to the side rails. This may be difficult since the treadmills were not designed for this manner of use. Some models provide a built-in incline, which increases aerobic value, as I shall explain later.

2. Medium-priced ($385): A new model available in this price group is motor-driven with a speed selection of three, four, or five miles per hour, which covers the range of walking and slow jogging. Elevate the front end with blocks and you can operate the treadmill at an incline to earn more aerobic points. The design of this treadmill is very good.

3. Expensive ($1000–1500): Motor driven treadmills in this price range offer variable speeds up to 7–8 miles per hour, which is fast enough for most people. Also they provide a built-in adjustable incline. Such treadmills are highly effective indoor exercise devices.

4. Very expensive ($3500 or more): These are research models, similar to the one I use in my laboratory. The speed is variable from 1.5 to 25 miles per hour and the incline can be adjusted from zero to 40 percent. It is an excellent device but prohibitive in cost for the average home user.

Whatever treadmill you may buy, you must follow certain basic rules. Leave the treadmill at zero inclination and use either the Category I running or walking program and follow it exactly as if you were exercising outdoors. If you want to get more points, add some incline. As you can see from the chart below, walking or running up an incline is worth considerably more aerobic points than exercising with no incline.

POINT VALUE FOR WALKING AND RUNNING ONE MILE ON A
TREADMILL SET AT VARIOUS INCLINES

Treadmill Speed (MPH)	Mile Time (Min)	Incline (% grade)				
		0%	5%	10%	15%	
10	6:00	6	7	9	—	
7.5	8:00	5	6	7	10	
6	10:00	4	5	6	7	
5	12:00	3	4	5	6	Points
4.14	14:30	2	4	5	6	
3	20:00	1	1.5	2.5	3	
2.5	25:00	0	1	1.5	2	
		0°	3°	6°	9°	

Incline (degrees)

You can use a motorized treadmill in still another way, providing it is equipped with a speedometer. You leave your treadmill at zero incline and set it at a certain speed. Then stay on the treadmill at that speed for the required number of minutes. The point value of such exercise can easily be determined from the following chart:

POINTS FOR WALKING OR RUNNING ONE MILE ON A
MOTORIZED TREADMILL (No Incline)

Mile Time	Treadmill Speed	Points
6:00 Min	10 MPH	6
6:30 Min	9¼ MPH	6
7:00 Min	8½ MPH	5
7:30 Min	8 MPH	5
8:00 Min	7½ MPH	5
8:30 Min	7 MPH	4
9:00 Min	6⅔ MPH	4
9:30 Min	6⅓ MPH	4
10:00 Min	6 MPH	4
12:00 Min	5 MPH	3
13:30 Min	4½ MPH	2
15:00 Min	4 MPH	1
17:30 Min	3½ MPH	1
20:00 Min	3 MPH	1

If you prefer, you can even use a motorized treadmill for taking the 12-minute fitness test, providing you have an accurate speedometer. Set the treadmill at the required speed for a given fitness category, then see if you can stay on the treadmill for 12 minutes. If so, you know that you meet the requirements for that particular fitness category. For example, the following chart provides guidelines for the 12-minute fitness test for men under 30 years of age.

REQUIREMENTS FOR 12-MINUTE FITNESS TEST ON
MOTORIZED TREADMILL

(for men under 30 years of age)

Treadmill Speed	Time Endured on Treadmill	Fitness Category
5 MPH	less than 12 Min	I. Very Poor
5–6 MPH	12:00 Min	II. Poor
6¼–7¼ MPH	12:00 Min	III. Fair
7½–9 MPH	12:00 Min	IV. Good
Over 9 MPH	12:00 Min	V. Excellent

There is no inherent advantage in taking a fitness test on

the treadmill instead of running out in the open. But it does eliminate such difficulties as finding a track, measuring off the distance you cover in 12 minutes, and worrying about what the neighbors will think when they see you huffing and puffing down the road.

In this chapter, I have discussed some of the devices that may be used in an indoor aerobics program, or to augment an outdoor program when weather conditions or other circumstances make outdoor exercise impractical. There are other kinds of indoor exercise machines, but the ones mentioned here are the most efficient and the easiest to use.

It has been my observation, however, that many people who purchase expensive exercise equipment use it for only a short time and then store it, evidently preferring outdoor exercise (or no exercise at all). That is why, at the conclusion of this chapter, I want to reemphasize what I have said many times before: to practice aerobics you really don't need equipment of any kind.

11: I'm Glad You Asked Me . . .

QUESTIONS AND ANSWERS are one of the best ways to clear up areas of confusion. That's why, after a lecture, I usually invite questions from the audience. It is encouraging to see how many excellent and thought provoking questions are asked during these discussion periods.

From the thousands of questions posed by my lecture audiences and correspondents, I have picked a typical sampling. Some of them touch on basic principles of aerobic exercise, others on specific exercise problems; many are concerned with the point value of certain activities, the effect of smoking and drinking on fitness, the special requirements for athletes, and a variety of personal situations.

Despite the often personal character of these questions, I feel that they are of general interest. After all, it is the personal experience with exercise that puts basic principles in sharper focus, linking theory and practice.

BASIC PRINCIPLES

Q. I am 45 years old and have been working my way through the running conditioning program. But after about 12 weeks I hit a snag and still can't manage to reach 30 points per week. What should I do?

A. If you find that you cannot reach the 30-point-per-week level within the 16-week conditioning period suggested in the chart, just repeat the weekly assignment at whatever level you *can* reach. If necessary, lengthen the distance and increase the time to build up your point total. Remember it is possible to reach 30 points per week just by walking.

Q. You say that the vast majority of your test subjects respond to the 30-point per week routine and easily meet the minimum test requirement. Why don't the others respond?

A. One always has to allow for individual differences. However, most of those who failed to respond were handicapped by heavy smoking, obesity, or both. Some quit smoking and reduced their weight. After that, even they responded to the 30-point regimen and showed improved aerobic capacity.

Q. My brother and I are having an argument. He says it's speed that really counts in earning your points. I say the most important thing is the distance you cover. Who's right?

A. Neither. Aerobic points are earned by a combination of both factors. Concentrate on earning points, and don't worry about setting speed or distance records. As a general rule I advise against striving for speed, which increases strain and fatigue. You can earn your points more safely and more comfortably by exercising at a slower rate for a longer time.

Q. After a game of handball, my pulse checks out around 160. That's what you say it should be. But I still don't understand what pulse rate means in term of aerobics.

A. Two factors are essential in producing the aerobic training effect. The exercise must be 1) strenuous enough, and 2) long enough. Your pulse shows that your handball game is certainly strenuous enough.

In the average person under 30 years of age, a heart rate of 150 beats per minute means that he is working at about 60 percent of his maximum capacity. For young, healthy people, that's a good energy level for producing a training effect.

However, the training effect can be reached in other ways: you may either work for a short time at a high heart rate or you may work for a longer time at a slower heart rate. The following chart, in simplified form, shows some of the possible combinations which can be used in producing a training effect.

	Training Effect				
Daily Time Requirements (Min)	180	90	45	20	10
Working Capacity (% of Maximum)	20	30	40	50	60
Heart Rate (beats per min)	110	120	130	140	150

The longer exercise periods are more realistic for older people whereas the exercise for younger people can be harder and shorter.

Q. I've been lifting weights for many years. After pushing up a heavy bar, I can feel my heart pounding very fast. Does this mean that I'm getting an aerobic effect?

A. Weight lifting is an isotonic exercise, and even though it accelerates the heart rate, it has little aerobic effect. If you just strain against the heavy weight, you tense your muscles, but there is no rapid movement. Such static exercise does not increase blood flow. The heart beats under the strain, but the static muscles return little blood to the heart. Therefore, the fast beat does not produce greater blood flow volume. This deprives the exercise of its aerobic value.

You'd be better off to use light weights and push them up and down rapidly to create continuous movement. Even so, it would require at least 30–45 minutes of activity to yield any appreciable number of aerobic points. Weight lifting is fine for muscle building. But remember that muscle size and strength are not always indicative of aerobic fitness.

Q. I'm with you when you say that exercise should be a family affair. Fortunately, my whole family is crazy about bowling. We've got a regular bowling date twice a week and spend about two hours at the alley. How do we figure points for that?

A. Sorry to disappoint you. I realize that bowling is great fun, but from an aerobic viewpoint, it's of little value. When you swing the ball, you're doing intense muscular work. But that lasts only a few seconds. Then you stand around again, waiting for the strike, waiting for the second ball, or just waiting your turn. Out of the whole game you only get very few minutes of actual muscular effort, and even that is not continuous. That's why I can't award points for bowling.

Q. One of my favorite summer recreations is skulling, and I keep in condition during the cold months with an indoor rowing machine. Can I earn my aerobic points that way?

A. Indeed you can, at the rate of 1 point for every six minutes if you row at a rate of 20 strokes per minute with both oars. Remember, though, that rowing does not involve the legs extensively. Therefore, you might supplement your rowing with running, cycling, walking, etc. Whenever the weather permits.

Q. I'm 56, and my doctor says aerobics is too tough for a man of my age. Walking 20 minutes twice a day, he says, is all the exercise I need. What do you think?

A. Ask your doctor to look up the charts. He'll find that covering 1.5 miles in 21:30 minutes earns 3 points. Twice a day, five times a week, this adds up to 30 points. So it seems that your doctor suggests exactly what I suggest. If he'd figure it out according to the charts, he may find that aerobics isn't "too tough" after all.

SMOKING AND DRINKING

A surprising number of questions come from people worried about the effect of smoking and drinking on their physical fitness. I had a feeling that some of my questioners were looking for reassurance, hoping I'd tell them that smoking and drinking don't really matter. My answers must have disappointed them.

Q. I have been smoking for 15 years. I try to hold it down to a pack a day, but I can't quit. I know I may get cancer, emphysema, bronchitis, and whatnot. But right now I'm basically healthy. I don't have any of these ailments. So how does smoking limit my physical performance?

A. An athlete I know was asked why he quit smoking. His simple, direct answer, based on his personal experience, sums up the problem: "It cuts your wind."

Behind this simple fact lie some grim medical details. You consider yourself "basically healthy." Frankly, I doubt that there is such a thing as a basically healthy smoker. Even if lung cancer and other smoking-related diseases have yet to catch up with you, you are partially disabled as soon as you smoke your first pack. According to information compiled by the American Medical Association, just ten puffs of a cigarette increase resistance in the air pathways of the lungs. This choked-up condition persists for an hour after each smoke.

Your physical performance is affected when you smoke because the body loses some of its ability to transport oxygen from the lungs to the muscles. Carbon monoxide in cigarette smoke is a potent poison that rapidly enters the blood, combines with the hemoglobin in the red blood corpuscles and renders many of them incapable of carrying oxygen.

The lung capacity of habitual smokers gradually shrinks, the membranes of their air passages thicken and become less efficient in gas exchange. Moreover, the cilia (tiny hairlike structures acting as brooms to sweep out the windpipe and the bronchial tubes) become paralyzed by cigarette smoking. Without this natural defense, the lungs are vulnerable to airborne intruders, dust particles and other pollutants.

The total picture is this: Smoking creates the opposite effect from aerobics. It wrecks the body's ability to absorb and distribute oxygen.

Q. How can I, as a compulsive smoker, benefit from aerobics?

A. Smoking has been called slow suicide. It may take longer to kill yourself if aerobics is able to counteract some of the damage from smoking.

Q. Like the guy in the joke, I quit smoking—twice a week. Each time I try, I backslide. Can aerobics do anything for someone like me?

A. If you have a sincere desire to quit, aerobic conditioning can help you break the habit. Several reformed smokers tell me that aerobics helped them get rid of their craving for tobacco.

We still don't know for sure why this is so. It may be that regular exercise gives you a sense of positive achievement that bolsters your willpower. Very likely, the physical changes resulting from exercise also play a role in curing the habit. This area has yet to be explored.

Q. Everybody says alcohol and athletics don't mix. I like to keep in shape, but I also like a drink before dinner—a small one. Will this interfere with my fitness training?

A. It depends on your individual reaction. Some people can tolerate small amounts of alcohol without impairing their physical performance. Others find it impossible to get anywhere near their top performance with any alcohol intake, no matter how small. That is why many professional athletes refrain from alcohol for at least 36 to 48 hours before a sports event.

Since individual tolerance varies so greatly, it is difficult to set standards other than to say that abstinence is the only absolute way to assure no impairment in performance.

MAINLY FOR ATHLETES

Those preparing for competitive sports approach aerobics with a point of view different from those interested mainly in personal fitness. Their questions reflect this difference.

Q. Everyone on our team is sold on aerobics, we play soccer—and that takes a lot of running and endurance. But the head of our physical education department still believes that calisthenics is better for athletic conditioning. So which is it—calisthenics or aerobics?

A. Many college, university and professional athletic teams have asked me this question. I usually suggest an aerobics program supplemented by short-distance sprinting and calisthenics. An athlete so trained gains a blend of speed, coordination and endurance that gives him an edge in almost any sport.

Q. As a college athlete (track and basketball), I'm interested in building up my staying power for competition. How many points per week do you recommend for this purpose?

A. For athletic conditioning I suggest at least 50 points per week off-season and at least 100 points per week during the season. Many athletes in training do considerably more, earning up to 300 and 400 points per week.

Q. I timed myself for a quarter mile. Sixty-three seconds! How does this rate for fitness?

A. It doesn't. You're fast all right. But dash speed (anaerobics) is unrelated to basic fitness, for short bursts of energy are not indicative of heart-lung reserve. What counts is endurance (aerobics) which is a direct measure of heart-lung capacity. Take the 12-minute test or the 1.5 mile test and find out how fit you really are.

Q. I'm a pretty fast runner and worked my way up into Category V. Now I'd like to find out how I stack up in competition with people of my age. I'm not in college and don't belong to any sports club. Where could I find out?

A. Your best bet is to check with the National Jogging Association, P.O. Box 19367, Washington, D.C. 20036; the Mile-a-Thon International, c/o Long Beach Community Hospital, 1720 Termino Avenue, Long Beach, California, 90804; Road Runners Club of America, 1584 Spruce Drive, Kalamazoo, Michigan, 49005 or your local "Y." Chances are that one of them would know about amateur sports competitions in your area. An increasing number of communities are now organizing public "Run-for-Fun" programs. Perhaps you can join one of those. The best known event open to male competitors of all ages is the Boston Marathon, an annual 26-

mile race from Hopkinton to Boston, Massachusetts. Last year, more than a thousand people came to Boston from all over the world to join in.

Q. I go out for track at my high school, so I'm naturally interested in speed. But the aerobic charts don't list point values for fast running—nothing at all for a guy who breaks 5:00 minutes for a mile. Why don't you figure out points for fellows who are really fast on their feet?

A. I have not measured oxygen consumption or assigned aerobic points in that speed range because I consider it of very limited applicability. The charts are intended primarily for fitness training rather than competitive sports. Besides, I don't encourage high speed as a goal in running exercise— at any rate not for the general public. Speed makes massive demands on the heart that may be dangerous to older or deconditioned persons. As a rule I favor earning points in a less strenuous manner by running at a slower rate for a longer distance.

Q. As a basketball player, I use aerobics to build up my endurance. Some weeks I earn as many as 200 points. But at the end of a workout I sometimes get a strange feeling in my chest. It's not a pain. It just feels hollow, as if there were an empty space around my heart. Is that normal?

A. That hollow feeling in your chest is probably a premature ventricular contraction (PVC). It's a kind of extra heartbeat sandwiched into the regular heart rhythm. This is fairly common among athletes engaged in strenuous exercise. It's not dangerous as such, but it may be a sign that you are driving yourself too hard, and there is always a certain risk in getting close to the limit of your capacity. I'd suggest that you reduce the intensity of your exercise but first, let your family doctor evaluate you.

Q. I saw a TV commercial in which professional athletes endorsed a vitamin product. They claim vitamin C and E improve their performance. What is your opinion?

A. As yet, it has not been conclusively demonstrated that vitamin supplements beyond the daily minimum requirement have any effect at all on athletic performance. At the Squadron Officers School, Maxwell Air Force Base, Alabama, a test of vitamin C involved 286 men engaged in a 12-week vigorous conditioning program. Half of the men received ten times the daily requirement; the other half received no supplement to a normal diet. Everyone participated in games of flickerball, volleyball, and soccer and, in addition, they were tested on the 12-minute endurance test at the beginning and end of training. At the conclusion of the study, the two groups revealed no significant difference in athletic or endurance performance, the frequency of injuries, or the speed of recovery.

A similar research project on vitamin E is being contemplated, but so far the study has not been performed.

INDOOR EXERCISE

A surprising number of inquiries concern indoor exercise. Here are a few samples of more than routine interest.

Q. I exercise at home on a stationary bike. But mine doesn't have a speedometer or mileage counter. This makes it impossible for me to use the charts of the cycling program. Can you give me some other guidelines?

A. It may be possible for you to have a speedometer/ odometer installed on your stationary bike. But if not, you might try to do the following. Start with a 5:00 minute exercise period and add 1:00 minute per week until you work up to 20:00 minutes per day, six days per week. Continue to increase the brake resistance as your physical condition improves. Adjust the brake force so that at the end of each exercise period you feel moderately fatigued but not uncomfortably exhausted. By this I mean that your breathing should be back to normal and your heart rate 100 or less ten minutes after the exercise. If you cannot meet these requirements, adjust the bike for easier pedaling.

Q. I use a treadmill for indoor exercise, but I find that I have to hold on to the rails to keep my balance. I realize that grasping the rail lessens the aerobic effect. How many points should I deduct? I usually walk an 18-minute mile up a 15 percent incline.

A. Normally, an 18-minute mile on a self-propelled treadmill with a 15 percent incline is worth 3 points. Yet, it is difficult to measure the energy requirement when holding on to the rails. For this reason, I would encourage you to learn to walk without holding on to the side rails but if necessary hold on and subtract one point per mile.

Q. As a young girl I used to go to ballet class. Now that

I'm a middle-aged housewife, I still like to do an occasional pirouette in the living room. I wonder if dancing earns me any aerobic points?

A. It depends on what kind of dancing you do. Slow ballet movements in the style of the "Dying Swan" will do little to increase your aerobic capacity. By contrast, fast-moving ballet numbers, many kinds of modern dancing, and vigorous folk dances with fast footwork unquestionably have some aerobic effect. But because dances differ so greatly, it has not been possible to assign representative point values.

KEEPING SCORE

Questions about point credits are by far the most frequent. Some of these queries are about the charts themselves while others concern modes of exercise not specifically covered by the charts.

Q. One of the things I like about aerobics is that everything follows quite logically from a basic principle. But the logic of the point charts sometimes puzzles me. For example, you're giving me 5 points for running a mile in 6:30 minutes. And you're giving me 5 points for running a mile in 7:59 minutes. How come? Shouldn't I earn more points for running faster?

A. Of course you should. But I set up the charts so that the point credits increase in steps rather than as a continuous curve. Credit represents the slowest performance within each step. This is the reason for the apparent discrepancy.

Setting up the charts in this way allows a certain margin for error. It assures that you are getting all the exercise you need for effective conditioning even if there is a slight error in your measurement of time or distance.

Q. I get most of my walking exercise near my home in the Green Mountains of Vermont. A beautiful path near my house leads up to a fine lookout point. I go there almost every afternoon, and then back home again. Should I get extra credit because of the hilly terrain?

A. If the uphill and downhill parts of your course are approximately equal, the effect of incline cancels out and you get no extra points. But if you walked a course that is more uphill than downhill, you certainly should award yourself extra points.

You can figure the added points for various grades of climb from the Inclination Chart in Chapter Ten (Page 151). For example, walking at a speed of 3.4 mph (18:00 minutes per mile) is worth 1 point on a level grade. But if you walk at the same speed up a 15 percent grade, the point value jumps to 3.

Q. I earn about 50 points per week, cycling on New Jersey back roads on my English three-speed racer. Would I have to figure my credit in a different way if I used a ten-speed racing bike or a standard no-shift bike?

A. Experience has shown that the difference in energy expended on various types of bicycles is not great enough to require adjustment of the point chart. Since the chart is set up to allow a certain margin for error, you'll be getting the total point value from your exercise even if you ride a ten-speed racer.

Q. I'm a commuter and ride my bike to and from the railroad station, a distance of one mile. I do this every day. How many points do I get?

A. Riding a mile on a bike probably doesn't take you more than four minutes. That's not long enough to reach a steady state of energy expenditure. As a result, no aerobic training effect can take place and you earn no points. Remember that to gain aerobic benefits (and point credits) your exercise must be long enough and must challenge the heart and lungs to supply higher than ordinary amounts of oxygen.

Q. Ever since we read about aerobics, my husband and I go out regularly for an early evening run. It's doing wonders for our health as well as our disposition. But there's one problem. He's 6'1" and I'm 5'3". With my short legs, I have to take almost twice as many steps as he. So I feel I'm entitled to some extra points.

A. Sorry to disappoint you, but laboratory measurements say "no extra points." I know this sounds unfair, but the energy expenditure of tall and short people running on the treadmill has been measured, and there is no significant difference once you compensate for body weight. Only the very short ones—below five feet in height—have to work harder to keep up.

Q. Do I get more points for running three continuous

miles in 24 minutes than for three separate miles, each one in less than eight minutes?

A. The training effect is the same in both cases, so you get the same number of points. I realize that instinctively you may feel a continuous three-mile run would earn more aerobic benefit than three separate mile runs. But according to our current data, it just doesn't seem to work out that way.

Q. I've been doing yoga exercises for some time and find them wonderfully relaxing. I wonder if I can get any aerobic points that way?

A. I know of no aerobic benefit from standing on your head or other yoga-type exercises. Many people derive muscular relaxation and other benefits from such exercises, but so far there has been no indication that they have any aerobic value.

TEACHER'S SEMINAR

Q. As head of the physical education department of a Georgia high school, I wish I could provide an incentive for exercise. How do you motivate boys and girls from 12 to 14 who are too young to care much about fitness?

A. At that age, children can be readily motivated by competition. Unlike younger age groups, they are mature enough not to be damaged in their character development by the competitive element. I know of several schools awarding patches to students achieving 30 points per week, another patch for 50 points, and a special "Century Club" emblem for 100 points. Of course, it should be made clear to the students that the "Century Club" is not for everyone. Nobody needs to feel left out for not getting in. Such intense level of exercise is primarily for athletes developing their "staying power." But the entire student body —except for those medically screened out—should be motivated to go for the 30 and 50 point patches.

Grades are also a good motivator. I was recently told of a high school in California that awards grades to boys in physical education based on performance in a one-mile run. You can't earn an "A" unless you run a mile faster than six minutes, seven minutes is required for a B, eight minutes for a C and longer than eight minutes means a D. During a recent semester, 97 percent of the students got passing grades.

Q. I supervise physical education classes for children from seven to 14 years. Can you suggest types of exercise and aerobic goals for this age group?

A. Walking, running, cycling and swimming are excellent even for the younger children. The older children, from about ten years up, may take part in more competitive team sports. As yet, we do not have enough data to set aerobic norms for children in the six to ten age bracket. I assume that about 20 points per week would not be an unrealistic requirement. Above the age of ten, the weekly minimum is the same as for adults—30 points per week.

SPECIAL SITUATIONS

Q. I'm 55 years old and, try as I may, I can't meet the time goals in the chart. What do you advise?

A. You probably have been trying to meet the time goal in the original charts which did not provide for age adjustment. Instead, follow the age-adjusted chart in this book. You may find it much easier. Then, if you still have trouble meeting the specified time goals, exercise at a slower speed. That way you can still get your 30 points per week and remember that it is more important to get your points than it is to reach a specific time goal.

Q. Back in 1960 I had a slight myocardial infarction. In October I suffered another slight heart attack. With this history, do you think aerobics is safe for me?

A. Only your own doctor can tell you, because only he has detailed knowledge of your condition. However, the cardiac walking program outlined in the Chart Pack has proved successful in the rehabilitation of many people who have suffered heart attacks. The objective is to train yourself so that you gradually reach the point where you can comfortably walk a mile in less than 14:30 minutes. Then you work up to three miles a day, or 1½ miles twice a day, five days a week. This gives you 30 points per week, which gives you enough of an aerobic training effect to build up your cardiovascular reserve. It may take you 32 weeks or even longer to reach this point. Do not rush it. And do not even start any exercise program without the specific approval of your physician.

Q. My pulse rate at rest is between 48 and 52—about six beats per minute slower than when I started the aerobics program about four months ago. But I notice that it takes nearly an hour for my heart rate to return to normal after I run an eight-minute mile. After a two-mile run it takes even longer. Is that okay?

A. It's all right as long as your heart rate returns to about 100 after ten minutes of rest. To drop back to the normal resting rate may take a good deal longer. What happens is this: The oxygen debt you build up during aerobic exercise is mostly "paid back" during the first few minutes after exercise, and your heartbeat slows considerably during that period. But to pay back the rest of the accumulated oxygen debt may take as long as one to three hours, depending on how hard you exercised. As long as you are repaying, your heart must pump more than the normal amount of blood. Hence your heart rate will remain slightly elevated.

Q. An old knee injury prevents me from running, and even walking isn't comfortable. Yet with my 215 pounds and 48 years, I definitely need exercise. My doctor suggests swimming, since that would put the least strain on my knee. The problem is that I can't afford a swimming pool. Any other suggestions?

A. I realize that a standard-size, concrete swimming pool would be expensive, but you might consider one of those inexpensive round plastic pools that are entirely above ground and can be easily put up in the yard. Then get a swimming harness and tether it to the rim of the pool. That way you can "swim in place" in a small pool.

One man I know exercises in this way, using the time chart for the swimming program. Of course he can't gauge his "distance" while swimming on a tether. Instead, he checks his pulse after the specified time period, making sure he is swimming fast enough to drive his heart rate to 140. Occasionaly he swims at a friend's regular pool where he can measure his distance. This gives him a chance to check his performance directly against the chart.

Another possibility you and your doctor might consider is an indoor rowing machine. Many people handicapped in the use of their legs have found such machines a suitable exercise device. The seat could be screwed down in a fixed position so that no flexing of the knees occurs.

Q. Sunday is my only chance to get in a few sets of tennis. Frankly, I think a once-a-week workout is better than nothing at all. Why then are you so hard on us "weekend athletes"?

A. Your motives are fine, but your methods are something else again. For one thing, Sunday-only exercise gives you very little aerobic benefit. The intervening week is too long an interruption. No significant training effect can possibly occur. Worse yet, weekend athletes are a danger to themselves. The sudden Sunday exertion can be harmful unless you are conditioned by regular weekday exercise.

Q. I'm about 20 pounds too heavy and have been trying to shake off some of that extra fat by running. How many calories can I burn up that way?

A. Figure about 100 calories for an eight-minute mile. That's not enough to whittle down that extra weight of yours rapidly. You'd have to run three miles a day to burn enough calories to obtain a significant weight reduction. But if you supplement your running with a moderate diet, even one mile a day will soon give you results.

Q. How can I tell if I push myself too hard during the conditioning period?

A. Fatigue is a good general indicator. If you feel tired most of the time—not just for an hour or so after exercising—you are probably driving yourself too hard. More specifically, you can check your recovery heart rate. As I have mentioned before, five minutes after exercise your heart rate should be less than 120, ten minutes after exercise it should be less than 100. If your heart rate at those time points is faster than that, cut back on your exercise.

Q. I've just an ordinary cold. Should I continue to exercise? I hate to miss out on my conditioning program.

A. You should never exercise while you suffer from an acute infection—and a common cold is just that. Also stop exercising if you have the flu, an intestinal upset or other virus disorders. If you have a fever, wait until your temperature returns to normal. Then wait at least an additional 24 hours. Not before then should you resume exercise—and then at a slower pace than before your illness.

Q. I never had any trouble with brittle bones before, but after five weeks of running on the aerobics program, I cracked a bone in my left foot. It's six weeks later now and it no longer hurts. Can I go back to the conditioning program now?

A. Better wait a while yet. It is important to give a fracture enough time to heal completely before putting renewed stress on it. Absence of pain is a sign that the fracture is at least partially healed, but your doctor should make the final decision about your reentry into the conditioning program.

It may interest you to know that frequently a bone becomes stronger after a break. The strengthening effect results from the thickening of the bone at the point of fracture and from drawing more calcium into the tissue during the healing process.

When your doctor says you can resume exercise, don't start running right away. Stick with the walking program for a few weeks. If no complications occur, you may then switch to running again.

Q. About six weeks after I started on the running program, I began to feel stiff around neck and shoulders. What do you think is the reason?

A. Very likely you are not using your arms properly while running. Chances are that you are tense and carry your arms far too high. Relax and let your arms swing loose as you run. The natural rhythm of their swing will add to your forward momentum, making your overall body movement more efficient. Also, you may benefit from some calisthenic exercises for the arms.

Q. Sometimes I feel quite giddy during or after exercise, sort of light-headed and dizzy. Is that normal?

A. Your symptom is not normal. It may be due to hyperventilation, which means that you're breathing in and out more than you need to. That way you blow off carbon dioxide, changing the chemical balance of the blood. This, in turn, affects the brain and makes you dizzy.

It is also possible that your dizziness is caused by insufficient blood supply to the brain due to a heart or blood vessel problem. In that case you should not be exercising at all. So let your doctor check you out, just to be sure.

Q. Should I exercise when I'm fatigued from overwork or lack of sleep?

A. No, skip exercising that day. Unusual fatigue, inadequate sleep or excessive emotional strain, added to vigorous exercise, may cause undesirable consequences.

I would like to finish up this chapter with one of the toughest questions I ever fielded from the lecture platform. I was speaking in Oklahoma City, Oklahoma, when a large man rose in the audience and said: "I've been trying to explain aerobics to my wife. But the more I try, the more I get mixed up. Finally she asked me, 'Can you define aerobics in a single sentence?' So that's what I'm asking you."

Being accustomed to talking for hours on aerobics, I must admit that momentarily I was stumped. But then I made a brave try at a simple answer: "Aerobics is a system of exercise designed to improve your overall health, but particularly the condition of the heart, lungs and blood vessels." This doesn't tell all, of course, but it does sum it up.

An Afterthought

IN THE RELATIVELY short span of fifty years, the automobile has so altered our way of life that walking—the most natural mode of locomotion—now seems almost discreditable.

I once expressed this thought to a friend who is a successful car dealer.

Predictably, he responded.

"I hate to see cars getting the blame for everything," he said irritably. "I bet people didn't walk any more in the old days than they do now. They just went by horse and buggy."

"When you went to school," I asked, "how did you get there?"

He admitted that he had walked more than three miles to and from school.

"And your children?"

"The bus picks them up."

"And does your wife use a car much?"

"Oh yes, you should see our monthly gasoline bill."

I didn't press my point further.

No, the automobile is not just a mechanical replacement for the horse. It represents an entirely new attitude, a new set of customs, and it is ushering in an era of physical passivity.

I remember when people walked to church, to the store and the post office. Today, we have the "drive-in craze." There are drive-in restaurants, drive-in cleaners, drive-in theaters and drive-in banks. Not only have we given up walking; we don't even get out of the car when we reach our destinations!

Paradoxically, this passion for passivity extends even to sports, robbing them of much of their healthful effects. The golf cart and the ski lift are but two of many examples of our unwillingness or inability to move under our own power. And we are becoming so engrossed with television that a major portion of our leisure time, formerly spent in outdoor activities, is now spent in watching television. To top that, remote control is making it "out of style" to leave the comfortable, cushioned chair to change television stations. Where will it end?

But all of these changes have been too swift for the human organism. Over many thousands of years, since before the dawn of civilization, our bodies have been geared to and sustained by habitual and extensive physical activity. Now, with dramatic suddenness, this functional pattern has been broken. Our legs are technologically unemployed. And our entire health suffers for it.

Even in other areas of our modern life, strenuous physical activity is a thing of the past. Mechanization has placed the farmer in the driver's seat, the construction worker at the controls of a crane, and the road builder on his bulldozer. The warehouseman has his fork lifts, the carpenter his power tools, and the office-worker his elevators to eliminate the occasional effort of climbing a flight of stairs. Even the trucker—thanks to power steering and power brakes—exerts little more muscular effort than the housewife driving to a bridge party.

Unquestionably, these developments represent progress. Modern technology has created immense benefits and satisfied many human needs. I am not criticizing these accomplishments, and I am certainly not suggesting that we tear up our highways, junk our cars, and eliminate the elevators. But, as a physician, I am concerned about the medical consequences of the machine age. The high tension and low activity of modern life make a deadly mixture. Biologically, we're in the midst of a crisis, and the statistics on cardiovascular disease show it.

At this point in the history of civilization, it is evident that technical progress may backfire unless it is matched by a balancing regard for human health and well-being. In its broadest sense, the question is whether man can prosper in the technological environment he has created. He must learn to protect the natural resources that sustain his life. He must learn to clean up the air and the water, and to preserve the land. But first of all, he must protect his own body against the ravages imposed by modern life.

It is my hope that aerobics will help him do so.

Appendix: The Point System Expanded. With the Addition of Endurance Points

1. WALKING/RUNNING

(at 1/10-Mile Increments)

In measuring a course that starts and finishes in front of their home, many people have found that it is impossible to end on an even mile or half-mile. Consequently, hundreds have asked for a chart that gives the point value for walking and running distances measured in 1/10 miles. The following special chart is in response to this request and gives the point value for walking and running one to five miles at 1/10-mile increments.

1.0 Mile

19:59—14:30 min	1
14:29—12:00 min	2
11:59—10:00 min	3
9:59— 8:00 min	4
7:59— 6:31 min	5
6:30— 5:45 min	6
under 5:45 min	7

1.1 Miles

21:59—15:57 min	1⅛
15:56—13:12 min	2¼
13:11—11:00 min	3⅓
10:59— 8:48 min	4½
8:47— 7:09 min	5½
7:08— 6:20 min	6⅔
under 6:20 min	7¾

1.2 Miles

23:59—17:24 min	1¼
17:23—14:24 min	2½
14:23—12:00 min	3⅔
11:59— 9:36 min	5
9:35— 7:48 min	6
7:47— 6.55 min	7⅓
under 6:55 min	8½

1.3 Miles

25:59—18:51 min	1⅜
18:50—15:36 min	2¾
15:35—13:00 min	4
12:59—10:24 min	5½

1.3 Miles (Cont.)

10:23— 8:27 min	6½
8:26— 7:30 min	8
under 7:30 min	9¼

1.4 Miles

27:59—20:18 min	1½
20:17—16:48 min	2¾
16:47—14:00 min	4½
13:59—11:00 min	6
10:59— 9:06 min	7
9:05— 8:05 min	8⅔
under 8:05 min	10

1.5 Miles

29:59—21:45 min	1½
21:44—18:00 min	3
17:59—15:00 min	4½
14:59—12:00 min	6
11:59— 9:45 min	7½
9:44— 8:40 min	9
under 8:40 min	10½

1.6 Miles

31:59—23:12 min	1⅝
23:11—19:12 min	3¼
19:11—16:00 min	4⅔
15:59—12:48 min	6½
12:47—10:24 min	8
10:23— 9:15 min	9⅔
under 9:15 min	11¼

1. WALKING/RUNNING (CONTINUED)
(at 1/10-Mile Increments)

1.7 Miles

33:59—24:39 min	1¾
24:38—20:24 min	3½
20:23—17:00 min	5
16:59—13:36 min	7
13:35—11:03 min	8½
11:02— 9:50 min	10⅓
under 9:50 min	12

1.8 Miles

35:59—26:06 min	1⅞
26:05—21:36 min	3¾
21:35—18:00 min	5⅓
17:59—14:24 min	7½
14:23—11:42 min	9
11:41—10:25 min	11
under 10:25 min	12¾

1.9 Miles

37:59—27:33 min	1⅞
27:32—22:48 min	3¾
22:47—19:00 min	5⅔
18:59—15:12 min	7½
15:11—12:21 min	9½
12:20—11:00 min	11½
under 11:00 min	13½

2.0 Miles

40:00 min or longer	1*
39:59—29:00 min	2
28:59—24:00 min	4
23:59—20:00 min	7
19:59—16:00 min	9
15:59—13:00 min	11
12:59—11:30 min	13
under 11:30 min	15

2.1 Miles

42:00 min or longer	1*
41:59—30:27 min	2⅛
30:26—25:12 min	4¼
25:11—21:00 min	7½

2.1 Miles (Cont.)

20:59—16:48 min	9⅔
16:47—13:39 min	11¾
13:38—12:05 min	13¾
under 12:05 min	16

2.2 Miles

44:00 min or longer	1*
43:59—31:54 min	2¼
31:53—26:24 min	4½
26:23—22:00 min	7¾
21:59—17:36 min	10
17:35—14:18 min	12¼
14:17—12:40 min	14½
under 12:40 min	16⅔

2.3 Miles

46:00 min or longer	1*
45:59—33:21 min	2⅜
33:20—27:36 min	4¾
27:35—23:00 min	8⅓
22:59—18:24 min	10⅔
18:23—14:57 min	13
14:56—13:15 min	15⅓
under 13:15 min	17⅔

2.4 Miles

48:00 min or longer	1*
47:59—34:48 min	2½
34:47—28:48 min	4¾
28:47—24:00 min	8⅔
23:59—19:12 min	11
19:11—15:36 min	13½
15:35—13:50 min	16
under 13:50 min	18¼

2.5 Miles

50:00 min or longer	1*
49:59—36:15 min	2½
36:14—30:00 min	5
29:59—25:00 min	9
24:59—20:00 min	11½
19:59—16:15 min	14

* Exercise of sufficient duration to be of cardiovascular benefit. At this speed, ordinarily no training effect would occur. However, the duration is of such extent that a training effect does begin to occur.

1. WALKING/RUNNING (CONTINUED)
(at 1/10-Mile Increments)

2.5 Miles (Cont.)

16:14—14:20 min	16½
under 14:20 min	19

2.6 Miles

52:00 min or longer	1*
51:59—37:42 min	2⅝
37:41—31:12 min	5¼
31:11—26:00 min	9¼
25:59—20:48 min	12
20:47—16:54 min	14½
16:53—15:00 min	17
under 15:00 min	19½

2.7 Miles

54:00 min or longer	1*
53:59—39:09 min	2¾
39:08—32:24 min	5½
32:23—27:00 min	9½
26:59—21:36 min	12½
21:35—17:33 min	15
17:32—15:35 min	18
under 15:35 min	20¼

2.8 Miles

56:00 min or longer	1*
55:59—40:36 min	2⅞
40:35—33:36 min	5¾
33:35—28:00 min	10
27:59—22:24 min	13
22:23—18:12 min	15½
18:11—16:10 min	18½
under 16:10 min	21

2.9 Miles

58:00 min or longer	1*
57:59—42:03 min	2⅞
42:01—34:48 min	5¾
34:47—29:00 min	10½
28:59—23:12 min	13¼
23:11—18:51 min	16¼
18:50—16:45 min	19
under 16:45 min	22

3.0 Miles

1 hr or longer	1½*
59:59—43:30 min	3
43:29—36:00 min	6
35:59—30:00 min	11
29:59—24:00 min	14
23:59—19:30 min	17
19:29—17:15 min	20
under 17:15 min	23

3.1 Miles

1 hr 2:00 min or longer	1½*
1 hr 1:59—44:57 min	3⅛
44:56—37:12 min	6¼
37:11—31:00 min	11½
30:59—24:48 min	14½
24:47—20:10 min	17¾
20:09—17:50 min	20¾
under 17:50 min	24

3.2 Miles

1 hr 4:00 min or longer	1½*
1 hr 3:59—46:24 min	3¼
46:23—38:24 min	6½
38:23—32:00 min	11¾
31:59—25:36 min	15
25:35—20:49 min	18½
20:48—18:25 min	21¾
under 18:25 min	24⅔

3.3 Miles

1 hr 6 min or longer	1½*
1 hr 5:59—47:51 min	3⅜
47:50—39:36 min	6¾
39:35—33:00 min	12
32:59—26:24 min	15½
26:23—21:28 min	19
21:27—19:00 min	22½
under 19:00 min	25⅓

3.4 Miles

1 hr 8:00 min or longer	1½*
1 hr 7:59—49:18 min	3⅜

* Exercise of sufficient duration to be of cardiovascular benefit. At this speed, ordinarily no training effect would occur. However, the duration is of such extent that a training effect does begin to occur.

1. WALKING/RUNNING (CONTINUED)
(at 1/10-Mile Increments)

3.4 Miles (Cont.)

49:17—40:48 min	6¾
40:47—34:00 min	12½
33:59—27:12 min	16
27:11—22:07 min	19½
22:06—19:35 min	23
under 19:35 min	26

3.5 Miles

1 hr 10:00 min or longer	1½*
1 hr 9:59—50:45 min	3½
50:44—42:00 min	7
41:59—35:00 min	13
34:59—28:00 min	16½
27:59—22:45 min	20
22:44—20:10 min	23½
under 20:10 min	27

3.6 Miles

1 hr 12:00 min or longer	1½*
1 hr 11:59—52:12 min	3⅝
52:11—43:12 min	7¼
43:11—36:00 min	13½
35:59—28:48 min	17
28:47—23:24 min	20½
23:23—20:45 min	24¼
under 20:45 min	27¾

3.7 Miles

1 hr 14:00 min or longer	1½*
1 hr 13:59—53:39 min	3¾
53:38—44:24 min	7½
44:23—37:00 min	14
36:59—29:36 min	17½
29:35—24:03 min	21
24:02—21:15 min	25
under 21:15 min	28½

3.8 Miles

1 hr 16:00 min or longer	1½*
1 hr 15:59—55:06 min	3⅞
55:05—45:36 min	7¾
45:35—38:00 min	14

3.8 Miles (Cont.)

37:59—30:24 min	18
30:23—24:42 min	21¾
24:41—21:50 min	25¾
under 21:50 min	29¼

3.9 Miles

1 hr 18:00 min or longer	1½*
1 hr 17:59—56:33 min	3⅞
56:32—46:48 min	7¾
46:47—39:00 min	14½
38:59—31:12 min	18½
31:11—25:21 min	22½
25:20—22:25 min	26¼
under 22:25 min	30

4.0 Miles

1 hr 20:00 min or longer	4*
1 hr 19:59—58:00 min	7
57:59—48:00 min	11
47:59—40:00 min	15
39:59—32:00 min	19
31:59—26:00 min	23
25:59—23:00 min	27
under 23:00 min	31

4.1 Miles

1 hr 22:00 min or longer	4*
1 hr 21:59—59:27 min	7
59:26—49:12 min	11¼
49:11—41:00 min	15⅓
40:59—32:48 min	19½
32:47—26:39 min	23½
26:38—23:35 min	27½
under 23:35 min	31¾

4.2 Miles

1 hr 24:00 min or longer	4*
1 hr 23:59—60:54 min	7¼
60:53—50:24 min	11½
50:23—42:00 min	15⅔
41:59—33:36 min	20
33:35—27:18 min	24

* Exercise of sufficient duration to be of cardiovascular benefit. At this speed, ordinarily no training effect would occur. However, the duration is of such extent that a training effect does begin to occur.

1. WALKING/RUNNING (CONTINUED)
(at 1/10-Mile Increments)

4.2 Miles (Cont.)

27:17—24:10 min	28
under 24:10 min	32½

4.3 Miles

1 hr 26:00 min or longer	4*
1 hr 25:59—1 hr 2:21 min	7½
1 hr 2:20—51:36 min	11¾
51:35—43:00 min	16
42:59—34:24 min	20½
34:23—27:57 min	24½
27:56—24:45 min	28¾
under 24:45 min	33¼

4.4 Miles

1 hr 28:00 min or longer	4*
1 hr 27:59—1 hr 3:48 min	7¾
1 hr 3:47—52:48 min	12
52:47—44:00 min	16½
43:59—35:12 min	21
35:11—28:36 min	25¼
28:35—25:20 min	29½
under 25:20 min	34

4.5 Miles

1 hr 30:00 min or longer	4½*
1 hr 29:59—1 hr 5:15 min	8
1 hr 5:14—54:00 min	12½
53:59—45:00 min	17
44:59—36:00 min	21½
35:59—29:15 min	26
29:14—25:55 min	30½
under 25:55 min	35

4.6 Miles

1 hr 32:00 min or longer	4½*
1 hr 31:59—1 hr 6:42 min	8¼
1 hr 6:41—55:12 min	12¾
55:11—46:00 min	17½
45:59—36:48 min	22
36:47—29:54 min	26½
29:53—26:30 min	31
under 26:30 min	36

4.7 Miles

1 hr 34:00 min or longer	4½*
1 hr 33:59—1 hr 8:09 min	8¼
1 hr 8:08—56:24 min	13
56:23—47:00 min	18
46:59—37:36 min	22½
37:35—30:33 min	27
30:32—27:00 min	31½
under 27:00 min	37

4.8 Miles

1 hr 36:00 min or longer	4½*
1 hr 35:59—1 hr 9:36	8½
1 hr 9:35—57:36 min	13¼
57:35—48:00 min	18
47:59—38:24 min	23
38:23—31:12 min	27½
31:11—27:35 min	32
under 27:35 min	38

4.9 Miles

1 hr 38:00 min or longer	4½*
1 hr 37:59—1 hr 11:03 min	8¾
1 hr 11:02—58:48 min	13½
58:47—49:00 min	18½
48:59—39:12 min	23½
39:11—31:51 min	27½
31:50—28:10 min	33
under 28:10 min	38

5.0 Miles

1 hr 40:00 min or longer	5*
1 hr 39:59—1 hr 12:30 min	9
1 hr 12:29—1 hr	14
59:59—50:00 min	19
49:59—40:00 min	24
39:59—32:30 min	29
32:29—28:45 min	34
under 28:45 min	39

* Exercise of sufficient duration to be of cardiovascular benefit. At this speed, ordinarily no training effect would occur. However, the duration is of such extent that a training effect does begin to occur.

1. WALKING/RUNNING (CONTINUED)
(at 1/2-Mile Increments)

5.5 Miles

1 hr 50:00 min or longer	5½*
1 hr 49:59—1 hr 19:45 min	10
1 hr 19:44—1 hr 6:00 min	15½
1 hr 5:59—55:00 min	21
54:59—44:00 min	26½
43:59—35:45 min	32
35:44—31:35 min	37½
under 31:35 min	43

7.5 Miles

2 hrs 30:00 min or longer	7½*
2 hrs 29:59—1 hr 48:45 min	14
1 hr 48:44—1 hr 30:00 min	21½
1 hr 29:59—1 hr 15:00 min	29
1 hr 14:59—60:00 min	36½
59:59—48:45 min	44
48:44—43:10 min	51½
under 43:10 min	59

6.0 Miles

2 hrs or longer	6*
1 hr 59:59—1 hr 27:00 min	11
1 hr. 26:59—1 hr 12:00 min	17
1 hr 11:59—1 hr	23
59:59—48:00 min	29
47:59—39:00 min	35
38:59—34:30 min	41
under 34:30 min	47

8.0 Miles

2 hrs 40:00 min or longer	8*
2 hrs 39:59—1 hr 56:00 min	15
1 hr 55:59—1 hr 36:00 min	23
1 hr 35:59—1 hr 20:00 min	31
1 hr 19:59—1hr 4:00 min	39
1 hr 3:59—52:00 min	47
51:59—46:00 min	55
under 46:00 min	63

6.5 Miles

2 hrs 10:00 min or longer	6½*
2 hrs 9:59—1 hr 34:15 min	12
1 hr 34:14—1 hr 18:00 min	18½
1 hr 17:59—1 hr 5:00 min	26
1 hr 4:59—52:00 min	32½
51:59—42:15 min	39
42:14—37:22 min	45½
under 37:22 min	52

8.5 Miles

2 hrs 50:00 min or longer	8½*
2 hrs 49:59—2 hrs 3:15 min	16
2 hrs 3:14—1 hr 42:00 min	24½
1 hr 41:59—1 hr 25:00 min	33
1 hr 24:59—1 hr 8:00 min	41½
1 hr 7:59—55:15 min	50
55:14—48:50 min	58½
under 48:50 min	67

7.0 Miles

2 hrs 20:00 min or longer	7*
2 hrs 19:59—1 hr 41:30 min	13
1 hr 41:29—1 hr 24:00 min	20
1 hr 23:59—1 hr 10:00 min	27
1 hr 9:59—56:00 min	34
55:59—45:30 min	41
45:29—40:15 min	48
under 40:15 min	55

9.0 Miles

3 hrs or longer	9*
2 hrs 59:59—2 hrs 10:30 min	17
2 hrs 10:29—1 hr 48:00 min	26
1 hr 47:59—1 hr 30.00 min	35
1 hr 29:59—1 hr 12:00 min	44
1 hr 11:59—58:30 min	53
58:29—51:45 min	62
under 51:45 min	71

* Exercise of sufficient duration to be of cardiovascular benefit. At this speed, ordinarily no training effect would occur. However, the duration is of such extent that a training effect does begin to occur.

1. WALKING/RUNNING (CONTINUED)

9.5 Miles

3 hrs 10:00 min or longer	9*
3 hrs 9:59—2 hrs 17:45 min	18
2 hrs 17:44—1 hr 54:00 min	27½
1 hr 53:59—1 hr 35:00 min	37
1 hr 34:59—1 hr 16:00 min	46½
1 hr 15:59—1 hr 1:45 min	56
1 hr 1:44—54:40 min	65½
under 54:40 min	75

10.0 Miles

3 hrs 20:00 min or longer	10*
3 hrs 19:59—2 hrs 25:00 min	19
2 hrs 24:59—2 hrs	29
1 hr 59:59—1 hr 40:00 min	39
1 hr 39:59—1 hr 20:00 min	49
1 hr 19:59—1 hr 5:00 min	59
1 hr 4:59—57:30 min	69
under 57:30 min	79

12:5 Miles

3 hrs 1:15—2 hrs 30:00 min	36½
2 hrs 29:59—2 hrs 5:00 min	49
2 hrs 4:59—1 hr 40:00 min	61½
1 hr 39:59—1 hr 21:15 min	74
under 1 hr 21:15 min	86½

15 Miles

3 hrs 37:28 min—3 hrs	44
2 hrs 59:59—2 hrs 30:00 min	59
2 hrs 29:59—2 hrs	74
1 hr 59:59—1 hr 37:30 min	89
under 1 hr 37:30 min	104

20.0 Miles

4 hrs 49:59 min—4 hrs	59
3 hrs 59:59—3 hrs 20:00 min	79
3 hrs 19:59—2 hrs 40:00 min	99
2 hrs 39:59—2 hrs 10:00 min	119
under 22 hrs 10:00 min	139

25.0 Miles

6 hrs 2:25 min—5 hrs	74
4 hrs 59:59—4 hrs 10:00 min	99
4 hrs 9:59—3 hrs 20:00 min	124
3 hrs 19:59—2 hrs 42:30 min	149
under 2 hrs 42:30 min	174

MARATHON (26 Miles, 385 Yards)

Less than 2 hrs 30 min 45 sec	209
2 hrs 30:45—2 hrs 50:25 min	182
2 hrs 50:26—3 hrs 29:45 min	156
3 hrs 29:46—4 hrs 22:12 min	130
4 hrs 22:13—5 hrs 14:40 min	104
5 hrs 14:41—6 hrs 20:12 min	78
6 hrs 20:13—8 hrs 40:25 min	51

* Exercise of sufficient duration to be of cardiovascular benefit. At this speed, ordinarily no training effect would occur. However, the duration is of such extent that a training effect does begin to occur.

2. CYCLING

INSTRUCTIONS:

1. Points determined considering equal uphill and downhill course.
2. Points determined considering equal time with and against the wind.
3. For cycling a one-way course constantly against a wind exceeding 5 mph, add ½ point per mile to the total point value.

2.0 Miles

12 min or longer	0
11:59— 8:00 min	1
7:59— 6:00 min	2
under 6:00 min	3

3.0 Miles

18 min or longer	0
17:59—12:00 min	1½
11:59— 9:00 min	3
under 9:00 min	4½

4.0 Miles

24 min or longer	0
23:59—16:00 min	2
15:59—12:00 min	4
under 12:00 min	6

5.0 Miles

30 min or longer	1*
29:59—20:00 min	2½
19:59—15:00 min	5
under 15:00 min	7½

6.0 Miles

36 min or longer	1*
35:59—24:00 min	3
23:59—18:00 min	6
under 18:00 min	9

7.0 Miles

42 min or longer	3½*
41:59—28:00 min	5½
27:59—21:00 min	9
under 21:00 min	12½

8.0 Miles

48 min or longer	3½*
47:59—32:00 min	6½
31:59—24:00 min	10½
under 24:00 min	14½

9.0 Miles

54 min or longer	5*
53:59—36:00 min	7½
35:59—27:00 min	12
under 27:00 min	16½

10.0 Miles

1 hr or longer	5½*
59:59—40:00 min	8½
39:59—30:00 min	13½
under 30:00 min	18½

11.0 Miles

1 hr 6 min or longer	6½*
1 hr 5:59 min—44:00 min	9½
43:59—33:00 min	15
under 33:00 min	20½

12.0 Miles

1 hr 12 min or longer	7*
1 hr 11:59 min—48:00 min	10½
47:59—36:00 min	16½
under 36:00 min	22½

13.0 Miles

1 hr 18 min or longer	8*
1 hr 17:59 min—52:00 min	11½
51:59—39:00 min	18
under 39:00 min	24½

* Exercise of sufficient duration to be of cardiovascular benefit. At this speed, ordinarily no training effect would occur. However, the duration is of such extent that a training effect does begin to occur.

2. CYCLING (CONTINUED)

14.0 Miles

1 hr 24 min or longer	8½°
1 hr 23:59 min—56:00 min	12½
55:59—42:00 min	19½
under 42:00 min	26½

15.0 Miles

1 hr 30 min or longer	9½°
1 hr 29:59 min—1 hr	13½
59:59—45:00 min	21
under 45:00 min	28½

16.0 Miles

1 hr 36 min or longer	10°
1 hr 35:59 min—1 hr 4:00 min	14½
1 hr 3:59 min—48:00 min	22½
under 48:00 min	30½

17.0 Miles

1 hr 42:00 min or longer	11°
1 hr 41:50 min—1 hr 8 min	15½
1 hr 7:59 min—51:00 min	24
under 51:00 min	32½

18.0 Miles

1 hr 48:00 min or longer	11½°
1 hr 47:59 min—1 hr 12 min	16½
1 hr 11:59 min—54:00 min	25½
under 54:00 min	34½

19.0 Miles

1 hr 54:00 min or longer	12½
1 hr 53:59 min—1 hr 16 min	17½
1 hr 15:59 min—57:00 min	27
under 57:00 min	36½

20.0 Miles

2 hrs or longer	13°
1 hr 59:59 min—1 hr 20 min	18½
1 hr 19:59 min—1 hr	28½
under 1 hr	38½

25.0 Miles

2 hrs 30:00 min or longer	17°
2 hrs 29:59 min—1 hr 40 min	23½
1 hr 39:59 min—1 hr 15 min	36
under 1 hr 15:00 min	48½

30.0 Miles

3 hrs or longer	20½°
2 hrs 59:59 min—2 hrs	28½
1 hr 59:59 min—1 hr 30 min	43½
under 1 hr 30:00 min	58½

° Exercise of sufficient duration to be of cardiovascular benefit. At this speed, ordinarily no training effect would occur. However, the duration is of such extent that a training effect does begin to occur.

3. SWIMMING

200 Yards

6:40 min or longer	0
6:39— 5:00 min	1
4:59— 3:20 min	1½
under 3:20 min	2½

250 Yards

8:20 min or longer	0
8:19— 6:15 min	1¼
6:14— 4:10 min	2
under 4:10 min	3

300 Yards

10:00 min or longer	1*
9:59— 7:30 min	1½
7:29— 5:00 min	2½
under 5:00 min	3½

350 Yards

11:40 min or longer	1*
11:39— 8:45 min	2
8:44— 5:50 min	3
under 5:50 min	4½

400 Yards

13:20 min or longer	1*
13:19—10:00 min	2½
9:59— 6:40 min	3½
under 6:40 min	5

450 Yards

15:00 min or longer	1*
14:59—11:15 min	3
11:14— 7:30 min	4
under 7:30 min	5½

500 Yards

16:40 min or longer	1*
16:39—12:30 min	3
12:29— 8:20 min	4
under 8:20 min	6

550 Yards

18:20 min or longer	1*
18:19—13:45 min	3½
13:44— 9:10 min	4½
under 9:10 min	7

600 Yards

20:00 min or longer	1½*
19:59—15:00 min	4
14:59—10:00 min	5
under 10:00 min	7½

650 Yards

21:40 min or longer	1½*
21:39—16:15 min	4
16:14—10:50 min	5½
under 10:50 min	8

700 Yards

23:20 min or longer	1½*
23:19—17:30 min	4½
17:29—11:40 min	6
under 11:40 min	8½

750 Yards

25:00 min or longer	1½*
24:59—18:45 min	4¾
18:44—12:30 min	6½
under 12:30 min	9½

800 Yards

26:40 min or longer	2¼*
26:39—20:00 min	5¾
19:59—13:20 min	7¼
under 13:20 min	10¾

850 Yards

28:20 min or longer	2½*
28:19—21:15 min	6¼
21:14—14:10 min	8
under 14:10 min	11½

* Exercise of sufficient duration to be of cardiovascular benefit. At this speed, ordinarily no training effect would occur. However, the duration is of such extent that a training effect does begin to occur.

3. SWIMMING (CONTINUED)

900 Yards

30:00 min or longer	3¼*
29:59—22:30 min	6¾
22:29—15:00 min	8¾
under 15:00 min	12½

950 Yards

31:40 min or longer	3½*
31:39—23:15 min	7¼
23:14—15:50 min	9½
under 15:50 min	13½

1000 Yards

33:20 min or longer	4*
33:19—25:00 min	8¼
24:59—16:40 min	10½
under 16:40 min	14½

1100 Yards

36:40 min or longer	4½*
36:39—27:30 min	9½
27:29—18:20 min	11½
under 18:20 min	16¼

1200 Yards

40:00 min or longer	5½*
39:59—30:00 min	10½
29:59—20:00 min	13
under 20:00 min	18

1300 Yards

43:20 min or longer	6*
43:19—32:30 min	11½
32:29—21:40 min	14½
under 21:40 min	19¾

1400 Yards

46:40 min or longer	6½*
46:39—35:00 min	12¾

1400 Yards (Cont.)

34:59—23:20 min	15½
under 23:20 min	21½

1500 Yards

50:00 min or longer	7½*
49:59—37:30 min	14
37:29—25:00 min	17
under 25:00 min	23¼

1600 Yards

53:20 min or longer	8*
53:19—40:00 min	15
39:59—26:40 min	18¼
under 26:40 min	25

1700 Yards

56:40 min or longer	9¾*
56:39—42:30 min	17¼
42:29—28:20 min	20¾
under 28:20 min	28

1800 Yards

1 hr or longer	9½*
59:59—45:00 min	17
44:59—30:00 min	21
under 30:00 min	28½

1900 Yards

1 hr 3:20 min or longer	10*
1 hr 3:19—47:30 min	18½
47:29—31:40 min	22¼
under 31:40 min	30¼

2000 Yards

1 hr 6:40 min or longer	10½
1 hr 6:39—50:00 min	19½
49:59—33:20 min	23½
under 33:20 min	32

ADDITIONAL COMMENTS:
Points calculated on overhand crawl, i.e., 9.0 Kcal per min. Breaststroke is less demanding: 7.0 Kcal per min. Backstroke, a little more: 8.0 Kcal per min. Butterfly, most demanding: 12.0 Kcal per min.

* Exercise of sufficient duration to be of cardiovascular benefit. At this speed, ordinarily no training effect would occur. However, the duration is of such extent that a training effect does begin to occur.

4. POINT VALUE FOR STATIONARY RUNNING

TIME	*60-70 STEPS/MIN	POINTS	*70-80 STEPS/MIN	POINTS	*80-90 STEPS/MIN	POINTS	*90-100 STEPS/MIN	POINTS	*100-110 STEPS/MIN	POINTS
2:30			175-200	¾	200-225	1	225-250	1¼	250-275	1½
5:00	300-350	1¼	350-400	1½	400-450	2	450-500	2½	500-550	3
7:30			525-600	2¼	600-675	3	675-750	3¾	750-825	4½
10:00	600-700	2½	700-800	3	800-900	4	900-1000	5	1000-1100	6
12:30			875-1000	3¾	1000-1125	5	1125-1250	6¼	1250-1375	7½
15:00	900-1050	3¾	1050-1200	4½	1200-1350	6	1350-1500	7½	1500-1650	9
17:30			1225-1400	6¾	1400-1575	8½	1575-1750	10¼	1750-1925	12
20:00	1200-1400	7	1400-1600	8	1600-1800	10	1800-2000	12	2000-2200	14
22:30			1575-1800	9¼	1800-2025	11½	2025-2250	13¾	2250-2475	16
25:00	1500-1750	9¼	1750-2000	10½	2000-2250	13	2250-2500	15½	2500-2750	18
27:30			1925-2200	11¾	2200-2475	14½	2475-2750	17¼	2750-3025	20
30:00	1800-2100	11½	2100-2400	13	2400-2700	16	2700-3000	19	3000-3300	22

* Count only when the left foot hits the floor. Knees must be brought up in front raising the feet at least eight inches from the floor.

5. HANDBALL/BASKETBALL/SQUASH

DURATION *	POINTS	DURATION *	POINTS
10 min	1½	1 hr 10 min	10½
15 min	2¼	1 hr 15 min	11¼
20 min	3	1 hr 20 min	12
25 min	3¾	1 hr 25 min	12¾
30 min	4½	1 hr 30 min	13½
35 min	5¼	1 hr 35 min	14¼
40 min	6	1 hr 40 min	15
45 min	6¾	1 hr 45 min	15¾
50 min	7½	1 hr 50 min	16½
55 min	8¼	1 hr 55 min	17¼
1 hr	9	2 hrs	18
1 hr 5 min	9¾		

* Continuous exercise. Do not count breaks, time-outs, etc.

6. ADDITIONAL EXERCISES

EXERCISE	DURATION	POINTS*	COMMENTS
Badminton	1 game	1½	Singles, players of equal ability, and a duration per game of 20 minutes.
	2 games	3	
	3 games	4½	
Fencing	10 min	1	
	20 min	2	
	30 min	3	
Football	30 min	3	Count only the time in which you are actively participating.
	60 min	6	
	90 min	9	
Golf	9 holes	1½	No motorized carts!
	18 holes	3	
Hockey	20 min	3	Count only the time in which you are actively participating.
	40 min	6	
	60 min	9	
	80 min	12	
Lacrosse and Soccer	20 min	3	Count only the time in which you are actively partcipating.
	40 min	6	
	60 min	9	
Rope skipping	5 min	1½	Skip with both feet together or step over the rope alternating one foot at a time.
	10 min	3	
	15 min	4½	

*Points based on caloric requirements expressed in the scientific literature.

6. ADDITIONAL EXERCISES (CONTINUED)

EXERCISE	DURATION	POINTS*	COMMENTS
Rowing	6 min	1	2 oars, 20 strokes a minute, continuous rowing.
	18 min	4	
	36 min	8	
Skating	15 min	1	Either ice or roller skating. For speed skating triple the point value.
	30 min	2	
	60 min	4	
Skiing	30 min	3	Water or snow skiing. For cross-country snow skiing triple the point value.
	60 min	6	
	90 min	9	
Tennis	1 set	1½	Singles, players of equal ability, and duration per set of 20 minutes.
	2 sets	3	
	3 sets	4½	
Volleyball	15 min	1	
	30 min	2	
	60 min	4	
Wrestling	5 min	2	
	10 min	4	
	15 min	6	

* Points based on caloric requirements expressed in the scientific literature.

7. TARGET HEART RATES TO BE USED DURING STRESS TESTING TO DETERMINE THE PRESENCE OR ABSENCE OF HEART DISEASE

AGE (years)	HEART RATE (beats per minute)
under 30	175
30—34	170
35—39	165
40—44	160
45—49	155
50—54	150
55—59	145
60—64	140
65 and up	135

8. DETERMINATION OF THE HEAT STRESS
Wet Bulb Globe Temperature (WBGT) Index *

A. To determine the WBGT index, it is necessary to take readings from (1) a standard thermometer shaded from the sun (2) a black globe thermometer exposed to the sun and prevailing wind and (3) a stationary wet bulb thermometer similarly exposed.

To measure the black globe temperature, obtain a 6-inch hollow copper sphere painted flat black on the outside. Insert a thermometer into the sphere with its bulb at the center. The thermometer is supported by means of a rubber stopper tightly fitting into a brass tube soldered into the sphere. The sphere is supported by two wires or strings and it must be kept dull black by repainting when necessary.

To measure the wet bulb temperature, cover the bulb of a standard laboratory thermometer with a wick (heavy white corset- or shoe-string). Insert the wick into a flask of clean, perferably distilled, water. The mouth of the flask should be about ¾ to 1 inch below the tip of the thermometer bulb and the water level in the flash should be high enough to insure thorough wetting of the wick. The water should be changed daily and the wick washed with soap and water.

B. The WBGT heat stress index is determined as follows:
.7X wet bulb temperature plus .2X black globe temperature plus .1X standard temperature (shade) = WBGT Index

C. How to use the WBGT Index in controlling physical activity.
   1. When the WBGT Index exceeds 85° F., only those people who have been exercising in the heat for at least 10 days can continue their workouts.
   2. When the WBGT Index exceeds 88° F., only those individuals who have been exercising in the heat for at least 30 days can continue vigorous outdoor workouts.
   3. If the WBGT Index exceeds 90° F., it is best for all individuals to stop vigorous outdoor exercise regardless of the state of conditioning or heat acclimatization.

* Taken from Air Force Pamphlet 160-1 (25 April 1969), page 9.

METHOD FOR CONSTRUCTING A WBGT INDEX FIELD APPARATUS

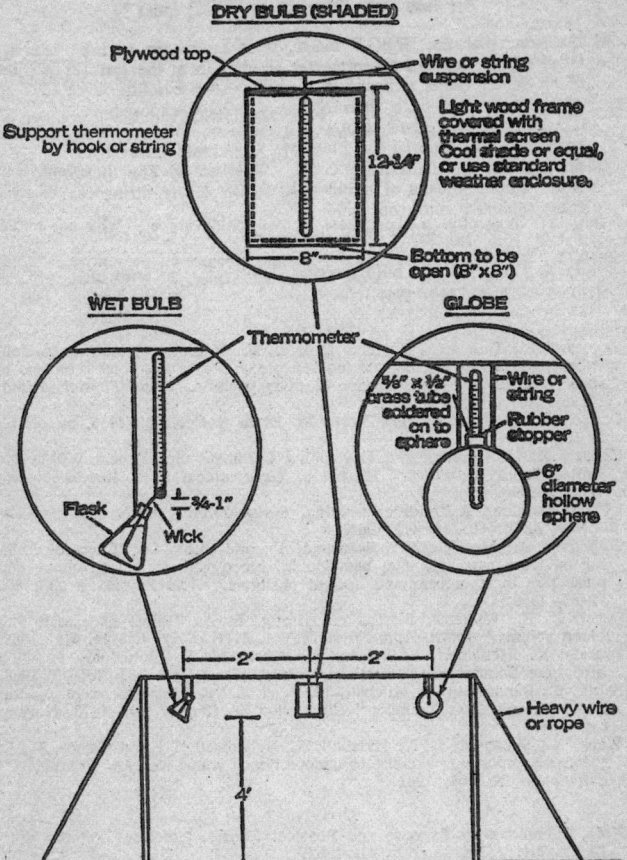

DRY BULB (SHADED)

Plywood top

Wire or string suspension

Support thermometer by hook or string

Light wood frame covered with thermal screen Cool shade or equal, or use standard weather enclosure.

12-¾"

8"

Bottom to be open (8" x 8")

WET BULB

Thermometer

GLOBE

⅛" x ½" brass tube soldered on to sphere

Wire or string

Rubber stopper

6" diameter hollow sphere

Flask

Wick

¾-1"

2'

2'

Heavy wire or rope

4'

Bibliography

CHAPTER 1

The Texas Poll—Belden Associates—Southland Center, Dallas, Texas, 17 July 1968.

The Coronary Prevention Program For Vermont Communities—Directed by Otto A. Brusis, M.D. Asst. Professor Community Medicine, University of Vermont, Burlington, Vt., April 1969.

Fox, S. M. and Haskell, W. L. "Physical Activity and the Prevention of Coronary Heart Disease." *Bulletin of the New York Academy of Medicine.* Second Series Vol. 44 (No. 8): 950-67, Aug. 1968.

Mitchell, J. H., and Blomqvist, C. G. "Role of Exercise in Prophylaxis Against Coronary Disease." Editorial. *Dallas Medical Journal* Vol. 54: 534-35, November 1968.

Raab, W. "Preventive medical mass reconditioning abroad—Why not in the U.S.A.?" *Ann. Int. Med.* 54:1191, 1961.

Raab, W. R., and Gilman, L. B. "Insurance-Sponsored, Preventive, Cardiac Reconditioning Centers in West Germany." *Amer. J. of Cardiol.* Vol. 13 (No. 5): 670-73, May 1964.

CHAPTER 2

Bevegard, S., Holmgren, A., and Jonsson, B. "Circulatory studies in well-trained athlete at rest and during heavy exercise with special reference to stroke volume and the influence of body position." *Acta Physiol. Scand.* 57:26, 1963.

Cooper, K. H. *Aerobics.* New York: M. Evans & Co. Inc., 1968, pp. 22-30; 56-102.

Cooper, K. H. "Testing and Developing Cardiovascular Fitness Within the United States Air Force." *Journal of Occupational Med.* 10:636-39, November 1968.

Konditionstraning & Konditionstestning. Fysisk Träning Häfte 1 Chefen For Armen Ao nr 80: 56, 4/2 1964.

Holmgren, A.; Mossfeldt, F.; Sjöstrand, T.; and Ström G. "Effect of training on work capacity, total hemoglobin, blood volume, heart volume and pulse rate in recumbent and upright positions." *Acta Physiol. Scand.* 50: 72-83, 1960.

Oscai, L. B., Williams, B. T., and Hertig, B. A. "Effect of exercise on blood volume." *Journ. App. Physiol.*, Vol. 24 (No. 5): 622-24, May 1968.

Pyorala, K., Heinonen, A. O., and Karvonen, M. J. "Pulmonary Function in Former Endurance Athletes," *Acta Med. Scand.* Vol. 183; 263-73, 1968.

Saltin, B.; Blomqvist, G.; Mitchell, J. H.; et al. "Response to Exercise After Bed Rest and After Training." *Circulation* 38 (Suppl. 17): 1-78, November 1968.

Wang, Y.; Shepherd, J. T.; Marshall, R. J.; Rowell, L.; and Taylor, H. L. "Cardiac response to exercise in unconditioned young men and in athletes." *Circulation* 24:1064, 1961.

CHAPTER 3

AMA Committee on Exercise and Physical Fitness. "Is Your Patient Fit?" *JAMA* 201: 117-118, (July 10) 1967.

Cooper, K. H. "Guidelines in the Management of the Exercising Patient." *JAMA.* (in press)

"Catch Larry Lewis; He's Only 102" *Fort Smith* (Ark). *Southwest Times-Record.* July 15, 1969.

Grimby, G. and Saltin, B. "Physiological Analysis of Well-trained Middle-aged and Old Athletes." *Acta Med. Scand.* Vol. 179 (fasc 5): 513-526, 1966.

Lester, M.; Sheffield, L. T.; Trammell, P. and Reeves, T. J. "The effect of age and athletic training on the maximal heart rate during muscular exercise." *American Heart Journal* Vol. 76 (No. 3): 370–76, September 1968.

Master, A. M.: "The Master Two-Step Test." *Amer. Heart J.* 75:809–37, June 1963.

CHAPTER 4

Adams, A. "Effect of exercise upon ligament strength." *Res. Quart* 37: 163–67, 1966.

Letter from Coach Thomas L. Bateman III. 30 July 1969. Calvert Hall High School, Towson, Maryland 21204.

Cooper, K. H. "A Means of Assessing Maximal Oxygen Intake," *JAMA* 203: 201–04, 15 January 1968.

Kattus, A. A. Jr.; Hanafee, W. N.; Longmire, W. P. Jr.; McAlpin, R. N.; and Rivin, A. U. "Diagnosis, Medical and Surgical Management of Coronary Insufficiency. *Annals of Internal Medicine* 69:115, July 1968.

"Packers Run to Get Their 2nd Wind." *Milwaukee Journal*, June 29, 1969.

Tipton, C. M., Schild, R. J., and Tomanek, R. J. Influence of physical activity on the strength of knee ligaments in rats. *Amer. J. Physiol.* 212: 783–87, 1967.

Personal communication from Hptn Arthur Zechner, Salzburg, Austria. (27 January 1969).

CHAPTER 5

Air Force Pamphlet 160-4-1. The Etiology, Prevention, Diagnosis and Treatment of Adverse Effects of Heat. 7 August 1957.

Anderson, K. L., Hellström, B., and Eide, R. Strenuous Muscular Exertion in the Polar Climate. *Ergonomics* Vol. 11 (No. 3): 261–74, 1968.

Bowerman, W. From a presentation given to the San Diego Heart Association, San Diego, Calif. 17 June 1968.

Coleman, W. Summer Conditioning Cuts Football Heat Stroke. *Medicine in Sports Newsletter* Vol. 8: No. 4, July 1968.

Hellström, R. and Linroth, K. Physical Working Capacity, Training and Climate. *Acta Med. Scand.* Suppl 472: 207–14, March 11, 1967.

Peter, J., and Wyndham, C. H. Activity of the human eccrine sweat gland during exercise in a hot, humid environment before and after acclimatization. *J. Physiol.* 187: 583–94, 1966.

Stampfer, M.; Epstein, S.; Beiser, G.; Goldstein R.; and Braunwald, E. From a presentation given at the American Heart Association Meeting. "Effect of cold air on peripheral arteries." Bal Harbour, Fla., 24 November 1968.

Strydom, N. B.; Wyndham, C. H.; Williams, C. G.; Morrison, J. F.; Bredell, G. A. G.; Benade, A. J. S.; and Von Rahden, M. Acclimatization to humid heat and the role of physical conditioning. *J. Appl. Physiol.* Vol. 21: 636–42, March 1966.

Taylor, C. L. and Allen, S. C. "Unpublished Report to the National Research Council," 1941.

CHAPTER 6

None

CHAPTER 7

Behling, F. L. (Stress fractures) from an article in *Hospital Tribune*, May 5 1969.

Glick, J. M. and Katch, V. L. Orthopaedic Aspects of Jogging. Presented at the Postgraduate Course on Sports Medicine, July 30, 1969, San Francisco, Calif.

Hoffman, M. S. Jogging and Foot Problems. Letters to the Journal, *JAMA* Vol. 207 (No. 12): 2283–4, March 24, 1969.

Siegel, I. M. Joggers Heel. Letters to the Journal, *JAMA* Vol. 206 (No. 13); 2899, December 23–30, 1968.

CHAPTER 8

Barach, A. L., Bickerman, H. A., and Beck, G. J. Advances in Treatment of Non-Tuberculous Pulmonary Disease. *Bull N. Y. Acad Med* 28:353, 1952.

Campbell, D. E. Influence of several physical activities on serum cholesterol concentrations in young men. *Journal of Lipid Research* Vol. 6: 478–80, 1965.

Carlsson, C., Physician in charge of alcoholics at the mental hospital in Göteborg, Sweden (Lillhagens sjukhus, Hisings-Backa). Communication 13 February 1969. A special report is to be printed in *Quart J.* on Studies of Alcoholism.

Christie, D. Physical Training in Chronic Obstructive Lung Disease. *Brit. Med J* pp 150–151, 20 April 1968.

Frommeyer, W. B. From a Speech given to San Antonio Heart Association, 27 June 1969, San Antonio, Texas.

Golding, L. A. Effects of Physical Training Upon Total Serum Cholesterol Levels. *Rsch Quarterly* Vol. 32 (No. 4): 499, December 1961.

Hellerstein, H. K.; Hornsten, T. R.; Goldbarg, A. N.; Burlando, A. G.; Friedman, E. H.; and Hirsch, E. Z. "The Influence of active conditioning upon coronary atherosclerosis" in *Atherosclerotic Vascular Disease.* Edited by A. N. Brest and J. H. Moyer. New York: Appleton-Century-Crofts, 1967. p 115 (Mood & anxiety changes in response to exercise).

Millman, M.; Grundon, W. G.; Kasch, F.; Wilkerson, B.; and Headley, J. Controlled Exercise in Asthmatic Children. *Annals of Allergy* Vol. 23: 220–25, May 1965.

Paez, P. N.; Phillipson, E. A.: Masangkay, M.; and Sproule, B. J. The Physiologic Basis of Training Patients with Emphysema. *Amer. Review of Respiratory Disease* Vol. 95 (No. 6): 944–53, June 1967.

Pierce, A. K.; Taylor, H. F.; Archer, R. K.; and Miller, W. F. Responses to Exercise Training in Patients wtih Emphysema. *Arch Int. Med* Vol. 113: 78–86, January 1964.

Rochelle, R. H. Blood plasma Cholesterol Changes during a Physical Training Program. *Rsch Quart* Vol. 32 (No. 4): 538, December 1961.

Siegel, W., Blomqvist, G., and Mitchell, J. H. Effects of a Quantitated Physical Training Program on Middle-Aged Sedentary Males. Unpublished report from Southwestern Medical School, Dallas, Texas. (Self image changes in response to exercise.)

CHAPTER 9

Biddulph, L. G. Athletic Achievement and the Personal and Social Adjustment of High School Boys. *Rsch. Quart.* 25 (No. 1), March 1954.

Bier, R. A. How Fit Are Our Youth? *Chicago Medicine* Vol. 71 (No. 19): 731–36, September 14, 1968.

Biörck, G. The Biology of Myocardial Infraction *Circulation* Volume XXXVII: 1071–1085, June 1968.

Brummer, P. Coronary Heart Disease and the Living Standard. *Acta Medica Scandinavica* Vol. 182 (fasc. 4): 523–27, 1967.

Cooper, K. H. A Means of Assessing Maximal Oxygen Intake. *JAMA* 203: 201–204, 15 January 1968.

Doolittle, T. L. and Bigbee, R. The twelve-minute run-walk: A test of cardiorespiratory fitness of adolescent boys. *Rsch. Quart.* 39(3): 491–95, October 1968.

Gallagher, J. R. and Brouha, L. Dynamic Physical Fitness in Adolescence. *Yale Journal of Biology and Medicine* Vol. 15 (No. 5): 657–70, May 1943.

Gendel, E. S. Pregnancy, Fitness, and Sports. *JAMA* Vol. 201 (No. 10): 751–54, September 4, 1967.

Hammerton, M. and Tickner, A. H. Physical Fitness and Skilled Work After Exercise. *Ergonomics* Vol. 11 (No. 1): 41–45, 1968.

Hart, M. E. and Shay, C. T. Relationship Between Physical Fitness and Academic Success. *Rsch. Quart.* 35 (No. 3): 443–45, October 1964.

Rasch, P. J. and Hamby, J. W. Physical Fitness of Women Marines. Vol. XVII (No. 1): January 1967. Bureau of Medicine and Surgery. Navy Dept. Work Unit M.F. 022 01-04-8003.2.

Rose, L. I.; Bradley, E. M.; Kudzma, D. J.; and Cooper, K. H. Changes in Body Composition During Intensive Physical Conditioning (abstract). *Clinical Research* Vol. 17 (No. 2): 393, April 1969.

Walker, A. Coronary Heart Disease and Future Expectation of Life. *Circulation* Vol. XXXVII: 126–31, January 1968.

Weber, R. J. Relationship of Physical Fitness to Success in College and to Personality. *Rsch. Quart.* 24: 471, December 1953.

CHAPTER 10

Gordon, E. E. Energy Cost of Activities in Health and Disease. *AMA Archives of Internal Med* Vol. 101: 702–13, January–June 1958.

Lehmann, G., Arbeitsbedingungen. Praktische Arbeitsphysiologie, Thieme Stuttgart, West Germany, page 154. (Reference on Stairclimbing.) 1953.

Margaria, R.; Cerretelli, P.; Aghemo, P.; and Sassi, G. Energy Cost of Running. *Journ of Applied Physiology* Vol. 18: 367–70, 1963.

CHAPTER 11

Banister, E. W.; Ribisi, P. M.; Porter, G. H.; and Cilio, A. R. The Caloric Cost of Playing Handball. *Rsch. Quart.* 35(3) Part 1: 236–40, October 1964.

"1152 Start, Most Finish" *The Boston Globe*, April 22, 1969.

Bouchard, C.; Hollmann, W.; Venrath, H.; Herkenrath, G.; and Schlussel, H. Minimal Amount of Physical Training for the Prevention of Cardiovascular Diseases. A report from the Dept. of Phys. Ed., Universiteé Laval, Quebec, and Institut fur Kreislaufforschung and Sportmedizin, Köln, Deutschland, June 1968.

Cooper, K. H.; Gey, G. O.; and Bottenberg, R. A. Effects of Cigarette Smoking on Endurance Performance. *JAMA* Vol. 203: 189–92, 15 January 1968.

Doyle, J. T.; Dawber, T. R.; Kannel, W. B.; Kinch, S. H.; and Kahn, H. A. The Relationship of Cigarette Smoking to Coronary Heart Disease. *JAMA* Vol. 190: 886–90, December 7, 1964.

Gey, G. O., Cooper, K. H., and Bottenberg, R. A. Effect of Vitamin C on Endurance Performance and the Incidence, Severity, and Duration of Athletic Injury (A Negative Study). *JAMA* (in press)

Gordon, E. E. Energy Costs of Activities in Health and Disease. *AMA Archives of Internal Medicine* Vol. 101: 702–13, January–June 1958.

Jacobs, E. Smoking Versus Myocardial Infarction: Two Hundred Consecutive Well-Documented Cases. *Military Medicine* Vol. 133: 908–10, 1968.

Karvonen, M. J.; Kentala, E.; and Mustala, O. The Effects of Training on Heart Rate: A Longitudinal Study. *Ann. Med. Exp. Biol. Fenn.*, 35: 307–15, 1957.

MacAlpin, R. N. and Kattus, A. A. Adaptation to Exercise in Angina Pectoris. *Circulation* Volume 33: 233–69, February 1966.

Pollack, M. L., Cureton, T. K., and Greninger, M. S. Effects of frequency of training on working capacity, cardiovascular function, and body composition of adult men. *Medicine and Science in Sports* Vol. 1 (No. 2): 70–74, June 1969.

Roskamm, H. Optimum Patterns of Exercise for Healthy Adults. *Canad. Med. Ass. J.* 96:895–99, March 25, 1967.

Smith, J. E. and Kidera, G. J. Treamtnt of Angina Pectoris with Exercise Stress. *Aerospace Medicine* Vol. 38 (No. 7): 742–45, July 1967.

KENNETH H. COOPER, M.D.
ON
THE AEROBICS WAY

In 1968 *Aerobics* was published in an effort to make the American people more aware of their need for exercise and to encourage them to use exercise in the practice of preventive medicine. *Aerobics* resulted from years of research, working with relatively young U.S. Air Force personnel.

Yet, much to my surprise, the majority of the people who purchased the book were over forty, and many were women. This necessitated the publication of *The New Aerobics*. In this book we deemphasized initial field testing (the twelve-minute test), particularly for people over thirty-five years of age, and encouraged a six-week starter program followed by age-adjusted progressive programs. Greater emphasis was placed on the initial screening physical examination. The point system incorporated the concept of endurance points, awarding more points for longer-endurance-type activities. The emphasis in *The New Aerobics* was on exercising safely.

Aerobics for Women followed when we realized that women have special needs and problems. Written with my wife Millie, this book is specifically for women, and answers the questions and needs that many women had brought to our attention.

Now, in the last five years, knowledge in the area of exercise as it applies to the practice of preventive and rehabilitative medicine has increased tremendously. Some of this information has come from research being conducted at our own Aerobics Center in Dallas, Texas. As a result of the studies being conducted at the Aerobics Center and the research of countless others, we have probably learned more in the past five years than we did in the previous twenty.

This new information plus the consolidation of all the programs is the basis for *The Aerobics Way*. Readers of the previous books will find some repetition of concepts and ideas first introduced in the original books, but they will also find considerable new information further substantiating the need for exercise in the maintenance of good health.

Get fit . . . keep fit . . . and may you enjoy life to its fullest!

AEROBICS, THE NEW AEROBICS, AEROBICS FOR WOMEN and THE AEROBICS WAY are now available in Bantam Books, wherever paperbacks are sold.